In the Name of Allah,
The Compassionate, the Merciful

Wahhabism

2nd Edition

Author
Ayatullah Ja'far Subhani

Revised, Edited and Annotated

by

Ahmad Abdullah Martin

Book Title: Wahhabism

Edition: 2nd

Author: Ayatullah Ja'far Subhani

Revision, Editing and Annotation: Ahmad Abdullah Martin

Graphics: Abu Yahya al-Hussaini

Publisher: Jerrmein Abu Shahba

ISBN: 978-1-7330284-7-9

Copyright © 2020

Owned by the Editor and Publisher. No part of this book can be published without written permission by the copyright owners.

CONTENTS

Editor's Note 1
Preface by the Author 3
Familiarity with the Life of the Founder of Wahhabism 19
Wahhabis and the Renovation of Graves of *Awliya Allah* 31
Construction of Mosque near the Graves of Pious People 67
Visitation *(Ziyarat)* of Graves of Believers from the View-Point of the Holy Qur'an and Sunnah ... 79
Valuable Effects of *Ziyarat* of the Graves of Religious Personalities 89
Performance of Prayer and Supplication near Graves of the Holy Personalities ... 101
Tawassul (Recourse) to the *Awliya Allah* 107
Is it an Innovation to Commemorate the Birth and Death Anniversaries of *Awliya Allah*? ... 127
Seeking Benediction and Cure from the Signs and Traces of *Awliya* 135
Tawhid in *'Ibadah* and Worship (or Pretext of Wahhabis) 141
Seeking Help from *Awliya Allah* during Their Lifetime 159
Seeking Help from the Spirits of *Awliya Allah* 169
Seeking *Shafa'a* (Intercession) from *Awliya Allah* 185
Examining the Reasoning of Wahhabis about the Prohibition of Seeking *Shafa'a* ... 193
Is Belief in Invisible Power the Basis of *Shirk* (Polytheism)? 203
Pleading Allah by the Right and Position of *Awliya* 215
Nadhr (Vow) to the People in Grave 233
'Calling' the Divine Personalities 239
Political and Social Dimensions of Hajj 247
Conclusion 265
Glossary of Important Terms 267

APPENDIX

APPENDIX I 271
List of *Ayahs* of Holy Qur'an used by Wahhabi Scholars to prove their deviant ideology and the rebuttal of their argument 271

APPENDIX II 273
Najd and Wahhabi *fitna* as mentioned in the hadithes of Prophet Muhammad (s) ... 273

APPENDIX III 279

List and brief description of few books written by leading Muslim scholars in rebuttal of Wahhabism 279

APPENDIX IV 285

A description of Ibn Taymiyyah by the famous Muslim scholar and explorer Ibn Battuta..........285

APPENDIX V 287

Wahhabism in Contemporary Western Literature 287

A. Books on Wahhabism and its various forms and aspects published by international publishers..287

B. Scholarly articles on Wahhabism and its various aspects published in peer reviewed international journals 293

Selected Bibliography...305

INDEX 309

Editor's Note

Wahhabism is one of the most important books that deals in depth with the history and reality of its fake and deviated ideology when seen in the light of Holy Qur'an and *Sunnah* of Prophet Muhammad (s). The author, Ayatullah Ja'far Subhani needs no introduction as he is an authority on the topic and has written several books on related issues. It will be evident for the reader that Wahhabism has nothing to do with real Islam – neither *Sunni* nor *Shia*. The author has discussed the creed of Wahhabism from various aspects from the ayahs of Qur'an and hadithes of Prophet Muhammad (s) and the history of Islam from authentic Sunni sources.

The second edition has been thoroughly revised by the author with addition of one more chapter. The translation of the first edition by Jalil Durrani was adopted as base for the preparation of second edition. It was reviewed word for word and errors were corrected. Transliteration was minimized for easy word search and to avoid confusion. References to traditions were checked and corrections were made as well as the translation of ayahs of Qur'an. Footnotes were added extensively to provide additional details about famous historians, religious scholars and intellectuals and their leading books. Selected bibliography was added to enlist books referred by the author to discuss various aspects of Wahhabism. Appendices are added to provide additional information for the interested readers. In particular, appendix 2 provides few hadithes of Prophet Muhammad (s) predicting the sedition of Wahhabism from Najd. Appendix 4 provides complete citation of books and articles published in modern Western literature about Wahhabism and its various forms and its role in global terrorism especially Middleeast. Appendix 5 provides a list of important books written by leading Muslim scholars for the rebuttal of Wahhabism. Glossary is added to provide simple definitions of relevant religious concepts and terms. We hope that this book will be a source of valuable information for the readers against ever growing threat of Wahhabism.

Ahmad Abdullah Martin

2019

Preface by the Author

Ka'ba is the first and foremost house of *Tawhid* (monotheism) that was destroyed before Nuh (a)[1] and was damaged in the storm at the time of Nuh (a), after sometime Ibrahim (Abraham) *Khalilullah* (a) repaired and reconstructed it[2] and then invited all the worshippers of God for the *ziyarat* (visitation) to this center of the lovers and devotees of 'Allah'.[3]

God has declared His house (*Ka'ba*) the focal point of gathering for monotheists and the center of 'peace' for God worshippers and that no one should make it unsafe or create disturbance there.[4]

God has made *ziyarat* of His house (*Ka'ba*) the basis of sustenance of the life of monotheists and it is reminded that attending Hajj rituals secures their individual, collective and social, material and spiritual life.[5]

In the divine inspiration of this verse, Imam al-Sadiq (a) said:

لاَ يَزَالُ اَلدِّينُ قَائِماً مَا قَامَتِ اَلْكَعْبَةُ.

The religion will exist until the Ka'ba exists.[6]

The special characteristics and specific attributes of the house of God (*Ka'ba*) and the *haram*[7] of God is more than what is reflected in this preface. What is important and requiring attention is the current situation of *Ka'ba* that its custodians call themselves as 'Servants of Two Holy Shrines' (*Khadimayn Harmayn Sharifayn*) and express their pride and joy over its management.

From the special attributes (pointed above), we will mention two of them:

---

[1] إِنَّ أَوَّلَ بَيْتٍ وُضِعَ لِلنَّاسِ لَلَّذِي بِبَكَّةَ مُبَارَكًا وَهُدًى لِلْعَالَمِينَ
Indeed the first house to be set up for mankind is the one at Bakkah, blessed and guidance for all nations. [Aale Imran:96]

[2] وَإِذْ يَرْفَعُ إِبْرَاهِيمُ الْقَوَاعِدَ مِنَ الْبَيْتِ وَإِسْمَاعِيلُ رَبَّنَا تَقَبَّلْ مِنَّا إِنَّكَ أَنْتَ السَّمِيعُ الْعَلِيمُ
As Abraham raised the foundations of the House with Ismael, [they prayed]: 'Our Lord, accept it from us! Indeed, You are the All-hearing, the All-knowing. [Baqarah: 127]

[3] وَأَذِّنْ فِي النَّاسِ بِالْحَجِّ يَأْتُوكَ رِجَالًا وَعَلَىٰ كُلِّ ضَامِرٍ يَأْتِينَ مِنْ كُلِّ فَجٍّ عَمِيقٍ
And proclaim the Hajj to all the people: they will come to you on foot and on lean camels, coming from distant places. [Hajj:27]

[4] وَإِذْ جَعَلْنَا الْبَيْتَ مَثَابَةً لِلنَّاسِ وَأَمْنًا
And [remember] when We made the House a place of reward for mankind and a sanctuary [Baqarah:125]

[5] جَعَلَ اللَّهُ الْكَعْبَةَ الْبَيْتَ الْحَرَامَ قِيَامًا لِلنَّاسِ
Allah has made the Ka'bah, the Sacred House, a [means of] sustentation for mankind [Maida:97]

[6] *Al-Kafi*, vol.4, page 271

[7] *Haram* (حرم), means 'sanctuary' or 'holy shrine' in the Islamic teachings.

1. Are the current Hajj ceremonies in accordance with 'قِيَامًا لِّلنَّاسِ'?

Do the mass gatherings of over 2 million Muslims around the *Ka'ba* and for its *ziyarat* ensures their material and spiritual lives? If it is like that, then let us know in which year in the recent past, the custodians and the preachers of two holy shrines have discussed or engaged in the solving common problems of Islamic world during the great gatherings and came up with guidelines and solutions?

In the year 1356 S.H. (1978 A.D.), I went to perform *'Umra mufarrada*[8] with a group of young memorizers of Qur'an and visited the house of God (*Ka'ba*). During the days our visit there, news of attack of Israel on South Lebanon for killing and destruction of Palestinians was projected in the news media. On Friday we went to 'Tahfiz al-Qur'an al-Kareem' adjacent to holy *haram* to participate in the recitation of Qur'an competition. Conference meeting session was chaired by one of the high-level officials of Saudi Arabia. The competition ended and after sometime, Friday prayers *azan* was called and the Imam of the Masjid al-Harām went on pulpit (*mimbar*) for delivering the sermon. I said to myself that he will mention about the latest incident (attack of Israel on Palestinians in South Lebanon). But he didn't mention anything and my 'good opinion' (*Husne Zan*) changed to 'bad opinion' (*Suye Zan*). He mentioned about the etiquette of participating in the prayers in mosque and Friday prayers and that the cleanliness of mouth and feet should be taken care of! But he didn't say a word about the incident! Beside me a personality from 'Ikhwan al Muslimeen' from Egypt was sitting and he was living as a refugee in Mecca. I asked him: "Is this sermon according to what the current situation demanded?" Because he was a righteous person, he gave expression of sadness and didn't answer.

All the Friday prayer sermons in the grand mosques in Saudi Arabia are routinely checked and their contents are formally approved. Not a word is allowed about the colonialistic policies of blood thirsty and savage United States and Zionist entity and their dangers for the world. However, what is freely allowed is that Shias are Magus![9] This is to the extent that after Islamic

---

[8] There are two kinds of *'umra: 'umrat al-mufrada* and *'umrat al-tamattu'. 'Umrat al-mufrada* is not related to hajj rituals and is undertaken independently.
[9] Followers of Zoroastrianism.

Revolution of Iran, a book entitled "جاء دورالمجوس" (The start of Reign of Magi[10]) was published from Saudi Arabia!

Keeping in view this situation, can it be questioned that are the current rulers of Najd and Riyadh, really the custodians of House of God and are they preparing the ground for ... قِيَامًا لِلنَّاسِ in the Islamic World?!

2. Is the House of God (Ka'ba) a place of peace?

Qur'an has declared Mecca and its suburbs as *Haram* (peaceful sanctuary) of God and says:

$$وَمَن دَخَلَهُ كَانَ آمِنًا$$

... and whoever enters it shall be secure... [Aale Imran:97]

The ancestor of Muslims (Ibrahim Khalilullah (a)) requested God to declare Mecca as a city of peace and said:

$$رَبِّ اجْعَلْ هَٰذَا الْبَلَدَ آمِنًا$$

'My Lord! Make this city a sanctuary... [Ibrahim:35]

Now the question is: Are the present Custodians of Holy Harams, Guarantors of this Divine order? Does in reality do the Leaders of all Islamic sects enjoy security in this place to bring forth the political issues, inform about the important problems of Islamic world[11] and guide the true representatives of Islamic nations who have gathered there? Or among all the Islamic sects only Hanbalis have right to speak? And from the lofty Islamic teachings and thoughts only the fossilized and dry views of 'Ibn Taymiyyah', 'Ibn Qayyim' and lately 'Mohammad bin 'Abd al-Wahhab' be allowed to propagated and discussed? And from among the hundreds of important social, cultural and political discussion topics, only issues related to *ziyarat* of dead, commemoration of Prophet (s) birthday, holding respect for *Awliya Allah* be echoed every year and undefended opposers are whipped as they are *kafirs* and any injury and harm

---

[10] Plural of Magus

[11] Saudi Arabia is a key ally of USA and Zionist regime for the last several decades. Following the dictation of its masters, it has initiated several sectarian and military conflicts and invasions in the Middle East and beyond. Wahhabi ideology and petrodollars recently created Daesh and ISIS that has killed hundreds of thousands of innocent human beings and displaced millions from Syria and Iraq. In addition, Saudi led war on Yemen that started in 2015 has killed hundreds of thousands of innocent civilians and has led to death of thousands of children because of starvation.

be inflicted upon them and they be declared as apostates with abusive language and offended in all possible ways!

Is this the meaning of 'حَرَامًا آمِنًا'? Keeping in view the above-mentioned limitations, if we say: *Ka'ba* is occupied by…. Have we said something really harsh?

The culture of Wahhabism in founded on 'Apostasing Islamic sects', 'Creation of sectarian discord between Muslims', 'Giving extremist outlook to the teachings of Islam', 'Destruction of physical sites related to Prophethood and Divine Revelation' and 'Conspiring with oppressors and world arrogant powers.' Even Yazid Ibn Mu'awiyah is a steadfast ruler for them. The missionaries and authors that work under their control are 'Preachers of Despotic Kings' and coward paid agents who will not speak a word other than whatever is whispered in their ears by their masters.

Perhaps respected reader of this book might think that we with this description are talking illogically and without any proof. But for an example, we are presenting below the front cover of a book that is published and propagated in Saudi Arabia. In this book, the person (Yazid) who bombarded and damaged the holy *Ka'ba* with catapult, and for three days allowed his soldiers to plunder, loot and attack the lives, honor and property of inhabitants of Medina[12], is defended, praised and honored.

Front cover image of the book published from Saudi Arabia

---

[12] For details of this horrific historic event in which several companions of the Prophet were also massacred, please read the book '*Battle of Harrah*' by Muhammad Ali Chenarani available at: https://www.al-islam.org/battle-of-harrah-muhammad-ali-chenarani

Preface by the Author

on '*Ameer al-mominin*' Yazid

Keeping in view this fundamental point, it can be said that in this country (Saudi Arabia), there is a kind of 'absolute freedom' maintained with an utterly suffocating authoritarian government system. Books that contain praise of oppressors and tyrants Umayyid and Abbasid rulers are allowed to be liberally written and published. However, books that defend Ahlul Bayt (as) are banned. Not only these books, but any book that enters the country is strictly controlled and should be approved by the Security and Intelligence Ministry.

Last year (1404 A.H. / 1984 A.D.), when I entered Medina airport, I had 10 copies of the book 'مصدرالوجود' (*Masdar al-Wujud*) with me. This book is related to affirming proofs and arguments on the existence of God. The aim for carrying this book that I am myself the author was to contribute to the culture of this country. However, unfortunately it was confiscated at the airport. And even after reading it, the relevant in charge of the section at the airport said: 'Even though this book is very good and informative but it must be sent to Security and Intelligence Ministry and you can get it back from there.' This is the meaning of بَلَدَ آمِنًا !!

'*Shirk*' (Polytheism) – The most abundant and the cheapest commodity of Saudi Arabia

Accusation of '*shirk*' and being a polytheist by many of the 'ulama and seniors is a common and routine practice in this country. When a person encounters the officials of 'enjoining the good', before anything, he hears such words (*shirk, mushrik,* etc.) from them. In their stock of talks, there is nothing to sell except '*shirk*' or to accuse one of being a polytheist!

While writing this foreword, I got a book entitled '*Shias and Shiaism: Their Genesis and Evolution*' from a Pakistani author[13] but was published in Saudi Arabia. On page 20 of the book, the author quotes sentences from famous scholar Sheikh Mohammad Husayn Mozaffari and then describes and interprets them based on his personal opinion. We will cite below text of both of them to shed light on how madly these Wahhabi authors accuse people of 'inviting to *shirk*'.

---

[13] Ehsan Elahi Zaheer; also written as Ihsan Ilahi Zaheer

Late Mozaffari writes: 'Shiaism started on the very first day when the Prophet (s) of God started inviting people towards one God and his own prophethood.'

There he writes: 'Invitation to follow Abul Hasan (Imam Ali (a)) pleasantly continued with invitation to *Tawhid* and Prophethood.'

This Pakistani author criticizes these writings of Mozaffari as:

'The Prophet (s), according to the writing of Mozaffari, used to include Ali in the Prophethood'

If this author was not taken over by his personal inclinations and whims and had not sold himself to the Wahhabis; and if he had basic knowledge of the beliefs of Shia, he would not have made such ridiculous criticism on one of the great writers of the world of Islam.

If such invitation is the 'invitation to *shirk*' or '*shirk* in prophethood', before anyone else, the Qur'an itself has done it. The reason is, Qur'an, in addition to invitation to follow 'God and Prophet', also invited to follow the أُولِي الْأَمْر (those vested with authority) and says:

أَطِيعُوا اللَّهَ وَأَطِيعُوا الرَّسُولَ وَأُولِي الْأَمْرِ مِنكُمْ

Obey Allah and obey the Apostle and those vested with authority among you... [Nisa:59]

Based on the beliefs of this author, the Prophet of God (s) instead of inviting people to *tawhid*, invited them to polytheism and dual worshipping! Because Prophet (s) brought أُولِي الْأَمْر in the same position as 'following God' and it's basically known that the term أُولِي الْأَمْر no matter how it is interpreted is evidently used for Imam Ali (a).

We all know that the day when Prophet (s) was entrusted to invite his relatives and when the verse

وَأَنذِرْ عَشِيرَتَكَ الْأَقْرَبِينَ

"Warn the nearest of your kinsfolk" [Ash Shu'ra:214]

was revealed, he invited his close family members and in that gathering known as *Yawm al-Inzar* (يَوْمُ الْإِنذَار)[14] announced his prophethood and said:

---

[14] *Hadith* of Warning. The occasion is known as دعوة ذو العشيرة (*Da'wat dhul-'Ashirah*).

فَأَيُّكُمْ يُوَازِرُنِى عَلَى هَذَا الْأَمْرِ عَلَى أَنْ يَكُونَ أَخِى وَ خَلِيفَتِى فِيكُمْ؟

"Who will share the burden of this work with me? Who will respond to my call? Who will become my brother, my vicegerent and my successor among you?"

In that gathering, no one except Ali (a) stood up and responded, and Prophet (s) after repeating his call twice and not having any response from family members except Ali (a), said:

إِنَّ هَذَا أَخِى وَ وَصِيِى وَ خَلِيفَتِى فِيكُمْ فَاسْمَعُوا لَهُ وَ أَطِيعُوا

"This is my brother, my vicegerent and my successor among you. Listen to him and obey his commands."[15]

Based on the historic order, Shias believe: On the day when Prophet (s) was entrusted to invite to *tawhid* and his own Prophethood, that he ordered, he also invited them to the successorship of Ali (a) and so the invitation to 'Prophethood' was accompanied with the invitation to 'Imamat'[16].

Now is it right to accuse Shias by saying: 'Prophet was entrusted to include Ali in the Prophethood and announce it? Was the invitation to successorship that too after death of Prophet (s) meant invitation to Prophethood?!'

The disastrous situation of the books that Sunni authors and especially the Wahhabis write about the beliefs of Shia, is because of two reasons:

1. Lack of knowledge about the beliefs of Shias: This pathetic situation has been prevalent for centuries and the reason for it was Umayyid and Abbasids ruling dynasties that didn't allow Shias to express their belief in the gatherings of scholars of Ahl al-Sunnah and let the Shia religion be known as a school of thought. Everyone was allowed to speak and discuss about their school of thought in the centers of knowledge and learning and worship except Shia, with few exceptions that are beyond the scope of this book.

2. Depth of knowledge of Ahl al-Sunnah scholars: Revolution that took place in the community and society of scholars of Ahl al-Sunnah from the point of view of teaching and learning of religious sciences, the new styles of teaching, and the books that lacked depth of knowledge in beliefs and discourse. For this

---

[15] The authentic reports of this *hadith* which is known among the experts of the science of *hadithes* as *hadith* of يَوْمُ الْإِنْذَارِ and بَدْءُ الدَّعْوَةِ are found in books of history and *hadithes*. Tabari has reported his famous book of history *Tarikh al-Tabari* in volume 2, page 63.

[16] Divine Guardianship or Successorship after Prophet (s). For details visit: https://www.al-islam.org/ghadir/

reason, in this Islamic country (Saudi Arabia), there is no one to teach the historic, classical and in-depth theology books such as المواقف [17] and شرح المقاصد [18] written in 8th century A.H.

It is because of this shallow approach and teachings in Wahhabi seminaries that lack depth of knowledge that produces authors such as 'Ehsan Elahi Zaheer'[19] who does not know the difference between 'Invitation to Caliphate' and 'Invitation to Prophethood' and writes the book فِرَق وتاريخ and with unlimited financial support from oil money of Saudi Arabia, he publishes his books while not knowing even the ABC of the beliefs of Shias.

In-depth Investigation

The great grandson of Prophet (s), Imam al-Sadiq (a) said:

الْعَالِمُ بِزَمَانِهِ لَا تَهْجُمُ عَلَيْهِ اللَّوَابِسُ

"A person knowledgable about the conditions of his time will not suffer from onslaughts of unfavorable incidents."[20]

It's the right time now that we think about the current disastrous situation and the calamities that have descended upon the world of Islam and recognize the real enemies of Islam. At present it's about hundred years ago that the ideological and intellectual battle against Islam has started and camps from both East and West, with their masters and supporters have united against Islam and almost every week or month with different titles and on different topics, a book with is published against Islam and its teachings.

Is it appropriate that under this difficult situation and condition that in a very short time, only in one country i.e., Saudi Arabia, books are written about Shia religion giving impression that currently in the world of Islam there is no

---

[17] *Al-Mawaqif* is the famous book of *Ahl al-Sunnah* written by Qadhi Ezzuddin Aiji (d. 752 A.H.) in 8th century. It's a master piece of *Ilm al-Kalam* (discourse) from Asharites point of view and taught in both Shias and Sunni seminaries.

[18] *Sharh al-Maqasid* is another classical book of *Ilm al-Kalam* written in 784 A.H. by Sunni Hanafi Asharite scholar from Persia, Sa'aduddin Mas'ud bin Umar bin Abdullah Taftazani (d. 792 A.H.).

[19] Ehsan Elahi Zaheer was a Pakistani Wahhabi theologian and leader of the Ahl-e-Hadith movement who studied Wahhabi brand of Islam at the Islamic University of Madinah. He died from an assassin's bomb blast in 1987. He wrote several books (translated to different languages) against all sects of Islam based on Wahhabi style of accusation and labelled them as *kafirs* (unbelievers) and *mushriks* (polytheists). He sowed seeds of discord between various Islamic sects in Pakistan and other Islamic countries such as Egypt, Indonesia and Malaysia.

[20] *Al-Kafi*, vol. 1, page 26

problem, and there is no difficulty other than the beliefs of Shias and there is no solution other than criticism of their beliefs?!

I wish these books were written on logical and reasonable grounds which was not a problem at all. The Shia scholars ('ulama) should either answer the logical arguments or accept them. However, unfortunately, all these books are loaded with abusive and malicious accusations against Shias, their scholars and possibly insulting the holy personality of Ameer al-Mominin Imam Ali (a).

The book entitled 'الشيعه و التشيّع'[21] (*Shias and Shiaism: Their Genesis and Evolution*) is a glaring example of what was pointed out earlier about the dirty business of writing deviated books. The author of this book while citing from the historic books written by Tabari[22], Ibn Kathir[23] and Ibn Khaldun[24], conceived that Shias are products and outcomes of a Jew by the name of 'Abdullah Ibn Saba. He then cites Ahmad Amin Misri[25], from his book *Fajr al-Islam* as a testifier to it and then for completing his arguments he takes assistance from the writings of a group of Jewish and Christian experts of Middle East, such as Miller, Douzi and Wellhausen. But he never refers or cites works of Shia *'ulama* for their own beliefs that comes from the personalities such as Sheikh al-Sadduq (d. 381 A.H.)[26] and Sheikh Mufid (d. 413 A.H.)[27] who have extensively written on the topic. He doesn't even accept and doesn't mention any of them and says: These books are the books just for the outwardly propagation of Shia religion and the real beliefs of Shia are not in these books! Worse than all he takes the traditions

---

[21] Written by Ehsan Elahi Zaheer.
[22] Abu Ja'far Muhammad ibn Jarir al-Tabari (839 – 923 A.D.). Famous historian and author of *History of the Prophets and Kings* (تاريخ الرسل و الملوك) a.k.a. *Tarikh al-Tabari*.
[23] Isma'il bin 'Umar bin Kathir (1300 – 1373 A.D.). Famous Syrian Sunni Shafi'i Islamic scholar and historian, author of several books including the classical historic book *Al-Bidayah wal Nihayah*.
[24] Abu Zayd 'Abd ar-Rahman ibn Muhammad ibn Khaldun al-Hadrami (1332 – 1406 A.D.) aka as Ibn Khaldun was an Arab historiographer and historian. His famous book on History was *Muqaddimah* (Introduction to history) written in 1377 A.D.
[25] Ahmad Amin (1886–1954 A.D.) was an Egyptian historian and writer. He wrote several books on the history of the Islamic civilization.
[26] Abu Ja'far Muhammad ibn 'Ali ibn Babawayh al-Qummi (918 – 991 A.D.), also known as Sheikh al-Sadduq was great Iranian Shi'ite Islamic scholar and author of several important books including *Man la yahduruhu al-Faqih, Kamal al-din wa Tamam al-Ni'mah, Al-Khisal, Ma'ani al-Akhbar* and *Ilal al-shara'i*.
[27] Muhammad ibn al-Nu'man al-'Ukbari al-Baghdadi (948 – 1022 A.D.), known as al-Sheikh al-Mufid, was a prominent Shia theologian. He was student of Sheikh al-Sadduq and author of famous books including *Al-Irshad, Al-Muqni'ah,* and *Tashih al-Itiqadat*.

mentioned in *Bihar al-Anwar*[28] and *Anwar al-Naumaniyah*[29] to prove the beliefs of Shia while we all know that among the sources of hadithes of all Islamic sects, there are weak and false hadithes and citing one tradition from among them doesn't not always reflect the belief of the sect on that topic or concept.

We now attract the attention of author of *Shias and Shiaism: Their Genesis and Evolution* to few points:

1. Is *Tarikh al-Tabari* from the point of view of authenticity and validity, a fundamental work that we can say all of its contents are precise and correct? Or is there need for further investigation of the sources *Tabari* has used for making a decision about authenticity of its contents and the views mentioned by *Tabari* in it? The reason for this is because the number of false, liars, weak and unauthentic reporters and individuals in the books of history and exegesis is very high and we cannot mention all of them here.

2. As a worth remembering example, we mention here something that the author of the book *Shias and Shiaism: Their Genesis and Evolution* writes: Shias accepted Islam by following the views of 'Abdullah Ibn Saba,[30] a Yemeni Jew who according to the views of *Tabari*, had only outwardly accepted Islam and propagated Jewish ideology (*Isra'iliyyat*)[31] among Muslims under the cover of invitation to follow Ali (a). Seems this had impressive influence! However, fundamentally, was there any real person in the world by this name? Or is this character, a part of fictional stories of past mythology? Right now, we are not going to discuss it in detail. It is to be mentioned here that *Tabari* cites reference

---

[28] Compiled by great Shiite scholar Mohammad Baqir Majlisi, known as 'Allama Majlisi (d. 1110 A.H./1698 A.D.). The book has 110 volumes and was completed after his death. According to many leading Shia scholars, traditions collected in this book are authentic subject to scrutiny.

[29] Compiled by Ni'mat Allah al-Musawi Jaza'iri (d.1112 A.H./1701 A.D.). He was student of 'Allama Majlisi. The collection of traditions by him had methodological issues and is subject to thorough investigation. This book is not popular among Shia scholars for citing as a source of authentic hadithes.

[30] 'Abdullah Ibn Saba was a fictitious character of the 7th century in the history of Islam invented by an agnostic Yemeni Jew and an unreliable story teller Saif Ibn Umar. For more details kindly see the scholarly book "'*Abdullah Bin Saba and other myths*" written by Sayyid Murtaza Al-Askari (d. 2007 A.D.). The book is available at: https://www.al-islam.org/abdullah-ibn-saba-and-other-myths-sayyid-murtadha-al-askari

[31] *Isra'iliyyat* is an Arabic term used by Muslim exegetes to designate Islamic traditions seen as deriving from the Hebrew Bible and later Jewish exegetical traditions. For a detailed inquiry, refer to the article entitled '*Isra'iliyyat or Traditions of Jewish Origin: A Major Instance of Transferred Traditions*' by Moaddab et al., *Religious Inquiries* available at: http://ri.urd.ac.ir/article_43965.html

for this text (about belief of Shia and 'Abdullah Ibn Saba) from the following chain of narrators of traditions as:

كتب به إلى السري عن شعيب عن سيف عن عطية عن يزيد الفقعسي قال كان عبد الله بن سبأ يهوديا من أهل صنعاء[32]

'Among the things he wrote to al-Sirri on the authority of Shu'ayb from Sayf, from 'Atiyya from Yazid al-Faq'asi who said: 'Abdullah b. Saba' was Jew from Ṣan'a.''

3. Let us now investigate the above quote, the content of which is cited by historians like Ibn Kathir, Shami and Ibn Khaldun. All of them have taken this text from *Tarikh al-Tabari*. Let us now see whether any tradition or contribution from these individuals is worthy of being reliable and can be cited or not:

a. Al-Sirri: Whether he is Maqsud Al-Sirri bin Isma'il Kufi or Al-Sirri bin 'Asim (d. 258 A.H.). Both of them were notorious liars of their time and fabricators of traditions and historic fables.[33]

b. Shuayb bin Ibrahim Kufi: Unknown and unidentified[34]

c. Sayf Ibn 'Umar: Narrator of false reports from the authentic persons[35]

d. Yazid al-Faq'asi: Individual reported as unknown[36] and unidentified in the books of narrators of traditions.

4. Tabari is his history book (*Tarikh al-Tabari*) volumes 3, 4 and 5 cites 701 historic accounts about the events during the years 11 to 37 A.H. (the caliphates of Abu Bakr, 'Umar and 'Uthman) from these five individuals mentioned above and has vehemently highlighted the results of historic facts.

Reports from these five individuals in context of historic incidents during that period (11 to 37 A.D.) are mentioned in volumes 3, 4 and 5 of *Tarikh al-Tabari* and at the end of volume 5, the *hadithes* also end there in such a manner that for all other historic incidents (except for one *hadith* in volume 10) not a single *hadith* is reported by these five individuals.

---

[32] *Tarikh al-Tabari*, vol.3, page 378
[33] *Tahdhib al-Tahdhib*, vol.2, page 46, *Tarikh al-Khatib*, vol. 9, page 193, *Mizan al-I'tidal*, vol.1, page 37, *Lisan al-Mizan*, vol.3, page 13.
[34] *Mizan al-I'tidal*, vol.1, page 447, *Lisan al-Mizan*, vol.3, page 145.
[35] *Mizan al-I'tidal*, vol.1, page 438, *Tahdhib al-Tahdhib*, vol.4, page 295
[36] Several companions mentioned in the *Tarikh al-Tabari* and other history books were fictious characters never existed. For detailed inquiry, refer to book '*One Hundred and Fifty Fictitious Companions of Prophet*' by Sayyid Murtaza Al-Askari.

Is the historic information of Al-Sirri and Sayf Ibn 'Umar specifically related to this particular historic period? That too even only related to a specific religious sect?

5. Isn't it that because the historic events of that period form the basis and fundamental beliefs and are counted as the views of Muslims, the actual aim of quoting these hadithes[37], is distortion of facts and to paint an opposite picture of the real historic events of that particular period of Islamic history?

6. Anyone who carefully pays attention to these historic reports, will conclude that all of these have been factiously made up and fabricated by a group or one individual and all the details serve one specific purpose. It cannot be supposed that these fabricated reports were not known to Tabari. What can be done! There is no other reason for this other than actions based on blind love, hate and ignorant selflessness.

7. Unfortunately and sadly these fabricated traditions and bizarre reports, after Tabari mentioned in his book, were reported by later books of Islamic history such as *Tarikh Ibn 'Asakir*[38], *Tarikh Kamil Ibn Athir*[39], *Al-Bidayah wal Nihayah*[40], *Tarikh Ibn Khaldun*[41] and others. All of them cited these reports directly from *Tarikh al-Tabari* without doing any research or investigation about their authenticity claiming that whatever Tabari has mentioned is the reality. And so, continuing the similar trend, the historians of later periods too quoted these 'fabricated and preserved lies' one after the other in their works taking these accounts as 'historic facts'.

---

[37] For detailed inquiry to this topic, refer to the book '*A probe into the history of hadith*' by Sayyid Murtaza Al-Askari at: https://www.al-islam.org/probe-history-hadith-allamah-sayyid-murtadha-askari/part-two

[38] Ibn 'Asakir (1106 – 1175 A.D.) was a Sunni Shafi'i Syrian Islamic scholar. The book referred to here is تاريخ دمشق لإبن عساكر (The History of Damascus by Ibn Asakir) popularly known *Tarikh Ibn Asakir*. It is one of the most voluminous books (74 volumes) of history of Syria. The author tried to collect everything that has been said about personalities and events, true or false, with full chain of narration. It also contains a huge collection of Arabic poems.

[39] *Al-Kamil fi al-Tarikh* was written by Ali 'Izz al-Din Ibn al-Athir al-Jazari (d. 1233 A.D.). Ibn al-Athir was a famous Kurdish Sunni scholar from Turkey.

[40] Written by Isma'il ibn Kathir (1300 – 1373 A.D.).

[41] Original name of the book is *Muqaddimah*.

Of course, it's very fortunate that *Tarikh al-Tabari* is a 'musnad'[42] type of collection of traditions and reports and so the documentation of traditions is mentioned clearly. It's thus possible to investigate and authenticity of each tradition and differentiate true and authentic ones from false and baseless. As we have pointed out earlier, individuals who are documented as narrators of these traditions in *Tarikh al-Tabari* lack authenticity and are untrustworthy.

8. A book whose resources are these types of manufactured traditions and the narrators that are liars, fabricators and forgers of lies such as Al-Sirri and their likes… Does it really have a worthy place to withstand in-depth research and thorough investigation by experts? And is it appropriate that a great Islamic community[43] that has treasures of Islamic knowledge and that has great wealth of Prophetic traditions and that takes pride to be at forefront in fighting on ground and globally resisting against 'despotic, usurper and fake Zionist' regime, to attribute such fabricated and fictional lies to it synthesized by an individual who is a Jew unknown and unidentified in the history books?

Machiavellian Ideology

This obstinate author under the cover of questions and answers and very implicitly criticizes Amir al-mu'minin (a) as to why he acted hastily in dismissing Mu'awiyah (from governorship)? Why he, … why, … why? …[44]

This criticism lacks a base because the author imagines that Imam Ali (a) was like other common rulers or commanders who would give preference to personal reasons and motives over the commands of God duties made incumbent by God and take his aim with an excuse of means. For this very reason he levels such criticism in the form of a question.

If Imam Ali (a) was a Michiavellist individual, it was possible to think like this author and for personal reasons, he would impose tyrant oppressors on the

---

[42] A *musnad* collection is the one in which the chain of narrators who have heard a particular hadith or tradition or historic account is known.
[43] The author refers to full support of Islamic Republic of Iran to Hizbullah movment in Lebanon that defeated Zionist Israel for the first time in its history and to the Palestinan resistance movments.
[44] *Shias and Shiaism*, page 144.

life and property of common people. But he is the human being, who in response to an advice by Mughira ibn Shu'ba[45] said:

$$\text{وَمَا كُنتُ مُتَّخِذَ الْمُضِلِّينَ عَضُدًا}$$

"nor do I take those who mislead others as assistants" [Al-Kahf:51]

Here we will shorten our discussion and hope that this brief explanation will provide reader with enough information about the personality and approach of author, level of his knowledge of the fundamentals of Islamic, reasons behind his choices and selections from the history of Islam. I give you my pledge that very soon we will give an appropriate response to this book (*Shias and Shiaism: Their Genesis and Evolution*) which will be published with the contribution of great scholars of Islam.[46]

Need for Organizing International Islamic Conferences and Seminars

For the solution of several controversial issues, organizing annual international Islamic conference in which different beliefs and point of views should be presented in a rational and logical manner would be very beneficial and effective. In the present times, one category of problems is related to *tawhid* and *shirk* between the followers of Wahhabism and all other Islamic sects. Isn't it appropriate in order to bring these two groups closer to each other, Academic Seminar or even Conferences be organized so that the controversial problems can be presented and discussed with the hope that for all the sects and groups a new horizon of proximity and a new way opens up and all come out of the prevalent friction due to diverse beliefs? However, this mission should be undertaken seriously and following conditions should be taken care of:

1. All the leading intellectuals and scholars of Islamic sects, who are in reality the representatives of fundamentals and beliefs of their sect should be invited. Those who are paid from Saudi money from countries such as Pakistan, India

---

[45] Mughira ibn Shu'ba (d. 50 A.H./670 A.D.) was a companion of Prophet (s). He played role in attacking Lady Fatima's (a) house and he cursed Imam Ali (a) and his followers in the Masjid al-Kufa. In the time of Mu'awiyah, he became the governor of Kufa.

[46] The author has published two other valuable books on Wahhabism. 1. *A Teaching Course on Criticism of Wahhabism*, published by Mo'assasa Darul A'alam li Madressa Ahlul Bayt, Qom, 2017. 2. *Wahhabism – Ideological Foundations and Course of Actions* published by Mo'assasa Imam al-Sadiq Publications, Qom, 2016.

and Egypt that have suffered (because of sectarian conflicts caused by Wahhabism) should not be invited.

2. In these conferences, leading scholars and intellectuals of four major Islamic sects (Hanafi, Maliki, Shafi'i and Hanbali)[47] as well as from Zaidiyah sect should be invited, and so that the conference should be aimed to be an Islamic event with far-reaching and long-term objectives.

3. There should be respect for logical expression of freedom so that the participants can freely defend their ideology and beliefs and any kind of violence and accusations that is prevalent in Saudi Arabia against the scholars of Islam, should be banned.

4. All the sessions and proceedings of the conference should be managed and supervised by the group of neutral persons or at least an organizing committee comprising of members and participants from different sects should organize and supervise the meetings and sessions.

5. List of important problems to be discussed should be clearly be announced to the participants before the conference so that every participant can choose topic and discuss about it.

6. All the proceedings of the conference without a smallest change or distortion should be published and be made accessible to centers of religious learning so the interested persons can get information about the results of conference.

In case of becoming practical, it can be hoped that the above project and the proposals will help in achieving proximity at least in one category of problems.

Aim of Writing the Book

In this book, overall controversial issues between the Wahhabis and all other Islamic sects are discussed and through Qur'an and *Sunnah*, I have presented and highlighted the original Islamic views. This is not the first work presented by me on the topic. I have written and published two other books before and in each of these I had analyzed these issues. These are:

---

[47] For comparison of jurisprudence laws and practices between these four Sunni Schools and Shia school of Thought, please see book *The Five Schools of Islamic Law* written by Allamah Muhammad Jawad Maghniyyah. Available at: https://www.al-islam.org/five-schools-islamic-law-allamah-muhammad-jawad-maghniyyah

1. *Mafaheem al-Qur'an*[48]: The first volume of this book, chapter entitled *'Tawhid in Worship'*, (pages 387-528) is related to the relevant issues of *'Tawhid* and *shirk* from the Qur'anic point of view' which was taught in the Islamic Academic *Howzah* of Qum and was written by the famous expert scholar Ja'far Ilhadi. This book has been published in Iran and Beirut, Lebanon.

2. *Tawassul* with the Holy Spirits[49]: This book is related to the issue of *'Tawassul* with the holy spirits' that the Wahhabis are spreading their hearsay and baseless teachings everywhere.

For these reasons, the present book is presented to the Islamic Community. We want the Wahhabis and the authors in Riyadh and the Holy Harams and all their supporters in other cities to write a logical critic on this book if they find the contents of this book against their views and reduce the damage it will inflict on their deceived followers. In other case (if they cannot do it), leave the Muslim pilgrims in the Holy Harams free to worship, in the peaceful House of God do not hurt or offend them, stop propagating Wahhabism which only leads to sectarian discord and division among Muslims and finally allow Muslim scholars and intellectuals of the Islamic Community to manage the Holy Shrines.

Ja'far Subhani
Howzah Ilmiyah
Imam al-Sadiq (a) Institute
Qom
26th Shawwal, 1405 A.H. / 15th July, 1985

---

[48] مفاهيم القرآن is thematic exegesis of Holy Qur'an published in 10 volumes by Mo'assasa Imam al-Sadiq, Qom, 2000. First 2 volumes of this tafsir were written by Ja'far Ilhadi.
[49] توسل به ارواح مقدّسه

1

Familiarity with the Life of the Founder of Wahhabism

The origin of religion and path of Wahhabism is ascribed to Sheikh Muhammad, the son of 'Abd al-Wahhab of Najd, Saudia Arabia. This ascription has been derived from the name of his father 'Abd al-Wahhab. And as some scholars put it, the reason why this creed has not been attributed to Sheikh Muhammad himself and has not been called Muhammadiyyah is for fear lest the followers of this creed would find a kind of association with the name of the Holy Prophet (s)[1] and would misuse this ascription.

Sheikh Muhammad was born in 1115 A.H. (1703 A.D.) in the city of 'Uyayna[2] which was located in Najd.[3] His father was a judge in this city. Ever since his childhood, Sheikh Muhammad had a great liking for the study of books on *tafsir* (Qur'anic interpretation), *hadith* (tradition), and *aqa'id* (principles of beliefs). He learned the Hanbali jurisprudence from his father who was one of the Hanbali scholars. From the bloom of youth, he regarded as indecent many of the religious practices of the people of Najd. After going on a pilgrimage to the house of Allah and performing its rites, he headed for Medina where he rejected the resorting of the people to the Holy Prophet (s) near his shrine. He then returned to Najd, and from there he went to Basrah with the aim of later leaving Basrah for Damascus. He spent some time in Basrah and embarked on opposing many religious practices of the people. The people of Basrah, however, casted him out of their city. While on his way from Basrah to the city of al-Zubayr,[4] he was about to die due to the intensity of the heat, thirst, and toll of

---

[1] Farid Wajdi, *Da'irat al-Ma'arif al-Qarn al-'Ishrin*, vol. 10, p. 871, quoting from the magazine *Al-Muqtataf*, vol. 27, p. 893.
[2] 'Uyayna or Al-'Uyaynah is a village in central Saudi Arabia, 30 km northwest of the Saudi capital Riyadh.
[3] Najd or Nejd (Arabic: نجد) is a historic central region of Saudi Arabia that has almost a third of the population of the country. Najd consists of modern administrative regions of Riyadh, Al-Qassim, and Ha'il. In a famous hadith, Prophet Muhammad (s) predicted that horns of Satan (devil) will emerge from Najd. For the hadith text, refer to: *Sahih al-Bukhari* vol. 2, book 17, *hadith* 147 and vol. 9, book 88, *hadith* 214. Appendix II of the book as a collection of few hadithes on this *fitnah*.
[4] Al-Zubayr or Az-Zubayr is small city in the south of Basrah at a distance of about 20 km.

walking in the desert. But a man from al-Zubayr, seeing the Sheikh clad like the clergy, endeavored to save him. He gave the Sheikh a gulp of water, set him on a mount, and took him to the city of al-Zubayr. The Sheikh wanted to travel from al-Zubayr to Damascus, but as he did not have sufficient provisions and could not afford the expenses of the journey, he changed his destination and headed for the city of al-Ahsa.[5] From there, he decided to go to Huraymala,[6] one of the cities of Najd.

At that time which was the year 1139 AH, his father 'Abd al-Wahhab had been transferred from 'Uyayna to Huraymala. Sheikh Muhammad accompanied his father and learned (text of) some books from his father. He then set out on rejecting the beliefs of the people of Najd. For this reason, disputes and debates ensued between him and his father. In like manner, serious and violent disputes erupted between him and the people of Najd. This matter lasted several years until his father Sheikh 'Abd al-Wahhab passed away in the year 1153.[7]

After the death of his father, Sheikh Muhammad embarked on openly expressing his own beliefs and rejecting part of the religious acts of the people. A group of the people of Huraymala followed him and his work won fame. He departed from Huraymala for the city of 'Uyayna. At that time, 'Uthman ibn Hamd was the head of 'Uyayna. 'Uthman received the Sheikh, honored him and made the decision to assist him. In return, Sheikh Muhammad also expressed hope that all the people of Najd would obey 'Uthman ibn Hamd. The news of Sheikh Muhammad's call and doings reached the ruler of al-Ahsa. He wrote a letter to 'Uthman. The consequence of this letter was that 'Uthman summoned the Sheikh and dismissed him. Sheikh Muhammad replied that if you help me, you will become the leader of the entire Najd. 'Uthman, however, avoided him and expelled him out of the city of 'Uyayna.

In the year 1160 A.H., after being expelled from 'Uyayna, Sheikh Muhammad headed for al-Dar'iyya,[8] one of the renowned cities of Najd. At that time,

---

[5] Al-Ahsa, Al-Hasa, or Hadjar (Arabic: الأحساء) is a traditional oasis historical region in eastern Saudi Arabia.
[6] A.k.a. as Huraymila. Located at a distance of about 90 km North West of Riyadh.
[7] Summarized from the *Ta'rikh Najd* of al-Alusi, pp. 111-113.
[8] A.k.a. as Diriyah. Located 22 km north-western outskirts of Riyadh. It was the original home of the Saudi royal family. It was capital of the Emirate of Diriyah under the first Saudi dynasty from 1744 to 1818 A.D.

Muhammad ibn Sa'ud (the ancestor of Al-Sa'ud tribe) was the emir of al-Dar'iyya. He went to see the Sheikh and gave him tidings of glory and goodness. The Sheikh too gave him tidings of power and domination over all the cities of Najd. And in this way, the relationship between Sheikh Muhammad and al-Sa'ud commenced.[9]

At the time when Sheikh Muhammad went to al-Dar'iyya and made an agreement with Muhammad ibn Sa'ud, the people of al-Dar'iyya lived in utmost destitution and need.

Relating from ('Uthman) Ibn Bishr al-Najdi, al-Alusi[10] writes:

"I (Ibn Bishr) initially witnessed the poverty of the people of al-Dar'iyya. I had seen that city at the time of Sa'ud, when its people had enjoyed enormous wealth, their weapons were decorated with gold and silver and they mounted thoroughbred horses. They wore sumptuous clothes and were well provided with all the means of prosperity, so much so that it is beyond the scope of expression.

One day in a bazaar in al-Dar'iyya, I saw men on one side and women on the other. In the bazaar, there was a huge amount of gold, silver, and weapons and a large number of camels, sheep, horses, expensive clothes, and much meat, wheat, and other edibles, so much so that they could not be recounted. The bazaar extended as far as the eye could see. And I could hear the call of the sellers and buyers, a sound which hummed like the buzz of the bee. One (of them) would say, "I sold (my goods)", and the other (one) would say, 'I bought (something)'."[11]

Of course, Ibn Bishr had not given an account as to how and from where such an enormous wealth had been amassed. But the trend of history indicates that it had been accumulated by attacking the Muslims of other tribes and cities (on the charge of not accepting his beliefs) and by plundering and taking as booty their properties. With regard to the war booties which Sheikh Muhammad took (from the Muslims of that region), his policy was to spend it in any way he desired. At times, he granted unto only two or three people all the war booties which amounted to a very large amount. No matter what the booties were, they

---

[9] An Ottoman writer in his book *Tarikh Baghdad*, p. 152, has noted that the relationship between Sheikh Muhammad and Sa'ud dynasty began in another manner. But what has been stated here is more correct.
[10] Shihab ad-Din Sayyid Mahmud ibn 'Abdullah al-Alusi (1802 – 1854 A.D.) was an Iraqi Sunni Hanafi scholar and exegete of Qur'an. His most work is *Ruh al-Ma'ani*, an exegesis of the Qur'an.
[11] 'Uthman ibn Bishr al-Najdi, *'Unwan al-majd fi tarikh Najd*, pp. 117-118.

were in the possession of the Sheikh, and the Emir of Najd could have a share of the booties on permission of the Sheikh.

One of the biggest flaws during the Sheikh's life was the fact that he treated Muslims who did not follow his notorious beliefs as infidels deserving to be fought against. He had no respect for their life or property.

In short, Muhammad ibn 'Abd al-Wahhab called (the people) to *tawhid* (**monotheism**) but an erroneous *tawhid* which he created himself, not the real *tawhid* promulgated by the Qur'an. Whoever adhered to it would have immunity as far as his life and property were concerned, otherwise (the dissolution of) his life and property would, like that of the infidels, be religiously lawful and permissible.

The wars which the Wahhabis waged in Najd and outside Najd such as in Yemen, Hijaz, the vicinity of Syria and Iraq were on this basis. Any city which they conquered by war and domination was religiously lawful for them. If they could, they would establish it as their own possession, otherwise they would be content with the booty they had taken.[12]

Those who adhered to his beliefs and hearkened to his call had to pledge allegiance to him. If anyone rose up in rebellion, he was killed and his property divided. On the basis of this policy, for instance, they killed three hundred men from a village called al-Fusul, located in the city of al-Ahsa and pillaged their property.[13]

Sheikh Muhammad ibn 'Abd al-Wahhab died in the year 1206 A.H. (1792 A.D.).[14] After the demise of Sheikh Muhammad, his followers also pursued this policy and kept alive his innovation and misguidance. For instance, in the year 1216 A.H., the Wahhabi emir Sa'ud mobilized an army of twenty thousand warriors and invaded the city of Karbala. At this time, Karbala enjoyed utmost fame and grandeur. Iranian, Turkish, Arab, and other pilgrims turned to it. After laying siege to the city, the army of Sa'ud finally entered it and brutally massacred the defenders and inhabitants of the city.

---

[12] *Jazirat al-'Arab fi al-Qarn al-'Ishrin*, p. 341.
[13] *Tarikh al-Mamlakat al-'Arabiyya al-Sa'udiyya*, vol. 1, p. 51.
[14] The date of birth and death of Muhammad ibn 'Abd al-Wahhab (1115-1206 A.H / 1703 – 1792 A.D.) has variations in reports. He died in the Emirate of Diriyah.

Familiarity with the Life of the Founder of Wahhabism

The Wahhabi army created such a public disgrace in the city of Karbala that it cannot be put to words. They killed over five thousand people. After emir Sa'ud found leisure from the affairs of the war, he turned to the treasures in the shrine of Imam Husayn (a). These treasures consisted of various properties and precious objects. He took away and plundered whatever he found there. After this incident, Karbala was transformed into such a pathetic situation that the poets composed elegies for it.[15]

For over twelve years, the Wahhabis, every now and then, invaded and looted the city of Karbala and its suburbs, as well as the city of Najaf. The first of these invasions took place in the year 1216 A.H. as already mentioned. According to the writings of all Shi'i scholars, this invasion took place on *Eid al-Ghadir*[16] (a religious festival celebrating the designation by Prophet Muhammad (s) of Imam Ali's (a) as his successor on 18th of Dhul-Hajjah) the same year.

The late 'Allama Sayyid Muhammad Jawad al-'Amili writes:

"This part of the book Miftah al-Kirama was completed by the writer after midnight of the ninth of the holy month of Ramadan 1225 A.H. while in anxiety and apprehension, for the 'Unayza Arabs who are Wahhabi had laid siege on the Najaf al-'Ashraf and on the place where Imam Husayn (a) had been martyred. They blocked the roads, plundered the pilgrims to the shrine of Imam Husayn (a) who were returning to their own lands after pilgrimage in the middle of Sha'ban, and massacred a large number of them (mostly from among Iranian pilgrims). It is said that the number of those killed (this time) probably amounted to one hundred and fifty, some say less..."[17]

The *tawhid* to which Sheikh Muhammad and his followers invited the people in which they made permissible the taking of life and the confiscation of property of whoever did not accept it, consisted of proving a location for Allah the Almighty and regarding Him as having limbs and organs, going by the apparent meaning of some of the Qur'anic verses and traditions.

In this regard, Alusi has noted that the Wahhabis, adhering to Ibn Taymiyyah, confirm the traditions which express Allah's descent into the heavens. They say: Allah descends into the heavens from the empyrean[18] and says:

---

[15] Dr. 'Abd al-Jawad al-Kalidar, *Tarikh Karbala*, pp. 172-174.
[16] For details of the incident of Ghadir, visit: https://www.al-islam.org/ghadir/
[17] Sayyid Muhammad Jawad al-'Amili, *Miftah al-Kiramah*, vol. 7, p. 653.
[18] The highest point in heaven known in 'Arabic as عرش

$$\text{هَلْ مِنْ مُسْتَغْفِرٍ}$$

"Is there a person who seeks forgiveness for his sins?"[19]

In like manner, they also acknowledge that on the Judgment Day, Allah comes to the place where mankind is gathered because He Himself has said:

$$\text{وَجَاءَ رَبُّكَ وَالْمَلَكُ صَفًّا صَفًّا}$$

"And your Lord comes and (also) all the angles in ranks (Fajr:22)."

And Allah can draw near to any of His creations in any way He wants as He Himself says:

$$\text{وَنَحْنُ أَقْرَبُ إِلَيْهِ مِنْ حَبْلِ الْوَرِيدِ}$$

"...and We are nearer to him than his life vein (Qaf:16)"[20]

As indicated in his book entitled *al-Radd 'ala al-'Ikhna'i*, Ibn Taymiyyah regarded the traditions related to going on pilgrimage to the shrine of the Holy Prophet (s) as forged. He has pointed out that it is a grave mistake if a person thinks that the Holy Prophet's being is the same as that of his lifetime even after his demise. Sheikh Muhammad and his followers have expressed similar statements in a more vehement manner.

The false beliefs and statements of the Wahhabis has prompted some people, who have studied Islam from their viewpoint, to say that Islam is a strict and rigid religion and that it is not suitable for all ages (of human history).

An American scholar, Lothrop Stoddard, says:

"The Wahhabis have gone to extremes as far as prejudice is concerned. In the meantime, a group of fault-finders have risen and, voicing out the Wahhabi course of action, have said that the essence and nature of Islam does not fit in with the demands of different times. Therefore, it does not have conformity with progress and evolution of the society and does not follow changes brought about by time."[21]

---

[19] *Hadithe Qudsi* # 52 and 53
[20] al-Alusi, *Tarikh Najd*, pp. 90-91; Ibn Taymiyyah, *al-Risalah al-'Aqida al–Hamawiyya al-Kubra*, risalah no. 11 from his *Majmu' al-Rasa'il al-Kubra*, pp. 429-432.
[21] Lothrop Stoddard, *The New World of Islam*, (London, 1922), vol. 1, p. 264

From the time that Sheikh Muhammad ibn 'Abd al-Wahhab expressed his views and called on the people to accept them, a large group of eminent scholars voiced opposition to his beliefs. The first person to oppose him severely was his father 'Abd al-Wahhab and then his brother Sulayman ibn 'Abd al-Wahhab, both of whom are deemed as Hanbali scholars.

His own brother Sheikh Sulayman compiled a book entitled *al-Sawa'iq al-Ilahiyya fi al-Radd 'ala al-Wahhabiyyah*[22] in which he refuted the views of his brother.

Zayni Dahlan[23] says:

"The father of Sheikh Muhammad was a righteous man of learning. His brother Sheikh Sulayman was also regarded as a scholar. Sheikh 'Abd al-Wahhab and Sheikh Sulayman both reproached Sheikh Muhammad and warned the people against him from the very beginning. This was from the time when Sheikh Muhammad was still studying in Medina. It was through Sheikh Muhammad's words and deeds that very soon they had realized he had such deviant views."[24]

Egyptian scholar 'Abbas Mahmoud al-'Aqqad[25] said:

"The greatest opponent of Sheikh Muhammad was his own brother Sheikh Sulayman, the writer of al-Sawa'iq al-Ilahiyya, who did not acknowledge for his brother a position of ijtihad and correct understanding of the Qur'an and sunnah."

Al-'Aqqad has also noted that Sheikh Sulayman said the following while severely refuting his brother's statements:

"Matters in which the Wahhabis have regarded as polytheism and unbelief, and used as pretexts to make permissible the taking of life and property of the Muslims existed at the time of the A'imma (religious leaders) of Islam. But no one has heard or narrated from the Imams of Islam that those who commit these acts are infidels or apostates. Neither have the Imams issued order of Holy war (jihad) against them. Nor have they called the cities of Muslims as the cities of polytheism and unbelief, as you have."[26]

---

[22] This was the first book written in rebuttal of Wahhabi ideology.
[23] Ahmad Zayni Dahlan (1816 – 1886 A.D.) was famous Sunni Shafi'i scholar. He was also the Grand Mufti of Mecca and Shaykh al-Islam (highest religious authority) in the Hijaz region of the Ottoman empire. He wrote several important books against Wahhabi ideology including *Fitnat al-Wahhabiyyah* and *Al-Durar al-Saniyyah fi al-Radd 'ala al-Wahhabiyyah*.
[24] Zayni Dahlan, *Al-Futuhat al-Islamiyyah ba'da Mudhiy al-Futuhat al-Nabawiyyah*, vol. 2, p. 357
[25] 'Aqqad (1889 – 1964 A.D.) was a famous Egyptian scholar and a literary critic. He wrote over 100 books.
[26] 'Abbas Mahmoud Al-'Aqqad, *Al-Islam fi al-Qarn al-'Ishrin*, (Egypt), pp. 126-137.

In conclusion, it must be noted that Sheikh Muhammad ibn 'Abd al-Wahhab was not the originator and innovator of the beliefs of the Wahhabis. But centuries before him, his ideas had been expressed in different forms by people such as Ibn Taymiyyah al-Harrani and his disciple Ibn al-Qayyim. However, it had not been turned into a new creed and had not found many followers at that time.

Refutations of the Founder of Wahhabism

Abu al-'Abbas Ahmad ibn 'Abd al-Halim, known as Ibn Taymiyyah, was a Hanbali scholar who died in 728 A.H. As he expressed views and beliefs opposite to the views held by all the Islamic sects, he was constantly opposed by other scholars. Investigators are of the view that the beliefs of Ibn Taymiyyah later formed the principles of beliefs of the Wahhabis.

When Ibn Taymiyyah made his views public and wrote books in this regard, the scholars of Islam, headed by the Sunni scholars', did two things to prevent the prevalence of ideological corruption of Muslims:

A. They criticized his views and beliefs. In this regard, we will refer to some books that have been written as a criticism to his beliefs:

1. *Shifa' al-Saqam fi Ziyarat Qabr Khayr al-Anam* by Taqi al-Din al-Subki.[27]
2. *Al-Durrat al-Mudi'a fi al-radd 'ala Ibn Taymiyyah* by Taqi al-Din al-Subki.
3. *Al-Maqalat al-Mardiyya,* compiled by the supreme Judge (*qadi al-qudat*) of the Malikis by the name of Taqi al-Din Abi 'Abdillah al-'Ikhna'i.[28]
4. *Najm al-Muhtadi wa Rajm al-Muqtadi* by Fakhr bin Mu'allim al-Qurashi (d. 725 A.H.).
5. *Daf' Shubah* by Taqi al-Din al-Hisni.
6. *Al-Tuhfat al-Mukhtara fi al-radd 'ala Munkir al-Ziyarah,* by Taj al-Din al-Subki.[29]

---

[27] Abul Hassan Taqi al-Din Ali Ibn Kafi al-Subki (1284-1355 A.D.) was a famous Egyptian Shafi'i Ash'ari scholar and expert in hadithes, Qur'anic exegesis and jurisprudence. He was the chief judge (*qadi*) of Syria for 17 years. He wrote books to refute Ibn Taymiyyah and Ibn Qayyim's deviant ideas.

[28] Taqi al-Din Abi 'Abdillah al-'Ikhna'i (d. 1361 A.D.) was the Sunni Maliki chief justice of Damascus who ordered Ibn Taymiyyah to be imprisoned.

[29] Abu Nasr Taj al-Din 'Abd al-Wahhab ibn 'Ali al-Subki (1327 -1370 A.D.). He was son of Taqi al-Din al-Subki. Like his father, he was Shafi'i Ash'ari scholar and expert in hadith and jurisprudence (*fiqh*) as well as history and wrote famous book *Tabaqat al-Shafi'iyya*. He was appointed chief justice of Syria after his father's death.

These are some of the refutations written on the beliefs of Ibn Taymiyyah. In this way, the baselessness of his views has become evident.

B. The Sunni scholars and *fuqaha* (jurisprudents) of his time have accused him of immorality and have even at times excommunicated him and have revealed his heresy.

When his views about going on pilgrimage to the shrine of the Holy Prophet (s) were expressed in written form for the Supreme Judge of Egypt, al-Badr ibn Jama'ah,[30] he wrote the following at the bottom of the page:

"Going on pilgrimage to the (shrine of the) Holy Prophet (s) is a virtue, the Sunnah and all scholars unanimously accept it. He who regards going on pilgrimage to the shrine of the Holy Prophet (s) as being religiously unlawful, must be rebuked by the scholars and must be barred from making such statements. If these measures are not effective, he must be imprisoned and exposed to the people, so that the latter would not follow him."

Not only did the supreme Judge of the Shafi'i school of thought express such a view about him, but also the Supreme Judges of the Maliki and Hanbali schools of thought in Egypt also confirmed his views in one way or the other. You can refer to *Daf' Shubah (Rebutting the Doubts)* written by Taqi al-Din al-Hisni[31] for more details.

Apart from this, his contemporary al-Dhahabi[32], who was a great writer of the eighth century A.H. and who has written valuable works on history and biography, has, in a letter to him, called Ibn Taymiyyah an equal match to al-Hajjaj al-Thaqafi as far as spreading corruption and deviation are concerned. (This letter has been disseminated by the writer of *al-Sayf al-Saqil fi al-Radd 'alá*

---

[30] Badr al-Din Abu Abd Allah Muhammad Ibn Jama'ah (d. 1333 A.D.) was a famous Sunni Shafi'i jurist of Mamluk Egypt and served as chief justice of Cairo and Damascus during a period when Shafi'i jurisprudence was favored by the state.

[31] Taqi al-Din Abu Bakr bin Muhammad al-Hisni al-Shafi'i (d. 829 A.H./1425-6 A.D.) was a Shafi'i scholar who refuted Ibn Taymiyyah's deviated views in his famous book *Daf' Shubah man Shabbaha wa-Tamarrada wa-Nasaba Dhalik ila al-Sayyid al-Jalil al-Imam Ahmad wa-yalihi al-Fatawa al-sahmiyah fi ibn Taymiyyah*, published from Cairo 1350 A.H./1931–32 A.D.

[32] Famous Syrian Sunni Shafi'i scholar, Shams al-Din al-Dhahabi (1274 – 1348 A.D.) wrote a long letter to correct Ibn Taymiyyah's deviant views and arrogant behavior. He wrote: *"Is it not the proper time that you give up ignorance and do repentance? Know that the repentance in age of 70s is one's last step and is near to death. By God! I don't think you remember your death, but you insult and humiliate those who remember death. I don't think that you will accept my advices and listen to my guidance..."*

ibn Zafil[33] on page 190 of his book, as recorded by the late 'Allama al-Amini[34] in the fifth volume of *Al-Ghadir* on pages 87-89. Those interested may refer to these books.)

When Ibn Taymiyyah died in 728 A.H. in a prison in Damascus, his movement underwent a decline. Though his renowned student Ibn al-Qayyim embarked on propagating the views of his master but did not succeed. No trace of such beliefs and ideas was left in later periods.

But when the son of 'Abd al-Wahhab came under the influence of the beliefs of Ibn Taymiyyah, and when al-Sa'ud supported him to strengthen the foundations of their own rule over Najd, once again the hereditary beliefs of Ibn Taymiyyah spread in the minds of some of the people of Najd like cancer in the body. In the wake of rigid bias, and unfortunately in the name of *tawhid* (*monotheism*), a blood bath was perpetuated under the title of *jihad* against the unbelievers and polytheists. Tens of thousands of men, women, and children were victimized by it.

Once again, a new sect sprang up in the Muslim community and regret arose from that day the *haramayn sharifayn* (*the two holy sanctuaries of Mecca and Medina*) were put under the possession of this group as a result of compromise with Britain and the other superpowers of that time. Also due to the dissolution of the Ottoman Empire[35] and division of the Arab countries among the superpowers, the Wahhabis of Najd gained control over Mecca and Medina, as well as other vestiges of Islam. They exerted utmost effort in annihilating the graves of the *awliya Allah* and in transgressing in disrespect against the progeny of the Prophet (s) by destroying their shrines and other historical remains attributed to them.

In this regard, the Shi'a scholars, alongside the Sunni scholars as we have mentioned above, made tremendous efforts to refute the views of 'Abd al-

---

[33] Written by Taqi al-Din Subki.
[34] 'Abd al-Husayn Amini (b. 1320 – 1390 A.H. / d. 1903 -1970 A.D.), known as 'Allama Amini was a famous Shi'a jurist, *muhaddith*, theologian and historian of 14th century. He was the author of the well-known book *al-Ghadir* that has detailed description of the event of Ghadir.
[35] The Ottoman Empire was a Sunni Hanafi caliphate based in Constantinople, Turkey that controlled much of Southeast Europe, Western Asia and North Africa from 1299 to 1922 A.D. It was dissolved after World War I by the world powers mainly Britain, France and Russia at that time.

Wahhab. Both groups commenced logical and scholarly *jihad* in the best possible manner.

The first refutation which the Sunni scholars wrote on the views of Muhammad ibn 'Abd al-Wahhab was the book entitled *Al-Sawa'iq al-Ilahiyya fi al-radd 'ala al-Wahhabiyyah*[36] written by Sheikh Sulayman ibn 'Abd al-Wahhab (d. 1209 A.H.), the brother of Muhammad ibn 'Abd al-Wahhab.

The first book written by the Shi'a scholars to refute the views of Muhammad ibn 'Abd al-Wahhab was *Manhaj al-Rashad li man Arad al-Sadad*, penned by the honorable late Sheikh Ja'far Kashif al-Ghita[37] (d. 1228 A.H.). He wrote this book as a reply to a treatise which one of the Emirs from among House of Sa'ud by the name of 'Abd al-'Aziz ibn Sa'ud[38] had sent to him. In that treatise, 'Abd al-'Aziz ibn Sa'ud had gathered all views of Muhammad ibn 'Abd al-Wahhab and tried to prove them from the Qur'an and *Sunnah*. This book was published in 1343 A.H. in Najaf. After the work of this dignitary, numerous refutations and criticisms were written against the movement of Wahhabism in the region. Most of these books have been published.

But now, the Wahhabi movements have increased as a result of the massive wealth that the Sa'udis has amassed by way of selling oil. Every day and month, the modern Abu Jahls and Abu Lahabs who have taken control of Holy *Ka'ba*, attack the Islamic sanctities in one way or the other. Each day, the vestiges of Islam are ruined. That which has given impetus to their movement is the secret signs and go-aheads given by their Western masters who are appalled by the unity of the Muslims.

They fear this unity more than they fear international communism. Therefore they have no choice, but to expedite the creation of new religions and faiths (cults), so as to spoil a part of the money they pay to the Wahhabi government

---

[36] Translated to English entitled '*The Divine Lightening*' by Al-Hajj Abu Ja'far Al-Hanbali. Available for sale on internet.
[37] Ja'far Ibn Khidr al-Hilli al-Najafi (1743 – 1812 A.D.), known as Kashif al-Ghita (كاشف الغطاء), was a famous Shiite Scholar from Iraq. He was student of famous scholar Allama Bahr al-'Ulum. The family of Kashif al-Ghita was a well-known Shiite family of scholars in 13th and 14th centuries.
[38] Known as Ibn Saud (1875 – 1953 A.D.), was the first monarch and founder of Saudi Arabia. Ibn Saud in Riyadh in the region called Najd in central Arabia. His family, the House of Saud, had been a power in central Arabia for the previous 130 years. With the full support of British government, he used Wahhabism to gradually gain control of whole Arabian Peninsula in 1932, now known as Saudi Arabia.

for oil and ultimately to severely harm the unity of the Muslims and engage them in branding one another as immoral and in excommunicating one another.

In this book, we will try to reveal their beliefs and remove the obscurities regarding Wahhabism. We will remove the dark veils of doubts and hope to clarify the facts that the beliefs of all Muslims of the world, originate from the Qur'an and the blessed *Sunnah* and that the movements of Wahhabism and its deeds are against the teachings of the Qur'an and the *Sunnah* of the Messenger of Allah (s).

2

Wahhabis and the Renovation of Graves of *Awliya Allah*

Amongst the matters about which the Wahhabis are most sensitive is the matter of renovation of graves and construction over the graves of Prophets, Imams and the pious ones.

This matter was at first initiated by Ibn Taymiyyah and his famous student Ibn al-Qayyim[1] and they gave their verdicts (*fatawa*) in prohibiting the construction of a structure over graves and the necessity of its destruction.

Ibn al-Qayyim in his book *Zad al-Ma'ad fi Huda Khayr al-'Ibad*[2] says as such:

يجب هدم المشاهد التي بُنِيَت على القبور، ولا يجوز إبقاءها بعد القدرة على هدمها وإبطالها يوماً واحِدا

"It is obligatory to destroy the structure constructed over the grave and after gaining power for their destruction it is not permissible to reinstate them even for one day."

In the year 1344 A.H. (1925 A.D.) when the Sa'udi family had gained control over Mecca, Medina and its surroundings, they planned a pretext for destroying the graves of Baqi' and the traces of household and companions of the Holy Prophet (s). By getting verdict (*fatwa*) from the scholars of Medina they wanted to pave the way for demolition and preparing the minds of the people of Hijaz who were never in favor of such action.

For this reason, they sent the Chief Judge (*qadi*) of Najd, Sulayman bin Bulayhid to Medina for the purpose of deriving benefit from the scholars of that place regarding this matter. Thus, he planned the questions in such a manner that the answers (as per the viewpoint of the Wahhabis) were hidden in the questions itself. And in this way, he declared to the *muftis* that their replies should match the answers that had come with the questions; otherwise they would be called as polytheists (*mushrikin*) and be killed if they would not repent.

---

[1] His real name was Muḥammad ibn Abi Bakr ibn Ayyub al-Zur'i al-Dimashqi al-Hanbali (691–751 A.H. / 1292–1350 A.D.). He belonged to the Hanbali sect and was a staunch follower of Ibn Taymiyyah with whom he was imprisoned in 1326 A.D. in Damascus. They were imprisoned for their deviated and heretical beliefs by the *ijma'* (collective decision) of the Sunni scholars at that time.

[2] Ibn al-Qayyim, *Zad al-Ma'ad fi Huda Khayr al-'Ibad*, page 661.

The questions and answers were published in the newspaper *Umm al-Qura* in Mecca in the month of Shawwal 1344 A.H. (1925 A.D.).[3] As a result of this publication, a severe reaction took place among the Muslims mainly Sunnis and Shi'as because they were aware that after taking the verdict (*fatwa*) even if it was by way of force, the destruction of graves of the leaders of Islam would commence.

Incidentally, after taking the verdict from fifteen scholars of Medina and publishing it in Hijaz, the destruction of the traces of the household of the Prophet (s) began on the 8th of Shawwal of the same year. The entire traces of Ahl al-Bayt (a) and the companions of the Holy Prophet (s) disappeared and the valuable properties of the shrine of the Holy Imams (a) at Baqi' were plundered and the graveyard of Baqi' was turned into a heap of dung which would fill one with horror while looking at it.

Now we will mention some of the questions so that it becomes clear as to how the answers had been placed in the question itself. That is to say, the aim was not to ask any questions but gain a pretext for destroying the traces of Messengership. If the aim was truly conception and realism it was meaningless for the inquirer to place the answers in the questions itself.

Instead we can conclude from it that the questions and answers were written on a piece of paper which they took to the scholars ('*ulama*) of Medina only for getting their signature since it is un-imaginable that the famous scholars of Medina who for years were propagators and protectors of the traces of the Holy Prophet (s) and the visitors to his grave would, all of a sudden, accept the views of others and give their verdict for the prohibition of construction and the necessity of its destruction.

Sulayman bin Bulayhid says in his questions:

---

[3] The late Agha Buzurg al-Tehrani in his book *al-Dhari'a ila Tasanif al-Shi'a*, vol. 8, p. 261, writes as such: "The Wahhabis gained control over Hijaz on 15th Rabi' al-'Awwal 1343 A.H. and on 8th of Shawwal 1343 A.H. they destroyed the graves of the Imams (a) and companions in Baqi'." On the other hand, the newspaper *Umm al-Qura* published the questions and answers in publication No.17th Shawwal from the year 1344 A.H. and fixed the date of reply of the scholars of Medina as 25th Ramadan. It should be said that invasions and destruction of the graves both occurred in the year 1344 A.H. and Sayyid Mohsin al-Amin suggests that the year 1344 A.H. was the date of complete destruction. Please refer to the book *Kashf al-'Irtiyab* pages 56 to 60.

ما قول عُلماء المدينة المُنوَّرة زادهم الله فَهماً وعِلماً في البِناء على القبور واتخاذها مساجِد هل هُو جائز أولاً وإذاكان غير جائز بل ممنوع مَنهِيٌ عنه نهياً شديداً فهل يجب هدمها ومنع الصلاة عندها أم لا؟ وإذا كان البناء فيمسبلة كالبقيع وهو مانع مِن الإنتفاع بالمقدار المبني عليه فهل هو غصبٌ يجب رفعه لِما فيه من ظلم المستحقينومنعهم استحقافهم أم لا؟

"What are the views of the scholars of Medina who, may God increase their knowledge and insight, about the construction over the graves and setting them as mosques? Is it permissible or not? And if it is not permissible, and is strictly prohibited in Islam, then is it necessary and compulsory to destroy them and prevent the people from reciting prayers near it or not? If in one endowed (waqf) land like Baqi' construction over the grave becomes an obstacle from making use of those sections which are over that, then is this act not usurpation of a portion of the waqf?"

The scholars of Medina under threat and compulsion gave replies to the questions of Sheikh as follows:

أما البِناء على القبور فهو ممنوع إجماعاً لصحة الأحاديث الواردة في منعه ولِهذا افتى كثير من العلماء بوُجوب هَدمه مستندين بحديث عليُ رضي الله عنه أنه قال: لأبي الهياد ألا ابعثُك على ما بعثتني عليه رسول الله (صلى الله عليه وآله) أن لا تدع تمثالاً إلا طمسته ولا قبراً إلا سوَّيته

"Construction over the graves is forbidden. Based on some traditions proving its prohibition, a group has given verdict (fatwa) for the destruction of the same. In this matter they have made use of the tradition which Abu al-Hayyaj has narrated from 'Ali (r). The latter told him - I am entrusting you with a work which the Messenger of God (s) had entrusted me with the same. Don't see any picture but that you erase it and don't see any grave but that you level it."

Sheikh Najdi in an article, which was published in the newspaper *Umm al-Qura* No. Jamadi al-thani 1345 A.H. (1926 A.D.), says: *"Construction of dome and structure was in vogue from 5th century A.H."*

These are a few examples of the sayings of Wahhabis about renovation of graves and mostly they put forth two reasons in support of their sayings:

1. Consensus of the scholars of Islam about its being prohibited.
2. Tradition of Abu al-Hayyaj from Ali (a) and some other similar ones.

It should be known that our discussion at present is about renovation of graves and construction of bower or ceiling over them. However, the matter of *ziyarat* - visitation to graves, will be discussed separately.

For making the matter clear, we will discuss this issue from three perspectives:

1. What is the view of the Qur'an regarding this matter? Can we derive the judgement from the Qur'an?

2. Does the Islamic *ummah* in reality have consensus in its being prohibited or is it that throughout the history of Islam this matter was something else and renovation of graves and construction of house was in vogue during the period of the Holy Prophet (s) himself and his companions?

3. What is the derivation of the tradition of Abu al-Hayyaj, Jabir, Umm Salama and Na'im which the Wahhabis utilize?

A. Qur'anic View-Point Regarding Renovation of Graves

The Qur'an has not directly passed a judgement about this matter but it is possible to derive its ruling from some of the relevant verses. The details follow.

1. Renovating and protecting the graves of the Prophets (a) is nothing but paying respect to the Divine Rites.

The Holy Qur'an reckons the respect of Divine rites to be a sign of piety and purity of heart. It says:

ذَٰلِكَ وَمَن يُعَظِّمْ شَعَائِرَ اللَّهِ فَإِنَّهَا مِن تَقْوَى الْقُلُوبِ

"And whoever respects the signs of Allah, this surely is (the outcome) of the piety of hearts. (Hajj:32)."

What is meant by respect of Divine rites? شعائر is the plural of شعيرة and gives the meaning of sign and symbol. This verse does not show the sign of existence of God since the whole Universe is the sign of His existence. And nobody has said that respecting whatever things that exist in this Universe is the sign of piety. Instead, it shows the signs of His religion and thus the exegetes interpret this verse as "the Signs of religion of Allah".[4]

If in the Qur'an, Safa and Marwa[5] and the camel which is to be sacrificed in Mina[6] are reckoned to be the rites of God it is for the reason that these are the signs of straight religion (*Din-e-Hanif*) and beliefs of Ibrahim. If Muzdalifa is considered to be *al-mash'ar*, it is because it is the sign of religion of God and

---

[4] al-Tabarsi, *Majma' al-Bayan*, (Sayda edition), vol. 4, p. 83.
[5] *Baqarah*: 158 (إِنَّ الصَّفَا وَالْمَرْوَةَ مِن شَعَائِرِ اللَّهِ). *[Indeed Safa and Marwa are among Allah's sacraments.]*
[6] *Hajj*:36 (وَالْبُدْنَ جَعَلْنَاهَا لَكُم مِّن شَعَائِرِ اللَّهِ لَكُمْ). *[We have appointed for you the [sacrificial] camels as part of Allah's sacraments.]*

stopping at this sign (during Hajj) is practically acting on the religion and obedience to God.

If the entire Hajj rites are named as *al-sha'air* it is because these actions are the signs of divine and true religion.

In short, whatever are the signs and symbols of divine religion, respecting them is the source of nearness towards God. Indisputably, the Prophets (s) and *Awliya Allah* (friends of God) who were the channel for propagating religion among the people are the greatest and the most evident signs of the divine religion. No just person can deny this fact that the existence of the Holy Prophet (s) and Imams (a) are from the proofs of Islam and are the signs of this holy religion and one of the ways of respecting them is protecting their graves and their remains and safeguarding them from any kind of destruction.

Anyhow, the matter of respect for the graves of *Awliya Allah* becomes clear when we consider two things:

(a) The Prophets and *Awliya Allah*, in particular those who have sacrificed their lives in the path of religion are from the divine *sha'air* (rites) and signs of religion.

(b) One of the ways of respecting this group after their demise is to safeguard and renovate their graves as well as protecting their school of thought. For this reason, throughout the world, great religious and political leaders whose graves are a symbol of their school of thought are buried in such selected places which remain permanently safe. Safeguarding their grave from destruction is the sign of protection of their existence and eventually the sign of protection of their school of thought.

For understanding this fact, it is necessary to examine and analyze accurately verse number 36 of *Surah Hajj*. Some of the pilgrims to the House of God take a camel along with themselves right from their houses to be sacrificed near the House of God. They earmark on this camel for sacrifice in the way of God and distinguish it from the other camels by putting a collar round its neck.

As this camel is somehow related to God then according to the same verse it is considered to be the *sha'air* (rites) of God and according to the contents of verse 32 of *Surah Hajj* (Surah 22) وَمَنْ يُعَظِّمْ شَعَائِرَ اللَّهِ should be respected. For example, no one should ride on that camel and water and grass should be given to her at the appropriate time till the time she is slaughtered.

When one camel which is earmarked for being sacrificed near the House of God is considered to be a part of *sha'air* (rites) and its honor and respect is found to be necessary, then why the Prophets (s), Imams, Scholars, Martyrs and those who right from the beginning of their life have put the collar of obedience and submission to God around their neck and have become a channel between God and His creatures are not to be considered a part of *sha'air* (rites) of God and their respect and honor not necessary?

If really *Ka'ba*, Safa, Marwa, Mina and Arafat, which are all inanimate objects and no more than stone and mud, are part of the *sha'air* (rites) because of being related to the divine religion and each one requires obligatory honor and respect, then why the Divine Leaders, who are the preachers and protectors of the divine religion, and those things which are related to them not part of the *sha'air* (rites)!?[7]

We put the conscience of Wahhabis to justice in this matter. Do they doubt the Prophets and Messengers to be amongst the *sha'air* (rites) of Allah and do not they consider the protection of their traces and things related to them as honorable!? Does respect and honor mean renovating their graves and keeping them clean or rather destroying and turning them into a heap of ruins?

2. The Holy Qur'an very clearly instructs us to love the near ones of the Holy Prophet.

The Qur'an says:

$$\text{قُلْ لَا أَسْأَلُكُمْ عَلَيْهِ أَجْرًا إِلَّا الْمَوَدَّةَ فِي الْقُرْبَىٰ}$$

"Say; I do not ask of you any reward for it but love for my near relatives. (Shura:23)"

From the view point of the general people who are referred to by this verse, is not the matter of the grave and its renovation as one of the ways of expressing love towards the household of the Holy Prophet (s)? We see that this custom was and is still prevailing amongst all the nations and they think this to be one way of expressing their love to the people in grave. Thus, great political and religious personalities have been buried in the church or in famous shrines surrounded by flowers and trees.

---

[7] Protection of graves is an expression of love and affection.

3. Renovation of graves and the past nations

From the Qur'anic verses we come to know that respect towards the grave of a believer was one kind of practice which was in vogue amongst the nations prior to Islam.

About the companions of *Kahf* (the Cave), Qur'an narrates that when their condition became known to the people of that time and they came near the entrance of the cave, they expressed two views about their graves:

ابْنُوا عَلَيْهِمْ بُنْيَانًا

"…..*Build a building over them*…., (Al-Kahf:21)"

قَالَ الَّذِينَ غَلَبُوا عَلَى أَمْرِهِمْ لَنَتَّخِذَنَّ عَلَيْهِمْ مَسْجِدًا

"….*Those who prevailed in their affair said: We will certainly raise a mosque over them*….. (Al-Kahf:21)"

The Qur'an narrates these two views without any criticism. Of course, it can be said that if either of these two views were wrong then surely Qur'an would have criticized them or would have narrated their action with condemnation. Anyhow these two views show that one of the ways of respect of the *Awliya Allah* and virtuous people has been the protection of their shrines.

By paying attention to these three verses we can never declare the matter of renovation of graves of the *Awliya Allah*, Prophets and the virtuous ones as prohibited and or an abominable affair. Instead we can interpret it to be one kind of respect to the *sha'air* (rites) of God and manifestation of *mawadda fi al-qurba* (love towards kinsfolk).

4. Elevation of Special Houses

The Qur'an sets forth one novel parable wherein the Light (*nur*) of Allah is compared to a lamp which is having a light within it, and this elegant and profound parable begins with the sentence الله نور السموات والأرض and ends with the sentence والله بكل شئ عليم.

After setting forth this parable which itself is having a lengthy discussion, Qur'an says:

فِي بُيُوتٍ أَذِنَ اللَّهُ أَنْ تُرْفَعَ وَيُذْكَرَ فِيهَا اسْمُهُ يُسَبِّحُ لَهُ فِيهَا بِالْغُدُوِّ وَالْآصَالِ رِجَالٌ لَا تُلْهِيهِمْ تِجَارَةٌ وَلَا بَيْعٌ عَنْ ذِكْرِ اللَّهِ

"In houses which Allah has permitted to be exalted and that His name may be remembered in them; there, glorify Him therein in the mornings and the evenings, Men whom neither trade nor selling diverts from the remembrance of Allah. (Nur:36 & 37)"

Argumentation of this verse requires, before anything else, two points to be clarified:

(a) What is meant by بيوت (houses)?

(b) What is meant by يرفع which has come in the meaning of raising and elevation?

Regarding the first word, we have to remind you that its objective is not limited to mosques. Instead it refers to mosques and houses such as the houses of Prophets (s) and *Awliya Allah* which possesses the aforesaid specialties mentioned in the verse and there is no reason to confine the meaning of the word to mosque.

The whole of this بيوت most common being the mosques and houses of the Prophets and the pious ones who have never been forgetful of the Hereafter, is the center of Light (*nur*) of Allah and the flames of *tawhid*, purification and glorification. Instead it can be said that بيوت here excludes the mosques because a house consists of four walls and surely a ceiling and if *Ka'ba* is called as بيت الله (house of Allah) it is because it possesses a ceiling.

But we see that it is recommended (*mustahab*) that a mosque should be devoid of a ceiling and at present even Masjid al-Harām is without a ceiling. The verses of the Qur'an too show that by *house* is meant a place possessing a ceiling. It says:

وَلَوْلَا أَنْ يَكُونَ النَّاسُ أُمَّةً وَاحِدَةً لَجَعَلْنَا لِمَنْ يَكْفُرُ بِالرَّحْمَنِ لِبُيُوتِهِمْ سُقُفًا مِنْ فِضَّةٍ

"And were it not that all people had been a single nation, We would certainly have assigned to those who disbelieve in the Beneficent God (to make) of silver the roofs of their houses. (Zukhruf:33)"

Anyhow بيوت either refers to a place other than mosque or it consists of both mosque and house.

Now it is time to explain the meaning of the second word i.e. يرفع

The word يرفع in the Arabic language means 'to raise' or 'to elevate' and the verse explicitly says that God has permitted these houses to be elevated. This elevation either refers to physical elevation i.e. raising the base and the walls and protecting them from tumbling down as Qur'an has used the same meaning in the following verse,

$$وَإِذْ يَرْفَعُ إِبْرَاهِيمُ الْقَوَاعِدَ مِنَ الْبَيْتِ وَإِسْمَاعِيلُ$$

"And when Ibrahim and Ismail raised the foundations of the House (Baqarah:127)"

or it refers to spiritual elevation i.e. God has given a special privilege to such houses and has raised their rank and position.

If we take the meaning of physical elevation, then it clearly shows that the houses of the Prophets (s) and *Awliya Allah* who are the true proofs of these houses, are worthy of renovation - whether during their lifetime or after their demise, whether they are buried there itself (like the house of the Holy Prophet (s), Imam al-Hadi (a) and Imam al-'Askari (a) where their houses are their graves because they were buried in their own houses) or in some other place. Under any condition such houses are to be renovated and protected from ruin and destruction.

And if we take the meaning of spiritual elevation, then we conclude that God has permitted such houses to be honored and respected and one of the ways of manifesting our respect to such houses is safeguarding them from destruction and renovating them and keeping them clean.

All these physical and spiritual elevation is because these houses belong to the divine men who were God's obedient servants and were submissive to His commands.

Despite these and such other verses it is a matter of shock as to how the Wahhabis have destroyed the traces of Messengership and ruined their houses and have turned into a heap of rubble, these lustrous places where men and women used to glorify and praise God, day and night, and gather in these places and recite supplications because of the spiritual connection the owners of these houses had with God! This shows as to how they have openly and apparently disclosed their old enmity with the Holy Prophet (s) and his household (a) and his sincere companions!

In this connection we draw the attention of our readers to one tradition.

Anas bin Malik says: The Holy Prophet (s) recited this verse. At that time a person stood up and asked:

"بيت refers to which house?"

The Holy Prophet (s) said: "The house of the Prophets."

Abu Bakr stood and said: "Is this house (referring to the house of 'Ali and Fatima) included amongst them?"

The Holy Prophet (s) replied:[8]

$$نعم مِن أفضلها$$

"Yes, it is the most important of all of them."

B. The Islamic Ummah and Renovation of Graves

The day when Islam spread out in the Arabian Peninsula and its light gradually spread to the important areas of the Middle East, the graves of the Prophets (s) whose place of burial were known to the people were not only having ceiling and bower at that time but also had a dome and place of gathering. Presently also a part of their graves stands intact in the same form.

In Mecca itself, the graves of Isma'il (a) and his mother Hagar (Hajar) lie on a rock. The grave of Danial (a) is in Shush, Iran, and of Hud (a), Salih (a), Yunus (a) and Dhu'l Kifl (a) at Iraq. The graves of the Prophet Ibrahim (a) and his sons Ishaq (a), Ya'qub (a) and Yusuf (a) who were brought from Egypt to Baitul Maqdis by Musa (a) are in the occupied Quds and all of them possess structure, signs and symbols.

The grave of Hawwa (wife of Adam (a)) is in Jeddah where the traces of it were destroyed after the conquest of tribe of Sa'uds and the reason this land is called as Jeddah is because of her grave in that place although this relationship may not be correct.

When the Muslims gained control over this place they never got disturbed and never issued any orders for its demolition.

If truly the renovation of graves and burial of the dead in a covered shrine is forbidden in Islam, then the first and foremost task of the Muslims of that time was to destroy all the graves existing in Jordan and Iraq and secondly prevent

---

[8] al-Suyuti, *al-Durr al-Manthur*, vol. 5 p. 50.

the restoration of any structure at all times. Not only have they not destroyed these shrines but also during the entire 14 centuries they have strived in protecting and renovating any traces left from the previous Prophets (s).

By their God-gifted wisdom they took the protection of the remains of the Prophets to be one way of expressing their respect towards them and by this action reckoned themselves to be pious and virtuous.

Ibn Taymiyyah in his book *al-Sirat al-Mustaqim* says:
"At the time of victory of al-Quds the graves of Prophets consisted of a constructed structure but its doors were closed till the fourth century hijri." [9]

If truly the construction over the graves was a prohibited affair, then its demolition was naturally necessary and its continuity not justified. In short, the existence of these structures during this period and before the very sight of Islamic scholars is itself an evident sign of its being permissible in the religion of Islam.

Islamic Remnants are the Signs of Originality of Religion[10]

Fundamentally, protecting the remnants of Prophethood especially the traces of Holy Prophet (s) such as his shrine, the graves of his wives, children and companions, the houses in which he lived and the mosques wherein he recited prayers, all have great significance which we shall now discuss.

Today, after the lapse of twenty centuries following the birth of ('Isa) Jesus Christ (a) and his mother (Maryam) Mary (a), his book Bible and his companions and disciples, all have been looked upon as a fairy tale in the West. A group of Orientalists have doubted the existence of this heavenly man by the name of Christ whose mother was Mary (a) and his book Bible and described them as a fairy tale like the fairy tale of Layla and Majnun. Why!?

Because not even one genuine trace of Jesus Christ is at hand. For example, his true place of birth, his house where he lived in and the place of his burial according to Christian belief are not known. His heavenly book fell victim to distortion and these four gospels where in the last chapter of each of them there

---

[9] *Kashf al-'Irtiyab*, p. 384 by Sayyid Mohsin al-Amin (1284-1371 A.H. / 1867 – 1952 A.D.). He was a famous Lebanese Shia scholar from Jabal Amel. Wrote more than 70 books including *Haqq al-yaqin*, *A'yan al-Shi'a, al-Rahiq al-Makhtum* and *Naqd al-washi'a*.

[10] Refer to *al-Tabaqat al-Kubra*, vol. 1 pp. 360 to 503 by Ibn Sa'd. In these pages we find the special characteristics of the life of the Prophet (s).

is the description of death and burial of Jesus Christ is certainly not related to him and it clearly shows that they have been compiled after his demise. Thus most of the researchers recognize them to be the literary works of the second century A.D. However, if all the specifications related to him had been protected, then there would have been a clear proof and confirmation to his originality and there would have been no excuse for these fictional and skeptical persons.

Muslims openly announce to the world that: "O people! 1400 years ago a man was appointed in the land of Hijaz for the guidance of the human society and he was fully successful in his mission. All the specifications of his life have been protected as seen in his life without the slightest ambiguity and even the house where he was born is known to us. The mount of Hira is a place where divine revelation (*wahy*) used to descend upon him and it is in this mosque where he used to pray and this is the house where he was buried in and these are the houses of his wives, children and relatives and these are the graves of his children, wives, Caliphs, and….

Now, if we remove all these traces or signs, then obviously we have erased all the traces of his existence and the signs of his originality and prepared the ground for the enemies of Islam. Therefore destroying the traces of Messengership and household of the Prophet is not only one kind of disrespect but also a war against the original manifestations of Islam and authenticity of Messengership of the Prophet (s).

The constitution of religion of Islam is a permanent and everlasting program and till the day of Judgement it will remain as the religion of mankind. The generations that will follow after thousands of years have to believe in its authenticity. Therefore, for ensuring this objective, we have to always protect all the traces and signs of the Holy Prophet (s) and in this way take a step in safeguarding the religion for the coming years. We should not do anything that will make the fate of Prophethood of the Holy Prophet (s) meet the same end as that of Prophet ('Isa) Jesus (a).

The Muslims have strived for the protection of the traces of the Holy Prophet (s) to such extent that they have accurately recorded all the specifications of his life during Prophethood, such as the details of his ring, shoes, brush and the signs of his sword, spear, shield, horse, camel and slave. Even the wells from where he used to draw water and drink and the territory which he has bequeathed and still more the style of his walking and eating and the kinds of food which he liked and the appearance of his beard and his way of applying dye, etc., have been recorded and to a certain extent these signs have still remained till today.

By referring to the history of Muslims and touring the expansive Islamic countries, it becomes clear that renovation of graves and their protection and preservation was one of the customs of the Muslims. At present, throughout the Islamic countries, the graves of Divine Prophets, *Awliya Allah* and the pious people exist in the form of shrines and for their protection endowments are available where their revenues are used for their preservation, etc.

Before the birth of faction of Wahhabism at Najd and before their domination over the two holy shrines and the outskirts of Hijaz, the graves of *Awliya Allah* had been erected, thriving and worthy of attention of everyone. None of the Islamic scholars had any objection towards them.

It is not only in Iran where the graves of *Awliya* and virtuous people have been sanctified in the form of shrines but throughout the Islamic countries, especially Egypt, Syria, Iraq, the western countries and Tunisia the shrines of scholars and great personalities of Islam are flourishing and Muslims depart in groups towards these shrines to visit their graves and recite *Fatiha* and Holy Qur'an for the souls of these great personalities. All these holy places are having servants and protectors responsible for maintenance and keeping them clean.

With such propagation and dissemination throughout the Islamic countries, is it possible to regard the renovation of graves as a forbidden act when this long-drawn custom was existing and still exists from the beginning of Islam till today and this custom is known in the language of the scholars as 'the ways or conduct of Muslims'? The existence of such behavior without any objection from any corner shows that it is permissible, desirable and popular.

This matter is so fundamental that one of the Wahhabi writers too confesses to it as such:

هذا امر عمَّ البلاد وطبَّق الأرض شرقاً وغرباً بحيث لا بلدة مِن بلاد الإسلام إلا فيها قبور ومشاهد بل مساجد المُسلمين غالباً لا تخلو عن قبرٍ ومشهد ولا يَسع عقل عاقل أن هذا مُنكر يبلُغ الى ما ذكرت من شناعة ويسكُت عُلماء الإسلام.

"This matter has reached the common places, East and the West to such an extent that there is no Islamic country where there is no holy grave or shrine. Even the mosques of the Muslims are not devoid of it and reason does not accept that such an affair remains forbidden and the scholars of Islam have kept silent towards this matter."[11]

However, in spite of such confession they have not left their obstinacy and say that the prevalence of such matter and the silence of scholars are no reason for it to be permissible. And if a group remains silent due to some reason or the other, another group under different situation will reveal the fact.

But the answer to such talks is obvious since last seven centuries, the scholars of Islam had remained silent and did not utter a word regarding this matter. Were all of them conservative during this period!? Why at the time of the victory over Baitul Maqdis, the second Caliph did not destroy the traces of graves of the Prophets? Did he too compromise with the polytheists of his time!?

Surprising is the reply of scholars of Medina who say:

اما البناء على القُبور فهو ممنُوع غجماعاً لصحّة الأحاديث الواردة في منعِها ولهذا افتى كثير مِن العُلماء بوُجوب هدمِه.

"Construction over the graves is forbidden according to the consensus of scholars because of the correct traditions that have come in this regard. Thus a great many of scholars have given their verdict (fatwa) for their destruction."

How can the claim of consensus be made for the prohibition of construction over graves when we see that the Muslims buried the Holy Prophet (s) in the house where his wife - Ayesha (r) was living. Later Abu Bakr (r) and 'Umar (r) were buried near the Holy Prophet (s) in the same chamber. Thereafter, the chamber of Ayesha (r) was divided from the middle and a wall was put up there. A portion of it was earmarked for Ayesha (r) and the other portion was related to the grave of the Holy Prophet (s) and the two Caliphs. During the time of Abdullah bin Zubayr, the wall was raised to a higher level due to its low height.

From then on, in every period, the house in which the Holy Prophet (s) was buried was either renovated or reconstructed based on the special architecture of that time. Even during the period of the caliphate of the Umayyads and

---

[11] *Tathir al-I'tiqad*, (Egyptian edition), p. 17, cited from *Kashf al-'Irtiyab*. *Tathir al-I'tiqad* was written by a Wahhabi scholar Muhammad ibn Isma'il al-San'ani (d. 1768 A.D.).

Abbasids the matter of construction of grave was in vogue and graves were constructed in every period with the special architecture of that time.

And the last of the construction over the grave which still exists was the construction of Sultan Abdul Hamid that started in the year 1270 A.H. and lasted for four years. You can read the detailed history of renovation and reconstruction of the house of the Holy Prophet (s) throughout the Islamic history till the time of Samhudi in the book *Wafa' al-Wafa"* of Samhudi[12] and some other related books about the history of Medina.

C. Hadith of Abu Al-Hayyaj

Now it is the time to closely examine the hadith which the Wahhabi scholars narrate. Here we produce a tradition from *Sahih Muslim*:

حدثنا يَحيى بن يحيى وأبو بكر بن أبى شيبة وزُهير بن حربٍ قال: يحيى اخبرنا وال الأخران ، حدَّثنا وكيعُ عن سفيان عن حبيب بن أتى ثابت عن أبى وائل عن أبى الهياج الأسجى قال لي عليٌّ بن أبي طالب ألا ابعثك على ما بعثني عليه رسول الله (صلى الله عليه وآله) أن لا تدع تمثالاً إلا طمسه ولا قبراً مُشرفاً إلا سوَّيته.

Narrated to us Yahya bin Yahya, Abu Bakr bin Abi Shayba and Zuhayr bin Harb (on the authority of) Waki' who narrates from Sufyan who narrates from Habib bin Abi Thabit who narrates from Abu Wa'il who narrates from Abu al-Hayyaj that 'Ali told him: "I assign you for a task which the Holy Prophet (s) assigned me for the same. Do not leave any picture but that which you erase nor any high grave but that you level it."[13]

The Wahhabis have utilized this tradition as a pretext without paying attention to the authenticity and logic of the tradition.

Our Views about this Tradition

Whenever we wish to derive an Islamic ruling from a *hadith*, it should possess two conditions:

1. The authenticity of tradition should be correct; that is to say, the narrators of tradition should be such people that one could rely on their sayings.

---

[12] al-Samhudi, *Wafa' al-Wafa' fi Akhbar dar al-Mustafa*, pp. 383 to 390. Ali bin Ahmad al-Samhudi (1466-1533 A.D.) was Egyptian Sunni Shafi'i Islamic scholar and historian. In this book he has presented Islamic history of the city of Medina.

[13] *Sahih Muslim*, book *al-jana'iz*, vol. 3 p. 61; *Sunan al-Tirmidhi*, chapter *ma ja'a fi taswiyat al-qabr*, vol. 2 p. 256; and *Sunan al-Nasa'i*, chapter *taswiyat al-qabr*, vol. 4, p. 88.

2. The instruction of tradition should be clear upon the purpose.

That is to say the words and the sentences of the tradition should clearly prove our purpose such that if we give the same tradition to a person well versed in language and aware of its specifications, he would be able to derive the same meaning as we derive.

Unfortunately, this tradition is worthy of criticism from both these points especially the second, where one can find no relation with its purpose.

From the viewpoint of authenticity (*isnad*), the traditionalists (those expert in the science of *hadith*) do not accept the reliability of the persons narrating this tradition because we see that its narrators are people like (1) Waki' (2) Sufyan al-Thawri (3) Habib bin Abi Thabit and (4) Abu Wa'il al-'Asadi.

A traditionalist such as Hafiz Ibn Hajar al-'Asqalani[14] has criticized them in his book *Tahdhib al-Tahdhib* to such an extent that it throws doubt and uncertainty on the authenticity of the aforementioned tradition and other traditions narrated by them.

1. For example, he narrates from Ahmad bin Hanbal about Waki' that:

إنه أخطأ في خمس مائة حديثٍ

"*He has committed mistakes in 500 traditions.*"[15]

He also narrates from Muhammad ibn Nasr al-Marwazi about Waki' that:

كان يحدُث بالمعنى ولم يكُن مِن أهل اللسان

"*He used to narrate the tradition according to its meaning (rather than narrating the precise text) while his mother-tongue was not Arabic.*"[16]

2. About Sufyan al-Thawri, he narrates from Ibn al-Mubarak that:

حدث سُفيان بحديث فجسته وهو يُدلسه فلما رانى إستحيى

"*Sufyan was narrating a tradition when I suddenly arrived and noticed that he was deceiving in tradition. When he saw me, he felt ashamed.*"[17]

---

[14] Shihab al-Din Muhammad Ibn Hajr 'Asqalani (1372-1449 A.D.) was a famous Egyptian Shafi'i Ash'ari scholar of Jurisprudence. He was chief judge of Egypt. He wrote over 150 books including *Fath al-Bari* (commentary on *Sahih al-Bukhari*), *al-Isaba fi Tamyiz al-Sahaba, Lisan al-Mizan* and *Risalah Tadhkirat al-Athar*.

[15] *Tahdhib al-Tahdhib*, vol. 11, p. 125. The book enlists narrators of hadithes in alphabetical order and published in 12 volumes.

[16] *Ibid.*, vol. 11 p. 130.

[17] *Ibid.*, vol. 4 p. 115.

Deception in any tradition in whatever meaning it may be interpreted shows that there had been no equity, truthfulness and realism in such a man that he has presented the untrue things to be true.

In the translation of Yahya al-Qattan[18], he narrates from him that Sufyan tried to present to me an unreliable person to be reliable but eventually he was unsuccessful.[19]

3. About Habib ibn Abi Thabit, he narrates from Ibn Hibban[20] that:

كان مُدلَّسا

"He was deceiving in tradition."

He also narrates from al-Qattan that:

لا يُتابع عليه وليست محفوظةً

"His traditions cannot be followed because they are not firm."[21]

4. About Abi Wa'il, he says:

"He is from the *nawasib* and from the deviators from (the path) of Ali (a)."[22] It is worthy of attention that in the entire *Sihah al-Sittah* (six authentic books of *Ahl al-Sunnah*) only one tradition is narrated from Abu al-Hayyaj and that is the same which we have discussed already. It shows that a person, whose share from the Prophetic knowledge was only one tradition, was not a man of tradition at all. Therefore, it becomes difficult to rely on him. When the reference of tradition possesses such shortcomings, then no jurisprudent (*faqih*) can pass a verdict (*fatwa*) based on such a weak reference.

The 'instruction' of tradition is no less important than its reference as the following words in this tradition testify:

ولا قبراً مُشرفاً إلا سوَّيته

Now we will discuss the meaning of these two words i.e. (a) مُشرفاً and (b) سوَّيته

(a) The word مشرف in dictionary means high and elevated and it has been said that:

المُشرف من الأماكن: العالي والمُطلُّ على غيره

---

[18] Imam Yahya bin Saeed Al-Qattan (d.198 A.H.) was a *muhaddith* and contemporary of Imam Abu Hanifah.
[19] *Ibid.*, vol. 11 p. 218.
[20] Abu Hatim Muhammad al-Busti (884 – 965 A.D.) was a Sunni scholar, *muhaddith* and historian from Afghanistan. His most famous book *Sahih Ibn Hibban* is collection of hadithes.
[21] *Ibid.*, vol. 2 p. 179.
[22] *Sharh Nahj al-Balagha*, vol. 9 p. 99. Written by Ibn Abi al-Hadid al-Mu'tazili (1190-1258 A.D.). He was Iraqi Shafi'i Mu'tazili scholar from Baghdad. Famous for his 20 volumes commentary (*Sharh*) on *Nahj al-Balagha*.

مشرف is a high place overlooking the other place."²³

The author of *al-Qamus*²⁴ who has greater validity in the arrangement of meaning of words says:

الشرف مُحركه : العُلو ومن البعير سنامه

شرف with vowel of (راء) is named as something 'high' and 'the hump of a camel'.

Therefore the word (مشرف) in absolute term is called as 'height' and in particular that height which is in the shape of a hump of a camel. By referring to the past, we have to see the objective pertains to which kind of height.

(b). The word سوّيته in dictionary means 'to restore equilibrium', 'to make equal' and 'to set right the crooked'.

سوّى الشيئ: جعله سوياً يُقال: سوّيت المُعوج فما استوى ، صنعه مُستوياً

سوّى الشئ: He made it straight. Arab says - I wanted to set right the crooked which was not smoothened. It also comes in the meaning of 'a faultless product'.

The Holy Qur'an says:

الَّذِي خَلَقَ فَسَوَّىٰ

"Who created and proportioned. (A'la:2)"

After knowing the meanings of phrases and words, we have to see what this tradition actually means!

Two possibilities exist in this tradition. We have to select one of the two by paying attention to the individual meanings and other logical possibilities, the first one of it is:

1. One possibility is that Prophet (s) ordered Abul-Hayyaj to destroy the elevated graves and level them to the ground.

This possibility which the Wahhabis rely upon is rejected due to the following reasons:

Firstly, the word سوّيته does not mean 'to destroy' or 'to demolish' and if it meant so then they should have said:

ولا قبراً مُشرفاً إلا سوّيته بالأرض

'Level them to the ground' while we do not find such words in the tradition.

---

²³ *Al-Munjid*, root word شرف

²⁴ *Al-Qamus al-Muhit* is a famous comprehensive Arabic dictionary compiled by Persian lexicographer Majid al-Din Muhammad al-Shirazi al-Firuzabadi (1329 - 1414 A.D.).

Secondly, if it is meant what they say then why the scholars of Islam have not given such a verdict (*fatwa*)? It is because levelling of grave to the ground is against the Islamic *Sunnah* which says that a grave should be slightly higher than the ground level and all the jurisprudents (*fuqaha*) of Islam have given verdict (*fatwa*) over this matter that a grave should be higher than the level of ground by one span.

In the book *Al-Fiqh 'ala al-Madhahib al-Arba'ah*, as per the verdicts (*fatawa*) of the four well-known Imams (Hanifa, Malik, Shafi'i and Hanbal), we read as such:

ويندُب ارتفاع التُراب فوق القبر بقدر شِبرٍ

"*It is recommended (mustahab) that the soil of grave be higher than the ground by one span.*"[25]

By paying attention to this matter we are bound to interpret the tradition in some other way to which we shall now refer.

2. Second possibility is that he was ordered to make the top of the grave uniform, even or flat and not like the graves which are made in the shape of the hind of a fish or the hump of a camel.

Therefore, the tradition is a witness to this fact that the top of a grave should be even and flat and not in the shape of the hind of a fish or a hump which is common among some of the *Ahl al-Sunnah*. All the four well-known Imams of *Ahl al-Sunnah*, except al-Shafi'i, have given *fatwa* that the grave is recommended to be so. Thus this tradition conforms to the Shi'a scholars who say that a grave apart from being above the ground should be even and flat.[26]

Incidentally, Muslim[27], the author of *Sahih* has himself brought this tradition and another tradition which we shall soon discuss under the title

باب الأمر بتوسية القبر

---

[25] *Al-Fiqh 'ala al-Madhahib al-Arba'ah*, vol. 1, p. 420. Written by famous Egyptian Shafi'i scholar Abdul Rahman al-Jaziri (1882 – 1941 A.D.) who was a scholar of al-Azhar University. In this famous 5 volumes book he compares differences in jurisprudence of 4 Sunni schools of thought.

[26] al- *Fiqh 'ala al-Madhahib al-Arba'a*, vol. 1, p. 420. Therefore, no groups from the Islamic tradition have acted upon this tradition, except the Shafi'i's and the Shi'a.

[27] Asakir ad-Din Muslim ibn al-Hajjaj ibn Muslim ibn Ward Nishapuri (815 – 875 A.D.), popularly known as Imam Muslim, famous Islamic scholar, *muhaddith* (scholar of hadith) from Khorasan, Iran. His hadith collection, known as *Sahih Muslim*, is one of the six major hadith collections in Sunni Islam.

and similarly al-Tirmidhi and al-Nasa'i[28] have brought this tradition in their *Sunan* under the aforementioned title. This title gives the meaning that the surface of grave should be even and flat and if it meant that the graves should be made level to the ground then it was necessary to change the title and name it as الأمر بتخريب القبور وهدمها.

Incidentally, in Arabic language if سوّيته is ascribed to anything (like grave) it means that the thing itself should be flat and even and not that it should be made equal with anything (like ground).

Here we produce another tradition which Muslim has narrated in his *Sahih* and this tradition too contains the same contents which we have approved.

كُنا مع فضالة بن عُبيد بأرض الرُّوم برودسٍ فتَوَفّى صاحب لنا فامر فضالة بن عُبيد بقبره فسوَّى ثم قال سمعت رسول الله يأمر بتسويتها.

The narrator says: "We were with Fudalah bin 'Ubayd in Rome when one of our companions died. Fudalah ordered that his grave be made uniform and said that he had heard the Holy Prophet (s) giving instructions for the levelling of graves."[29]

The key to understanding this tradition lies in acquiring the meaning of the word سوّيته which possesses three possible meanings. By paying attention to the legal presumptions one of them should be selected. Here are the three possibilities:

1. One meaning is 'to destroy the structure over the graves!' This possibility is false because the graves which were in Medina were not possessing structure or dome.

2. Another meaning is 'to level the surface of the grave to the ground'. This is against the *Sunnah* (practice) of the Prophet (s) which is conclusive that the grave should be above the ground by one span.

3. Lastly it could mean 'to surface the grave and make even the uneven portions and hence bring it out from the shape of hind of a fish or hump of a camel'. This meaning is exact and precise and needs no reason for proving this interpretation.

---

[28] Ahmad ibn Shu'ayb ibn Ali ibn Sinan al-Nasa'i (829 – 915 A.D.) was a great Sunni Shafi'i scholar from Nasa, Turkmenistan. He was expert in hadith collection and compiler of *Sunan al-Nasa'i*. which is one of the six authentic books, *Sihah al-Sittah*.

[29] *Sahih Muslim*, book *al-jana'iz*, vol. 3 p. 61.

Now let us see how the famous commentator of *Sahih Muslim*, al-Nawawi, interprets the tradition. He says:

إن السُنة أن القبر لا يُرفع عن الأرض رفعاً كثيراً ولا يُسنَّم بل يُرفع نحو شبرٍ ويُسطَّح

"It is Sunnah (tradition) that the grave should not possess excessive height above the ground and should not have a shape of a hump of a camel. However, it should be one span above the ground and should be even."[30]

This sentence shows that the commentator of *Sahih Muslim* has derived the same meaning as we have derived from the word سوَّيته. That is to say, Imam al-Nawawi recommended and advised that the surface of the graves should not possess the shape of the hind of a fish and they should be made uniform, flat and even, not that they should be levelled with the ground or that the grave and the structure on it should be destroyed.

It is not only we who have interpreted the tradition as such but al-Hafiz al-Qastallani too in his book *Irshad al-Sari fi Sharh Sahih al-Bukhari* has interpreted the tradition as we have. He says:

"It is the sunnah that a grave should be surfaced and we should never abandon this sunnah just because surfacing of the grave is the motto of the rawafid. When we say that the sunnah is surfacing of grave (having no difference with the tradition of Abu al-Hayyaj) it is because

لأنه لم يُرد تسوئيته بالإرض وإنما أراد تسطيحه جمعاً بين الأخبار...

The objective is not to make the grave on par with the ground but the objective is to make the surface of the grave flat and even although being above the ground level."[31]

Moreover, if the objective of recommendation was to destroy the structures and domes over the graves then why didn't Ali (a) himself destroy the domes over the graves of the Prophets existing during his own time!? Besides, he was the ruler over the Islamic lands and places like Palestine, Syria, Egypt, Iraq, Iran and Yemen, which were full of such structures over the graves of the Prophets and were within his sight.

Forgoing all that we have said even if we assume that Imam (a) ordered Abu al-Hayyaj to level all the elevated graves on par with the ground, still the

---

[30] al-Nawawi, *Sharh Sahih Muslim*, vol. 7, p. 36.
[31] *Irshad al-Sari fi Sharh Sahih al-Bukhari*, vol. 2 p. 468. Written by Shihab al-Din Ahmad ibn Muhammad al-Qastallani (1448 - 1517 A.D.), an eminent Egyptian Shafi'i Ash'ari scholar and expert in hadithes. He was contemporary of al-Suyuti, This book is a commentary on *Sahih al-Bukhari* published in 15 volumes.

tradition never bears testimony over the necessity of destroying the structures over the graves since Imam (a) has said:

ولا قبراً إلا سوَّيته

i.e. 'destroy the graves', but has not said:

ولا بناءً ولا قُبة إلا سوَّيتهما

'There is no building and no dome (dome of grave) unless I made them separate'.

Moreover our discussion is not about grave itself but about construction and structures over the graves where people occupy themselves under the shade of these structures and recite the Qur'an, invocations and prayers. Which part of this sentence bears testimony for the destruction of the structures surrounding the graves which in fact facilitates the visitors to worship and recite Qur'an and protects them from extreme heat or cold!?

Two More Possibilities in interpretation of Tradition

In the end we are bound to present two more possibilities in the interpretation of tradition:

1. It is possible that this and some other similar traditions are pointing to a series of graves of the past people where people took the graves of the pious and virtuous people as their *qibla* instead of performing prayers towards the true *qibla*. They used to perform prayers over the grave and the picture which was near the grave and were refraining from facing the true *qibla* which God has selected.

Thus, the tradition has no connection to the graves which have never been prostrated upon by the Muslims but have recited prayers near them facing the divine *qibla* (Holy Ka'ba).

And if they expedite in visiting the graves of the pious people and worship God near their pure bodies and the holy graves, it is because of the high esteem these dignified places have acquired due to the burial of their bodies. We shall discuss about them later on.

2. By تمثالاً is meant the portrait of idols and by قبر is meant the graves of polytheists that were still respected by their near and far ones.

Over here we shall narrate the verdicts of the four scholars of Sunni school of thought:

يُكره ان يُبنى على القبر بيت أو قُبة أو مدرسة أو مسجد

"It is *makruh* (abominable) to build a house, dome, school or mosque over the grave."[32]

With such consensus existing amongst the four Imams how can the judge of Najd insist that construction over the grave is *harām*[33] (prohibited)!?

Moreover, its being *makruh* is itself not having a decisive and correct reference especially when construction over the grave provides a means of worship for the visitor to the grave of Prophets and pious people.

D. Analysis of Hadith of Jabir

The tradition of Jabir is one of the references which the Wahhabis rely on to prove the matter of prohibition of construction of the grave. This tradition has been narrated in different ways in the books of *Sihah* and *Sunan* of the *Ahl al-Sunnah* and in all the references we see the names of Ibn Jurayh and Abu al-Zubayr.

We shall investigate them by narrating all the phases of tradition with their references and then mention our own views regarding the scale of its competency based on logical reasoning.

Muslim narrates in his *Sahih* in the chapter:

النهى عن تجصيص القبر والبناء عليه

'Prohibition to plaster-mould or make construction on a grave'

The tradition of Jabir is reported with three chains of narration, and with two texts. The first one is:

1. حدثنا أبو بكر بن أبي شيبة ، حدثنا حفص بن غياث ، عن ابن جريج ، عن أبى الزُبير ، عن جابر
قال نهى رسول الله أن يُجصص القبر وأن يُقعد عليه وأن يُبنى عليه

"It is narrated from Abu Bakr bin Shaybah, (who said) Hafs bin Ghiyath narrated to us, from Ibn Jurayh, and from Abu al Zubayr from Jabir who said that The Prophet of God (s) prohibited the plastering of graves and prohibited anyone from sitting or constructing over them."

2. حدثني هارون بن عبد الله ، حدثنا حجاج بن محمد وحدثني محمد بن رافع حدثنا عبد الرازق جميعاً عن ابن جُريج قال اخبرني أبو الزبير ، أنه سمع جابر بن عبد الله يقول سمعت النبي بمثله

Here the text of the tradition is indicated to be the same but its chain of narrators differs slightly from the first.

---

[32] *Al-Fiqh 'ala al-Madhahib al-Arba'ah*, vol. 1, p. 421.
[33] *Harām* (حَرَام) means 'forbidden'.

3. حدثنا يحيى بن يحيى ، اخبرنا اسماعيل بن عُلَيَّة عن أيُّوب عن ابي الزُّبير عن جابر قال نهى عن تجصيص القبور.

"The Holy Prophet (s) prohibited the plastering of graves."[34]

Sahih al-Tirmidhi narrates one tradition with one chain of narrators in the chapter:

كراهية تجصيص القبور والكتابة عليها

'Abominability of plaster moulding and writing on graves'

4. حدثنا عبد الرحمن بن الأسود ، اخبرنا محمد بن ربيعة عن ابن جُريج ، عن ابي الزبير عن جابر قال: نهى رسول الله (صلى الله عليه وأله) عن تجصيص القبور وان يُكتب عليها وأن يُبنى عليها وأن توطاء

"It is narrated to us from Abdur Rahman bin Aswad, who reported from Muhammad ibn Rabi' from Ibn Jurayh from Ibn Zubayr from Jabir who said that The Messenger of God (s) prohibited us from plastering the graves and writing on them, and from making and doing construction over them."

Thereafter al-Tirmidhi[35] narrates from al-Hasan al-Basri and al-Shafi'i that they have permitted growing of flowers over the grave.[36]

Ibn Majah[37] narrates a tradition with two texts and two chains of narration in his *Sahih* in the chapter entitled:

ما جاء في النهى عن البناء على القبور وتجصيصها والكتابة عليها

'What it is been said, is about prohibition of building, plaster-moulding and writing on graves (engraving)'

5 & 6. حدثنا ازهر بن مروان ، ومحمد بن زياد قال حدثنا عبد الوارث ، عن أيوب عن أبى الزُّبير عن جابر قال نهى رسول الله عن تجصيص القُبور. حدثنا عبد الله بن سعيد ، حدثنا حفص عن ابن جُريح عن سُليمان بن مُوسى عن جابر قال: نهى رسول الله ان يُكتب على القبر شئ

"It is narrated from Azhar ibn Marwan, Muhammad-ibn-Ziad said Abdul Warith has narrated to us from Ayub from Abi-Zubair from Jabir that Prophet (s) of God has prohibited from plaster-moulding on graves. Abdullah-ibn-Sa'eed narrated us, Hafs

---

[34] *Sahih Muslim*, book *al-jana'iz*, vol. 3 p. 62.
[35] Muhammad ibn 'Isa as-Sulami ad-Darir al-Bughi al-Tirmidhi (824 – 892 A.D.) Persian Islamic scholar and collector of hadith from Termez (Uzbekistan). He was student of Imam Bukhari. His famous work *Jami' al-Tirmidhi* a.k.a. as *Sunan al-Tirmidhi* is one of six authentic books of hadithes of Ahl al-Sunnah.
[36] *Sunan al-Tirmidhi*, (ed. by 'Abd al-Rahman Muhammad 'Uthman, al-Maktaba al-Salafiyya), vol. 2 p. 208.
[37] Abu 'Abdilluh Muḥammad ibn Yazid Ibn Majah al-Qazwini (824 – 887 A.D.) was great Persian Sunni Shafi'i scholar of hadithes from Qazwin. He compiled the last of Sunni Islam's six canonical hadith collections, *Sunan Ibn Majah*.

from Ibn Jarih from Sulayman Ibn Musa from Jabir that Prophet (s) of God has prohibited to engrave anything on graves."[38]

After narrating this tradition, the commentator al-Sindi[39], quotes al-Hakim al-Nishapuri[40] and says:

"The tradition is Sahih but not practical because the Islamic leaders from East to West have been writing over the graves. This is a practice which the people have adopted from the past generations."

al-Nasa'i narrates in his *Sahih* in the chapter of البناء على القبر with two chains of narrators and two texts:

7 & 8. اخبرنا يُوسف بن سعيد قال حدثنا حجاج عن ابن جُريح قال اخبرني ابو الزُبير انه سمع جابر يقُول سمعت رسول الله نهى عن تجصيص القُبور أو يُبنى عليها أو يجلس عليها أحد. أخبرنا عمران بن موسى قال حدثنا عبد الوارث قال حدثنا ايُوب عن ابى الزُبير عن جابر قال نهى رسول الله عن تجصيص القُبور.

"Yousuf bin Saeed reported to us that Hajjaj narrated from ibn Jarih who said I heard from Abu Zubair who heard Jabir he said that Prophet (s) of God prohibited to plaster-mould or build on a grave or someone sitting on it. Imran ibn Musa reported to us who said, narrated to us Abdul Warith, who said narrated to us Ayub, from Abi Zubair, from Jabir who said that Prophet (s) of God prohibited plastering mould graves."[41]

In the *Sunan* of Abu Dawud[42] (vol. 3, p. 216) chapter of البناء على القبر tradition of Jabir is narrated with two chains of narrations and two texts:

9 & 10. حدثنا احمد بن حنبل ، حدثنا عبد الرزاق حدثنا ابن جريح ، اخبرني ابو الزبير انه سمع جابراً يقول سمعت النبي نهى ان يُقعد على القبر وان يُجصص ويُبنى عليه. حدثنا مسدد وعثمان بن ابى شيبة قال حدثنا حفص بن غياث عن ابن جُريح عن سُليمان بن موسى وعن ابى الزبير عن جابر بهذا الحديث قال ابو داود قال: عثمان أو يُزاد عليه وزاد سُليمان بن موسى أو أن يُكتب عليه.

"……Abu Dawud says: "The Holy Prophet (s) has prohibited us from writing over the grave or from raising it."

---

[38] *Sunan Ibn Majah*, book *al-jana'iz*, vol. 1, p. 473.
[39] Abu Ma'shar Al-Sindi, (d.170 A.H.) was a scholar of hadith literature and a pioneer in the compilation of hadith from Mansura, Sindh now the part of Pakistan. He lived at Medina for a number of years and later shifted to Baghdad where he died. He was contemporary of famous religious scholars of his time.
[40] Abu Abdullah Muhammad al-Hakim al-Nishapuri (933 – 1012 A.D.) was a Persian Sunni Shafi'i scholar and expert in hadithes. His famous book *Al-Mustadrak alaa al-Sahihain* popularly known *al-Mustadrak* is a collection of hadithes from *Sahih al-Bukhari* and *Sahih Muslim*.
[41] *Sunan al-Nasa'i* (printed with commentary of Jalal al-Din al-Suyuti), vol. 4 pp. 87-88.
[42] Sulayman ibn al-Ash'ath ibn Ishaq al-Azdi al-Sijistani (817 – 889 A.D.) was Persian Sunni Hanbali scholar of hadithes and compiler of *Sunan Abu Dawud*, the third of the six authentic books.

Imam Ahmad bin Hanbal[43] in his *al-Musnad* has narrated the tradition of Jabir as follows:

1. عن عبد الرزاق عن ابن جُريج اخبرني ابو الزبير انه سمع جابر بن عبد الله يقول سمعت النبي ينهى ان يقعد الرجل على القبر وان يُجصص وان يُبنى عليها.

"*From Abd al-Razzaq from Ibn Juraih who reported from Abu Zubair that Jabir Ibn Abdullah said that I heard from Prophet (s), he prohibited people from sitting on grave or plaster- moulding or building on it.*"[44]

These were the various forms of the tradition that have been narrated with different chains of narration and texts. Now let us see whether the tradition can be rationalized or not.

Points of Weakness in this Tradition

The tradition of Jabir is faced with a series of problems that no logical reasoning can be based on it.

Firstly: In all the chains of transmission of this tradition, Ibn Jurayh[45] and Abu al-Zubayr[46] have either both come together or at least one of them has been mentioned. Now if the position of these two persons is clarified, then it would be needless to discuss about other people who have come in the chains of transmission of this tradition. Although a section of the narrators are from the unknown and weak, still by clarifying the position of these two people, it is not required to discuss and talk about the others.

Ibn Hajar al-'Asqalani narrates in *Tahdhib al-Tahdhib* about Ibn Jurayh quoting from the distinguished scholars as follows:

Yahya bin Sa'id was asked about the *hadith* of Ibn Jurayh to which he said: 'If Ibn Jurayh does narrate a tradition from the book, he cannot be relied upon'. It was said to him that he uses *akhbarani* (technical term used in *isnad* followed by identification of the transmitter from whom the report was obtained), to which he said, "It's nothing... all of it is weak."

He narrates from Ahmad bin Hanbal that if Ibn Jurayh says:

---

[43] Abu 'Abdilluh Ahmad Ibn Muhammad Ibn Hanbal (780 – 855 A.D.), Ibn Hanbal for short, was a famous Muslim jurist, theologian, hadith traditionist, and founder of the Hanbali school of Sunni jurisprudence.
[44] Ibn Hanbal, *al-Musnad*, vol. 3 p. 295 & p. 332, and he narrates from Jabir in the *mursal* form on p. 399.
[45] He is 'Abd al-Malik bin 'Abd al-'Aziz bin Jurayh al-'Umawi.
[46] He is Muhammad bin Muslim al-'Asadi.

قال فلان قال فلان واخبرتُ جاء بمناكيرٍ

"..that so and so said such and such then he has narrated a false tradition."

Malik bin Anas says: In the matter of traditions Ibn Jurayh is like one who collects twigs in the darkness of night. (where his hand will be bitten by snake and scorpion).

From al-Daraqutni,[47] who says:

تجنب تدليس ابن جُريح فإنه قبيح التدليس لا يُدلس إلا فيما سمعه مِن مجروج

"Keep away from the craftiness (presenting the false to be true) of Ibn Jurayh for he plays a dirty hypocrisy. Whenever he hears a tradition from a weak person, he presents it in such a manner that as if it was from a reliable person."

From Ibn Hibban who says that: Ibn Jurayh plays trickery in tradition.[48]

With such judgements from the scholars of *'ilm al-rijal* (the science of studying chain of narrators of *hadith*) can one rely on the tradition of such a person and in contrast to the decisive path of the Muslims who were always renovating the graves of *Awliya Allah* and respecting them, is it possible to have confidence in such a narrator?

About Abu al-Zubayr's position, Ibn Hajar narrates the following sentences from the scholars of *rijal*:

The son of Ahmad bin Hanbal narrates from his father who narrates from Ayyub that he (i.e. Abu al-Zubayr) was weak in *hadith*.

Ibn Hajar narrates from Shu'ba that Abu al-Zubayr did not know how to recite his prayers properly. Again he narrates from him as such: "I was in Mecca when a person came to Abu al-Zubayr and asked him some questions to which the latter started to defame him. I told him that he was accusing a Muslim. He replied: He has made me angry. I informed him that since he was defaming everyone who made him angry I would no longer narrate any tradition from him."

Again Ibn Hajar asked Shu'ba as to why he stopped narrating tradition from Abu al-Zubayr. He replied: "I saw him openly performing bad deeds."

---

[47] Abul-Hasan 'Ali ibn 'Umar al-Baghdadi al-Daraqutni (918— 995 A.D.) was Iraqi Sunni Shafi'i scholar and *muhaddith*. *Sunan al-Daraqutni*, a collection of hadithes is his most famous book.
[48] Ibn Hajar al-'Asqalani, *Tahdhib al-Tahdhib*, (Dar al-Ma'arif al-Nizamiyya), vol. 6 p. 402, 404 and p. 506.

Ibn Hajar narrates from Ibn Abi Hatim that he asked his father about the character of Abu al-Zubayr to which he replied: "His traditions are written but they cannot be relied upon."

Ibn Hajar further narrates from him that the latter informed Abu Zur'a that people were narrating traditions from Abu al-Zubayr and asked him whether he could be relied or not.

He replied: 'The tradition of only a trustworthy person can be used as an argument (a sarcastic remark to indicate that he was not a trustworthy person).'

This is the position of these two persons who have come in all the chains of narration of the tradition. Is it possible to rely on a hadith that is reported by these two persons?

Even if we assume that others mentioned in the references are reliable (while in fact some of them like 'Abd al-Rahman bin Aswad were accused of being liars), can such a tradition be used as argument when its narrators are these two people?

Is it really fair that with such a tradition that is having such a weak authenticity, one can destroys the traces of household of the Prophet and his companions and find fault with the actions of the Muslims in these fourteen centuries?

Secondly: The tradition is a matter of concern from the viewpoint of text. This is because of the fact that the narrators have not heeded sufficient attention to memorizing its text. And this concern is such that a person loses confidence in them. Now we shall describe the kind of concern:

The tradition of Jabir has been narrated in seven forms whereas the Holy Prophet (s) has mentioned that in one form. Here are the descriptions of the seven forms:

1. The Holy Prophet (s) has prohibited plastering of the graves and resting or constructing a structure over them. (Traditions no. 1, 2 and 9).

2. The Holy Prophet (s) has prohibited plastering of graves. (Traditions no. 5 and 8).

3. The Holy Prophet (s) has prohibited plastering, writing, constructing and walking over the graves. (Tradition no. 4).

4. The Holy Prophet (s) has prohibited writing over the graves. (Tradition no. 6).

5. The Holy Prophet (s) has prohibited sitting over the grave or plastering and constructing and sitting over it. (Tradition no. 10)

6. The Holy Prophet (s) has prevented from sitting, plastering or constructing over the grave. (Tradition no.11) This one differs from the first where in the first form resting is prohibited while here sitting is prohibited).

7. The Holy Prophet (s) has prohibited from sitting, plastering, constructing and writing over the grave or raising the grave. Here, the prohibition of writing over the grave and raising the grave is added.

Apart from this, there are some differences and contradictions among the interpretations. In the first case, resting is mentioned; in the third case walking is mentioned and in the fifth and sixth case we find sitting. With such problems, no jurisprudent (*faqih*) can rely upon this tradition.

Thirdly: Assuming that the chains of narration of this tradition are reliable, it does not indicate more than that the Holy Prophet (s) prevented construction over graves. However, preventing one thing is no proof of its being prohibited because prohibition sometimes is of *harām* type and sometimes of *makruh* type and prohibition has been mostly used in the *makruh* sense in the discourse of the Holy Prophet (s) and other religious leaders.

It is true that the first meaning of prohibition that is to say in real term is '*nahi*' which is same as *harām* and till a proper terminology for another meaning is not found, we can never take it to be *makruh*, yet the scholars and the *fuqaha* have not taken this tradition to be anything but in the *makruh* sense. For example, al-Tirmidhi in his *Sahih* narrates the tradition under the chapter:

كراهية تجصيص القُبور

A clear proof that it is *makruh* is the same which al-Sindi, commentator of *Sahih Ibn Majah* narrates from al-Hakim al-Nishapuri who says that none of the Muslims have acted upon this prohibition. That is to say he has not presented it to be a prohibition in the *harām* sense calling to witness the fact that all Muslims have been writing on the graves.

Another proof that this prohibition is in the *makruh* sense is the consensus of the Islamic scholars upon the permissibility of construction over the grave except that if the land is endowed.

The commentator of *Sahih Muslim* in his commentary of this tradition writes:

أما البناء فإن كان في مِلك الباني فمكروه وإن كان في مقبرة مسبلة فحرامٌ نصَّ عليه الشافعيِ والأصحاب.

"Construction over the grave in the land belonging to the owner of the grave is makruh and in the endowed land is harām. Al-Shafi'i has emphasized upon this matter and even brought the tradition under the title of chapter."[49]

كراهة تجصيص القبر والبناء عليه

However, it is obvious that a thing being *makruh* does not become an obstacle. The fact being that sometimes due to a series of affairs that *makruh* gets eliminated. Whenever renovation of grave becomes the source of protection of the originality of Islam or the source of manifestation of love for the owner of grave which God has made their love obligatory or the source of protection of Islamic signs or becomes the cause for the visitors to recite Qur'an and invocation under the shade of the structure over the grave than surely not only such benefits (which arise from the construction over the grave) eliminate the *makruh* element but make them *mustahab* (recommended).

The decree of *mustahab* or *makruh* changes under various pretexts. It is likely that a *makruh* becomes good due to some pretext or a series of *mustahabi* (recommended) affairs become abominable due to some other events because *makruh* and *mustahab* of one thing is nothing but expedient for being hated or loved respectively. But these expedients are effective under the condition that no obstacle nullifies their expediences and effects and this matter is clear for those people who are acquainted with Islamic jurisprudence (*fiqh*).

Logical Analysis of Two More Traditions

Now that our discussion has reached this stage, it is worthy that we examine some more traditions which are referred to by the Wahhabis.

1. Ibn Majah narrates in his *Sahih* as such:

حدثنا محمد بن يحيى ، حدثنا محمد بن عبد الله الرقاشى ، حدثنا وهب ، حدثنا عبد الرحمن بن يزيد بن جابرة ، عن القاسم بن مخيمرة عن ابي سعيد: إن النبي نهى أن يُبنى على القبر

"Mohammad Ibn Yahya, Muhammad Ibn Abdullah, Al-Riqashi, Wahab, Abdur Rahman Ibn Yazid Ibn Jaber, have narrated to us from Qasim ibn Mokhaimara from Abi Saeed: "Verily Prophet Muhammad (s) prohibited make construction on graves."[50]

---

[49] *Sahih Muslim*, (Egypt), vol. 3 p. 62. (published by Maktabah Muhammad Ali Sabih, Cairo, Egypt)
[50] *Sunan Ibn Majah*, vol. 1 p. 474.

2. Ahmad bin Hanbal in his *al-Musnad* narrates one tradition with two chains of narrators. Here we mention both of them:

حدثنا ، حسن ، حدثنا ابن لهيعه ، حدثنا بُريد ابن أبى حبيب عن ناعم مولى أم سلمة عن أم سلمة قالت: نهى رسول الله ان يُبنى على القبر أو يُجصص

"Narrated Hassan, Ibn Lahi'ah narrated, Buraid Ibn Abi Habib narrated from Naim servant of Umme Salamah. She said: 'Prophet of God prohibited to build (construction) on grave or plaster-moulding.'"[51]

عليّ بن اسحاق حدثنا عبد الله ، ابن لهيعه ، حدثني بُريد بن أبى حبيب عن ناعم مولى أم سلمة ، أن النبي نهى أن يُجصص قبر أو يُبنى عليه أو يُجلس

"Ali Ibn Ishaq narrated, Abdullah ibn Lahi'ah, narrated Buraid ibn Abi Habib from Naeem, servant of Umme Salama: 'Prophet prohibited to plaster-mould a grave or build (make construction) on it or sit on it.'"[52]

To prove the weakness of the first tradition suffice it is to say that one of the narrators is Wahab who is completely مجهول (unknown) and it is not known which 'Wahab' is the narrator of this tradition. In *Mizan al-I'tidal* seventeen Wahabs are mentioned and it is not known that this Wahab is which one of them where most of them are regarded to be fabricators of traditions and known liars.[53]

The major problem of the second and third traditions is the presence of 'Abdullah ibn Lahi'ah. Al-Dhahabi writes about him as such:

قال ابن معين ضعيف لا يحتج به قال الحميدى عن يحيى ابن سعيد انه كان لا يراه شيئاً

"Ibn Ma'in has said that he is weak and his tradition cannot be argued upon."[54]

Al-Humaydi[55] narrated from Yahya bin Sa'eed that he does not count him to be of any significance.

We shall now pass from the controversies in the *sanad* and turn over to the following matter. All the historians and Islamic *muhaddithun* (traditionists) have narrated that the holy body of the Holy Prophet (s) was buried by the approval of his companions in the house and chamber of his wife Ayesha (r). In selecting

---

[51] Ibn Hanbal, *al-Musnad*, vol. 6 p. 299.
[52] *Ibid*.
[53] al-Dhahabi, *Mizan al-I'tidal*, vol. 3 pp. 350 to 355.
[54] *Ibid*., vol. 2 p. 476 under the title 'Abdullah ibn Lahi'ah; Ibn Hajar al-'Asqalani, *Tahdhib al-Tahdhib*, vol. 1 p. 444.
[55] Imam al-Humaydi was Shafi'i jurisprudence scholar and a hafiz. He was student Imam Shafi'i himself. He also narrated hadithes from Sufyan ibn Uyainah and Fudhail ibn Iyadh. His pupils included al-Bukhari, an-Nasa'i and al-Tirmidhi. He died in Mecca in 219 A.H. / 834 A.D.

the place of his burial, the companions have relied on the tradition narrated by Abu Bakr from the Holy Prophet (s) that any Prophet who dies in any place should be buried in that very place.[56]

The question arises here that if the Holy Prophet (s) had really prohibited construction over the grave then how was it that he was buried under the ceiling and his grave became such that it possessed a structure. It is a matter of laughter when some of the dry and rigid Wahhabis say that what is forbidden is making the structure over the grave and not the burial of body under the structure and the Holy Prophet (s) was buried under the structure and not that a structure was made over his grave.[57]

Such an interpretation of the tradition shows no motive other than explaining one external fact (burial of the body of the Holy Prophet (s) under a structure) and if one Wahhabi was not faced with such a fact he would have ordered both these acts to be *harām* (forbidden).

Basically, at this juncture we ask the Wahhabis some questions:

Is it that only the original construction over the grave of the dead person forbidden and if someone has already made such a construction then is its continuity not forbidden although its original construction was forbidden?

Or is it that the original construction and its continuity both are forbidden?

If only the original construction is forbidden and their continuity was not forbidden, then the question arises that why the Government of Sa'ud destroyed by force the traces of Messengership and the houses of the household of the Holy Prophet (s) and the domes of his children and companions who were already buried under the structures.[58]

Moreover, this supposition is against the verdicts (*fatawa*) of founders of Wahhabism such as Ibn al-Qayyim and Ibn Taymiyyah.

The former says:

---

[56] Ibn Hanbal, *al-Musnad*, vol. 1 p. 7; *Sahih al-Tirmidhi*, vol. 2 p. 139; Ibn Sa'd, *al-Tabaqat*, vol. 2 p. 71; and others.

[57] *Riyad al-Jannah*, p. 269 by Muqbil bin al-Hadi al-Wadi'i. Al-Wadi'i (1933 - 2001 A.D.) was a modern Salafi reviver in Yemen. With the heavy financial support of Saudi Arabian government, he founded Madrasa in Dammaj in Yemen which was center for propagation of Salafist ideology.

[58] For detailed inquiry on this topic, refer to the book '*Building of tombs in the light of Qur'an and Hadith*' by Sayyid Murtaza al-Askari, available at: https://www.al-islam.org/building-tombs-light-quran-hadith-sayyid-murtadha-al-askari

يجب هدم المشاهد التي بُنيت على القبور ولا يجوز إبقاءها بعد القُدرة على هدمها وإبطالها يوماً واحداً.

"It is obligatory to destroy the structures made over the graves and after gaining power for its destruction it is not permissible to let it remain and to preserve it even for one day."

With this explanation it is not correct for a Wahhabi to select the first alternative of our question. Thus, he is bound to select the second and say that the construction over the grave is *harām* in both the cases.

At this moment, a question will arise as to why the Muslims buried the holy body of the Prophet (s) under a roofed place. Although it is true that they did not originally construct over his grave yet they acted in such a way that the grave of the Holy Prophet (s) was already having a structure.

Here a Wahhabi has only one route of escape and that is for explaining the physical action of the Muslims he will say: Preservation and continuation of grave is forbidden when original construction takes place over the grave and if at the time of the original construction, there was no grave then its continuation (no matter if it is in the form of construction over grave) is not *harām*.

Such dissociation has no reason other than justifying one external fact (action of Muslims).

Wahhabism entangled in the contradiction between the school of thought and the practice of Muslims

This point is not the only instance where the Wahhabism has been caught in the scuffle of contradiction between its school of thought and the deeds of Muslims.

It has been aimlessly struggling in other instances too. It strictly prohibits *tabarruk* of the remains of the Holy Prophet (s) and say: "Stone, soil, etc. are of no use." On the other hand we see the Muslims constantly kissing and touching the stone (*hajr al-aswad*) or kissing the curtain of the *Ka'ba* or seeking *tabarruk* from its door and walls which according to Wahhabis bears no result.

They have prohibited construction of mosque near the grave of the *Awliya Allah* whereas in the entire Islamic lands, mosques exist near the graves. Even besides the grave of Hamza (r) there was a mosque which the transgressive Sa'udis have destroyed. At present the grave of the Holy Prophet (s) is in the mosque and the Muslims perform prayers around there.

Preparing an argument instead of adopting a realistic approach

In order to destroy the tombs of the graves of Imams (a) buried in Baqi' the Wahhabis embarked on resorting to arguments and so to speak have found an excuse. They say that the land of Baqi' is an endowed (*waqfi*) land and maximum use should be made from this land and every kind of obstruction from reaping the benefits should be removed.

Construction of a structure over the graves of the household of the Prophet (s) is an obstacle from utilizing a part of the land of Baqi', because, although burial is possible in the sanctuary and the shrine, the same cannot be done under the foundations and surrounding walls. Therefore, such constructions should be destroyed till the entire land of Baqi' is exploited for useful purposes.

The Response and Refutation

Undoubtedly such reasoning is nothing but a kind of biased judgment. The Wahhabi judge (*qadi*) wishes to destroy, by any means, the traces of the household of the Holy Prophet (s) and even if he was unable to find any reason, he would still think of destroying them under the cover of force. On account of such a mentality he started to conjure up a pretext and hence brought up the matter of endowment of the land of Baqi'.

Moreover the idea that Baqi' is an endowed land is nothing more than an imagination since:

Firstly, no book that we could rely on, whether of history or tradition (*hadith*), mentions that Baqi' is endowed (*waqfi*). Instead it is possible to say that Baqi' was a waste land where the people of Medina used to bury their dead. In this case, such a land will be considered to be amongst the 'properties belonging to no particular person' (*al-Mubahat al-'Awwaliyya*) and any kind of appropriation over it is permissible.

In previous times, greed and avarice of the people in possessing the dead and barren land was insignificant and there was no money and power in developing and flourishing them. Moreover, the people living in villages had not yet started to migrate to cities and no issues related to land and no people such as land profiteers existed and no institute by the name of land exchange had come into existence. Thus most of the lands were not having owners and they remained as they were and were counted to be part of wastelands.

During these periods the people of every city, village and hamlet allocated a part of the land for the burial of their dead or if someone would become the first in burying his dead once on a piece of land, others would follow suit. As such, they would convert the land into a graveyard without anyone seeking possession of it and making it a *waqf* for burying the dead.

The land of Baqi' was no exception to this rule. The lands in Hijaz and Medina were not of much value and with the presence of waste lands around Medina, no wise person would have created an endowment over cultivable land. In a place where waste land is plentiful and cultivable land very scanty, surely the waste land (which is counted to be the property belonging to no particular person) will be used.

Incidentally, history too confirms this reality. Al-Samhudi in *Wafa' al-wafa' fi Akhbar dar al-Mustafa* writes:

"The first person who was buried by the Holy Prophet (s) in Baqi' was 'Uthman ibn Maz'un (the companion of the Holy Prophet). When Ibrahim, son of the Holy Prophet, died, the Prophet (s) ordered him to be buried near 'Uthman. From then on, people were inclined to bury their dead in Baqi' and they cut off the trees (to make space). Each tribe appropriated one piece of the land for themselves".

Thereafter he says:

"The land of Baqi' was having a tree by the name of *gharqad*. When the people buried 'Uthman ibn Maz'un over there the tree was cut off."[59]

The tree of *gharqad* is the same wild tree found in the deserts of Medina.

From these words of al-Samhudi we draw a clear conclusion that the land of Baqi' was a dead land where, after the burial of one companion everyone took a part of it for their respective tribes and the name of *waqf* has never been seen in history. Instead, history shows that the part or section of Baqi' where the Imams (a) have been buried was the house of 'Aqil bin Abi Talib and the holy bodies of these four Imams (a) were buried in the house which was related to Bani Hashim.

---

[59] al-Samhudi, *Wafa' al-Wafa' fi Akhbar dar al-Mustafa*, vol. 2 p. 84.

Al-Samhudi writes:

"Abbas bin 'Abd al-Muttalib was buried near the grave of Fatima bint Asad in the cemetery of Bani Hashim which was in the house of 'Aqil."[60]

He also narrates from Sa'eed bin Muhammad bin Jubayr that he has seen the grave of Ibrahim, son of the Holy Prophet (s), in the house which was the property of Muhammad bin Zayd bin 'Ali.

He further narrates that the Holy Prophet (s) buried the body of Sa'd bin Mu'adh in the house of Ibn Aflah which was around Baqi' and possessed a structure and dome.

All these show that the land of Baqi' was not endowed (*waqfi*) and the pure bodies of our Imams (a) have been buried in the houses owned by themselves.

Under these circumstances, is it correct to destroy, under the pretext of *waqf*, the traces and signs of the household of the Holy Prophet (s)?

Let us suppose, just for argument's sake, that the land of Baqi' was a *waqf*. But is there any hint about the circumstances in which the *waqf* was made? Perhaps, the one making the *waqf* has given permission for construction over the grave of noble personalities. So, because we do not know, we should interpret a believer's deeds as right, and not accuse him of offence.

Under these situations, destroying these domes and houses will be considered forbidden (*harām*) and going against the divine laws.

The *qadi* Ibn Bulayhid and his supporters knew well that the idea of *waqf* was one kind of preparing a reason and carving an argument. Even if they were not having such reason, they would have still destroyed the signs of the Holy Prophet (s) because this is not the first time, they have destroyed the traces of Messengership. In the year 1221 A.H. when they gained control over Medina for the first time, they destroyed the traces of Messengership. Later, when they were expelled from the land of Hijaz by the 'Uthmani forces, all the structures were re-built.

---

[60] *Ibid.*, vol. 2 p. 96.

3

Construction of Mosque near the Graves of Pious People

Is construction of mosque near or in front of the grave of pious people permissible or not? Supposing it is permitted, then what is the main purpose of the tradition (*hadith*) of the Holy Prophet (s) regarding the actions of Jews and Christians as it has come in a tradition that the Holy Prophet (s) has cursed these two groups for considering the graves of their Prophets as objects of worship? Moreover, is construction of mosque near the graves of the *Awliya Allah* inseparable with what has come down in this tradition!?

Answer: By paying attention to the general principles of Islam, construction of mosques, in the vicinity of graves of the *awliya* and pious doesn't not have the least problem. This is because the purpose of construction of mosque is nothing more than worshipping Allah near the grave of His beloved who has become the source of receiving gifts. In other words, the aim of establishing mosque in these instances is that the visitors to the Divine leaders either before or after their *ziyarat*, perform their duty of worship (*'ibadah*) over there in as much as neither *ziyarat* to graves is forbidden (even from the viewpoint of Wahhabis) nor performing of *salat*, after or before *ziyarat*. Therefore, there is no reason to believe that the construction of mosque near the graves of *awliya* for the purpose of worshipping Allah and performing divine duties is forbidden.

By paying attention to the story of *Ashab al-Kahf* it is deduced that this action was a custom prevalent in the previous religions and Qur'an has narrated that without any criticism. When the incident of Companions of Kahf was disclosed to the people of that time after 309 years, they expressed their views about the ways of honoring the Companions of Kahf. One group said that a structure should be made over their grave (so that apart from honoring them their names, signs and memories are kept alive). Qur'an expresses this view as such:

فَقَالُوا ابْنُوا عَلَيْهِم بُنْيَانًا

"…..Build a building over them…., (Al-Kahf:21)"

Another group said that a mosque should be built over their grave (and in this way *tabarruk* sought). The Islamic commentators are unanimous in their views[1] that the suggestion of the first group was related to the polytheists and the suggestion of the second group was that of the monotheists. The Qur'an, while narrating this saying, says:

قَالَ الَّذِينَ غَلَبُوا عَلَىٰ أَمْرِهِمْ لَنَتَّخِذَنَّ عَلَيْهِم مَّسْجِدًا

Those who prevailed in their affair said: We will certainly raise a masjid over them. (Al-Kahf:21)[2]

History has it that the period of occurrence of the incidence of Companions of *Kahf* was the period of victory of monotheism over polytheism. There was no more of the sovereignty of the polytheists, nor their calling the people towards idol-worshipping. Naturally, this victorious group will be the same monotheist group, especially, that the content of their suggestion was the matter of construction of mosque for the sake of worshipping Allah. This itself is a witness that those making the suggestion were monotheists and God-worshippers.

If really the construction of mosque over or near the grave of the holy persons is a sin or polytheism, then why the monotheists made such a suggestion and why Qur'an narrates this without any criticism? Is not the narration of Qur'an together with this silence a testimony upon its permissibility? It is never proper that God narrates the sign of polytheism from a group but without specifically or implicitly criticizing them. And this reasoning is the same 'assertion' which has been explained in *'ilm al-'usul*. (Methodology)

This event shows that it has been one kind of lasting conduct amongst all the monotheists and was one way of honoring the one in grave or a means of seeking *tabarruk*.

It was reasonable and polite of the Wahhabis that before arguing about hadith, they should first have sought the reference from the Holy Qur'an and then attempted the analysis of the tradition.

---

[1] Refer to *Tafsir al-Kashshaf* of al-Zamakhshari, *Ghara'ib al-Qur'an* of al-Nishapuri, *Tafsir al-Jalalayn* of al-Mahalli and al-Suyuti (it was started by Jalaluddin al-Mahalli in 1459 and completed after his death by his student Jalaluddin al-Suyuti).

[2] *Sahih al-Bukhari*, book *al-Jana'iz*, vol. 2, page 111.

Reasoning of Wahhabis that Construction of Mosque near Grave is Forbidden

By presenting a series of traditions, the Wahhabis have analyzed the matter of construction of mosque near the grave of pious people to be forbidden. We shall examine all such traditions:

Bukhari[3] in his *Sahih* under the chapter of يكره من إتخاذ المساجد على القبور narrates two traditions as such:

لما مات الحسن بن الحسن بن عليّ ضربَت إمراته القُبة عل قبره سنة ثم رفعت فسمعوا صائحاً يقول الأهل وجدوا ما فقدوا فاجابه الأخر بل يئسوا فانقلبوا

1. *When al-Hasan bin al-Hasan bin 'Ali passed away his wife made a dome (a tent) over his grave and after one year she removed it. It was heard that one person cried out: "Have they found that which they had lost", another person replied: "No they have become disappointed and have given up."*

لعن الله اليهود والنَّصار إتخذوا قبور انبيائهم مسجداً قالت (عائشة) ولولا ذلك لابرزُوا قبره غير أنِّي أخش أن يُتخذ مسجداً

2. *May the curse of Allah be upon the Jews and Christians (for) considering the graves of their Prophets as mosques. She (Ayesha) said: "If it was not for this fear that the grave of the Holy Prophet (s) would become a mosque, the Muslims would have kept his grave open (and not put up a barrier around it).*

3. Muslim has narrated in *Sahih* the same tradition with slight variation. As such we confine ourselves to narrating only one text.[4]

ألا وإن من كان قبلكم كانُ,ا يتَّخذون قبور أنبيائهم وصالِحيهم مساجد ألا فلا تتخذوا القُبور مساجد إنى أنهاكم عن ذلك

Know that people before you took the graves of their Prophets and the pious people as mosques. Never take the graves as mosques, I forbid you from that.[5]

إن أم حبيبة وأم سلمة ذكرتنا كنيسة رأيتها بالحبشة فيها تصاوير لرسول الله (صلى الله عليه وأله) فقال رسول الله إن أولئك إن كان فيهم الرجُل الصالح فما بنوا على قبره مسجداً وصوَّروا فيه تلك الصُور أولئك شرار الخلق عند الله يوم القيامة.

4. *Umme Habiba and Umm Salama (Wives of the Holy Prophet) saw a prophet's picture in the country of Ethiopia (when they had travelled to that place along with a group).*

---

[3] Muhammad ibn Isma'il al-Ju'fi al-Bukhari (810 – 870 A.D.) also known as Imam Bukhari was a famous Islamic scholar from Bukhara (current Uzbekistan). He authored the hadith collection known as *Sahih al-Bukhari*, regarded by Sunni Muslims as one of the most authentic hadith collections.
[4] *Sahih al-Bukhari*, book *al-Jana'iz*, vol. 2, page 111; *Sunan al-Nasa'i*, book *al-Jana'iz*, vol. 2, p. 871.
[5] *Sahih Muslim*, vol. 2, p. 68.

The Holy Prophet (s) said: They are such people that whenever a pious man dies amongst them they construct a mosque over his grave and draw his picture on it. They are the worst of the people before God on the Day of Judgement.[6]

al-Nasa'i narrates from Ibn 'Abbas in his *Sunan* under the chapter:

التغليط في اتخاذ السُرج على القبور

as such:

لعن الرسول زائرات القبور والمُتخذين عليها المساجد والسُرج

5. The Holy Prophet (s) has cursed those ladies who visit the grave and those who take them as mosques and light a lamp over it.[7]

Ibn Taymiyyah who is the leader of such beliefs and Muhammad ibn 'Abd al-Wahhab sharing his views interpret the aforesaid traditions in such a manner that building mosque over or near the grave of pious people is not permitted.

Thus Ibn-Taymiyyah writes:

قال عُلماؤنا لا يجوز بناء المسجد على القبور

"*Our scholars have said that it is never allowed to construct a mosque over the grave.*"[8]

A Probe into the Context of Traditions

Now we have to pay attention to the contents of the traditions and derive its correct meanings. We should not remain negligent to this principle and it is as such: As one verse (*ayah*) can remove the ambiguity of another verse and help its correct interpretation, in the same way, one tradition too can remove the ambiguity and interpret another tradition.

The Wahhabis have stuck to the apparent meaning of one tradition and relied on that in such a manner that any kind of building of mosque over or near the graves of *awliya* is prohibited whereas if they would have collected all the traditions together, they would have understood the objective of the Holy Prophet (s) in sending this curse.

The Wahhabis have closed the door of *ijtihad* and thus committed too many mistakes in understanding many of the traditions.

---

[6] *Sahih Muslim*, book *al-masajid*, vol. 2, p. 66.
[7] *Sunan al-Nasa'i*, (ed. Mustafa Halabi), vol. 4, p. 77.
[8] *Ziyarat al-Qubur*, p. 106 by Ibn Taymiyyah.

Superficially, it is possible that the authenticity of the traditions be reliable and its narrators trustworthy. Since the deliberation on the references of these traditions will lengthen our discussion, we shall limit ourselves to their contents only.

Our Views about This Matter

Awareness about the objective of the traditions is related to throwing light on the actions of the Jews and Christians near the graves of their respective Prophets (s) because our Holy Prophet (s) has prevented us from the actions which they used to do. If the limits of their actions are clarified, then surely the limits of *harām* in Islam too would be clarified.

In the previous traditions there exist evidences which testified to the fact that they took the graves of their prophets as their *qibla* and refused from paying heed to the true *qibla*. More still, they were worshipping their prophets near their graves instead of worshipping Allah or at least were taking partners with God in their worship.

If the context of the traditions is this that we do not choose their graves to be their *qibla* and do not consider them as partners with God in worship, then we can never consider the construction of mosque over or near the graves of the pious and virtuous as *harām* where the visitors neither take their graves to be as their *qibla* nor do they worship them. Moreover, they worship the one God facing the *qibla* in their *salat* and the aim of constructing mosque near the graves of awliya Allah is only to seek *tabarruk* from their places.

What is important is that it should be proved that the aim of the tradition (that we should not take their graves as mosques) is the same as what we have just said. Here are the evidences:

1. The tradition of *Sahih Muslim* (4th tradition) elucidates the other traditions because when the two wives of the Holy Prophet (s) explained to him that they had seen a portrait of a Prophet in an Ethiopian church, the Holy Prophet (s) said:

"They are such people that whenever a pious person passes away they would construct a mosque over his grave and put up his portrait in that mosque."[9]

The purpose of putting portraits near the graves of pious people was that people would worship them such that they considered the portrait and grave to be their *qibla* or still more, consider them as idols for worship and prostration. Worshipping of idols is nothing but placing the idol in front and respecting and falling into humiliation before them.

The probability which we are having in this tradition, keeping in mind the actions of the Christians who were and are always inclined towards human worship and are always worshipping portraits and statues, is very worthy of attention. With such strong probability we can never rationalize with the help of this tradition, the prohibition of construction of mosque over or near the grave of *Awliya Allah* which is devoid of such embellishments.

2. Ahmad ibn Hanbal in his *al-Musnad* and Imam Malik[10] in his *al-Muwatta'* narrate the tradition that the Holy Prophet (s) after prohibiting the matter of construction of mosque said:

"Allah, do not make my grave as an idol which is subject to worship"[11]

This sentence shows that they were behaving with the grave and the portrait which was next to it like one idol and taking them as their *qibla* and still more is worshipping them in the form of idol.

3. Pondering over the tradition of Ayesha (2nd tradition) will elucidate this fact to a greater extent. After narrating the tradition from the Holy Prophet (s) she says:

"If it was not for the fear that the grave of the Holy Prophet (s) would be taken as mosque the Muslims would have kept his grave open". (They would have not constructed a barrier around the grave)

Now it should be seen that from what aspects the barrier and wall around the grave can become an obstacle? Undoubtedly the barrier will prevent the

---

[9] إن اولئك إذ كان فيهم الرجل الصالح فمات بنوا على قبره مسجداً وصوراً فيه تلك الصور

[10] Malik bin Anas bin Malik (711–795 A.D.) also known as Imam Malik was famous Muslim jurist, theologian, and hadith traditionist. He was founder of Maliki School of thought. His most work was *Al-Muwatta'* which combines hadith and *fiqh* (jurisprudence) together.

[11] Ibn Hanbal, *al-Musnad*, vol. 3, p. 248 and also mentioned in *al-Muwatta'* of Imam Malik.

people from reciting *salat* over the grave, from worshipping the grave as one idol or at least from taking it as a *qibla*. However, performing *salat* near the grave without worshipping the grave or considering it as a *qibla* is absolutely possible, whether there exists a barrier or not and whether the grave is open or hidden. This is because for fourteen centuries the Muslims have been performing *salat* near the grave of the Holy Prophet (s) facing the *qibla* and have been worshipping Allah without the barrier preventing them from doing this action.

To sum up, the appendix of the *hadith* which is the text of the sayings of Ayesha clarifies the contents of the tradition because *Umm al-mu'minin* says: 'In order that the grave of the Holy Prophet (s) would not be taken as mosque, they kept his grave hidden from the eyes of the people and constructed a barrier around it.' Now it should be seen as to what extent this barrier can serve as an obstacle.

A barrier can prevent from two things:

1. The grave from taking the shape of idol and the people from standing in front of it and worshipping it since with the presence of a barrier, people are unable to see his grave to be able to treat it as an idol.

2. The grave from becoming a *qibla* since fixing it as a *qibla* is the outcome of seeing and we can never compare it with the *Ka'ba* which is a *qibla* in all the situations whether it is seen or not. This is because *Ka'ba* is a universal conventional *qibla* in all the conditions, making no difference if it is seen or not. However taking the grave of the Holy Prophet (s) as a *qibla* for the attendants in the mosque will be related to those who offer *salat* in his mosque and such a deviation is more achievable in case the grave is uncovered and seen; but when the grave is concealed the thought of prostrating over his grave even in the form of *qibla* is much less. Due to this, *Umm al-mu'minin* says that if no possibility existed for considering the grave as mosque (i.e. prostrating over the grave) it would have been kept uncovered. Moreover, such a deviation takes place more when the grave is seen and much less when the grave is hidden.

3. Most of the commentators of the tradition offer the same interpretation as we have done.

Al-Qastallani in *Irshad al-Sari* says: For keeping alive the memories of their past ones, the Jews and Christians were fixing the portraits of their virtuous ones near their graves and worshipping their graves. However, their sons and successors, under the influence of whisperings of *shaytan,* started to worship the portraits near the graves. Thereafter he narrates from *Tafsir al-Baydawi*[12] as follows:

لما كانت اليهود والنصارى يسجدون لقبور الأنبياء تعظيماً لشأنهم ويجعلونها قبلة يتوجهون في الصلاة نحوها واتخذوها اوثاناً ، مُنع المسلمون في مثل ذلك فاما من إتخذ مسجداً في جوار صالح وقصد التبرك بالقُرب منه لا للتعظيم ولا للتوجيه إليه فلا يدخل في الوعيد المذكور.

"In view of the fact that the Jews and Christians were taking the graves of their Prophets as their qibla for the purpose of respect, and were paying attention towards them at the time of their prayers, their graves took the position of idols. For this reason the Muslims have been forbidden from this action. However, if someone constructs a mosque near the grave of a pious person for the purpose of seeking tabarruk and not for worshipping or paying attention towards them, he will never be included in this prohibition."[13]

It is not only al-Qastallani who in his commentary on *Sahih al-Bukhari* interprets this tradition as such but also al-Sindi, the commentator of *Sunan al-Nasa'i* speaks with the same effect. We mention some of them here.

إتخذوا قبور انبيائهم مساجد أي قبلة للصلاة ويُصلون إليها أو بنوا مساجد عليها يُصلون فيها ولعلَّ وجه الكراهة أنه قد يُفض إلى عباده نفس القبر.

"The outcome of his dispensation is this that construction over the grave is harām and occasionally makruh. If the grave is considered as qibla it is harām, since it may lead to the worship of the one buried, otherwise it is makruh."[14]

Again he says:

يُحذر أمته أن يصنعوا بقبره ما صنع اليهود والنصارى بقبور أنبيائهم من إتخاذهم تلك القبور مساجد إما بالسجود إليها تعظيماً لها أو يجعلها قبلة يتوجهون في الصلاة إليها.

"He (i.e. the Holy Prophet) prohibits his ummah from treating his grave in the same manner as what the Jews and the Christians have done to the graves of their Prophets.

---

[12] Written by Nasir al-Din Abu al-Khayr al-Baydawi (d. 1286 A.D.). He was a Sunni Shafi'i scholar from Fars, Iran. His most famous book *Anwar al-Tanzil wa-Asrar al-Ta'wil* is an exegesis of Qur'an popularly known as *Tafsir al-Baydawi.*

[13] al-Qastallani, *Irshad al-Sari*; and Ibn Hajar al-'Asqalani, *Fath al-Bari,* vol. 3, p. 208 approve this view. He mentions that the prohibition is applicable under circumstances where the grave appears in the manner which was in vogue amongst the Jews and Christians. Otherwise there is no problem and objection.

[14] *Sunan al-Nasa'i,* (al-Azhar edition), vol. 2, p. 21.

This is because, in the name of honor and respect, they were prostrating over the grave or considering it as their qibla." [15]

Regarding this matter, the commentator of *Sahih Muslim* says:

"If the Holy Prophet (s) has prohibited us from considering his grave and other graves as a mosque, it is due to this reason that the Muslims should stop from exaggerating his honor which might lead to infidelity. Thus, when the Muslims were compelled to develop the mosque of the Holy Prophet (s) and place the chamber of the prophet's wives and the chamber of Ayesha in the middle of the mosque, they fixed a round wall around the grave so that it could not be seen and the Muslims would not prostrate over it." The speech of *Umm al-mu'minin* too is a witness to the same:

لولا ذلك لأبرزوا قبره غير أنه اخش أن يُتخذ مسجداً

"If it was not for this fear that his grave (i.e. the grave of Holy Prophet) would become a mosque, the Muslims would have kept his grave open (and not put up a barrier around it)."

Another commentator says: *"The words of Ayesha are related to that period when the mosque was not developed nor extended. After extension and the admittance of her chamber inside the mosque, the chamber was made in the shape of a triangle so that nobody could perform salat over the grave. Thereafter he says that the Jews and Christians were worshipping their Prophets near their graves and were taking them as partners in their worship. With such evidence and perception of the tradition, one cannot understand any meaning other than this."*

We shall now overlook all these evidences and will approach this issue from another angle:

Firstly, the tradition is applicable to a situation where a mosque is constructed over the grave and this matter does not bear any relation to an adjacent place of the buried. In all the buried places, the mosque is placed near the grave of Imams (*a'imma*) and *awliya* in such a manner that the mosque is separated from the shrine. In other words, we are having one shrine and one mosque. The shrine is set aside for *ziyarat* and *tawwasul* and the mosque near that, for the worship of Allah. Therefore these adjacent places (shrines) are

---

[15] *Ibid.*

outside the scope and contents of the tradition assuming that the contents of the traditions are the same as what the Wahhabis say.

Basically speaking how can it be said that the construction of mosque over the grave is *harām* or *makruh* whereas Masjid al-Nabi (mosque of the Holy Prophet) is placed near his grave?

If the companions of the Holy Prophet (s) are like the stars which should be followed then why, in this case, we should not follow them. They extended the mosque in such a manner that the grave of the Holy Prophet (s) and the *Sheikhayn* have been placed in the middle of the mosque.

If really, construction of mosque near the grave of Holy Imams was unlawful, then why the Muslims expanded the mosque of the Holy Prophet (s) from every angle; while the mosque during the time of the Holy Prophet (s) was placed on the eastern side of the grave, after the expansion, the western side of the grave too became the part of the mosque.

Is it that following the سلف i.e. predecessors and being سلفي which the Wahhabis are always proud of, means that we should follow them in one instance and disobey them in another?

From this description, it becomes clear that to what extent the sayings of Ibn al-Qayyim that in Islam, grave and mosque do not exist together are baseless and against the path of Muslims. Secondly, we do not derive any meaning from these traditions other than the Holy Prophet (s) prohibiting construction of mosque over or near the graves of the *awliya*. However, no argument exists to prove that this prohibition is a *harām* prohibition. Instead, it is possible that this prohibition is a *makruh* prohibition just as Bukhari has interpreted the traditions and discussed them under the title:

باب ، يكره من اتخاذ المساجد على القبور

Chapter: It is aversion to build mosques on graves. [16]

Another testimony is that this matter has come along with the curse upon female visitors to the grave.[17] Surely visiting the graves is *makruh* and not *harām* for the ladies.

---

[16] *Sahih al-Bukhari*, vol. 2, p. 111.
[17] *Sunan al-Nasa'i*, (Egyptian edition), vol. 3, p. 77.

If the Holy Prophet (s) has cursed this group, this curse is no testimony of it being *harām* because in many of the traditions those committing *makruh* acts have been cursed too. In tradition, it is mentioned that those who travel alone or eat alone or sleep alone are cursed.

In the end we remind that the construction of mosque over the grave of pious people was an act which was in vogue in the beginning of Islam.

Al-Samhudi says: "When the mother of Ali (a), Fatima bint Asad, passed away, the Holy Prophet (s) ordered that she be buried in a place where today stands a mosque named as 'Grave of Fatima'. He meant that the place of grave of Fatima appear as a mosque in later time. Again he says: "Mus'ab bin 'Umayr and 'Abdullah bin Jahsh were buried under the mosque which was built over the grave of Hamza."[18]

He further says that in the 2nd century there existed a mosque over the grave of Hamza (r).[19]

This mosque existed till the domination of the Wahhabis. They demolished this mosque on these unfounded reasons.

---

[18] *Wafa' al-Wafa' fi Akhbar dar al-Mustafa*, Al-Samhudi, (ed. Muhammad Muhyiuddin), vol. 3, p. 897.
[19] *Ibid.*, vol. 3, p. 922 and 936.

4

Visitation *(Ziyarat)* of Graves of Believers from the View-Point of the Holy Qur'an and Sunnah

The scholars of Islam with the support of verses of Qur'an and traditions have recommended *ziyarat* of grave especially the *ziyarat* of the Holy Prophet's grave and those of the pious people and consider this to be a virtue and honor. However, Wahhabis do not consider the principle of *ziyarat* to be *harām* (in apparent terms) but declare that the journey for *ziyarat* towards the grave of the *Awliya Allah* as unlawful and *harām*. After completion of the principle of *ziyarat*, we shall discuss the matter of journey for *ziyarat* of the graves of the *Awliya Allah*

Ziyarat of graves has many ethical influences and is important for moral education and training that we shall mention here very briefly.

Looking at this silent valley (i.e. graveyard) which has blown off the light of life of everyone from the poor to the rich and the weak to the powerful and all of them being buried with only three pieces of cloth, purifies the mind and the heart and reduces greed and avarice of a person to a great extent. If a person possesses an eye which can see warnings he can thereby learn a lesson and think within himself as such: A transient life of 60 or 70 years ending in getting concealed under the soil and then decaying and getting destroyed is not so much valuable that a person strives hard to achieve wealth and position and does injustice upon himself and the others.

Witnessing this silent valley which softens the most adamant heart and makes the heaviest ear to hear and gives brightness to the poorest eye-sight, causes a person to review his plans in life and ponder over the great responsibilities which he has before Allah and the people and controls his desires.

The Holy Prophet (s) referring to this point in a tradition says:

زوروا القُبور فإنها تذكركم الأخرة

"Visit the graves; for visiting them becomes the cause of remembering the next world."[1]

While the authenticity and firmness of *ziyarat* of graves is so obvious that it is needless to produce proofs and reasoning to a great extent yet, we reflect here some of the proofs for those who are doubtful.

Qur'an and *ziyarat* of Graves

Qur'an clearly instructs that the Holy Prophet (s) should not perform prayer over the dead body of the hypocrites and should not stand near their graves. It says:

ولا تُصلِّ على أحدٍ منهم ماتَ أبداً ولا تقم على قبره إنهم كفروا بالله ورسوله وماتوا وهُم فاسقون.

"And never offer prayer for anyone of them who dies and do not stand by his grave, surely they disbelieve in Allah and His Apostle and they shall die in transgression. (Tawbah:84)"

In this verse, for destroying the character of the hypocrites and rebuking the members of this group, the God commands the Holy Prophet (s):
1. Not to perform *salat* over the dead body of anyone of them.
2. Not to stand over their graves; and this reality is presented with the sentence;

ولا تقُم على قبره

When the Holy Qur'an commands that one should avoid these two actions with regards to the hypocrites it means that for others who are not hypocrites these actions are good and worthy to be performed.

Now let us see what ولا تقم على قبره means? Does it refer only to the standing at the time of burial which in the case of hypocrites is not permissible and in the case of the believers good and necessary? Or it also refers to standing at the time of burial and at other instances?

Some of the commentators think that the verse refers to the matter of standing at the time of burial but some others like al-Baydawi see the verse from a far angle and interpret it as such:

ولا تقُم على قبره للدفن أو لزيارة

"Don't stand on grave for burial or pilgrimage."[2]

---

[1] *Sunan Ibn Majah*, vol. 1 chapter 'When visiting the graves', p. 113.
[2] *Tafsir al-Baydawi*, vol. 3, p. 77.

Paying attention to the contents of verse will show that it is having a wider meaning i.e. it concerns standing at the time of burial as well as stopping after the burial. This is because two sentences form the gist of the subject matter of this verse and these two sentences comprises of:

لا تُصلِّ على أحدٍ منهم مات أبداً

"And never offer prayer for anyone of them who dies...... (Tawbah:84)"

The word of احد which has been placed in the course of prohibition is good for all individuals.

The word of ابدا is good for all times and the meaning of the sentence will be as such: *"Do not perform salat for any one of the hypocrites at any time."*

By paying attention to these two words we can easily understand that the meaning of this particular sentence is not referring to recitation of *salat* over the dead body because reciting *salat* over the dead body takes place only once and that is before the burial and it cannot be repeated. If it specifically meant recitation of *salat* over the dead, then it was needless to bring the word ابدا. And to imagine that this word serves the purpose of expressing all individuals is completely irrelevant because the sentence لا تصل على أحد is sufficient for such inclusion and purpose and there is no need to mention it once again.

Moreover, the word ابدا in Arabic refers to time and not individuals such as:

وَلَا أَن تَنكِحُوا أَزْوَاجَهُ مِن بَعْدِهِ أَبَدًا

"Nor that you should marry his wives after him ever;... (Ahzab:53)"

Therefore the essence of the first sentence is: Never seek forgiveness and mercy for anyone of the hypocrites whether at the time of reciting *salat* or otherwise.

And now we will discuss the second sentence:

ولا تقُم على قبره

The meaning of this sentence in connection with the previous sentence is as such:

ولا تقُم على قبر أحدا منهم أبداً

Because the adverbs which are present in معطوف عليه are also applicable for معطوف.

Therefore it cannot be said that *qiyam* (standing) refers to the *qiyam* at the time of burial because it is presumed that *qiyam* at the time of burial for each one is not subject to repetition and the word ابدا too is commendable in this sentence which shows that this action is worthy of repetition. The reply to the supposition that this word is applicable for all individuals was given in the previous sentence since with the presence of احد it is needless to express that once again.

By paying attention to these two points in the words لا تصل and لا تقم one can say:

'God has prohibited the Holy Prophet (s) from seeking any kind of mercy for the hypocrites whether by means of reciting *salat* upon the dead body or merely by means of *du'a* and from any kind of standing over their graves whether at the time of burial or after the burial. This means that these two actions i.e. 'seeking forgiveness' and 'standing' is permissible and worthy for the grave of a believer in all the instances and one of such instances is standing for *ziyarat* and recitation of Qur'an for a believer who has been buried there for years.'

Now we shall discuss the virtue and excellence of *ziyarat* of graves from the viewpoint of traditions.

Traditions and *ziyarat* of Graves

From the Islamic traditions which the authors of *Sihah* and *Sunan* have narrated, we derive the conclusion that the Holy Prophet (s) had prohibited, due to a temporary reason, the *ziyarat* of graves and later on allowed the people to make haste for *ziyarat*.

Perhaps the reason for prohibition was that their dead ones were predominantly polytheists and idol-worshippers and Islam had cut off their relation and affection with the world of polytheism. It is also possible that the reason for prohibition was something else and that is the newly converted Muslims were writing elegies and saying un-Islamic things over the graves of the dead polytheists. But after the expansion of Islam and the 'faith' entering into the hearts of people, this prohibition was lifted and the Holy Prophet (s) permitted the people to go for the *ziyarat* of graves because of the educative benefits, so that people should hasten to visit graves. The writers of *Sunan* and *Sihah* narrate following hadithes:

Visitation (*Ziyarat*) of Graves of Believers from the View-Point of the Holy Qur'an and Sunnah

1. The Holy Prophet (s) says:

زوروا القُبور فإنها تذكركم الأخرة

"*Visit the graves; for visiting them becomes the cause of remembering the next world.*"³

كُنت نهيتكم عن زيارة القُبور فزُوروها فإنها تُزهّد في الدنيا وتُذكر الأخرة

"*I had prohibited you from ziyarat of graves. From now on, go for ziyarat because it will make you feel unattached towards this world and make you remember the hereafter.*"⁴

2. It is on the same basis that the Holy Prophet (s) was visiting the grave of his mother and informing the people to visit the graves since *ziyarat* is the source of remembering the hereafter. Here is the text of the tradition:

زار النبيّ قبر أمه فبكى وأبكى من حوله...إستأذنت ربي في أن أزور قبرها فاذن لي فزوروا القبور فإنها تُذكركم الموت

"*The Holy Prophet (s) visited the grave of his mother and cried near her grave and also made others around him to cry. Thereafter he said: I have taken permission from my Lord to visit the grave of my mother. You too should visit the graves because such a visit will remind you of death.*"⁵

3. Ayesha says that the Holy Prophet (s) freely allowed the *ziyarat* of graves:

إن رسول الله رخَّص في زيارة القبور

---

³ *Sunan Ibn Majah*, chapter of 'When visitng the graves' ما جاء في زيارة القبور vol.1, p.113.
⁴ *Sunan Ibn Majah*, chapter of 'When visitng the graves' ما جاء في زيارة القبور vol.1, p.114, (Indian edition); *Sahih al-Tirmidhi* chapter of جنائز vol. 3 p. 274 along with commentary of Ibn al-'Arabi Maliki, (Lebanon edition); After narrating the tradition from Burayda, *al-Tirmidhi* says:
حديث بريدة صحيح والعمل على هذا عند اهل العلم لا يُرون بزيارة القبور باساً وهو قول ابن المبارك والشافعي وأحمد واسحاق
'The tradition of Burayda is correct and the people of knowledge act upon it. They do not put forward any obstacle for performing *ziyarat* of graves and they are people such as Ibn al-Mubarak, al-Shafi'i, Ahmad and Ishaq.' Meanwhile, you may refer to the following documents:
Sahih Muslim, vol. 3. page 65 chapter of استئذان النبي ربه وجل غم في زيارة قبر امه
Sahih Abu Dawud, vol. 2. p. 195, book of جنائز chapter of زيارة القبور
Sahih Muslim, vol. 4 p. 73, book of جنائز chapter of زيارة القبور
⁵ *Sahih Muslim*, vol. 3, p. 65, chapter of استئذان النبي ربه وجل غم في زيارة قبر امه *Sunan Ibn Majah*, vol. 1, p. 114. According to the narrators of this tradition, the reason the Holy Prophet (s) took permission from Allah for visiting the grave of his mother was that his mother was a polytheist. Undoubtedly the mother of Holy Prophet (s) was a monotheist and a believer like her father, grandfather and ancestors. For this reason all the portion of this tradition is incompatible with the religious standards. *Sunan Abu Dawud*, vol. 2 p. 195. Book of جنائز Egyptian print along with the additional notes of Sheikh Ahmad Sa'd from the scholars of Azhar. *Sahih Muslim*, vol. 4 p. 74, book of جنائز chapter of زيارة قبر المشرك

"The Prophet of God permitted the visit of graves."⁶

4. Ayesha says: The Holy Prophet (s) taught me the manner of visiting the graves. Here is the text of the tradition:

فامرني ربي أتي البقيع فاستغفر لهم قلت كيف أقول : يا رسول الله قال قولي: السلام على أهل الديار مِن المؤمنين والمسلمين يرحم الله المُستقدمين منا والمستأخرين وإنا إن شاء الله بكم لاحقون.

*"My Lord commanded me to come to Baqi' and seek forgiveness for them. (Ayesha) says: I asked him how one should seek forgiveness to which the Holy Prophet (s) replied: Say Peace (Salaam) be upon the people of this place from the believers and Muslims, May God have mercy on those who have left and those who are to follow. We shall join you all very soon."*⁷

5. In another tradition, there are some sentences which the Holy Prophet (s) used when performing *ziyarat* of graves. It is as follows:

السلام عليكم دار قوم مؤمنين وإنا وإياكم مُتواعدون غداً ومُواكلون وإنا إن شاء الله بكم لاحقون اللهم اغفر لأهل بقيع الغرقد

"Peace be with you the groups of believers and we will be return to you and rely on you and certainly if God wishes, we will join you. O God, have mercy on all those (buried) in Baqi' al-Gharqad."⁸

Gharqad was a tree in Baqi' graveyard. And because of this tree, it was commonly called as the land of *Gharqad*.

6. In another tradition, the text of *ziyarat* is narrated in a different way:

السلام عليكم أهل الديار من المؤمنين والمسلمين وإنا إن شاء الله بكمك لاحقون أنتم لنا فرط ونحن لكم تبع اسئل الله العافية لنا ولكم.

*"Peace be with you the groups of believers and Muslims, and certainty we will join you. You will exhilarate us and we will follow you. We ask welfare from you for ourselves and for yourself."*⁹

7. From the tradition of Ayesha, we got knowledge that whenever the last part of night was approaching, the Holy Prophet (s) would go towards Baqi' and say:

---

⁶ *Sunan Ibn Majah*, vol. 1, p. 114.
⁷ *Sunan al-Nasa'i*, vol. 3 p. 76; and *Sahih Muslim*, vol. 3, p. 64 chapter of ما يقال عند دخول القبر
⁸ *Sunan al-Nasa'i*, vol. 40, pp. 76- 77.
⁹ *Ibid*.

السلام عليكم دار قوم مؤمنين واتاكم ما توعدون ، غداً مؤجلون وإنا إن شاء الله بكم لاحقون اللهم اغفر لأهل بقيع الغرقد.

"Peace be with you! The groups of believers and what has been promised to you will be given to you, soon in future your destiny will reach you. And certainly, we will be the joiners to you soon. And if God wishes, will be with you. O God! Have mercy on all those (buried) in Baqi' al-Gharqad."[10]

8. From another tradition we come to know that the Holy Prophet (s) used to hasten, along with a group of people for *ziyarat* of graves and teach them the manner of doing *ziyarat*:

كان رسول الله يُعلمُهم إذا خرجوا إلى المقابر فكان قائلُهم يقول: السلام على أهل الديار (يا) السلام عليكم أهل الديار من المؤمنين وإنا إن شاء الله لاحقون اسئل الله لنا ولكم العافية.

"The Prophet (s) used to teach them that when they go out to graves they should say: Peace be with those who live in houses (graves). Peace be with you the groups of believers and Muslims. Certainly if God wishes, we will be joiners to you. We ask safety for ourselves and you."[11]

9. In another tradition, the text is narrated still differently:

السلام عليكم دار قوم مؤمنين وإنا إن شاء الله بكم لاحقون

"Peace be with you the groups of believers and if God wishes, we will join you."[12]

Women and *ziyarat* of Graves

The only matter which is remaining is the matter of *ziyarat* by women which in some of the traditions, the Holy Prophet (s) has prohibited them from doing so:

لعن رسول الله زوارات القبور

"The Prophet of God has cursed the women who go excessively for ziyarat."[13]

But it should be known that utilizing this tradition for proving prohibition of *ziyarat* is not correct due to a number of reasons:

Firstly, most of the scholars think this prohibition to be in the *makruh* sense and the reason for it being *makruh* was because of the special conditions prevailing

---

[10] *Sahih Muslim*, vol. 3, p. 63 chapter of ما يقال عند دخول القبر
[11] *Sahih Muslim*, vol. 3, p. 11 chapter of ما يقال عند دخول القبر
[12] *Sunan Abu Dawud*, vol. 2, p. 196.
[13] *Sunan Ibn Majah*, (1st Edition, Egypt), vol. 1, p. 478, book of جنائز chapter of زيارة النساء ما جاء في النهى عن القبور

at that time. One of the commentators of tradition i.e., the writer of *Miftah al-haja fi Sharh Sahih Ibn Majah* refers to that and says:

إختلفوا في الكراهة هل هى كراهة تحريم أو تنزيه ذهب ألا كثر إلى الجواز إذا امنت بالفتنة.

"The scholars are having two opinions about the prohibition. That whether it is prohibited in the makruh sense or prohibited in the harām sense! But most of the scholars believe that women can go for ziyarat if they are certain of remaining safe from any trouble."[14]

Secondly, we have read in the previous traditions (kindly refer to tradition number 7) that Ayesha narrates from the Holy Prophet (s) that the latter declared free the *ziyarat* of graves. If the women were excluded from this declaration then it is necessary to remind that this declaration is exclusively for men especially when the narrator is a lady and amongst the people to whom he (i.e. Prophet) was addressing was a lady and every addressee will naturally think that the order and declaration is directed to him or her.

Thirdly, some of the traditions mention the manner in which the Holy Prophet (s) taught Ayesha to perform *ziyarat* of graves[15] and Ayesha herself used to personally visit the graves after the Holy Prophet (s).

Fourthly, al-Tirmidhi narrates that when Ayesha's brother i.e. 'Abd al-Rahman bin Abi Bakr died in Ethiopia, his body was taken to Mecca and buried there. When his sister Ayesha came to Mecca from Medina, she visited grave of her brother and by the side of his grave, recited two couplets in his sorrow and made speech (about him).[16]

The commentator of *Sahih al-Tirmidhi* Imam Hafiz Ibn al-'Arabi [al-Maliki] (435 - 543 A.H.) writes in his additional notes on *Sahih*:

"The fact is that the Holy Prophet (s) has permitted the men and the women to go for ziyarat. If some of the traditions mention it to be makruh it is because of restlessness and impatience near the grave or because of not observing proper hijab."

Fifthly, Bukhari narrates from Anas that the Holy Prophet (s) saw a woman crying over her beloved one and comforted her to have faith and be patient. The woman not recognizing the Holy Prophet (s), said: "you release me from the

---

[14] Footnotes of *Sunan Ibn Majah*, (Indian edition), vol. 1, p. 114.
[15] Refer to tradition no. 8.
[16] *Sunan al-Tirmidhi*, vol. 4, p. 275 book of جنائز chapter of زيارة القبور ما جاء في

calamity which has befallen upon me and not befallen upon you". When it was said to her that he was the Holy Prophet (s) she left the grave and went to the house of the Holy Prophet (s) pleading pardon for not recognizing him. The Holy Prophet (s) replied: "Patience is advised at the time of misfortunes."[17]

If *ziyarat* was forbidden, the Holy Prophet (s) would have prohibited her from this action while he only asked her to adopt patience. Moreover, after the women visited the house of the Holy Prophet (s) he talked of patience and steadfastness at the time of misfortunes and did not say anything about *ziyarat* of grave; otherwise he would have ordered her not to visit the grave of her beloved one anymore.

Sixthly, Fatima (a), daughter of the Holy Prophet (s), used to visit every Friday the grave of her uncle Hamza (r) and recite prayer (*salat*) and cry sadly at his grave.[18]

Seventhly, al-Qurtubi[19] says that the Holy Prophet (s) did not prohibit any lady going for *ziyarat*. Instead he cursed those ladies who were going for *ziyarat* very often as he uses the words زوارات القبور and زوار which is used for exaggeration.[20]

Perhaps the reason of cursing such a habit is that excessive *ziyarat* is the source of spoiling the rights of husband. If such factors are absent in the *ziyarat* of one lady then there is no problem as such since remembering death is a matter which is necessary for both men and women.

Eighthly, if *ziyarat* of grave is the source of getting unattached towards this world and a reduction of the greed of the person in helping him to remember the Hereafter, it also brings some benefit for the dead one i.e. for the one who is buried under the soil and is helpless from doing anything. This is because the Islamic *ziyarat* is usually accompanied by recitation of *al-Fatiha* and giving its reward to the deceased. In fact this is the best gift which an alive person can give to his or her beloved dead one.

The books of *Sahih* narrate that the Holy Prophet (s) said:

وَعَنْ مَعْقِلِ بْنِ يَسَارٍ رضى الله عنه أَنَّ اَلنَّبِيَّ ـ صلى الله عليه وسلم قَالَ: اقْرَءُوا عَلَى مَوْتَاكُمْ يس

---

[17] *Sahih al-Bukhari*, p. 100, book of جنائز chapter of زيارة القبور; *Sunan Abu Dawud*, vol. 2 p. 171.
[18] *Mustadrak al-Sahihayn*, vol. 1, p. 377 by al-Hakim; *Wafa' al-Wafa'*, vol. 2 p. 112 by al-Samhudi.
[19] Abu 'Abdullah Muhammad al-Ansari al-Qurtubi (1214 – 1273 A.D.) was a Sunni Maliki scholar, *muhaddith* and jurist from Cordoba during Andalusian Spain. His most famous book *Tafsir al-Qurtubi*, is a 20 volume commentary of Qur'an.
[20] *Sunan Abu Dawud*, vol. 2, p. 196 has narrated "زائرات"

"Ma'qil bin Yasar (r) narrated that the messenger of Allah (s) said: "Recite Surah Yasin upon your dead ones."[21]

Therefore, there is no difference between man and woman that one should be permitted and the other should be forbidden, except that if the women are faced with some special situations that we previously discussed. Now, that the matter of *ziyarat* of the graves of believers is clear for us and it is now necessary to refer to the valuable effects of *ziyarat* of the graves of the *awliya* Allah and the beloved ones of Allah.

---

[21] *Bulugh al-Maram,* book 3, جنائز hadith 5. p. 537. Narrated by *Sunan Abu Dawud, Sunan Nasa'i* and Ibn Hibban graded it as *Sahih.* For online version visit: https://sunnah.com/bulugh/3/5

5

Valuable Effects of *Ziyarat* of the Graves of Religious Personalities

The graves which attract the worshippers of God from all over the world and in particular the Muslims, are the graves of those who had a divine mission in the society and they fulfilled their mission befittingly. These people consist of:

1. Prophets and religious leaders who carried the divine message upon their shoulders and guided the people by giving their own lives, property and blood of their dear ones and bore the hardships and difficulties in this path.

2. Great scholars who, like a bright candle, have spread light to their surroundings and have labored in research and left behind a great treasure by the name of knowledge and wisdom in the service of mankind. They have acquainted men with the Divine Book, the Book of Nature and the language of creation and have laid the foundation of religious, human and natural sciences.

3. The group of people whose cup of patience had been overflowing from the social oppression, ever-increasing injustices and unfair discrimination. They are those who have put their life at stake against the oppressive rulers and washed with their blood the cruelties prevalent in the society (martyrs in the path of Islam). No revolution and reform in society will remain worthless and the significance of a holy revolution that wishes to bring down the palaces of the oppressors and suffocate them, is the holy blood of those combatants who wished to bring Justice, Equity, Liberty and freedom back to the society.

It is they to whom the people go for their *ziyarat* and shed tears near their graves or shrines and remember their valuable services and their holy sacrifices. By reciting some *Surahs* from the Qur'an they soothe their souls and by reciting poems about their sacrifices, lofty human merits and exalted morals, they enliven their memories and their school of thought and invite the people to follow their path.

Ziyarat of graves of such group of people is one kind of thanksgiving and appreciation of their heroism and self-sacrifices. It is a warning to the contemporary generation that the reward of the person who selects the true path and gives his or her life while defending true beliefs and propagating freedom and liberty is that he or she will never be forgotten.

The passage of time which turns everything old and extinct not only does not make their memories to fade or disappear but causes the flames of love to glow more in the pure and sincere hearts. Thus how good it is that the contemporary generation and the future generations too follow their path since they have seen with their own eyes the rewards of the sacrifices of the men of truth. What was said till now has acquainted us with the importance of honoring the great religious personalities and the combatants in the path of truth and reality.

Therefore, based on this, we should always honor and respect these people in their death time just as it was done during their life time and should protect and safeguard their signs and memories. We should celebrate their birthdays and declare the day of their deaths to be the day of grief and sorrow. By holding big gatherings and delivering good and effective speeches, we should invite the people to become acquainted with their school of thought and protect and safeguard them in the future. We should respect the soil and place of their burial and prevent any kind of insult and segregation. This is because respecting their graves means respecting their school of thought just as insulting and degrading their grave is insulting their path and their conduct.

At present, anyone who steps into the cemetery of Baqi' will see that the graves of the leaders of Islam and the dear companions of the Holy Prophet (s) who self-sacrificed and endeavored hard in the propagation of religion in such a insulted and dilapidated state that it will give him a severe shock and grief and he will be astonished by the attitude of the stone-hearted Wahhabis who reckon themselves to be the propagators of religion.

This is because on the one hand they respect the names of religious leaders and companions of the Holy Prophet (s) on the pulpits and on the other hand whenever it comes to the matter of their graves, they do not pay the least respect.

They do not even care about the animals contaminating the surroundings of their graves.

By using the words of *shirk* (polytheism) and *mushrik* (polytheist) as an excuse, they strike down the respect and honor of the *awliya* and in this manner, restrain the people from honoring them in any possible manner (tongue, thoughts, expressions, actions etc.) and to the extent that they consider all these actions (in consideration of the services of the *awliya Allah*) to be polytheism and label them as polytheists. They have such a severe enmity with the *awliya Allah* that any kind of respect manifested towards them will very much annoy them.

Now it is time to talk and discuss about *ziyarat* of the grave of the Holy Prophet (s) from Islamic proofs and reasonings.

Ziyarat of the Grave of the Holy Prophet (s)

We shall here bring forth the logical proofs from the Holy Qur'an and traditions and request the respected readers for more concentration in this section.

Evidence from Qur'an

The Holy Qur'an commands the sinners to approach the Holy Prophet (s) and request him to seek forgiveness for them from Allah since his request and plead is accepted by Allah. The Holy verse says:

وَلَوْ أَنَّهُمْ إِذْ ظَلَمُوا أَنْفُسَهُمْ جَاءُوكَ فَاسْتَغْفَرُوا اللَّهَ وَاسْتَغْفَرَ لَهُمُ الرَّسُولُ لَوَجَدُوا اللَّهَ تَوَّابًا رَحِيمًا

"And had they, when they were unjust to themselves, come to you and asked forgiveness of Allah and the Apostle had (also) asked forgiveness for them, they would have found Allah Oft-returning, Merciful. (Nisa:64)"

If in case we were having only one such verse, we could say that the verse is related to the day when the Holy Prophet (s) was living amongst the people. However, due to a number of reasons, we can derive from this verse, one general conclusion that it is not specific to this worldly life.

They are, firstly the verses of Qur'an that consider a *barzakhi* life[1] for the Prophet (s), *awliya* and some particular group of people and introduces them as

---

[1] *Barzakh* designates a place separating the living from the hereafter; a veil between the dead and their return to world of the living, but also to a phase happening between death and resurrection. For more detailed description, refer to the book '*The Hereafter (Ma'ad)*' by Sayyid Abdul Husayn Dastghaib Shirazi. Available at: https://www.al-islam.org/hereafter-maad-sayyid-abdul-husayn-dastghaib-shirazi

the ones who can see and hear in that world. This segment of verses will be discussed under the topic of *Tawassul* (recourse) to the Holy souls.

Secondly, the Islamic traditions (*hadiths*) clearly bear testimony to the fact that the angels transmit the messages of the people to the Holy Prophet (s). This tradition has come in *Sihah* as such:

إن رسول الله قال ما مِن احدٍ يُسلِّم على إلا ردَّ الله على روحى حتى أرُد عليه السلام

"The Holy Prophet (s) said: "There is no one who sends greetings upon me but that Allah makes his greetings reach me and I answer his greetings.""[2]

And:

وقال رسول الله... وصلُّوا علىَّ فإن صلاتكم يبلُغني حيث كُنتم

"And said the Prophet of God (s) ...... 'Send greetings upon me for your greetings reaches me'."[3]

Thirdly, right from the beginning, the Islamic society has grasped a general and wider meaning from this verse (mentioned above) and acted accordingly without the demise of the Holy Prophet (s) becoming any obstacle in this regard. After the passing of the Holy Prophet (s), a group from the Arabs would come for *ziyarat* of Holy Prophet (s) with clear and pure minds and recite this verse and request him to seek forgiveness on their behalf.

Taqi al-Din al-Subki and al-Samhudi have reported examples regarding it in their books *Shifa' al-Saqam* and *Wafa' al-Wafa'* respectively. We shall mention here some of them:

Sufyan bin 'Anbar, who is one of the learned scholars of the Shafi'i school, narrates from al-'Utabi - that latter was standing near the grave of the Holy Prophet (s) when an Arab came and said:

السلام عليك يا رسول الله سمعت الله يقول وَلَوْ أَنَّهُمْ إِذْ ظَلَمُوا أَنْفُسَهُمْ جَاءُوكَ فَاسْتَغْفَرُوا اللَّهَ وَاسْتَغْفَرَ لَهُمُ الرَّسُولُ لَوَجَدُوا اللَّهَ تَوَّابًا رَحِيمًا وقد جئتك مستغفراً من دنبي مستشفعاً بك إلى ربي .

"Peace be upon you Oh Prophet of God, I have heard Allah saying (in Quran) 'And had they, when they were unjust to themselves, come to you and asked forgiveness of Allah and the Apostle had (also) asked forgiveness for them, they would have found Allah Oft-returning, Merciful' and indeed as I have come near you, I seek forgiveness for my sins and make you intercessor towards my Lord."

---

[2] *Sunan Abu Dawud*, vol. 1 p. 470-471, book of Hajj chapter: زيارة القبور
[3] Sheikh Mansur Ali Nasif, *Al-Taj al-Jami' li al-'Usul fi Ahadith al-Rasul*, vol. 2, p. 189

Thereafter he cried and sought forgiveness and left the shrine of the Holy Prophet (s) after reciting this poem:

يا خير من دُفنت بالقاع اعظمه   فطاب من طيبهن القاع والاكم

نفسي الفداء بقبر انت ساكنه   فيه العفاف وفيه الجود والكرم⁴

Regarding this matter al-Samhudi narrates from Ali (a) that: *"Three days had passed after the burial of the Holy Prophet (s). One Arab came and threw himself over the Prophet's grave and sprinkling the soil of the grave over his head said: 'O Prophet, you spoke to us and we listened. You received from Allah what we received from you.'"* One sentence which has been revealed from God is the verse:

ولو أنهم إذا ظلموا

"And I have done injustice to myself and I have come to you to seek forgiveness for me."

This action shows that the level and position which has been given to the Holy Prophet (s) by order of this verse is not limited to his life in this world but also applicable to his *barzakhi* life.

Basically, the Muslims do not consider the verses that mention about the matter of respect of the Holy Prophet (s) to be restricted to his life-time. At the time of burial of Hasan ibn Ali (a), when a section of the people had made an uproar, Husayn ibn Ali (a), immediately recited the following verse in order to silence them:

يَا أَيُّهَا الَّذِينَ آمَنُوا لَا تَرْفَعُوا أَصْوَاتَكُمْ فَوْقَ صَوْتِ النَّبِيِّ....

"O you who believe! Do not raise your voices above the voice of the Prophet, and do not speak loud to him. (Hujurat:2)"

Nobody, not even the Umayyids have said that this verse and this respect is only related to the life-time of the Holy Prophet (s). At present, the Wahhabis themselves have written this verse facing the grave of the Holy Prophet (s) and put it over the wall and by this, they wish to say that we should lower our voice and not speak loudly.

Therefore, we can grasp a wider meaning from the verse and it is this, at present, the Muslims can approach the Holy Prophet (s) and request him to seek forgiveness from Allah for their sins. *Ziyarat* of the Holy Prophet (s) of Islam has no purpose other than mentioned in this *ayah* and has no parable in this regard.

This verse proves two matters:

---

⁴ *Wafa' al-Wafa' fi Akhbar dar al-Mustafa*, vol. 4, p. 1361.

1. After the demise of the Holy Prophet (s), it is possible to approach him and request him to seek forgiveness from Allah on one's behalf. This matter will be discussed later under the topic of *"Tawassul* (recourse) with the *Awliya Allah."*

2. This verse is a testimony to the fact that *ziyarat* of the Holy Prophet (s) is lawful since the reality of *ziyarat* is nothing but the presence of the visitor near the visited one. If one is allowed to visit the grave of Holy Prophet (s) and request him to seek forgiveness from Allah then in fact we have performed two actions:

1. We have requested him to seek forgiveness from Allah.

2. We have, by approaching him, conversed with him and *ziyarat* possesses no reality other than this and the subject matter of *ziyarat* is mainly shaped with the same theme.

Therefore, this verse is a testimony to both these matters.

Another Evidence

The unanimity and consensus of the Muslims in various periods in a decree related to the commandments of Islam is the most obvious testimony upon its correctness.

Consensus over the *ziyarat* of grave of the Holy Prophet (s) is one of the better evidences of this decree. By referring to the books of tradition, *fiqh*, morals and history - especially those related to Hajj rites - the reality of this matter will be clarified.

Allama al-Amini has narrated from forty-two Islamic sources, the recommendation of *ziyarat* of the shrine of the Holy Prophet (s). He has accurately narrated the texts and wordings of them in *Al-Ghadir*, volume 5, pages 106 to 129.

The books which we have referred to are the following:

A. *Shifa' al-Saqam fi Ziyarat Qabr Khayr al-Anam* written by Taqi al-Din al-Subki al-Shafi'i (died in 756 A.H.). He has narrated in this book a part of the texts and wordings of the scholars.

B. *Wafa' al-Wafa' fi Akhbar dar al-Mustafa* written by al-Samhudi (died in 911 A.H.). He has narrated in this book the texts and wordings of the scholars which all indicate emphatic recommendation.

C. *Al-Fiqh 'ala al-Madhahib al-Arba'ah* which has been written by four men from the four schools of thought and exposes the thoughts of the four Imams of *Ahl-al Sunnah* whom they follow. They have written as such:

زيارة قبر النبي أفضل المندوبات ورد فيها احاديث

"*The ziyarat of the grave of the Prophet (s) is the principal recommendation as repeatedly found in traditions.*"

Now it's time to reflect upon a section of the traditions which have been narrated by Islamic *muhaddithun* (traditionists).

Traditions Regarding Paying Homage to the Holy Prophet (s)

The Islamic traditions (*hadiths*) about *ziyarat* of the Holy Prophet (s) are so many from the Sunni *muhaddithun* that we don't feel need to pay attention to their references. The great Sunni scholars from each of the sects have narrated these in their books and it shows that *ziyarat* of the shrine of the Holy Prophet (s) has been one of their indisputable matters. Now we shall narrate only a few of them as mentioning all of the traditions will lengthen our discussion.

First Tradition:

عن عبد الله بن عمر: من زار قبري وجبت له شفاعتي

"*Anyone who visits my grave will never be deprived of my intercession.*"

This tradition has come down in the book of *Al-Fiqh 'ala al-Madhahib al-Arba'ah* in volume 1 page 590 and the Sunni scholars of the four schools of thought have given *fatwa* (verdict) based on them. For reference consult the book of *Wafa' al-Wafa' fi Akhbar dar al-Mustafa* vol. 4, page 1336.

Certainly, such a tradition which the scholars have recorded right from the middle of the 2nd century till now, cannot be said to be unfounded. For completion of the matter, Taqi al-Din 'Ali bin 'Abd al-Kafi al-Subki (d. 756 A.H). has discussed and investigated this matter and *isnad* of the traditions in his valuable book *Shifa' al-Saqam* on pages 3 to 11 and has proved the verity and accuracy of the methods of this tradition.

Second Tradition

من جاءني زائراً (ولا تحمله) إلا زيارتي كان حقاً عليَّ أن أكون شفيعاً يوم القيامة

"*Anyone who comes to me with the intention of paying homage to me will be having a right upon me to intercede for him on the Day of Judgement*".

Sixteen memorizers (of Qur'an) and *muhaddithun* have brought this tradition in their books and Taqi al-Din al-Subki (d. 756 A.H.) has discussed the narrators and *isnad* of the traditions in his book *Shifa' al-Saqam* page no.13. Also refer to the book *Wafa' al-Wafa' fi Akhbar dar al-Mustafa* vol. 4, page 1340.

Third Tradition

من حجّ فزار قبري بعد وفاتي كأن كمن زارني في حياتي

"Anyone who visits the House of Allah and then visits my grave is like one who has visited me during my life-time."

This tradition has been recorded by twenty-five of the renowned *muhaddithun* and *huffaz* in their books and Taqi al-Din 'Ali bin 'Abd al-Kafi al-Subki (d. 756 A.H.) has written extensively about the references of this tradition in his book *Shifa' al-Saqam*[5] pages 12 to 16. Also refer to *Wafa' al-Wafa'* volume 4, page 1340.

Fourth Tradition

من حجّ البيت ولم يزُرني فقد جفاني

"Anyone who visits the House of Allah and does not visit me has done injustice upon me."

This tradition has been narrated by nine men from the *shuyukh* and memorizers of tradition. Also refer to *Wafa' al-Wafa'* volume 4, page 1342.

Fifth Tradition

من زار قبري (أو من زارتي) كنت له شفيعاً

"I will become an intercessor for anyone who pays homage to me by coming to my shrine."

This tradition has been narrated by thirteen *muhaddithun* and *huffaz*. Refer to *Wafa' al-Wafa'* volume 4, page 1347.

Sixth Tradition

من زارني بعد موتى فكأنما زارتي في حياتي

"Anyone who visits me after my demise is like one who has visited me during my lifetime."

---

[5] It is the best book that has been written by any of the Sunni writers against the *fatwa* (verdict) of Ibn Taymiyyah regarding the prohibition of journey for *ziyarat* of the Holy Prophet's grave.

These are the examples from various traditions in which the Holy Prophet (s) has invited the people for his *ziyarat* and the number of such traditions according to research of *al-Ghadir* amounts to twenty-two.

Al-Samhudi has collected seventeen traditions in his book *Wafa' al-Wafa'* volume 4, pages 1336-1348 and has discussed their references in detail.

If the Holy Prophet (s) has invited the people for his *ziyarat*, it is because of a series of material and spiritual benefits which are hidden in the *ziyarat* of great Islamic personalities.

By paying homage to the grave of the Holy Prophet (s), people become acquainted with the propagation of religion of Islam and receive the correct traditions and knowledge and spread them around the world.

Reasonings of Wahhabis about Prohibition of Journey towards *Ziyarat* of Graves

Apparently, the Wahhabis permit the *ziyarat* of the Holy Prophet (s) but do not consider the journey for *ziyarat* of graves (of others) to be permissible.

Muhammad ibn 'Abd al-Wahhab writes in the second treatise in *al-Rasa'il al-Hadiyya al-Saniyya* as follows:

تُسنُّ زيارة النبيّ إلا أنه لا يُشد الرَّحل إلا لزيارة المسجد والصلاة فيه

"*Ziyarat* of the Holy Prophet (s) is mustahab (recommended) but journey specifically undertaken for *ziyarah* of mosques and reciting prayer there in is not allowed."

Their main reasoning for *ziyarat* being forbidden is the following tradition which has been narrated in the *Sihah*. The narrator of this tradition is Abu Hurayrah who says that the Holy Prophet (s) said:

لا تُشد الرحال إلا إلى ثلاثة مساجد مسجدي هذا ومسجد الحرام ومسجد الأقصى

"The load of journey cannot be fastened except for (journey towards) three mosques - my own Mosque, Masjid al-Harām and Masjid al-'Aqsa."

The text of this tradition is narrated in other wordings also and that is:

إنما يُسافر إلى ثلاثة مساجد ، مسجد الكعبة ومسجدي ومسجد ايليا

Still this text has been narrated in a third way:

تُشد الرحال إلى ثلاثة مساجد[6]

---

[6] These three texts have been narrated by Muslim in his *Sahih* vol. 4, page 126 book of Hajj, chapter of لا تُشد الرحال. It can also be found in *Sunan Abu Dawud*, vol. 1, page 469, book of Hajj and *Sunan al-Nasa'i* with *Sharh* of al-Suyuti vol. 2, pages 37-38.

That the tradition has come in the books of *Sihah* is not doubtful and we never dispute that its narrator is Abu Hurayrah. However what is important is to understand the context of the tradition.

Let us suppose the text of the tradition is as such:

لا تُشد الرحال إلا ثلاثة مساجد

Indisputably the word of إلا is an exception and requires مستثنى منه (that from which the exception is made) and before referring to the evidences we can presume the مستثن منه in two ways:

1. لا تُشد إلى مسجد من المساجد إلا ثلاثة مساجد
2. لا تشد إلى مكان من الأمكنة إلا إلى ثلاثة مساجد

Understanding the context of the tradition depends on selecting one of the two assumptions.

If we assume the context of the tradition to be the first one, then in such a case it would mean that no luggage for journey will be fastened towards any mosque except these three mosques and it does not mean that (شدالرحال) is not permissible for any place even if it is not a mosque.

Anyone who fastens the luggage of journey for *ziyarat* of the Holy Prophet (s), Imams (a) and virtuous men will never be included in the prohibition of this tradition since the topic of discussion is journey (only) towards mosque and amongst all the mosques these three mosques have been excluded. But going to journey for *ziyarat* of shrines which is out of our topic of discussion is not included in this prohibition.

If we assume the context of the tradition to be the second case, it would mean that except for the journey towards these three places, all spiritual journeys are prohibited, whether the journey is for *ziyarat* of mosque or for *ziyarat* of other places.

However, by paying attention to the decisive evidences it will become clear that the context of the tradition is the same as the first one.

Firstly the مستثنى (the thing excepted) is of the three mosques; in as much as the exception is a linked exception certainly مستثنى منه will be related to the mosque and not place.[7]

---

[7] If someone says: "ما جائني الأزيد", then we have to say that مستثنى منه is the word for human-beings and its like for example tribe etc. and it is not referring to a more comprehensive meaning by the name of "things" and "existence" which is either human-beings or other things.

Secondly, if the aim is prohibition of all the spiritual journeys, it will not be a correct restriction because, in the Hajj ceremonies people do (شدالرحال) and fasten their luggage for Arafat, Mash'ar and Mina. If religious journey (other than to these three places) is not allowed, then why it has been permitted for these three places?

Thirdly, journeys undertaken for *jihad* in the path of Allah, seeking knowledge, establishing bonds of relationship or visiting parents are such journeys that have been emphasized in Qur'an and traditions. Qur'an says:

فَلَوْلَا نَفَرَ مِنْ كُلِّ فِرْقَةٍ مِنْهُمْ طَائِفَةٌ لِيَتَفَقَّهُوا فِي الدِّينِ وَلِيُنْذِرُوا قَوْمَهُمْ إِذَا رَجَعُوا إِلَيْهِمْ لَعَلَّهُمْ يَحْذَرُونَ

"Why should not then a company from every party from among them go forth that they may apply themselves obtain understanding in religion, and that they may warn their people when they come back to them that they may be cautious? (Tawbah:122)"

Therefore great research scholars have interpreted the tradition in the way which we have mentioned.

Al-Ghazali in his book *Ihya' 'Ulum al-din* says:

"The second type of journey is to go on journey for worship like journey for jihad, hajj, ziyarat of the grave of Holy Prophet (s), his companions and the awliya.

Anyone whose ziyarat is the source of tabarruk during life-time will also be the same during his death-time and شدالرحال *for these motives is no problem and is not contradictory to the tradition which prohibits* شدالرحال *(other than the three mosques).*

This is because the matter under discussion is about the mosques and since other mosques are all equal as far as superiority is concerned it is said that journey towards these mosques is not permitted. However, if we overlook the matter of mosques, the ziyarat of Prophets and awliya are having a great virtue although they possess ranks and grades."[8]

Therefore what is prohibited is شد رحال towards the mosques (other than the three mosques) and not "شد رحال" for *ziyarat* and or other spiritual works.

Here we don't have an alternative but to mention that when the Holy Prophet (s) says that no luggage can be fastened for other than the three mosques, it does not mean شد رحال is forbidden (*harām*). Instead it means that it

---

[8] *Ihya' 'Ulum al-din*, book 'Etiquette of going to journey' vol. 2, p. 247. (Published by Dar al-Ma'rufah, Beirut). Also in *Al-Fatawa al-Kubra*, vol. 2, p. 24 by Ibn Taymiyyah.

is not having any merit that a person fastens his luggage towards them and takes the trouble of visiting them as all the mosques (other than the three mosques) are not having any difference as far as their superiority is concerned. The general mosque, the district mosque and the community mosque are all having equal rewards; it is needless that with the presence of the general mosque in a near locality a person fastens his luggage for the general mosque situated in another far-away locality. But it does not mean that if he does so, his action will be *harām* and his journey will be a sinful one.

The proof of this matter is what the writers of *Sihah* and *Sunans* narrate that the Holy Prophet (s) and his companions would visit Masjid Quba on Saturdays and recite prayer at that place. Here is the text of *Sahih al-Bukhari*:

إن النبيّ كان يأتي مسجد قباء كل سبت ماشياً وراكباً وإن ابن عمر كان يفعل كذلك

"*The Holy Prophet (s) used to go for ziyarat of Masjid Quba on every Saturday either on foot or on a mount. The son of 'Umar too would do the same.*"[9]

Fundamentally, how can travelling distances for performing *salat* for Allah in one of the divine mosques without the least taint of sham be considered as *harām* and unlawful? While establishing prayers in mosque is *mustahab* (recommended) its preliminary steps too, as a rule, will take the same color.

---

[9] *Sahih al-Bukhari*, vol. 2, p. 76. *Sahih Muslim* (with commentary of *al-Nawawi*) vol. 9, pp. 169-171; *Sunan al-Nasa'i* (with commentary of *al-Suyuti*) vol. 2, p. 37.

6

Performance of Prayer and Supplication near Graves of the Holy Personalities

Among the matters that has been discussed and debated in the books of Wahhabis is the issue of performing prayer and recitation of *du'a* near the graves of the holy personalities and the matter of lighting candles over their graves.

The founder of Wahhabi school of thought says in the treatise of *Ziyarat al-Qubur* as such:

لم يذكر أحد من أئمة السلف أن الصلاة عند القبور وي مشاهدها مستحبة ولا أن الصلاة والدعاء هُناك افضل بل إتفقوا كلهم على أن الصلاة في المساجد والبُيوت افضل منها عند قبور الأولياء والصالحين

"No one from the past leaders has said that salat near the graves is mustahab (recommended) or that salat and du'a at these places are more superior to other places. Instead all of them are of the same view that salat in mosques and houses are more useful than reciting them near the graves of the awliya and virtuous people."[1]

Moreover, in a reply attributed to the scholars of Medina we read as such:

أما التوجه إلى حجرة النبي (صلى الله عليه وأله) عند الدعاء فالاولى منعه كما هو معروف من معتبرات كُتب المذاهب ولأن افضل الجهات ، جهة القبلة.

"At the time of supplication, it is better to stop from concentrating over the grave of the Holy Prophet (s) and what is well-known in the reliable books is its prohibition. Moreover the best direction is the direction of qibla."

This matter, over the passage of time has reached the level of *shirk* (polytheism) from the level of prohibition and at present they consider such an action to be *shirk* and its performer a *mushrik* (polytheist).

We remind you that anyone who performs *salat* for and worships the one in the grave or takes his grave as a *qibla* will undoubtedly be called a *mushrik*.

But no Muslim from anywhere in the world performs such an action near the grave of the Holy Prophet (s) and the *awliya*. They neither worship them nor take their graves as *qibla*.

---

[1] *Ziyarat al-Qubur*, page 159-160 written by Ibn Taymiyyah in 1310 A.D.

Therefore the idea of *shirk* is no more than an imagination. The motive of Muslims in performing *salat* and *du'a* near the graves of the *awliya* is the very intention of *tabarruk* to the place where the beloved one of Allah has been buried.

They imagine that since such a place beholds a special dignity due to the burial of the beloved one of Allah, their actions will consequently be having a great reward.

Now it is necessary to discuss whether a place enjoys sanctification due to the burial of some virtuous and pious person or not?

If such a judgment is proved through the Qur'an and *sunnah*, then naturally performing *salat* and *du'a* near the graves of the divine leaders will be considered as commendable acts. And, even in other case, we cannot declare it to be prohibited and *harām*. Instead, like all the other places, performing *salat* and reciting *du'a* in those places too will be permitted and lawful even though it may not be considered admirable.

In this section we shall now focus our discussion on whether the burial places and graves of the Prophets and *awliya* are possessing special superiority and dignity or not and whether any proof exists in the Qur'an and *sunnah* about this matter or not?

This reality can be known by paying attention to the following verses:
1. About the grave of *'Ashaab al-Kahf'*, the group of monotheists, gave their views as such:

لَنَتَّخِذَنَّ عَلَيْهِم مَّسْجِدًا

"*......For we will set up a place of worship over them. (Al-Kahf:21)*"

Their aim in considering the graves as mosques was nothing but to perform their religious obligations or, so to speak, their prayer and *du'a* over there.[2] They imagined that this place possessed a special dignity keeping in mind the fact that it contained the dead bodies of the beloved servants of Allah. They thought of seeking *tabarruk* from the superiority of that place and hence a greater reward.

---

[2] In interpreting the afore-said tradition, al-Zamakhshari in *al-Kashshaf* says:
يصلى فيه المسلمون ويتبركون بمكانهم
About this verse Nishapuri writes in his Tafsir as such:
يصلى فيه المسلمون ويتبركون بمكانهم

Qur'an narrates this matter from the group of monotheists and does not say anything more. If this action was unlawful, vain and useless, then Qur'an would have never remained silent. It would have certainly found fault with it and not kept silent which is naturally the sign of approval.

2. The Holy Qur'an commands the people visiting the House of Allah to recite *salat* at *Maqam Ibrahim* i.e. the place where Ibrahim (a) was standing.

Thus it says:

وَاتَّخِذُوا مِنْ مَقَامِ إِبْرَاهِيمَ مُصَلًّى

"And appoint for yourselves a place of prayer on the standing-place of Ibrahim. (Baqarah:125)"

If you place this verse before anyone they will not understand anything from it except that this place has achieved superiority and dignity due to the standing of Ibrahim (a) over this spot and perhaps his worshipping of Allah in that place. Due to the auspiciousness and dignity this spot possesses, the Holy Qur'an orders the Muslims to recite salat at that spot and seek *'tabarruk'*.

When the *Qiyam* (standing) of Ibrahim (a) in one place gives holiness and dignity to such a place then, does not the burial of the bodies of martyrs and virtuous people become the source of dignity and excellence and does not prayers in such a place possess a greater value and dua's get better answered?

Is it true that this verse has been revealed only in the case of Ibrahim and we cannot derive a general judgement from it!?

Dawaniqi[3] entered into a debate with Imam Malik (the founder of Maliki School of thought) in the mosque of the Holy Prophet (s) and said: *"Should we stand facing the qibla at the time of du'a or should we face the grave of the Holy Prophet (s)?"* Malik replied: *"Why should you turn away from the Holy Prophet (s) while he is your channel and your father, i.e. Adam's (a) channel?! Instead turn towards the grave of the Holy Prophet (s) and take him as your intercessor and request him to intercede on your behalf."*[4]

This conversation and discussion shows that *du'a* near the grave of the Holy Prophet (s) was having no problem and difficulty and the question of Mansur

---

[3] Second Abbasid Caliph Abu Ja'far 'Abd Allah al-Mansur Dawaniqi (713 – 774 A.D.). He ruled from 753 to 774 A.D. and was contemporary of Imam al-Sadiq (a).
[4] *Wafa' al-Wafa' fi Akhbar dar al-Mustafa*, volume 4, page 1376.

to the leader of Medina was about the preference of one (act) over the other and Imam Malik replied that paying attention to the grave is like paying attention to the *qibla*.

3. Reference to the incident of *mi'raj* will make this fact more evident since it has come in the traditions of *mi'raj* that the Holy Prophet (s) recited *salat* in places like Taiyyaba, Mount Sinai and Bethlehem.

Jibra'eel came to him and said: 'O Prophet! do you know the place where you recited *salat*? You have performed your prayer at the birth place of 'Isa' (Jesus).[5]

From this tradition we come to know that performing *salat* in places that have been in contact with the body of a Prophet have great significance and *tabarruk* to this particular place was because of Hazrat Isa's birth in that place and nothing else.

4. 'Hajar' and 'Ismail', due to their patience in the path of Allah and their forbearance for being away from home, reached to such position that the places where they used to walk became the places of worship (i.e. the places between Safa and Marwa).[6]

The following is the saying of the student of Ibn Taymiyyah.

"If really the places of strides of these two persons who, because of their patience and forbearance in the path of Allah became so much Holy that the Muslims have been ordered to worship God in these places, then why the grave of the Holy Prophet (s) who has exhibited the greatest of patience and steadfastness on the path of rectifying the society cannot be considered as Holy and sacred and why salat and du'a cannot be recited near such a place?"

5. If truly performing *salat* near the grave is unlawful, then how *Umm al-Mu'minin* (Ayesha) during her remaining life time performed *salat* and worshipped in her chamber where the Holy Prophet (s) was buried.

The meaning of the Holy Prophet's tradition: ("*God has cursed the Jews and the Christians for considering the graves of their Prophets as mosques*"[7]) which the

---

[5] *al-Kasa'is al-Kubra*, vol. 1, p. 154 by al-Suyuti.
[6] *Jala' al-Afham fi Salat wa al-Salam 'ala Khayr al-An'am*, p. 228 by Ibn al-Qayyim al-Jawziyya.
[7] *Sunan al-Nasa'i*, vol. 4, p. 96 (Beirut edition). لعن الله اليهود والنصار اتخذوا قبور انبيائهم مساجد

Islamic traditionists narrate and which the Wahhabis utilize for proving the prohibition of *salat* near the graves of *awliya* is because they were prostrating over the grave of their Prophets or that they were taking their graves as *qibla* both of which were unlawful. If the meaning of the tradition is what they say then why Ayesha, narrator of the tradition, performed *salat* in her chamber for approximately fifty years.

6. If the burial place of the Holy Prophet (s) is not having any special significance, then why the two Sheikhs insisted that they should be buried in that place?

Why al-Hasan ibn Ali (a) mentioned in his will that his Holy body should be buried near his great grandfather and if not possible due to his enemies, he should be buried in the cemetery of Baqi'!?

And what relation this tradition has with the actions of the Muslims who perform *salat* for the sake of God, facing the *qibla* near the grave of the Holy Prophet (s) and their motive is only to derive virtue from that place!

The daughter of the Holy Prophet (s) whose happiness as per the decree of traditions of *Sihah* is the happiness of her God and Messenger and her anger is the anger of her God and Messenger used to visit every Friday the grave of her Uncle Hamza (r) and perform *salat* and mourn in that place. Here is the text of history:

كانت فاطمة رضى الله عنها تزور عمّها حمزة كل جُمعة فتُصلي وتبكي عنده[8]

These reasons jointly show us the path of the Muslims who were always reciting *salat* and supplications in places where the beloved ones of Allah and the self-sacrificers on the path of truth had been buried and gives the message that *salat* and supplication in such places enjoy more honor and superiority and the motive is only to seek *tabarruk* from that sacred place.

* * *

Let us suppose that there is no proof from Qur'an and traditions that such a place possesses distinction and performing salat and *du'a* in such a place is honorable. But why prayer in such a place should be considered as prohibited?

---

[8] *Sunan al-Bayhaqi* (*al-Sunan al-Kubra*), vol. 4, p. 788; *al-Mustadrak*, vol. 1, p. 377 by al-Hakim al-Nishapuri.

Why such a place should not be included in the general principles of Islam which considers all the places on earth to be the places of worshipping God[9] so that the Muslims are able to perform prayer near the graves of the beloved ones of Allah!?

Previously, we had mentioned to you about the motive of the traditions which says that the Jews and Christians have taken the graves of their Prophets as mosques and never such a tradition includes those who perform *salat* and *du'a* facing the *qibla* for the sake of God.

The matter of lighting candles and so on over the graves of the beloved ones of God which the Wahhabis strictly prohibit is not an important matter since their references is the same tradition of *Sunan al-Nasa'i* who narrates from Ibn Abbas that the Holy Prophet (s) has cursed the women visiting the graves and those who turn the graves into mosques and light the candles.[10] This tradition is applicable in the event that lighting candles etc. is having no benefits other than wastage of money or imitating some countries of the world.

However if the aim of lighting candle etc. is to recite Qur'an and *du'a* or perform *salat* and other legal things, then certainly it will not create any problem. Instead lighting candles etc. in such places and that too for such holy purposes will be the proof to:

وَتَعَاوَنُوا عَلَى الْبِرِّ وَالتَّقْوَىٰ

"…….*And help one another in goodness and piety. (Maida:2)*"

Under these circumstances why should it be considered *harām* and forbidden?

Incidentally a group of commentators of traditions have specified the same fact,

Al-Sindi mentions in the margins of *Sunan al-Nasa'i*:

والنهى عنه لإنه تضييع مالٍ بلا نفع

"*Prohibition for lighting of candles was only because such an action leads to wastage of wealth.*"[11]

---

[9] *al-Musnad*, vol. 2 page 222 by Ibn Hanbal. جعلت لي الأرض مسجداً وطهوراً
[10] *Sunan al-Nasa'i*, vol. 3, page 77 (Egyptian edition) and vol. 4, page 95 (Beirut edition)
لعن رسول الله زائرات القبور والمتخذين عليها المساجد والسُرج .
[11] *Sunan al-Nasa'i*, vol. 3, page 77 (Egyptian edition) and vol. 4, page 95 (Beirut edition). Also refer to *Sharh al-Jami' al-Saghir*, vol. 2, page 198.

7

Tawassul (Recourse) to the *Awliya Allah*

Tawassul to the beloved ones of Allah is a matter which is in vogue amongst the Muslims of the world and from the day the Islamic *Shari'ah* was conveyed through the Holy Prophet (s) its legality was also declared by the way of Islamic traditions.

It was only in the 8th century A.H. that *tawassul* was rejected by Ibn Taymiyyah and two centuries later Muhammad ibn 'Abd al-Wahhab intensified this objection. *Tawassul* was introduced to be unlawful and heresy and occasionally was labelled as worshipping the *awliya* and it is needless to mention that worshipping other than God amounts to polytheism and is forbidden.

We shall later on have a separate discussion regarding the meaning of worship (*'ibadah*) and we shall remind you that *tawassul* to the divine leaders on the one hand will be counted as worship and polytheism and on the other hand will be considered as desirable and *mustahab* having no sign of worship. However, we shall not discuss them here. What is important to know is that *tawassul* to the *Awliya Allah* is done in two ways:

1. *Tawassul* to themselves. For example, we say:

اللهم إني أتوسل إليك بنبيك محمد (صلى الله عليه وأله) ان تقي حاجتي

"O Lord I take recourse to your Messenger Muhammad (s) in order that you fulfil my wish."

2. *Tawassul* to their position and reverence before Allah and their rights. Like we say:

اللهم إني أتوسل إليك بجاه محمد (صلى الله عليه وأله) وحُرمته وحقِّه ان تقضي حاجتي

"O Lord I take their position and their respect which they have before Thee as the means for my need to be fulfilled by Thee."

From the viewpoint of the Wahhabis, both these types are declared to be forbidden whereas the Islamic traditions and the practice of the Muslims bear witness contrary to the views of the Wahhabis and recommend *tawassul* of both these types.

At first, we shall mention the Islamic traditions one by one and then state the practice of the Muslims. By paying attention to both these reasonings, the matter of heresy and unlawfulness will automatically cease to exist.

But, whether *tawassul* to divine leaders amounts to their worship or not will be discussed in the section of 'meaning of worship' and that section will be the most insightful part of our discussion.

Tawassul According to Prophetic Traditions

There are many traditions mentioned in the traditional and historical books which bear testimony to the correctness and verity of the matter of *tawassul* to the divine leaders themselves and their position. Here, we mention a part of those traditions:

First Tradition - Tradition of 'Uthman ibn Hunayf[1]

إن رجلاً ضريراً اتى إلى النبي (صلى الله عليه وآله) فقال ادعُ الله ان يُعافيني فقال إن شئت دعوت وإن شئت صبرت وهو خير قال فادعه ، فامره أن يتوضأ فيُحسن وضوه ويُصلّي ركعتين ويدعو بهذا الدعاء: اللهم إني أسالك ، وأتوجه بك إلى ربي في حاجتي لتقضي ، اللهم شفعه في. قال ابن حنيف فوالله ما تفرقنا وطال بنا الحديث حتى دخل علينا كان لم يكُن به ضُرّ.

"A blind person approached the Holy Prophet (s) and said: 'Request Allah to cure me.' The Holy Prophet (s) replied: 'If you wish so I will pray for you but be patient for that is much better.' The blind man asked the Holy Prophet (s) to pray for him. The Holy Prophet (s) ordered him to take proper Wuzu and then recite two Raka't (units) of salat and this 'Dua': O' Lord! I request from Thee; I pay attention to Thee through (the channel) of your prophet Muhammad, Your blessed prophet. O Muhammad, I turn to my Lord for the fulfilment of my need through you so that my need is answered.

O Lord, accept his intercession for me...."

A Word about the Reference of this Tradition

The authenticity and verity of the reference needs no word from us. Even the leader of the Wahhabis i.e. Ibn Taymiyyah has declared its reference to be

---

[1] 'Uthman ibn Hunayf al-Awsi al-Ansari was a companion of the Prophet (s) and during the caliphate of Imam Ali (a) he was the governor of Basrah until a while before the Battle of Jamal.

correct and has said that by Abu Ja'far whose name has come in the *Sanad* of the tradition means Abu Ja'far Al-Khutami and he is a reliable man.[2]

Al-Rifa'i, a contemporary Wahhabi writer who strives to cast down the credibility of the traditions on *tawassul*, says with regard to this tradition as such:

لا شك إن هذا الحديث صحيح ومشهور وقد ثبت فيه بلا شك

"Undoubtedly this tradition is correct and well-known."[3]

In the book of *al-Tawassul*, al-Rafa'i says: "This tradition has been mentioned by al-Nasa'i, al-Bayhaqi[4], al-Tabarani[5], al-Tirmidhi and al-Hakim in his *al-Mustadrak*[6] and two recent writers have inserted the sentence اللهم شفعني فيه instead of وشفعه فيه.[7]

Zayni Dahlan writes in *Khulasat al-Kalam* that: "This tradition has been narrated - with reliable chains of narration - by al-Bukhari, Ibn Majah, al-Hakim in his *al-Mustadrak* and Jalal al-Din al-Suyuti[8] in his *al-Jami*."

The writer narrates this tradition from the following references:

1. *Sunan Ibn Majah*, vol 1, page 441 from the publications of Dar Ihya al-Kutub al-'Arabiyya, (ed. by Muhammad Fu'ad 'Abd al-Baqi), tradition no. 1385.

Ibn Majah narrates from Abu Ishaq:

هذا حديث صحيح

'This tradition is correct.'

Thereafter he adds:

"al-Tirmidhi has narrated this tradition in the book of Abwaab-ul-Adeeya and said

هذا حديث حق صحيح غريب

'This tradition is truly correct and Gharib.'

---

[2] In *al-Musnad* of Ahmad, Abu Ja'far has come with the word of Khutami although in *Sunan Ibn Majah* Abu Ja'far has come independently.

[3] *al-Tawassul ila haqiqat al-tawassul al-mashru' wa-al-mamnu'*, page 158. Written by Muhammad Nasib al-Rifa'i al-Salafi.

[4] Abu Bakr Ahmad ibn Husayn al-Bayhaqi (994 -1066 A.D.) was Sunni Shafi'i scholar and hadith expert from Khurasan, Iran. His most famous book *Sunan al-Kubra lil Bayhaqi*, commonly known as *Sunan al-Bayhaqi* is a collection of over 200,000 hadithes.

[5] Abu'l Qawsim Sulayman al Tabarani (874 - 971 A.D.) was a Sunni Hanbali hadith scholar from Syria who travelled extensively and died in Isfahan, Iran. His most famous work is collection of hadithes *al-Mu'jam al-Kabir* in which he excluded the traditions reported by Abu Hurayra.

[6] *Al-Mustadrak alaa al-Sahihain*

[7] *Ibid*.

[8] Al-Suyuti (1445 - 1505 A.D.) was a great Egyptian Sunni Shafi'i Ash'ari scholar, juristic expert and teacher. He was a prolific writer on wide range of topics of Islamic theology. His famous works include *Tafsir al-Jalalayn, Tarikh Al Khulafa, Dur al-Manthur, Khasais al-Kubra, Khasais al-Sughra, Jami al-Kabir* and *Jami al-Saghir*.

2. *Musnad Ahmad ibn Hanbal* vol. 4, page 138. He has narrated this tradition in three ways from the *Musnad* of 'Uthman ibn Hunayf printed from al-Maktab al-Islami, Mo'assassa Dar Sadir, Beirut.

3. *al-Mustadrak* of al-Hakim vol. 1, page 313 printed from Hyderabad. After narrating the tradition, he says:

هذا حديث صحيح على شرك الشيخين ولم يُخرجاه

"This tradition is correct according to the criteria set by the Sheikhayn and they have not narrated it."

4. *Al-Jami' al-Saghir* written by al-Suyuti narrated from al-Tirmidhi and *Mustadrak* of Hakim, page 59.

5. *Talkhis al-Mustadrak*[9] written by al-Dhahabi (died in 748 A.H.) which is printed below *al-Mustadrak*.

6. *Al-Taj al-Jami'* vol. 1, page 286. This book is the collection of the traditions of the five books of *Sihah* except Ibn Majah.

Therefore it is needless to speak and discuss about the reference of this tradition.

You hand over this tradition to someone who is acquainted with Arabic language and a person whose mind is completely free from the controversies of the Wahhabis in the matter of *tawassul* and ask him what the Holy Prophet (s) has commanded him in the *du'a* which he taught the blind man and how he guided him as to how one's 'Du'as' are easily answered! He will immediately reply: "The Holy Prophet (s) has taught him to consider the blessed Prophet as a channel and to seek *tawassul* from him and ask God to fulfil his wish. This matter can easily be understood from the following sentences:

A. اللهم إني اسئلك وأتوجه إليك بنبيك

"O Lord, I ask Thee and turn towards Thee through the channel of your Prophet."

The word نبيك is pertaining to the previous two words اسئلك and أتوجه إليك

In clearer terms, he asks from God through the channel of 'Nabi' and also turns to God through him. Moreover by 'Nabi' is meant Nabi himself and not the '*Du'a*' of Nabi; to imagine that it means the *du'a* of Nabi is deficient of any reason.

---

[9] is an abridged version of *Al-Mustadrak alaa al-Sahihain* written by al-Dhahabi.

Anyone who predetermines the word of *du'a* has no reason other than pre-judgement since, the one who commends such a word and does not think *tawassul* to people to be correct forcibly strives to predetermine the word of '*Du'a*' so that nobody opposes his idea and eventually he may say: "It means *tawassul* to the '*Du'a*' of the Prophet (s) and not the Prophet himself and *tawassul* to the '*Du'a*' of someone is proper.

B. محمد نبي الرحمة

In order to clarify that asking God for the sake of the Prophet and paying attention to Him through His channel is the right purpose, the word of نبيك is mentioned along with the sentence محمد نبي الرحمة which clarifies the fact much better and makes the meaning more apparent.

C. The sentence يا محمد اني أتوجه بك إلى ربي shows that he (i.e. the blind man) is referring to Prophet Muhammad himself and not his *du'a*.

D. The sentence وشفعه فيّ means O God make him as my intercessor and accept his intercession towards me. In all of these sentences what is said and explained is the very personality of the Holy Prophet (s) and his great position and there is no talk of the *du'a* of the Holy Prophet.

With this explanation all the five objections which the Wahhabi writer al-Rifa'i has mentioned in the book *al-Tawassul ila Haqiqat al-Tawassul* is done away with and we have brought the details of the objections and their reply in our book, *al-Tawassul*. Interested readers can refer to them on pages 147 to 153.

Second Tradition: *Tawassul* to the (Right) of Questioner

'Atiyya al-'Awfi narrates from Abu Sa'eed al-Khudri that the Holy Prophet (s) said: "Anyone who leaves his house for *salat* and recites in this state the following *du'a*, he will meet the mercy of Allah and one thousand angels will seek forgiveness for him."[10]

اللهم إني أسئلك بحق السائلين عليك وأسئلك بحق ممشاي هذا فإني لم اخرُج اشراً ولا بطراً ولا رياءً ولا سُمعة وخرجت إتقاء سخطك وابتغاء مرضاتك فاسئلك ان تعيذني من النار وان تغفر لي ذنوبي إنه لا يغفر الذنوب إلا أنت.

---

[10] قبل الله بوجهه واستغفر له ألف ملك *Sunan* of Hafiz Muhammad Ibn Abi Abullah Ibn Majah al-Qazwini (824 - 887 A.D.) which is one of the six canonical collections of Sunni hadith books called *Sihah*. vol. 1, pp. 261-262 chapter of 'Mosques' Egyptian edition. *Sunan Ibn Majah* has 1,500 chapters and about 4,000 hadithes. Ibn Majah was Shafi'i scholar. Also refer to *al-Musnad* Imam Ahmad ibn Hanbal vol. 3, hadith no. 21.

"O God I ask Thee by the right of the questioners and by the honor of the steps which I take in Thy direction, I have not left the house for the purpose of disobedience or recreation or hypocrisy. I have left for keeping away from Thy anger and achieving Thy satisfaction. I ask Thee to keep me away from the Fire and forgive my sins for nobody forgives the sins except Thee."

This tradition clearly bears testimony to the fact that man, while asking God for his need to be fulfilled can take the position and status of a pious person as his channel and the reasoning of this tradition brings to light our objective.[11]

Third Tradition: *Tawassul* **to the Right of Holy Prophet (s)**

After disobedience of Allah, Adam (a) in the light of the words which were manifested from God, repented as Qur'an says:

فَتَلَقَّىٰ آدَمُ مِنْ رَبِّهِ كَلِمَاتٍ فَتَابَ عَلَيْهِ ۚ إِنَّهُ هُوَ التَّوَّابُ الرَّحِيمُ

"Then Adam received (some) words from his lord, so He turned to him mercifully; surely He is oft-returning (to mercy), the Merciful. (Baqarah:37)"

Regarding the interpretation of كلمات (words) which has come down in this verse, a group of commentators and traditionists, by relying on the following tradition are having a view, which by paying attention to its text will become clear for us.

Al-Tabarani in *Al-Mu'jam al-Saghir*, al-Hakim Nishapuri in *al-Mustadrak*, Abu Nu'aym al-Isfahani[12] and al-Bayhaqi in the book of *Dala'il al-Nubuwwah*[13], Ibn 'Asakir al-Shami in his *al-Ta'rikh*, al-Suyuti in *al-Durr al-Manthur* and al-

---

[11] The command which has come in the verse of ولا تقربا هذا الشجرة (*Surah al-Baqarah*:35) is not an authoritative command. Instead, it is an order in the guided sense or so to say an advisory aspect and opposition to such a command will not result in punishment and chastisement. Its result will be that the person will only be faced with the effect of the state of the action itself. If a doctor orders his patient suffering from cold not to eat sour things and muskmelon, opposing his command will have no result other than intensification of his cold. In the Holy Qur'an many verses testify that the divine prohibition was of a guided nature resulting in nothing but expulsion from heaven which is reckoned to be the effect of state of the action itself. Please refer to verses 118 and 119 of *Surah Taha* and the book of 'Correct Tafsir of difficult verses of Qur'an' (*Tafsir al-Sahih Ayatul Mushkilah al-Qur'an*) the tenth matter from pages 73 to 82.

[12] Abu Nu'aym al-Isfahani (948 – 1038 A.D.) was a Persian Sunni Shafi'i scholar expert in hadithes and Islamic history. His most famous books are *Dala'il al-Nubuwwah* and *Hilyat al-Awliya'*.

[13] These two scholars have written books with similar names. al-Bayhaqi: *Dala'il al-Nubuwwah Wa ma'rifat Ahwal Sahib al-Shari'ah*. al-Isfahani: *Dala'il al-Nubuwwah*.

Alusi in *Ruh al-Ma'ani*[14] have narrated from 'Umar ibn al-Khattab that the Holy Prophet (s) has said: [15]

لما اذنب ادم الذي اذنبه رفع رأسه إلى السماء فقال اسئلك بحق محمد إلا غفرت لي فأوحى الله إليه ومن مُحمد؟ فقال تبارك اسمك ، لما خلقت رفعت رأسى إلى عرشك فإذا فيه مكتوب لا إله إلا الله ومحمد رسول الله فقلت إنه ليس أحد اعظم عندك قدراً: ممن جعلت اسمه مع اسمك فاوحى إليه إنه اخر النبيين من ذريتك ولولا هو لما خلقتك .

"When Adam committed the sin he raised his head towards the sky and said (O God) I ask Thee by the right of Muhammad that You forgive me. God revealed to him: "Who is Muhammad?" Adam replied: When You created me, I raised my head towards the 'Arsh' (Throne) and I saw that on it was written "There is no God except Allah and Muhammad is the Messenger of Allah. I said to myself that Muhammad must be His greatest creature that Allah has kept His name besides his own name. At this moment, it was revealed to him that Muhammad was the last of the Prophets from his Progeny and if it was not for Muhammad, God would have not created him. "

Our View about this Tradition:

1. In the Holy Qur'an, the word كلمة or words كلمات are applied to personalities contrary to what is common amongst us. For example:

أَنَّ اللَّهَ يُبَشِّرُكَ بِيَحْيَى مُصَدِّقًا بِكَلِمَةٍ مِنَ اللَّهِ

"That Allah gives you the good news of Yahya verifying a Word from Allah, (Aale Imran:39)"

يَا مَرْيَمُ إِنَّ اللَّهَ يُبَشِّرُكِ بِكَلِمَةٍ مِنْهُ اسْمُهُ الْمَسِيحُ عِيسَى ابْنُ مَرْيَمَ

"O Maryam, surely Allah gives you good news with a Word from him (of one) whose name is the Messiah, Isa son of Maryam. (Aale Imran:45)"

إِنَّمَا الْمَسِيحُ عِيسَى ابْنُ مَرْيَمَ رَسُولُ اللَّهِ وَكَلِمَتُهُ

"The Messiah, Isa son of Maryam is only an Apostle of Allah and His Word, (Nisa:171)"

---

[14] *Mustadrak al-Hakim*, vol. 2, page 61; *Ruh al-Ma'ani* vol. 1, page 217; *al-Durr al-Manthur*, vol. 1, p. 59 narrated from al-Tabarani, Abu Nu'aym al-Isfahani and al-Bayhaqi.

[15] The text of the hadith is taken from *al-Durr al-Manthur* and differs slightly from the text of al-Hakim in his *al-Mustadrak* although both are same in their contents.

$$\text{قُلْ لَوْ كَانَ الْبَحْرُ مِدَادًا لِكَلِمَاتِ رَبِّي لَنَفِدَ الْبَحْرُ}$$

"Say: If the sea were ink for the words of my Lord. (Al-Kahf:109)"

$$\text{وَالْبَحْرُ يَمُدُّهُ مِنْ بَعْدِهِ سَبْعَةُ أَبْحُرٍ مَا نَفِدَتْ كَلِمَاتُ اللَّهِ}$$

"With seven more seas to increase it, the words of Allah would not come to an end. (Luqman:27)"

Considering that the word of كلمات has come in the verse under our discussion, we can say that by كلمات is meant the same noble personalities to whom *tawassul* is sought and in the aforesaid tradition, only the name of Muhammad is mentioned from amongst the names of those personalities. Therefore, in Shia traditions, this reality is narrated in two ways. Sometimes كلمات is interpreted as a name of these holy personalities and sometimes it refers to their sparkling light. Here are both the interpretations:

$$\text{إن أدم رأى مكتوباً على العرش اسماء معظمة مكرمة فسأل عنها فقيل له هذه اسماء اجل الخلق منزلة عند الله تعالى والأسماء محمد وعليّ وفاطمة والحسن والحسين ، فتوسَّل ادم عليه السلام إلى ربه في قبول توبته ورفع منزلته}^{16}$$

"Adam saw the names which were written in 'Arsh (throne) and did tawassul to them. It was told to him that these names were the most honorable creatures of Allah and they were Muhammad, 'Ali, Fatima, Hasan and Husayn. Adam repented by doing tawassul to them."

Another Shia tradition mentions that Adam saw the sparkling light of these five personalities. For knowing this tradition, please refer to *Tafsir al-Burhan*.[17]

2. By referring to the historical and traditional books it becomes clear that *tawassul* of Adam (a) to the Holy Prophet (s) was one famous and well-known matter. As, Imam Malik told Mansur al-Dawaniqi in the shrine of the Holy Prophet (s) as such:

$$\text{هو وسيلتك ووسيلة ابيك أدم}^{18}$$

---

[16] *Majma' al-Bayan*, vol. 1, p. 89; *Tafsir al-Burhan*, vol.1, pp. 86-88; hadiths: 2, 5, 11, 12, 14 and 27.

[17] *Tafsir al-Burhan*, vol. 1, p. 87 *ahadith* no.13, 15 and 16.

[18] Sayyid Ahmad Zayni Dahlan writes in the both *al-Durar al-Saniyya*, p. 10 that al-Qadi 'Iyad has narrated this incident with correct reference. Imam al-Subki in his book *Shifa al-Saqam*, al-Samhudi in *Wafa' al-Wafa'*, and al-Qastallani in *al-Mawahib al-Ladunniyya*. Ibn Hajar said in *al-Jawhar al-Munazzam* that this incident has been narrated with correct references. Al-'Allama al-Zurqani writes *in Sharh al-Mawahib* that Ibn Fahd has narrated this with a good (*hasan*) chain of narration and al-Qadi 'Iyad has narrated it with an authentic (*sahih*) chain of narration. The text of the conversation of al-Mansur with Imam Malik will be mentioned later in the text.

"He (Holy Prophet) is your channel and your father, Adam's channel."

The Islamic poets have put this reality into a form of verse:

به قد اجاب الله ادم دعا ونجى في بطن السفينة نوح قوم بهم عفرت خطيئة ادم وهم الوسيلة والنجوم الطُلع

"On account of him, Allah accepted the 'Dua' of Adam and saved Noah inside the ship. They are such people through whom Adam's sin was pardoned and they are those who are the channels to Allah and the sparkling stars."[19]

Fourth Tradition: *Tawassul* of Prophet (s) by the Right of Prophet (s) and by the Rights of Previous Prophets

لما ماتت فاطمة بنت أسد ، دخل عليها رسول الله (صلى الله عليه وآله) فجلس عند رأسها ، فقال رحمك الله يا أمي بعد أمي ثم دعا رسول اله (صلى الله عليه وآله) اسمامة بن زيد ، وابا أيُوب الأنصاري وعمر بن الخطاب وغُلاماً أسود ، يحفرون ، فحفروا قبرها ، فلما بلغوا الحد ، حفر رسول الله بيده واخرج تُرابه ، فلما فرغ دخل رسول الله (صلى الله عليه وآله) فاضطجع فيه ، ثم قال: الله الذي يُحيى ويُميت وهو حيٌ لا يموت إغفر لأمي فاطمة بنت اسد ووسّع عليها مدخلها بحق نبيك الدين من قلبي

"When Fatima, daughter of Asad passed away and the Holy Prophet (s) was informed about her death he came and sat beside her and said: 'O my mother after my mother, may God have mercy upon you. Then he asked Usama, Abu Ayyub, 'Umar ibn al-Khattab and a black slave to prepare one grave. When the grave was ready the Holy Prophet (s) made a niche in the side of the grave and buried her with his own hands and then recited this 'Dua': 'O Allah the One who gives Life and Death: the One who is All-Living and never dies, Have mercy on Fatima daughter of Asad and make her abode vast by the right of your Prophet and the Prophets who came before me.'"

The writer of *Khulasat al-kalam* says:

رواه الطبراني في الكبير والأوسط وابن حبان والحاكم وصحّحوه

"This tradition is narrated by al-Tabarani (in his al-Mu'jam), Ibn Hibban and al-Hakim and they have confirmed its authenticity."[20]

Sayyid Ahmad ibn Zayni Dahlan writes in the book *al-Durar al-Saniyya fi al-Radd 'ala al-Wahhabiyyah* as such:

روى ابن أبي شيبة عن جابر مثل ذلك ، وكذا روى مثله ابن عبد البر عن ابن عباس ، ورواه ابو نعيم في حلية الأولياء عن أنس ، ذكر ذلك كُله الحافظ جلال الدين السُيوطي في الجامع الكبير.

---

[19] *Kashf al-'Irtiyab*, pp. 307, 308.
[20] *Kashf al-'Irtiyab*, page 312 narrated from *Khulasat al-Kalam*.

"The famous traditionist Ibn Abi Shayba has narrated this tradition from Jabir. Ibn 'Abd al-Barr and Abu Nu'aym too have narrated this tradition from Ibn 'Abbas and Anas respectively. Jalal al-Din al-Suyuti has brought all these matters in al-Jami' al-Kabir."[21]

The writer narrates this tradition in the afore-mentioned form from two books that some of them contain the supplication related to our discussion while others do not.

1. *Hilyat al-Awliya* (Abu Nu'aym al-Isfahani), vol. 3, page 121.
2. *Wafa' al-Wafa'* (al-Samhudi) vol. 3, page 899.

Fifth Tradition: *Tawassul* to Prophet (s) Himself

Some of the Islamic traditionists have narrated that an Arab accompanied with some villagers approached the Holy Prophet (s) and said:

لقد اتيناك وما لنا بعير يطّ[22] لنا ولا صبيُ يعظّ[23]

"We have come to you while we are neither having a camel with us to groan nor a child to sleep."

Thereafter he recited these poems

وقد شُغلت أم الصبيّ عن الطفل	أتيناك والعذراء تُمى لبائها
سوى الحنظل العامي والعلهز الفسل	ولا شيئ مما تأكل الناس عندنا
واين فرار الناس إلا إلى الرُسل	وليس لنا إلا إليك فرارُنا

"We have come to you while blood drops from the bosom of the horses; the mother has been restrained from her baby. We are not having anything with ourselves for people to eat except for bitter leaves which they eat in the year of famine and some bad food from wool and blood. We are having no alternative but to seek shelter in you, and in whom can people seek shelter except the Prophets."

Then,

فقال رسول الله يجرر حتى صعد المنبر ، فرفع يديه: اللهم إسقنا غيثاً مُغيثاً...فما ردّ النبي يديه حتى ألقت السماء...ثم قال لله درابي طالب لو كان حياً لقرّت عيناه ، من يُنشدنا قوله؟ فقال عليُ بن أبي طالب ، وقال وكأنك تُريد يا رسول الله قوله:

ثِمَالُ ٱلْيَتَامَى عِصْمَةٌ لِلْأَرَامِلِ	وَ أَبْيَضُ يُسْتَسْقَى ٱلْغَمَامُ بِوَجْهِهِ
فَهُمْ عِنْدَهُ فِي نِعْمَةٍ وَ فَوَاضِلَ	يَطُوفُ بِهِ ٱلْهَلَاكُ مِنْ آلِ هَاشِمٍ

The Holy Prophet (s) said:

---

[21] *al-Durar al-Saniyya*, page 8.
[22] ينط is derived from اطيط which means the noise of a camel.
[23] اطيط is derived from غطيط which means the noise of a child while sleeping.

فأنشد عليّ ابياناً من القصيدة والرسول يستغفر لأبي طالب على المنبر ، ثم قام رجل من كنانة وأنشد. لك الحمد والحمد ممن شكر سُقينا بوجه النبي المطر

'Yes, my objective was the same as you have recited.' Then Ali (a) read a portion of his elegy and the Holy Prophet (s) asked blessings for Abu Talib on top of the pulpit.' After this a man from the tribe of Bani Kinana stood up and recited some lines where the first line meant as follows: "All the praise is for You. O Allah; praise from Your worthy slaves. By resorting to the Holy Prophet (s), we have become satiated by the rainfall."

Numerous references have been narrated for this portion but the writer has narrated from the following documents:

a. *'Umdat al-Qari fi Sharh Sahih al-Bukhari,* vol. 7, page 31 written by Badr al-Din Mahmud bin Ahmad al-'Ayni[24] (d. 855 A.H.) printed by *Idara al-Taba'a al-Muniriyya.*

b. *Sharh Nahj al-Balagha* by Ibn Abi al-Hadid, vol. 14, page 80.

c. *al-Sira al-Halabiyya* by 'Ali bin Burhan al-Din al-Halabi[25], vol. 3, page 263.

d. *al-Hujjah 'ala al-Dhahib ila Takfir Abi Talib,* written by Shams al-Din Abi 'Ali Fakhar bin Ma'ad (d. 630 A.H.), printed in Najaf, 'Alawi press, page 79.

e. *Sira Zayni Dahlan* in the margin of *al-Sira al-Halabiyya,* vol. 1, page 81.

Sixth Tradition: *Tawassul* to the Self of Prophet (s)

إن سواد بن قارب رضي الله ، انشد لرسول الله قصيدته اليىئ فيها التوسل ويقول: وأشهد أن الله لا رب غيره وأنك مأمون على كل غائب وأنك أدنى المرسلين وسيلة إلى الله يابن الأكرمين الأطائب فمُرنا بما يأتيك يا خير مُرسل وإن كان فيما فيه شيب الذوائب وكن لي شفيعاً يوم لا ذو شفاعة بمُغنٍ قتيلاً عن سواد بن قارب

"I bear witness that there is no God except Allah. You (O Prophet) are trustworthy upon every hidden thing from the senses. From amongst the Prophets you are the nearest channel towards Allah. O the son of the honorable and noble! you command us whatever you receive. O, the most righteous Apostle! Although acting upon your commands causes the hair on the head to turn white, you be my intercessor on the Day when the

---

[24] He was a Sunni Hanafi scholar, born in Turkey in 1361 A.D. He extensively travelled to acquire religious knowledge and finally settled in Egypt and was also appointed as Qadi. He died in Cairo in 1453 A.D.
[25] Popularly known as al-Halabi (1460 – 1549 A.D.) was a Sunni Hanafi scholar born in Halab, Syria. He then travelled to Cairo and finally settled in Istanbul, spending over 40 years during Ottoman Empire.

intercession of the intercessors will be useless for Sawad bin Qaa'reb even to the extent of string of dates."[26]

Till here we were able to mention some of the traditions of *tawassul* which have come in the historical and traditional books of *Ahl al-Sunnah*.

However, in the traditions of Shi'a leaders, the matter of *tawassul* to holy personalities is so clear and obvious that it can be witnessed in most of their 'Du'as' (supplications).

Should we learn Islamic teachings and instructions from Ibn Taymiyyah and Muhammad ibn 'Abd al-Wahhab or acquire them from the Household of the Messengership and the progeny of the Holy Prophet (s) who by the order of *Hadith al-Thaqalayn*, are (The Lesser Weight) and witness to Qur'an. Amongst the numerous 'Du'as' that have come in *al-Sahifa al-'Alawiyya*[27] or in *du'a 'Arafa* or in *al-Sahifa al-Sajjadiyya*, we shall content ourselves with only one of them which is most suitable in connection with the previous tradition.

Seventh Tradition: The Leader of the martyrs says in *Du'a 'Arafa*

اللهم إنا نتوجه إليك في هذه العشية التي فرضتها وعظمتها بمُحمد نبيك ورسولك وخيرتك من خلقك

"O Lord at such a moment that You have made it obligatory and honorable upon me, I turn towards You by Muhammad, Your Prophet, Your Messenger and Your best of those created by You."[28]

Practice of the Muslims Regarding *Tawassul*

The practice of the Muslims during the time of the Holy Prophet (s) and also after him was that they were always seeking '*tabarruk*' to the *Awliya Allah* themselves as well as to their position and status. Now we shall mention some of them here:

1. Ibn al-'Athir 'Izz al-Din 'Ali bin Muhammad bin Muhammad bin 'Abd al-Karim al-Jazari (died in 630 A.H.) writes in the book *Usd al-Ghabah fi Ma'rifat al-Sahaba* as such:

---

[26] *Al-Durar al-Saniyyah fi al-Radd 'ala al-Wahhabiyyah*, page 27 written by Sheikh Zayni Dahlan and *al-Tawassul ila Haqiqat al-Tawassul*, page 300.

[27] *al-Sahifat al-'Alawiyya*, ad'iya (prayers) of Amir al-mu'minin which al-Sheikh 'Abdallah Samahiji has collected. Available online at: http://www.duas.org/alaviya/

[28] *Mafatih al-Jinan*, du'a 'Arafa. Available online at: http://www.duas.org/zilhajj/arfday.htm

واستسقى عمر بن الخطاب بالعباس عام الرمادة لما اشتد القحط فسقاهم الله تعالى به واخصبت الأرض فقال عمر هذا: والله الوسيلة إلى الله والمكان منه وقال حسان:

سأل الإمام وقد تتابع جدبنا	فسقى الغمام بغرة العباس
عمّ النبي وصنو والده الذي	ورث النبي بذالك دون الناس
أحيا الإله به البلاد فأصبحت	مخضرة الأجناب بعد اليأس

ولما سُقي الناس طفقوا يتمسحون بالعباس ويقولون هنيئاً لك ساقي الحرمين

"In the year when famine reached its peak, 'Umar requested for rain through the channel of Abbas. God satiated them through him and every place became green. Thereafter 'Umar faced the people and said: 'I swear by Allah that al-'Abbas is our channel towards Allah and he is having a high station before Allah.'

Hassan ibn Thabit recited a poem in his honor and said: 'When famine had severely engulfed the entire area, the Leader requested for rain.' Thereafter the clouds in the sky, through the brightness of al-'Abbas satiated the people. Al-'Abbas who is the Uncle of the Prophet (s) and alike the father of the Prophet (s) has inherited such a position and status from him. Almighty Allah enlivened the places through him and every spot began to be filled with greenery after despair and disappointment. When it rained, people everywhere started seeking tabarruk by touching the body of al-'Abbas and they said: Bravo O Saqi (cupbearer) of the two holy sanctuaries."[29]

Observation of the period of history, an example of which has also been mentioned in *Sahih al-Bukhari*, shows that one of the means of *tawassul* was through the honorable personalities who were embodiment of nearness (to God) and meritorious and possessed virtues that make them suitable for *tawassul*. What an elegant manner to express this is to say:

هذا والله الوسيلة إلى الله والمكان منه

'This is by God a means for seeking nearness to God and at His House.'

2. Al-Qastallani (d. 923 AH), who was a contemporary to Jalal al-Din al-Suyuti, writes in his book *al-Mawahib al-Ladunniyyah bil-manha al-Muhammadiyyah fil Seerat al-Nabawiyyah* that has been printed in Egypt that:

إن عمر لنا استسقى بالعباس قال يا أيها الناس إن رسول الله (صلى الله عليه وأله) كان يرى للعباس ما يرى الولد للوالد فاقتدوا به في عمه واتخذوه وسيلةً إلى الله تعالى فيه التصريح بالتوسل وبهذا يبطُل قول من منع التوسّل مُطلقاً بالإحياء والأموات وقول من منع ذلك بغير النبي.

---

[29] *Usd al-Ghabah*, vol. 3 p. 111. Egyptian edition.

"When 'Umar requested for rain through Abbas he said: 'O people! The Holy Prophet (s) used to look at Abbas from a father's angle. You follow him and take him as your channel towards Allah.'" This action nullifies the notion and thought of those who have completely prohibited tawassul or have prohibited it for personalities other than Holy Prophet (s)."[30]

3. When Mansur asked the grand Mufti of Medina, Malik bin Anas, whether he should face the *qibla* and recite *du'a* or face the Holy Prophet (s), the latter replied:

لِم تصرف وجهك عنه وهو وسيلتك ووسيلة أبيك آدم (عليه السلام) إلى الله يوم القيامة بل استقبله واستشفع به فيشفعك الله قال الله تعالى ولو أنهم إذ ظلموا أنفسهم.

"Why do you turn your face away from him? He is your means and your father, Adam's channel on the Day of Judgement. You resort to him and take him as your intercessor as Almighty Allah accepts his intercession. Allah declares (in Quran) that if those who do injustice upon themselves..."[31]

4. Ibn Hajar al-Haythami[32] in the book of *al-Sawa'iq al-Muhriqah* (which al-Qadi Nurullah al-Shustari[33] refuted under the title of *al-Sawarim al-Muhriqah)*[34] has narrated the following two couplets:

إن النبي دريعتي   هم إليه وسيلتي
ارجوا بهم أعطى غداً   بيدى اليمين صحيفتي

"The Household of the Holy Prophet (s) is my channel towards Allah and it is through their means that I have hope that my book of deeds will be given in my right hand."[35]

By taking into consideration these testimonies and words, one can claim that the Holy Prophet (s) and the outstanding personalities are one kind of channel which Qur'an has ordered for that as:

---

[30] *al-Mawahib al-Ladunniyya*, vol. 3, p. 380 Egyptian edition and in Ibn Hajar 'Asqalani, *Fath al-Bari*, vol. 2, p. 413 (Lebanon print). Also reported in *Sharh al-Mawahib* by al-Zurqani (1055 A.H. - 1122 A.H.).
[31] *Wafa' al-Wafa'*, vol. 2, page 1376.
[32] Shibab al-Din Ahmad ibn Muhammad ibn Hajar al-Haytami al-Makki (1503 – 1566 A.D.) popularly known as Ibn Hajar al-Haytami was a famous Egyptian Sunni Shafi'i scholar and *muhaddith*. His famous book *Al-Jawhar al-Munazzam fi Ziyarati'l Qabr al-Mukarram* discusses in detail about *ziyarath* grave of of Prophets and *Awliya Allah*.
[33] Qazi Nurullah Shustari (1542 -1610 A.D.) also known as Shaheed-e-Salis (third martyr) was an eminent Iranian Shia scholar and jurist of the Mughal period. He served as the Qazi-ul-Quzaa (chief justice) during the reign of King Akbar. He was martyred by flogging at the age of 70 years during the reign of King Jahangir. He was author of several famous books including *Ahqaq-ul-Haq* and *Majalis al-Mu'minin*.
[34] *al-Sawarim al-Muhriqah fi Jawab al-Sawa'iq al-Muhriqah*
[35] *al-Sawa'iq al-Muhriqah*, page 178 (Cairo print).

يَا أَيُّهَا الَّذِينَ آمَنُوا اتَّقُوا اللَّهَ وَابْتَغُوا إِلَيْهِ الْوَسِيلَةَ

"O you who believe! be careful of (your duty to) Allah and seek means of nearness to Him. (Maida:35)"

And وسيلة (means, channel) is not confined to observance of the *wajib* (obligatory) and *harām* (prohibited) acts. Instead, even the *mustahab* (recommended) acts such as *tawassul* to Prophets is a وسيلة (channel) too. Can we find fault with so many scholars in understanding the meaning of وسيلة while they are the authorities in (passing) judgement and the protectors of traditions and are reckoned to be the Islamic scholars!

Those who do not give importance to these kinds of specifications and testimonies and think of their justification and interpretation are those who because of their prejudice do not intend to reap the benefits of these testimonies and evidences. For presenting an example of their prejudice and discrimination, we bring here a matter which al-Bukhari has narrated about this historical event and hence see with the vision of reality, how the curtain of prejudice has brought about deviation and chaos in this matter. We have replied to them in the book of *al-Tawassul* page 135 to 140.

5. al-Bukhari narrates in his *al-Sahih* as such:

إن عمر بن الخطاب كان إذ قُحطوا إستسقى بالعباس بن عبد المُطلب رضي الله عنه ، وقال اللهم كُنا نتوسل إليك بنبينا فتُسقينا وإنا نتوسل إليك بعمّ نبيينا فاسقنا قال فيُسقون.

"During the period of famine, 'Umar bin al-Khattab would take resort to al-'Abbas bin 'Abd al-Muttalib and say: 'O God! previously we were taking resort to Your Prophet and You were sending Your mercy on us; Now we take resort to Your Prophet's uncle send Your mercy on us.' At this moment it started to rain and everything got satiated."[36]

There is nothing to be said about the authenticity and consensus regarding this tradition. Even al-Rifa'i who, under various pretexts, rejects the reliable traditions on *tawassul* has admitted the authenticity of this tradition and says:

إن هذا الحديث صحيحٌ... فإن صحَّ هذا الجواز شرعاً فنحن مِن أسبق الناس إلى الأخذ به والعمل بمُقتضاه

---

[36] *Sahih al-Bukhari*, chapter of Salat al-'Istisqa, vol. 2, page 32.

"Certainly this tradition is correct....If the purpose of the tradition is a proof upon the correctness of *tawassul* to people then we are the first people to take the step to accept that purpose and act upon it."[37]

By paying attention to the sentences of the Caliph himself which he narrates to al-'Abbas about *tawassul* and especially when he swears by Allah

هذا والله الوسيلة إلى الله والمكان منه

"This is by God a means for seeking nearness to God and at His House."[38]

It becomes clear that the reality of *tawassul* in this case is *tawassul* to the self or to the position and status of al-'Abbas before God.

In this regard, Muhammad bin Nu'man al-Maliki (d. 683 A.H.)[39] narrates in his book *Misbah al-Zalam fi al-Mustaghithin bi Khayr al-An'am fi al-Yaqzah wa al-Manam* the manner of *tawassul* of 'Umar to al-'Abbas as such:

اللهم إنا نستقيك بعمّ نبيك (صلى الله عليه وآله) ونستشفع إليك بشيبته فسُقوا وفي ذلك يقول عباس بن عتبة بن أبي لهب:

بعمّي سقى الله الحجاز وأهله   عشية يستسقي بشيبته عمر

"O God we ask for rain through the channel of thy Prophet's uncle and we take his authority and previous record in Islam as our intercessor. At this moment, the mercy of Allah showered upon everyone. 'Abbas ibn 'Utba ibn Abi Lahab recited a poem in this regard and said: 'By the blessings of my Uncle, the land of Hijaz and its inhabitants got satiated. And at sunset, 'Umar did tawassul to his (Al-Abbas's) virtuousness.'"[40]

In the same way, Hassan bin Thabit too recited a poem regarding this matter:

فسقى الغمام بغُرة العباس

"The cloud satiated (everything) due to the sparkling face of Abbas."

Ibn Hajar al-'Asqalani says in the book of *Fath al-Bari fi Sharh Sahih al-Bukhari*:

Al-Abbas in his *du'a* said:

وقد توجه القوم بي إليك لمكاني من نبيك

---

[37] Although, it was worthy to say إن هذا التاريخ صحيح because technically, tradition is that which must be narrated from the Holy Prophet (s) and our discussion too is about historical events and we reminded you previously of the traditions of *tawassul*.

[38] *Usd al-Ghabah*, vol. 3, page 111.

[39] Muhammad bin Musa bin Nu'man al-Mazali al-Maliki (d. 683 A.H./1284 A.D.) was a Sunni Maliki Ash'ari scholar from Morocco. He was expert in hadithes and jurisprudence.

[40] *Wafa' al-Wafa'*, vol. 3, page 375 narrated from *Misbah al-Zalam*.

"The people resorted to me because of the bond of relationship which I have with Thy Prophet."[41]

As the respected readers have observed, there is no place of doubt that the aim was *tawassul* to the position and status of Abbas and we are aware that from ancient times there is a saying that:

تعليق الحُكم بالوصف مشعر بالعلية

"*Anytime, a judgement is derived from a topic, its content will be a testimony against the topic (and) a testimony upon the proof of judgement.*"

That is to say, if the Holy Qur'an says:

وَعَلَى الْمَوْلُودِ لَهُ رِزْقُهُنَّ

"*...Securing the necessities of life for the women is a matter concerning those whose wives bear children for them... (Baqarah:233)*"

It is a judgement due to expression of the reason of judgement and since women bring children for the men, their expenses in daily life should naturally be met by the men.

If we say: A learned man and a scholar should be respected, it is because of his knowledge and wisdom.

Therefore, if 'Umar says إنا نتوسل إليك بعمّ نبيّك he wishes to indicate the reason for doing *tawassul* to al-'Abbas. In other words, from among so many people, why should we do *tawassul* to him? As al-'Abbas himself said:

لمكاني من نبيك

"*Because of my status in relation to your Prophet.*"

Taking into consideration these reasonings, we can decisively say that the Muslims in the beginning of Islam were doing '*tawassul*' to the righteous and virtuous personalities.

6. Poem of Safiyyah in grief of the Holy Prophet (s):

Safiyyah, daughter of Abd al-Muttalib and aunt of the Holy Prophet (s) recited a poem in grief of the Holy Prophet (s). Two of its lines are:

ألا يا رسول الله أنت رجاؤنا وكُنت بنا برّاً ولم تك جافياً
وكنت بنا برّاً رؤوفاً نبينا ليبكِ عليك القوم من كان باكيا

---

[41] *Fath al-Bari*, vol. 2, page 413 (print of Dar al-Ma'rifa Lebanon).

"O Prophet of God you are our hope. You were a righteous person and never did you oppress anyone. You were good and kind to us; O our Prophet, amongst your nation whosoever (claims to be) in grief should shed tears for you."[42]

This part of the poem which was presented in the presence of the companions of the Holy Prophet (s) and which has been narrated by the historians informs us of the following points:

Firstly, conversation with the spirits or so to speak, the address to the Holy Prophet (s) after his demise was an action which was permitted and was a common practice. As she said: ألا يا رسول الله which is against the views of the Wahhabis, this kind of conversation is neither polytheism nor useless.

Secondly, by the decree of the sentence أنت رجاؤنا the Holy Prophet (s) was the hope of the Islamic society in all the conditions. Even after his demise, his relation with us is not disconnected. Here we shall mention some of the valuable writings of the great Sunni authors regarding 'tawassul' towards the Holy Prophet (s).

Referring to following books will clarify the position of Islamic scholars on this matter and will manifest the fact that the matter of *tawassul*, contrary to the views of the Wahhabis, was a practice in vogue amongst the Muslims:

1. Ibn al-Jawzi (died in 597 A.H.)[43] has written a book by the name of *al-Wafa bi Ahwal al-Mustafa*, and has earmarked one chapter for *tawassul* to the Holy Prophet (s) and another chapter for 'seeking *shifa* from his grave'.

2. Abu Abdullah Muhammad bin Musa bin Nu'man al-Mazali al-Marakishi (d. 683 A.H.) has written a book by the name of *Misbah al-Zalam fi al-Mustaghithin bi Khayr al-An'am fi al-Yaqzah wa al-Manam* and Sayyid Nur al-Din al-Samhudi has narrated a lot from him in his book *Wafa' al-Wafa'* in the chapter of '*Tawassul* to the Holy Prophet (s)'.

---

[42] *Dhakha'ir al-'Uqba fi Manaqib Dhawi'l Qurba*, page 252 (print of Maktab al-Quds, Cairo), written by al-Hafiz Muhibb al-Din al-Tabari (615 - 694 A.H.), Sunni Shafi'i scholar from Mecca. *Majma' al-Zawa'id*, vol. 9, page 36, (2nd edition), written by al-Hafiz Nur al-Din al-Haytami (1335 – 1404 A.D.) Sunni Shafi'i scholar from Cairo. Let it not remain unsaid that the sentence of أنت رجاؤنا in the first line has appeared as كنت رجاؤنا in the aforesaid book.

[43] 'Abd al-Rahman bin 'Ali al-Jawzi (1116 -1201 A.D.) was a famous Sunni Hanbali scholar of Baghdad. He was expert in history, jurisprudence and hadithes.

3. Ibn Dawud al-Maliki al-Shadhili (d. 732 A.H.) has brought in his book *al-Bayan wa al-Ikhtisar* the *tawassul* of scholars and pious people to the Holy Prophet (s) in difficulties and hardships.

4. Taqi al-Din al-Subki (d. 756 A.H.) has analyzed this matter in his book *Shifa al-Siqam* pages 120 to 133.

5. Sayyid Nur al-Din al-Samhudi (d. 911 A.H.) has discussed this matter and brought testimonies to it in his book *Wafa al-Wafa'*, vol. 2, pages 413 to 419.

6. Abu al-'Abbas al-Qastallani (d. 932 A.H.) in his book *al-Mawahib al-Ladunniyyah*.

7. Abu 'Abdullah al-Zurqani al-Maliki (d. 1122 A.H.) in his book *Sharh al-Mawahib al-Ladunniyyah* vol. 8, page 317.

8. al-Khalidi al-Baghdadi (d. 1299 A.H.) author of *Sulh al-'Ikhwan*. Apart from this, he has written a *risalah* (treatise) in reply to Sayyid Mahmud al-'Alusi Baghdadi about *tawassul* to the Holy Prophet (s) and has been printed in the year 1306 A.H.

9. al-'Adawi al-Hamzawi (d. 1303 A.H.)[44] has discussed about *tawassul* in the book of *Kanz al-Matalib*, page 198.

10. al-'Azami al-Shafi'i al-Quda'i', author of *Furqan al-Qur'an*. This book has been printed along with the book *al-'Asma wa al-Sifat* of al-Bayhaqi in 140 pages.

By referring to these books some of which have presented the facts and most prominent amongst them being *Sulh al-'Ikhwan* and *Furqan al-Qur'an*, one can know what was the practice of the Muslims in every period concerning *tawassul* to the Holy Prophet (s) and will reveal the exaggerations of Ibn Taymiyyah and followers of his deviated ideology of Wahhabism.

In the end, we shall once more remind you of what Qur'an says:

يَا أَيُّهَا الَّذِينَ آمَنُوا اتَّقُوا اللَّهَ وَابْتَغُوا إِلَيْهِ الْوَسِيلَةَ وَجَاهِدُوا فِي سَبِيلِهِ لَعَلَّكُمْ تُفْلِحُونَ

"O you who believe! be careful of (your duty to) Allah and seek means of nearness to Him and strive hard in His way that you may be successful. (Maida:35)"

---

[44] Sheikh Hasan al-'Adawi al-Hamzawi (1221 - 1303 AH.) was Egyptian Sunni Shsfi'i scholar, expert in hadithes and Islamic historian. He wrote famous books *Irshad al-Murid fi al-Tawhid*, *al-Nafahat al-Nabawiyya*, *al-Nur al-Sary 'ala al-Bukhari*.

This verse in general orders to seek *tawassul* but what exactly is *tawassul* is not mentioned in this very verse.

There is no doubt that performing the religious duties is a channel (for *tawassul*) but it is not confined to this meaning only. Instead by paying attention to the short history of *tawassul* to the *awliya Allah*, it will become clear that this action itself is one of the channels. Moreover, this matter will fully become clear by referring to the conversation of Imam Malik with Mansur and also the incident of the second Caliph requesting for rain by doing *tawassul* to al-'Abbas, the uncle of the Prophet (s).

8

Is it an Innovation to Commemorate the Birth and Death Anniversaries of *Awliya Allah*?

The Wahhabis consider the honoring of birth and death anniversaries of *awliya* and divine personalities to be forbidden and an innovation. They are the staunch enemies of the *Awliya Allah* and religious leaders and consider the gatherings on their birth and death anniversaries to be (*harām*) prohibited.

Muhammad Hamid al-Faqi, the leader of group 'Ansar al-Sunnat al-Muhammadiyyah' in his footnotes to his book *al-Fath al-Majid* writes:

الذكريات التي ملأت البلاد بإسم الأولياء هى نوعٌ من العبادة لهم وتعظيمهم

"Remembering and celebrating on the days of birth and death of awliya amounts to one kind of worshipping them and respecting before them."[1]

The root of all their mistakes is that because they have not determined any limit and margin for polytheism (*shirk*), *tawhid* and specially the meaning of *'ibadah*, they think that every kind of respect and honor is worship. As you must have noticed, he has brought the word of *'ibadah* and homage close to each other and imagines that both give the same meaning.

In the one of next chapters, we shall explain the meaning of *'ibadah* and clearly prove that every honor and respect to the virtuous servants of God with the intention that they are the 'servants' of Allah, does not result in their worship at all. Therefore, we shall examine this discussion from another angle (not polytheism in *'ibadah*).

Undoubtedly, Qur'an has repeatedly praised the Prophets and *awliya* with eloquent and rhetorical words.

About Zakaria, Yahya and others the Qur'an says:

---

[1] *al-Fath al-Majid*, page 154. At this time when these pages and papers are being composed, and in the entire Islamic countries celebrations are being held on the occasion of the birth of the Holy Prophet, the Grand Mufti of the House of Sa'ud, Abdullah ibn Baz has declared as forbidden and innovation any kind of respect for the birthday of the Holy Prophet (s). But the same person addressed King Faisal al-Sa'ud during his reign as 'Amir al-mu'minin' and this action was biting and shocking to the extent that the king too understood and excused for accepting this title.

إِنَّهُمْ كَانُوا يُسَارِعُونَ فِي الْخَيْرَاتِ وَيَدْعُونَنَا رَغَبًا وَرَهَبًا ۖ وَكَانُوا لَنَا خَاشِعِينَ

"Surely they used to hasten, one with another, in deeds of goodness and to call upon Us, hoping and fearing, and they were humble before Us. (Anbiya:90)"

Now, if in a gathering which is held under their name, someone portrays them in a similar manner which has come down in the contents of this verse and by this way honors them, has he done anything other than obeying the Holy Qur'an?

About the household of the Prophet, Allah (swt) says:

وَيُطْعِمُونَ الطَّعَامَ عَلَىٰ حُبِّهِ مِسْكِينًا وَيَتِيمًا وَأَسِيرًا

"And they give food out of love for Him to the poor and the orphan and the captive. (Dahr:8)"[2]

Now if the followers of Ali (a) come together on the birthday of Amir al-mu'minin and say that Ali (a) is one who used to give his own food to the poor, orphan and the captive, have they by this act worshipped him!?

If on the birthday of the Holy Prophet (s) we translate the verse which praises the Prophet into a non-Arabic language or write a poem on a tablet and recite it in a gathering, have we committed a forbidden action!?

They are having enmity with the matter of honoring the Holy Prophet (s) and *Awilya Allah* that they wish to stop this under the pretext of fight against innovation.

At this stage a question is brought up to which the loud-speakers amongst the Wahhabis lay great emphasis and it is this: 'Since these assemblies and gatherings are held under the name of religion and are labelled as Islamic, they should be approved specifically and generally by the Islamic rules. Otherwise it would be innovation (*bid'at*) and forbidden (*harām*).

The reply to this question is quite clear because the verses of Qur'an that draw our attention to the necessity of honoring the Prophet (s) is sufficient in this case and these kinds of gatherings are not held for any reason other than respecting the *awliya Allah*. That thing is considered to be 'innovation' which is not approved specifically or generally by Qur'an or the *Sunnah* of the Holy Prophet.

---

[2] Also known as Surah *Insan*

The purpose of these honorings and utmost respect that are common amongst all the nations of the world is nothing but paying respect and homage and this practice is common among all the Muslims of the world except for these handful of dry Wahhabi 'Najdis'. If it was innovation and something new and not confirming with the general Islamic principles, it was impossible that the Islamic scholars would celebrate the birthday of the Holy Prophet (s) and make splendid such gatherings by reading scholarly monographs and reciting sweet and elegant poems.

Here are some logical reasoning from Qur'an permitting such respect and honorings:

First Proof

The Holy Qur'an praises that group of people who honor the Holy Prophet (s):

فالذين امنوا به وعزّروه ونصروه واتبعوا النّور الذي أنزل معه أولئك هُم المُفلحون.

"So (as for) those who believe in him and honor him and help him, and follow the light which has been sent down with him, these it is that are the successful. (A'raf:157)"

The words which have appeared in this verse comprises of:

1. أمنوا به
2. عزّروه
3. نصروه
4. واتبعوا النّور

Is it possible for one to think that the words واتبعوا النّور and نصروه , أمنوا به are confined to the period of the Holy Prophet (s)? Certainly not! If such a probability cannot be given about these three words, the word of عزّروه which gives the meaning of honor and respect[3] cannot be assigned to the period of the Holy Prophet (s) and thus this sublime leader should be respected and honored at all times.

---

[3] Refer to al-Raghib Isfahani's *Mufradat al-Raghib*, under عزّر. Written by Hussein bin Mufaddal al-Isfahani (d. 1108 A.D.), popularly known as Raghib Isfahani was an Iranian Sunni Ash'ari Muslim scholar of Qur'anic exegesis and the Arabic language. *Al-Mufradat fi Gharib al-Qur'an* also known as *Mufradat al-Raghib* is a dictionary of Qur'anic terms.

Is it not that arranging memorial gathering on the day of *bi'that*[4] and birth of the Holy Prophet (s) and delivering speeches and poems on such occasions clear evidence to عزَّروه؟

Surprisingly, the Wahhabis pay homage and respect their own tribal leaders and rulers and honor even one ordinary person such that observing one hundredth of that with regard to the Holy Prophet (s), his pulpit and alter is considered to be innovation and anti-Islamic by them. As a result they introduce Islam to the world as one dry religion lacking any sentiments and affections and think that the *shari'ah* which is in fact simple and easy, matching with the human nature and feeling and generous enough to attract the people is a dry "*shari'ah*" which does not consider the respect of divine leaders to be of any significance and does not possess the ability to attract the people of the world.

Second Proof

What do the Wahhabis who oppose any kind of mourning ceremonies for the martyrs in the way of Allah have to say about the story of Ya'qub (a)? If today, this great Prophet was living amongst these Najdis and the followers of Muhammad bin 'Abd al-Wahhab how would have they judged him?

Day and night he was weeping for his separation from Yusuf and all the time he was asking the people about the whereabouts of his beloved son. He was so much sorrowful by the separation of his son that he lost his eye-sight.[5]

Sickness and loss of eye-sight did not deter Ya'qub (a) from forgetting his son Yusuf (a). Instead, as the promise of re-union was drawing closer the flames of love towards his son increased manifold and he could smell Yusuf miles away.[6]

And instead of the star (Yusuf) pursuing the sun (Ya'qub (a)) it was vice - versa.

Why expression of such affection during the life of the loved one (i.e. Yusuf) is correct and confirms to *tawhid* but after his death when the heart becomes more prone to pain and suffering it amounts to polytheism and becomes forbidden?

---

[4] 27th Rajab
[5] *Surah Yusuf*: 84. وابيضت عيناه من الحزن
[6] *Surah Yusuf*: 94 إني لاجد ريح يوسف لولا أن تفندون

Now if the Ya'qubs of our time gather together every year on the death anniversary of their Yusufs and speak about the value of his moral qualities due to which they start crying, will such an act amount to worshipping of their sons!?[7]

Third Proof

Undoubtedly, مودت ذوى القربى (love towards kinship) is one of the Islamic obligations which Qur'an explicitly commends us towards it. Now, after fourteen centuries if someone wishes to act upon the religious obligations then what should we do? Is it not that he should rejoice on their joyous days and become sorrowful on the days of their grief and sorrow?

Now, for expressing one's own pleasure, if someone holds a gathering wherein he reveals their historical life and sacrifices and describes their innocence and their deprivation from their rightful claims then, has he done anything other than expressing his affection and manifesting *mawadda dhawi'l qurba*? (مودت ذوى القربى)

If, for showing more affection, such a person visits their progeny and comes near their graves and holds such gatherings near their graves then, has he in the eyes of the wise and intelligent people, done anything other than manifesting his love and affection!?

Except that the Wahhabis may say: Such love and affection should be kept secret and confined to the heart and no one has the right to manifest and express them (openly).

During the time of the Holy Prophet (s) and the period after him which was the period of change of thoughts and beliefs, different tribes and nations with different cultures and customs were turning towards Islam and by reciting the *shahadatayn* (verbal testimony of acceptance of Islam) their Islam was accepted. The stance of Prophet (s) and the leaders was never to investigate, censor (by establishing the 'section for scrutinizing of beliefs') than forbid the entire

---

[7] Moreover, reliable traditions have come down from the Infallibles about holding of mourning ceremonies and in this connection, Allama al-'Amini has collected in one chapter of his book titled: سيرتنا وسنتنا all the traditions from Sunni books

prevalent rites and customs of the nations and tribes and bring them out in another form different from the previous ones.

Respect of leaders, establishing memorial ceremonies, visiting the graves and expressing love for their signs and traces was and is the custom of all nations and tribes. At present too, the people of East and West stand for hours in queue waiting to pay visit to the mummified bodies and graves of ancient leaders in order to express their love and shed tears in their grief. They consider this to be one way for expressing respect and honor.

It was never seen that the Holy Prophet (s) would accept the Islam of people only after investigating their beliefs and examining their practices and customs in practical life. Instead, expressing the '*Shahadatayn*' was enough for him. If these practices and customs were forbidden and or amounted to worshiping the ancestors, then it was necessary to accept the Islam of nations and tribes (only) after taking allegiance and promise from them about their exoneration (of such practices) while such was never the case.

Fourth Proof

We see Isa (a) asks for table (with food) from the Almighty Allah and introduces the day of its dissension as the day of celebration and says:

رَبَّنَا أَنْزِلْ عَلَيْنَا مَائِدَةً مِنَ السَّمَاءِ تَكُونُ لَنَا عِيدًا لِأَوَّلِنَا وَآخِرِنَا وَآيَةً مِنْكَ وَارْزُقْنَا وَأَنْتَ خَيْرُ الرَّازِقِينَ

"*O Allah, our lord! send down to us food from heaven which should be to us an ever-recurring happiness, to the first of us and the last of us, and a sign from Thee, and grant us means of subsistence, and Thou art the best of the Providers. (Maida:114)*"

Is the value of the Holy Prophet's (s) existence lesser than one heavenly table which Isa (a) declares the day of its dissension to be the day of 'Eid'. If such a day is declared to be the day of 'Eid' because of the table being a divine sign, then is not the Holy Prophet (s) the greatest divine sign!?

Woe to those who are ready to celebrate the day of dissension of one heavenly table that feeds the stomachs but ignore and label as innovation, the celebration of the day of dissension of Qur'an and the day of appointment (*bi'that*) of Prophet who blessed the minds of human beings with perfection of thought over the period of history !

Fifth Proof

The Qur'an says:

وَرَفَعْنَا لَكَ ذِكْرَكَ

"Did We not exalt your name? (Inshiraah:4)"

Is it that arranging gatherings for celebrating the days of birth of the Holy Prophet (s) having any purpose other than elevating his name and fame? Why in this case we should not follow the Qur'an? Is not Qur'an an example and the best model for us?

9

Seeking Benediction and Cure from the Signs and Traces of *Awliya*

The Wahhabis reckon *tabarruk* (seeking benediction) towards the traces of *awliya* to be polytheism and label the one who kisses the altar and pulpit of the Holy Prophet (s) as polytheist even though in doing that he doesn't believe in any kind of godliness in it. Rather, love and affection to the Holy Prophet (s) becomes the cause of kissing the signs and traces related to him. Here we ask, what have they to say about the shirt of Yusuf (a')?

اذْهَبُوا بِقَمِيصِي هَذَا فَأَلْقُوهُ عَلَى وَجْهِ أَبِي يَأْتِ بَصِيرًا

Yusuf (a) *says: 'Take my shirt and cast it over my father's face so that he regains his eye-sight. (Yusuf:93)"*

Ya'qub (a) too kept the shirt of Yusuf over his eyes and at that same moment realized that he could see. As he says:

فَلَمَّا أَنْ جَاءَ الْبَشِيرُ أَلْقَاهُ عَلَى وَجْهِهِ فَارْتَدَّ بَصِيرًا

"So when the bearer of good news came he cast it on his face, so forthwith he regained his sight." (Yusuf:96)"

If Ya'qub (a) would have done such a thing in front of the *Najdis* and followers of Muhammad bin 'Abd al-Wahhab, how would have they behaved with him? Now would they explain the action of an immaculate Prophet who is free from sins and mistakes!?

Now if the Muslims keep the soil of the grave of the last of the Prophets (s) or his shrine over their eyes and kiss out of respect, the grave and shrine of the divine leaders or seek *tabarruk* and say that God has exerted some effect in this soil and wishes to follow the Ya'qub (a) of today in so and so affair then why should they be subjected to curse and be accused of heresy?[1]

Those who are aware of the life history of the Holy Prophet (s) know that the companions of the Holy Prophet (s) were always taking precedence to each other in doing *tabarruk* to the water of his *wudhu* (ablution). It is sufficient in this case, to briefly refer to *Sahih al-Bukhari* and *Sahih Muslim* which are thought to be the most authentic among the six *Sihah*[2]. Here, we mention some of them:

1. About the event of 'Peace of Hudaybiyyah' Bukhari writes:

"Whenever the Holy Prophet (s) was taking ablution, his companions used to take precedence to each other in collecting the drops of water of his ablution."[3]

2. In the chapter of 'Last of the Prophets', Bukhari narrates from Sa'ib bin Yazid that: "My aunt took me to the Holy Prophet (s) and informed him about my illness. The Holy Prophet (s) made ablution and asked Allah for blessings for me and I drank from the water of his ablution."[4]

3. In the chapter of 'The characteristics of the Prophet', Bukhari narrates from Wahab bin 'Abdullah that: "People were rubbing the hands of the Holy Prophet (s) over their faces and I too took the hands of the Prophet and rubbed them over my face and his hands were more fragrant than musk."[5]

4. In the chapter of 'The characteristics of the Prophet', Bukhari narrates:

The Holy Prophet (s) was in '*Abtah*' standing beside the tents. Bilal came out from a tent and called the people for prayers. Again, he went inside and brought out the remaining drops of water of ablution of the Holy Prophet (s). The people rushed towards it and sought *tabarruk* from it.[6]

---

[1] All the Muslims, right from the time of the Holy Prophet (s) till now, have been seeking *tabarruk* from the traces of the Holy Prophet (s). Sheikh Muhammad Tahir Makki Kurdi (published by *Maktabtul Qahira*, Cairo, Egypt) has proved this matter with decisive historical evidences in his treatise which was printed in 1385 A.H. This treatise is entitled تبرک الصحابة بآثار رسول الله صلى الله عليه و سلم و بيان فضلة العظيم and has been translated into Persian.
[2] *Sihah al-Sittah*
[3] *Sahih al-Bukhari*, vol.3, page 255.
[4] *Sahih al-Bukhari*, vol.4, page 227; and *Sahih Muslim*, Chapter of 'Last of the Prophets'.
[5] *Sahih al-Bukhari*, vol.4, page 226.
[6] *Sahih al-Bukhari*, vol. 4, page 231.

5. Muslim narrates in his *Sahih* from Anas that: "When the Holy Prophet (s) was shaving his head, his companions were besides him and each one of them held one string of his hair in their hands.[7]

These were some examples of the affection of the companions and their *tabarruk* to the signs and traces of the Holy Prophet (s) and collecting these incidents necessitates the writing of one separate book.

By referring to the last chapter of *Sahih al-Bukhari* about *jihad* and also the chapter related to the armour, stick, sword, vessels, seal, ring, hair and shroud of the Holy Prophet (s) one can become aware of the evident examples of *tabarruk*.

These traditions expose and explain the baseless nature of the culture of the Wahhabism that prevents the people from seeking *tabarruk* to the holy shrine of Prophet (s) and have employed special groups of persons to beat physically and use foul language with those who seek *tabarruk* to the holy shrine of the Holy Prophet (s). They thus stop the Muslims from expressing such love and affection which had been in practice during the period of the Holy Prophet (s) in his very presence.

The matter of prevention of *tabarruk* to the traces of the Holy Prophet (s) and kissing of his shrine and pulpit is one of the greatest ideological expressions of the Wahhabism. The Wahhabi Government of Saudi Arabia under the garb of *'amr bi al-ma'ruf* (enjoining the good) and *nahi 'an al-munkar* (forbidding the evil) have stationed their agents around the holy shrine in order to prevent the pilgrims from performing such action and they too behave harshly and mercilessly with the pilgrims. Many times, at such occasions innocent blood is shed and many persons' honor and prestige got damaged. The root cause of their belief is that kissing and honoring the shrine amounts to worshipping the one in grave, as if 'every respect is worship.'

Since these helpless people who are far from the reality of Islamic teachings are unable to interpret *'ibadah* (worship) in the logical sense, they have become puzzled and confused and take every type of respect to the dead to be an *'ibadah*. In the next chapter, we shall draw a precise limit and boundary for *'ibadah*, but

---

[7] *Sahih Muslim*, vol. 4., Book of 'Virtues of Companions'

what is important now is to know what was the practice of the Muslims in this matter:

1. After the Holy prophet's burial, his daughter Fatima (a) stood near his grave and then taking some soil from the grave she put it over her face. She later cried and recited these two couplets:

ماذا على من شمَّ تُربة احمدا   أن لا يشُمَّ مدى الزمان غواليا

"What happens to the one who smells the soil of grave of Ahmad, who till he is alive, shall smell no more the expensive musks."

صُبَّت عليَّ مصائب لو أنها   صُبت على الأيام صرن لياليا

"I was faced with such calamities that if it had befallen on the bright day it would have changed to night."[8]

2. The great companion Bilal (r) who left Medina for some reason and settled by order of the frontier guards, in the districts of Syria saw in his dream that the Holy Prophet (s) was saying: "What kind of injustice is this, O Bilal? Has not the time come that you visit us!? He woke up from his sleep, in sadness and sat on his horse and left for Medina. When he reached the grave of the Holy Prophet (s) he started to cry and rubbed his face over it. Later he saw al-Hasan and al-Husayn and kissed both of them.[9]

3. Amir al-mu'minin Ali (a) says: "Three days had lapsed from the burial of the Holy Prophet (s) when a Bedouin Arab came and threw himself over the grave of the Holy Prophet (s). He sprinkled the soil of his grave over his head and started to converse with the Holy Prophet (s). He said: 'O Prophet of Allah, you spoke and we listened. You received the truth from Allah and we too received it from you. From the things which Allah revealed to you is this:

ولو أنهم إذ ظلموا أنفسهم

I have done injustice upon myself. So seek forgiveness for me from Allah. Suddenly he heard a voice saying: Your sins have been forgiven."

This incident has been narrated by most of the historians mainly al-Samhudi in *Wafa' al-Wafa'*, vol. 2, page 612 and Sheikh Dawud al-Khalidi (died in 1299 A.H.) in *Sulh al-'Ikhwan* and others.

---

[8] Many of the research scholars have narrated this incident such as al-Shabrawi in *al-Tuhaf* page 9 and al-Samhudi in *Wafa' al-Wafa'*, vol. 2 page 444 and al-Khalidi in *Sulh al-'Ikhwan*, page 57 and others.
[9] This incident has been narrated by a group such as, al-Subki in *Shifa al-Saqam* narrating from Ibn 'Asakir, and Ibn al-'Athir in *Usd al-Ghabah*, vol. 1 page 28.

4. al-Hakim narrates in *al-Mustadrak* that: Marwan bin al-Hakam entered the mosque and saw a man putting his face over a grave. Marwan caught hold of his neck and said: "Are you aware of what you are doing?" The man lifted his head and it became apparent that he was Abu Ayyub al-Ansari. He said: 'I have not come to visit a stone, but have come to visit the Holy Prophet (s). O Marwan, I have heard the Holy Prophet (s) saying: When the pious people bear the leadership do not cry for that. Do cry when unworthy men become the leaders (i.e. you and your Umayyid household).'[10]

This period of history reveals the root of 'creation of obstacle' to prevent seeking *tabarruk* from the grave of the Holy Prophet (s) and shows that the companions of the Holy Prophet (s) were constantly seeking *tabarruk* from the holy grave of the Holy Prophet. It was people like Marwan bin al-Hakam who used to prevent people from this well-known deed.

The historical incidents in this case are so numerous that narrating all of them will lengthen our discussion. Interested readers can refer to the book *Tabarruk al-Sahabah bi'l-Nabi wa Atharuh*[11] and the valuable book *al-Ghadir* vol. 5, page 146-156.

In the end, we are bound to mention that all these historical narratives can never be false and baseless. Now, even if we assume that all of them are false and baseless yet they will serve our purpose. Because, if such actions were heresy, polytheism, unlawful or forbidden, then the fabricators would have never attributed them to religious personalities since the liars fabricate instances that are worthy of approval by the society so that the people believe and accept their made-up stories. They never attribute anything which is heresy, polytheism, forbidden or unlawful to the pious people because in such a case they will be confronted with the resistance and non-acceptance of the people and their arrows will hit the stone and miss the target.

---

[10] *Mustadrak al-Hakim*, vol. 4 page 515
[11] Written by Sheikh Sa'id 'Abd al-Qadir Ibn Salim Bashanfar.

10

Tawhid in *'Ibadah* and Worship (or Pretext of Wahhabis)

Monotheism (worship of the one God) is the basis of the invitation of the Prophets in all ages. This means that all the human-beings must worship the one God and refrain from worshipping creatures.

Monotheism and shattering the chains of 'dualism' and 'polytheism' are the most fundamental heavenly commands and have been the epigraph of the program of all the divine Prophets.

Every Prophet had been appointed with one main aim and that is establishing monotheism and fighting against absolute polytheism and especially polytheism in worship.

The Holy Qur'an refers to this reality and says:

وَلَقَدْ بَعَثْنَا فِي كُلِّ أُمَّةٍ رَسُولًا أَنِ اعْبُدُوا اللَّهَ وَاجْتَنِبُوا الطَّاغُوتَ

"And certainly We raised an apostle in every nation [to preach:] 'Worship Allah, and shun fake deities. (Nahl:36)"

وَمَا أَرْسَلْنَا مِنْ قَبْلِكَ مِنْ رَسُولٍ إِلَّا نُوحِي إِلَيْهِ أَنَّهُ لَا إِلَهَ إِلَّا أَنَا فَاعْبُدُونِ

"And we did not send before you any apostle but we revealed to him that there is no god but Me, therefore serve Me. (Anbiya:25)"

The Holy Qur'an introduces monotheism as a common base among all the heavenly precepts:

قُلْ يَا أَهْلَ الْكِتَابِ تَعَالَوْا إِلَى كَلِمَةٍ سَوَاءٍ بَيْنَنَا وَبَيْنَكُمْ أَلَّا نَعْبُدَ إِلَّا اللَّهَ وَلَا نُشْرِكَ بِهِ شَيْئًا

"Say: O followers of the Book! come to an equitable proposition between us and you that we shall not serve any but Allah and (that) we shall not associate aught with Him. (Aule Imran:64)"

Tawhid in worship is a decisive and firm foundation which has never been opposed by any of the Muslims and all the sects hold a common view about it. Although the group of Mu'tazilites are having a different view in توحید افعالی (*Tawhid* in actions) and the group of 'Asharites differ in توحید صفات (*Tawhid* in attributes), still all the Islamic sects have had one opinion in this respect and no Muslim can deny this principle. And if there is any differences, they are all related to مصاديق (its applicability); that is to say some of the Muslims imagine some of the actions to be *'ibadah* (worship) whereas others consider that to be honor and respect. Whatever dispute which exists is in صغرى (minor type) i.e. whether so and so act is *'ibadah* or not and not in كبرى (of major type) i.e. *'ibadah* other than Allah amounts to polytheism and is forbidden. It is here that we should properly clarify the meaning of *'ibadah* from the viewpoint of dialect and the Qur'an and then the relevant duties and مصاديق (applicability) of the matters under discussion will automatically become clear.

Tawhid in *'ibadah* is not something which some particular group can attribute it to themselves. Instead, all the monotheists, especially the Muslims are of one view in this regard. What is of concern is the talk and discussion of a series of actions which some manifest them as *'ibadah* while others do not consider them to have any relation to *'ibadah*. Thus we have to talk and discuss about this matter in this section. We have to define *'ibadah* in logical terms and clarify its limits and boundaries and hand over a criterion to the other person so that under the light of this he can distinguish the true *'ibadah* from the false one.[1]

Limits of *'Ibadah* and its Comprehensive Meaning

'Ibadah in Arabic is equivalent to 'worship' in English. Just as the word 'worship' is having a clear and obvious meaning for us, in the same manner the word of *'ibadah* is having a clear meaning even though we may not be able to give it a logical definition, and interpretation.

Undoubtedly, the meaning of 'land' and 'sky' is very clear and obvious for all of us but still, most of us are unable to define and explain them perfectly. However this matter cannot prevent us from understanding the clear and obvious meaning of these two words if ever we hear them.

'Ibadah and worship too are similar to the words 'land' and 'sky' Everyone is aware of its actual meaning even though we may not be able to define it

---

[1] In the Holy Qur'an too, sometimes this meaning has been utilized such as in *Surah Shu'ra*, verse 22: وتلك نعمة تمنها علي ان عبدت بني اسرائيل '*That you have enslaved the Children of Israel—is that the favour with which you reproach me?*'

logically as the actual dispensations of each of the words of *'ibadah* and *ta'zim* or worship and honor is clear for us and differentiating the instance of each from the other is simple and easy.

A lover who kisses the door and walls of the house of beloved one or keeps dress or puts it over chest or after death, kisses the grave of beloved will never be taken as a worshipper in the eyes of anybody. The action of those who hasten for visiting the mummified bodies of great world leaders who are a center of attraction for a group of people or visit their traces, houses and haven or for honoring them go into a few seconds of silence and hold ceremonies, will not be reckoned as *'ibadah* (worship) even though their humility and manifestation of love is in the rank of humility of monotheists in front of God. In this discussion, only the awakened consciences can be the judges in order to differentiate between *ta'zim* (respect) and *'ibadah* (worship).

Now if we wish to explain *'ibadah* in the logical sense and wish to test and analyze it, we can define it in three ways and all the three explanation can pursue the same objective. However, before that we shall mention two defective introductions upon which the Wahhabis rely.

Two Defective Presentations of *'ibadah*
A. *'Ibadah*: Humility (خضوع) and Submissiveness (تذلل)

In dictionaries, the word of *'ibadah* has been interpreted as humility or humbleness (خضوع) and manifestation of meekness or submissiveness (اظهار تذلل). Such an interpretation cannot give a precise, correct and perfect meaning of the word of *'ibadah* because:

1. If *'ibadah* is synonymous to either humility (خضوع) and meekness, (تذلل) then we cannot issue an identity card of *tawhid* for anybody in this world and cannot call anyone as a monotheist because man, by nature, is humble and meek in front of the spiritual and material perfections of those who are above him and better than him, like a student in front of his teacher, a child in front of his teacher, a child in front of his father and mother, a lover in front of his beloved one and so on.

2. The Holy Qur'an commands the children to be low and humble before the parents. It says:

وَاخْفِضْ لَهُمَا جَنَاحَ الذُّلِّ مِنَ الرَّحْمَةِ وَقُل رَّبِّ ارْحَمْهُمَا كَمَا رَبَّيَانِي صَغِيرًا

"And make yourself submissively gentle to them with compassion, and say: O my Lord! have compassion on them, as they brought me up (when I was) little. (Bani-Israel:24)"

If an abject humility is the sign of *'Ibadah'* of that person, then all the obedient children have to be called as polytheists and all the disobedient ones as monotheists.

B. *'Ibadah*: Unlimited Humility

When some of the commentators became aware of the deficiency of interpretation of the compilers of dictionaries, they strived to amend it and interpreted it in another manner. They said: *'ibadah* is that unlimited humility in sensing, perfection and greatness.'

Such an interpretation is no less than the first interpretation because God orders the angels to prostrate before Adam (a). As Qur'an says:

وَإِذْ قُلْنَا لِلْمَلَائِكَةِ اسْجُدُوا لِآدَمَ فَسَجَدُوا إِلَّا إِبْلِيسَ

"And when We said to the angels: Make prostration to Adam they did prostrate except Iblis. (Baqarah:34)"

Prostration in front of a creature is evidence of meekness and the manifestation of unlimited humility.

If such an act is the sign of *'ibadah,* then all the obedient angels are to be declared as polytheists, and the disobedient Satan as a monotheist.

The sons of Ya'qub (a) and even he himself along with his wife prostrated before the magnificence of Yusuf as the holy Qur'an says:

وَخَرُّوا لَهُ سُجَّدًا وَقَالَ يَا أَبَتِ هَٰذَا تَأْوِيلُ رُؤْيَايَ مِنْ قَبْلُ قَدْ جَعَلَهَا رَبِّي حَقًّا

"And they fell down in prostration before him, and he said: O my father! this is the significance of my vision of old, my Lord has indeed made it to be true. (Yusuf:100)"

The Holy Qur'an narrates the dream of Yusuf (a) in his childhood and says:

إِنِّي رَأَيْتُ أَحَدَ عَشَرَ كَوْكَبًا وَالشَّمْسَ وَالْقَمَرَ رَأَيْتُهُمْ لِي سَاجِدِينَ

"Surely I saw eleven stars, and the sun and the moon: I saw them prostrating themselves before me. (Yusuf:4)"

Following the leader of the monotheists, the Holy Prophet (s) - all the Muslims honor *Hajar al-Aswad* (black stone) and rub their hands over it. That is to say, they act in the same way as idol-worshippers do to their idols with the difference that our action is purely *tawhid* and their action purely heresy.

By paying attention to this point, one should not search the reality of *'ibadah* only in the external form of action and in the absolute humilities and meekness even though humility and meekness are amongst the actual elements and essentials of *'ibadah*. However, the elements and essentials are not confined to that; rather humility and meekness should also be linked with some special belief and in fact if humility whether unlimited or to a lesser degree originates from a special belief, it will be counted as *'ibadah*. As a matter of fact, it is belief that gives the color of *'ibadah* to one's action and without it, the action cannot be regarded as *'ibadah*.

Now, what is this second element? This is what we are going to discuss in this section, i.e. the logical explanation of *'ibadah*.

First Definition of *'Ibadah*

'Ibadah is that practical, literal or verbal humility which originates from belief in the divinity of source entity.

Now we should see what is meant by 'Divinity' and the crucial point of our discussion lies in understanding the meaning of 'Divinity' الوهيت or Divinity gives the meaning of Godliness and الله gives the meaning of God. If incidentally, the word of الله (God) has been interpreted as 'deity', it necessitates explanation and not that deity is the actual meaning of الله. Rather, in view of the fact that the genuine الله and / or the imaginary الله have been the deity and object of worship among the people of the world, it is supposed that الله gives the meaning of deity; otherwise deity is from the requisites of الله and not its primary meaning.

A clearer evidence that the word of الله denotes the meaning of God and not deity is the very pure creed (of faith) i.e. لا إله إلا الله. If in this sentence, the word of الله is interpreted as 'deity' then this creed will be a false one because it is clear and obvious that with the exception of 'Allah', there are thousands of other deities too.

Therefore, for relieving themselves from the difficulty, some people have commended the word of بالحق so that in this way they remove the falsehood and thus the meaning of the sentence becomes لا معبود بالحق إلا الله (no deity with the truth except Allah). However appreciating such a sentence is nothing but a formality.

A clear proof of this definition is a verse which has come in this regard. Examining this verse will clarify the fact that *'ibadah* is that kind of speech and action which originates from the belief in divinity[2] and till such a belief does not exist in a person his humility and bowing down or honor and respect will not be counted as *'ibadah*. When Qur'an gives command to perform *'ibadah* of Allah, it immediately convinces that except for Him there is no god. As Qur'an says:

يَا قَوْمِ اعْبُدُوا اللَّهَ مَا لَكُمْ مِنْ إِلَهٍ غَيْرُهُ

"O (my) people, worship Allah; there is no god for you except Him. (A'raf:59)"

The main theme of this verse has come in nine or more instances and our dear readers can refer to *Surah A'raaf*, verses 65, 73, 58, *Surah Hud*, verses 5, 61 and 84 *Surah Anbiya*, verses 25 *Surah Mominun*, verses 23 and 32 and *Surah Taha*, verse 14.

Such interpretations indicate that *'ibadah* is that humility and meekness which originates from belief in divinity and if such a belief does not exist, then it cannot be regarded as *'ibadah*.

This verse and its contents is not the only verse which bears testimony to this matter. Rather other verses too bear testimony to this fact such as:

إِنَّهُمْ كَانُوا إِذَا قِيلَ لَهُمْ لَا إِلَهَ إِلَّا اللَّهُ يَسْتَكْبِرُونَ

"Surely they used to behave proudly when it was said to them: There is no god but Allah. (Safaat:35)

That is to say, they do not pay attention to this talk because they believe in the divinity of other creatures.

أَمْ لَهُمْ إِلَهٌ غَيْرُ اللَّهِ ۚ سُبْحَانَ اللَّهِ عَمَّا يُشْرِكُونَ

"Or have they a god other than Allah? Glory be to Allah from what they set up (with Him). (Tur:43)[3]

---

[2] When it is said that the idols are god it does not necessarily mean that they are the Creators or that they are managing the affairs of this world. Rather God is having a wider meaning which includes real and imaginary gods. Whenever we reckon some being to be the source of divine activities and imagine that some of the affairs of God like intercession and forgiveness has been entrusted to him, then we have considered him as god, of course a small god before a bigger God!

[3] Also refer to *Surah al-Tawbah* verse 43 and *Surah al-Nahl* verse 63.

In the above verse, the basis of polytheism has been shown to be belief in the divinity of someone other than Allah.

$$الَّذِينَ يَجْعَلُونَ مَعَ اللَّهِ إِلَٰهًا آخَرَ ۚ فَسَوْفَ يَعْلَمُونَ$$

"Those who set up another god with Allah; so they shall soon know. (Hijr:96)"

$$وَالَّذِينَ لَا يَدْعُونَ مَعَ اللَّهِ إِلَٰهًا آخَرَ$$

"And they who do not call upon another god with Allah…. (Furqan:68)"

The proof that the call of the polytheists was along with the belief in divinity of their idols are the following verses:

$$وَاتَّخَذُوا مِنْ دُونِ اللَّهِ آلِهَةً لِيَكُونُوا لَهُمْ عِزًّا$$

"And they have taken gods besides Allah that they should be to them a source of strength. (Maryam:81)"

$$أَئِنَّكُمْ لَتَشْهَدُونَ أَنَّ مَعَ اللَّهِ آلِهَةً أُخْرَىٰ$$

"Do you really bear witness that there are other gods with Allah? (An'am:19)"

$$وَإِذْ قَالَ إِبْرَاهِيمُ لِأَبِيهِ آزَرَ أَتَتَّخِذُ أَصْنَامًا آلِهَةً$$

"And when Ibrahim said to his sire Azar: Do you take idols for gods? (An'am:74)"

By referring to the verses that have come down about the polytheism of idol-worshippers, this reality becomes clear that the polytheism of idol-worshippers was the result of their belief in the divinity of their deities and they considered these deities which were man-made ones to be as various gods. They believed that some of the affairs of the great god had been entrusted to them and because of this, they used to worship them.

It was because of their belief in divinity of their idols that whenever they were invited to believe in the One God, they would deny this matter and if a partner was associated with Him they would readily believe just as the following verse confirms so:

$$ذَٰلِكُمْ بِأَنَّهُ إِذَا دُعِيَ اللَّهُ وَحْدَهُ كَفَرْتُمْ ۖ وَإِنْ يُشْرَكْ بِهِ تُؤْمِنُوا ۚ فَالْحُكْمُ لِلَّهِ الْعَلِيِّ الْكَبِيرِ$$

"That is because when Allah alone was called upon, you disbelieved, and when associates were given to Him, you believed, Judgement belongs to Allah, the High, the Great. (Ghafir:12)"

When (late) Ayatullah al-Sheikh Muhammad Jawad al-Balaghi[4] comes to the point of analyzing and interpreting the reality of *'ibadah* in his valuable *tafsir* called *'Aala al-Rahman* he explains it as such:

العبادة ما يرونه مستشعراً بالخضوع لمن يتخذه الخاضع إلهاً ليُوفيه بذلك ما يراه من حق الإمتياز بالإلهية.[5]

"*'Ibadah (worship) is that very action which arises from the humility of a person in front of the One whom he selects as God, so that he fulfils His superior right which He possesses due to His distinguished position (divinity).*"

Al-Balaghi has described *'ibadah* by his own conscience and perception and the afore-mentioned verses clearly confirm and elucidate the correctness and firmness of this description.

The great teacher, Ayatullah Khomeini (ra) has written the same view in his valuable book and says: *'ibadah* consists of glorifying someone as God either as a major God or a minor god.[6]

The most evident testimony to this view is the observation of the collective verses which speak against polytheism. All the polytheist sects would consider as (God, whether big or small and real or metaphorical) all such creatures whom they would pay homage and worship.

The key to this interpretation lies in this that by referring to the verses, we should clarify the point that means 'God' and not 'deity' and to be a God it is enough that a being (in the eyes of a worshipper) is the owner of some of the affairs and actions of the Creator God even though he himself may be a created one as was the view of the ignorant Arabs with respect to their idols.

Second Definition of *'Ibadah*

'Ibadah is humility (خضوع) in front of the one whom we consider as رب (Lord).

We can change our perception of *'ibadah* and say: *'Ibadah'* is a verbal and practical humility (خضوع) that arises from belief in the ربوبیت (Lordship) of the source entity and the word of عبودیت (submission) is in contrast to ربوبیت (Lordship).

---

[4] Mohammad Jawad Balaghi (1865–1933 A.D.), was an Iraqi Shia Muslim religious authority, author, poet, and polemicist. His two major works, *al-Hoda ila din al-Mostafa* and *al-Reḥla al-Madrasiya* were popular as rebuttal against Christian missionaries in Iraq.
[5] *Tafsir Aala al-Rahman*, vol.1, p. 57.
[6] *Kashf al-Asrar*, p. 29.

Whenever a person imagines himself to be a servant and slave and the opposite person to be his creator Lord and with this intention, he pays homage to his Lord (whether or not he is his actual Lord) such an action will be considered as *'ibadah'*.

From the verses mentioned hereunder we can derive this conclusion that *'ibadah'* is from the rank of ربوبیت (Lordship). Here are some of them:

وَقَالَ الْمَسِيحُ يَا بَنِي إِسْرَائِيلَ اعْبُدُوا اللَّهَ رَبِّي وَرَبَّكُمْ

"And the Messiah said: O Children of Israel! serve Allah, my Lord and your Lord. (Maida:72)"

إِنَّ اللَّهَ رَبِّي وَرَبُّكُمْ فَاعْبُدُوهُ ۚ هَٰذَا صِرَاطٌ مُسْتَقِيمٌ

"Surely Allah is my Lord and your Lord, therefore serve Him, this is the right path. (Aale Imran:51)"

Such contents have come in other verses too. In some of the verses, *'Ibadah'* is reckoned to be from the rank of خالفیت (creative power) as it says:

ذَٰلِكُمُ اللَّهُ رَبُّكُمْ ۖ لَا إِلَٰهَ إِلَّا هُوَ ۖ خَالِقُ كُلِّ شَيْءٍ فَاعْبُدُوهُ

"That is Allah, your Lord, there is no god but He, the Creator of all things, therefore serve Him. (An'am:102)"

What is meant by رب (Lord)?

In Arabic language, رب (Lord) is attributed to the One to whom the management and direction of all things is entrusted and their destiny rests in His authority. If in Arabic, the owner of a house; the nurse of a child and the farmer of a farm are called as رب (Lord), it is because the authority of their management is entrusted to them and their destiny lies in their hand. If we recognize God to be our Lord, it is because our entire destiny, right from existence, life, death, sustenance, legislation and forgiveness lies in His hands.

Now if someone imagines that one of the affairs related to our destiny lies in someone else's hand, for example, if God entrusts the affair of life, death, sustenance, legislation and forgiveness to some other person so that the person independently assumes the responsibility of all or one of these positions, we have taken him as Lord. If with this belief, we pay homage to him, we have worshipped him.

In other words, *'ibadah'* and worship originates from the feeling of bondage and the reality of bondage is nothing other than taking oneself as slave and the higher authority as the Master of existence, life, death and sustenance or at least the Master and authority of particularly forgiveness,[7] intercession,[8] and enactor of laws and responsibilities.[9] In such a case, he has imagined him to be his Lord and anyone who manifests such feelings either verbally or practically has undoubtedly worshipped him.

Third Definition of *'Ibadah*

Here we can interpret *'ibadah* in a different manner and that is: "*'Ibadah* is humility (خضوع) in front of the one whom we think as God or the source of divine works".

There is no doubt that the affairs connected with the world of creation and existence such as, planning of the affairs, bringing to life the human-beings, causing the people to die, giving sustenance to the living creatures and forgiving the sins of the people, are all from God. If you refer to the verses[10] related to planning of the affairs, creation of things, reviving the dead and causing the alive ones to die and other such verses, you will realize that Qur'an recognizes, with emphatic emphasis, all such affairs to be the work of God and strictly prohibits its connection to anyone other than Him.

On the other hand, we know that the world of creation is a well-organized and systematic world and every action which takes place in this world does not occur without the numerous causes which all finally lead to God. On various occasions the holy Qur'an has itself specified the causes of these actions which are the agents of God but act according to the command of God.

For example, Qur'an mentions with special emphasis that the Giver of Life and Death is God. As it says:

وَهُوَ الَّذِي يُحْيِي وَيُمِيتُ وَلَهُ اخْتِلَافُ اللَّيْلِ وَالنَّهَارِ

"And He it is Who gives life and causes death, and (in) His (control) is the alternation of the night and the day. (Mu'minun:80)"

---

[7] *Aale Imran*, verse 135. وَمَن يَغْفِرُ الذُّنُوبَ إِلَّا اللَّـهُ
[8] *Zumar*, verse 44. قُل لِّلَّـهِ الشَّفَاعَةُ جَمِيعًا
[9] *Tawbah*, verse 31. اتَّخَذُوا أَحْبَارَهُمْ وَرُهْبَانَهُمْ أَرْبَابًا مِّن دُونِ اللَّـهِ
[10] *Qasas* verse 73; *Surah Naml* verse 60-64; *Surah Zumar* verse 5-6.

But the same Qur'an in another verse introduces the Angels to be the Giver of death. It says:

حَتَّىٰ إِذَا جَاءَ أَحَدَكُمُ الْمَوْتُ تَوَفَّتْهُ رُسُلُنَا

"Until when death comes to one of you, Our messengers cause him to die. (An'am:61)"

Therefore the way of drawing a conclusion is that we say: The agency and causality of these natural causes whether material or non-material, such as the Angels is by the permission and command of God and the independent executor is God Himself. In other words, these two doers are besides each other, one being an independent doer and the other being a dependent one and this is one of the sublime gnosis of Qur'an which by referring to the numerous verses one can understand the actions of God.

Now if a person reckons the actions of God to be cut off from Him and says that these affairs have been entrusted to splendid creatures like Angles and Prophets and with such a belief, he pays homage and becomes humble in front of them, then certainly his humility is *''Ibadah'* and his action will amount to polytheism.

In other words, if he believes that God has bestowed the accomplishment of these affairs to them and that they independently fulfil all of them, then in such a case, he has likened them to God. Such a belief is undoubtedly polytheism and any kind of humility or request towards them will be *'ibadah*.

As the Qur'an says:

وَمِنَ النَّاسِ مَنْ يَتَّخِذُ مِنْ دُونِ اللَّهِ أَنْدَادًا يُحِبُّونَهُمْ كَحُبِّ اللَّهِ

"And there are some among men who take for themselves objects of worship besides Allah, whom they love as they love Allah. (Baqarah:165)"

No creature can be, to our imagination, the example and like of Allah except if he is independent or has absolute authority in fulfilling one or more affairs. However, if he works by the permission and command of God then not only will he not be likened to Him, but also he will be an obedient creature who performs his duty by His command.

Incidentally, the polytheists during the time of the Holy Prophet (s) were of the belief that the gods which they were worshipping had independent powers in fulfilling the affairs.

The lowest kind of belief in the form of polytheism during the period of ignorance was that a group of people were of the belief that the duty of legislation has been entrusted to the monks[11] and 'intercession' and 'forgiveness' which are specifically the right of Allah have been given to their idols and deities and that they are independent in these actions. Thus the verses which are related to intercession lay great emphasis that nobody can perform intercession without the permission of Allah.[12]

If they were of the belief that their deities could do intercession by the permission of God, then it was needless to emphasize the matter of negation of intercession without the permission of God. Some of the sages of Greece had imagined a god for everything in this world and thought that the management of these things (which is the action of God) had been entrusted to them. Those ignorant Arabs who used to worship the angels and the fixed and the moving stars were of the opinion that the management of the world of creation had been bestowed upon them i.e. the angels and stars and they were the Masters in managing this world and that God had been completely dethroned from the position of management.[13]

Therefore any kind of humility and bowing down which is accompanied by such a belief will amount to *'ibadah*.

Some other group of ignorant Arabs did not consider the wooden and metallic idols to be their Creator and / or the manager of the affairs of this world but regarded them to be the Masters of intercession. They would say:

هَٰؤُلَاءِ شُفَعَاؤُنَا عِندَ اللَّـهِ

"They are our intercessors towards Allah. (Yunus:18)"

Based on this false belief that they are the Masters of intercession, they worshipped them and thought that their worship was the source of gaining proximity to God. As they say:

مَا نَعْبُدُهُمْ إِلَّا لِيُقَرِّبُونَا إِلَى اللَّـهِ زُلْفَىٰ

"We do not worship them except that they may make us nearly to Allah. (Zumar:3)"

---

[11] *Tawbah*, verse 31. اتَّخَذُوا أَحْبَارَهُمْ وَرُهْبَانَهُمْ أَرْبَابًا مِّن دُونِ اللَّـهِ
[12] *Baqarah*, verse 255. مَن ذَا الَّذِي يَشْفَعُ عِندَهُ إِلَّا بِإِذْنِهِ
[13] *al-Milal wa al-Nihal*, vol. 2, page 244.

In short, any action which originates from such perception that shows some kind of devotion will be taken as *'ibadah*. As against this, any action which does not originate from such a belief and any person devoid of such belief exhibits his humility before someone and honors him then it will not be *'ibadah* and polytheism even though the action may be forbidden.

For example, the prostration of a lover before his beloved one or of a slave before his master or of a wife before her husband etc., are not *'ibadah* even though it is forbidden in the religion of Islam. This is because no one can prostrate (even if it does not amount to such *'ibadah*) before anyone without the permission of Allah.

Conclusion of Our Discussion

Up to this point, we were able to acquaint you clearly with the reality of *'ibadah*. Now it is necessary to derive a conclusion from the foregoing discussion. If someone becomes humble and shows humility in front of someone else without considering them as اله (God) or رب (lord) or the source of divine acts but respects them because of the fact that they are:

عِبَادٌ مُّكْرَمُونَ لَا يَسْبِقُونَهُ بِالْقَوْلِ وَهُم بِأَمْرِهِ يَعْمَلُونَ

"They are honored servants, they do not precede Him in speech and (only) according to His commandment do they act," then surely, such an act shows nothing but honor respect, humility and humbleness. (Anbiya:26-27)"

God has introduced a group of His servants with such qualities that will attract the interest of every person towards honoring and respecting them. As the holy Qur'an says:

إِنَّ اللَّهَ اصْطَفَى آدَمَ وَنُوحًا وَآلَ إِبْرَاهِيمَ وَآلَ عِمْرَانَ عَلَى الْعَالَمِينَ

"Surely Allah chose Adam and Nuh and the descendants of Ibrahim and the descendants of 'Imran above the nations. (Aale Imran:33)"

Almighty Allah (by specification of Qur'an) has appointed Ibrahim to the position of *Imamat* and leadership:

قَالَ إِنِّي جَاعِلُكَ لِلنَّاسِ إِمَامًا

".....He said, Surely I will make you an Imam of men..... (Baqarah:124)"

Almighty Allah has described Hazrat Nuh (a), Ibrahim (a), Dawud (a), Sulayman (a), Musa (a), 'Isa (a) and Muhammad (s) in the Holy Qur'an with such sublime qualities that each of these qualities is the source of attraction for the hearts to such extent that the love of some of them has been made compulsory.¹⁴https://www.al-islam.org/wahhabism-ayatullah-jafar-subhani/tawhid-ibada-and-worship-or-pretext-wahhabis - f_b2121fb4_13

If the people respect and honor these servants in their life-time and even after their death from this viewpoint that they are the honorable servants of Allah and without recognizing them as God or imagining them to be the source of divine affairs, then such respect will never be considered as *'ibadah* and no one can call them as polytheists.

As you are all well-informed, following the Holy Prophet's custom, we respect and sanctify *Hajar al-Aswad* which is no more than a black stone; we circumambulate around the House of God which is no more than stone and mud and strive between the two mountains named Safa and Marwa. That is to say, we perform the same actions which the idol-worshippers used to perform with regards to their idols. Under these circumstances, no one till now has thought that by these actions we are worshipping the stones and mud because we never imagine the least benefit or harm from them.

However, if we perform these actions with this belief that these stones and mountains are God and are the source of divine works, then in such a case, we will be equal to the idol-worshippers. Therefore, kissing the hands of the Holy Prophet (s) and Imams; master or teacher; parents or kissing Qur'an, religious books, shrines and all other things which are related to the honorable servants of Allah will only be an expression of respect and honor except that if we believe in their divinity or lordship.

The prostration of angels before Adam and prostration of brothers of Yusuf in front of Yusuf has come in the Holy Qur'an.¹⁵

No one interprets the action of the angels or the action of the brothers of Yusuf as *'ibadah* of Adam or Yusuf. The point is that the prostrators did not consider the least position of 'divinity' or 'lordship' for the prostrated ones and never did they take them as God nor the source of divine actions. Therefore, their actions were purely an expression of respect and not *'ibadah* or worship.

---

¹⁴ *Shura*, verse 23. لَا أَسْأَلُكُمْ عَلَيْهِ أَجْرًا إِلَّا الْمَوَدَّةَ فِي الْقُرْبَىٰ
¹⁵ *Baqarah*, verse 34 and *Yusuf*, verse 100.

When the Wahhabis are faced with such verses they at once say: *"The reason that these actions were not prostration of the prostrated ones was that it was performed by the command of God."*

Although it is true that all these actions together with the action of brothers of Yusuf in front of Yusuf was by the command and satisfaction of Allah, yet the Wahhabis are heedless of one point and it is this that the very essence of their action (i.e. prostration) too was not *'ibadah*. And it was due to this that God commanded for that action.

If the reality of the action amounted to worship of the prostrated one, then God would have never ordered it.

إِنَّ اللَّهَ لَا يَأْمُرُ بِالْفَحْشَاءِ ۖ أَتَقُولُونَ عَلَى اللَّهِ مَا لَا تَعْلَمُونَ

"Say: Surely Allah does not enjoin indecency, do you say against Allah what you do not know? (A'raf:28)"

In short, the order and command of God does not change the essence of action. Before the command of God, the essence or nature of action should be non-*'ibadah*; then only the command of God will pertain to it. It can never be imagined that the 'essence' of one action is *'ibadah* but due to the command of God in performing that action it automatically becomes non-*'ibadah*. This reply which we have repeatedly heard from the Wahhabi leaders in Mecca and Medina shows that they have closed the doors in their analysis of Qur'anic teachings.

'Ibadah has an independent essence and concept for itself which is sometimes commanded for and sometimes prohibited. That is to say, an affair which in its essence is *'ibadah*, is ordered by God such as salat and fasting and sometimes prohibits it for example fasting on the day of Eid. Whenever the prostration of angels and sons of Ya'qub (a) is, in its essence, *'ibadah* of Adam and Yusuf, then ordering for its performance will not change it to non-*'ibadah*.

The Basis of Solving the Dispute

Respected readers should realize that the basis of solving most of the controversial matters between the Wahhabis and us lies in analyzing the concept of *'ibadah* and unless and until *'ibadah* is not interpreted in logical terms and we cannot reach to an agreement with an impartial person with regards to it and any kind of talk or discussion will be useless.

Therefore, a person of research should deeply study and investigate this matter (more than what we have mentioned) and should not be deceived by the interpretation of most of the dictionaries which often intend to give an abstract explanation of a word and not its actual analysis. In this regard, pondering over the verses is the best guidance.

Unfortunately, all the Wahhabi writers and some of those writers who wish to refute their beliefs have given greater importance to secondary matters rather than laying emphasis on this point.

To sum up, a Wahabi says:

"Most of the actions which you perform with regard to the Holy Prophet (s) or Imam is *'ibadah* and necessarily results in polytheism in worship". For this reason we have to disarm him with the precise interpretation of the word of *'ibadah*.

For making our objective clear, we shall now bring examples of those actions which the Wahhabis show to be worshipping of the dead. We remind you that all of them like our other ordinary actions, can be fulfilled in two ways: Either it will be counted as *'Ibadah* or not.

1. Seeking intercession from the Holy Prophet (s) and the virtuous ones.
2. Asking for *shifa'* (cure) from the *Awliya Allah*.
3. Request for fulfilling one's need from the divine leaders.
4. Respecting and honoring the one in grave.
5. Seeking help from the Holy Prophet (s) and others.

They say: *Shafa'a* (intercession) by decree of the verse

قُل لله الشفاعة جميعاً

is from the actions of Allah just as *shifa'* is from the actions of Allah,

وإذا مرضتُ فهو يشفين

and asking or requesting from the actions of Allah from someone other than Him will amount to his worship.

Here, it is necessary to interpret the Actions of Allah and mention what are the Actions of Allah?

The reply to this is as such: "Any kind of *shafa'a* and *shifa'* of the sick which the doer is independent in fulfilling them (not that he has achieved this privilege from somewhere and that he is in need of the strength and power of some superior being) will be counted as the Divine Action.

To request such an action from anyone is accompanied with the belief in his 'divinity' and 'lordship' and naturally will amount to *'ibadah* and worship.

However, if seeking *shafa'a* and *shifa'* from someone is not accompanied with this belief but rather, the person seeking *shafa'a* reckons the intercessor to be a doer who while being a servant of Allah, relies on a superior power in his actions and affairs and accomplishes them by His Wish and Will, then in such a case making a request will not be accompanied with the belief in 'divinity' and 'lordship'.

The same explanation prevails for the matter of request for fulfilment of needs and or asking for help from someone other than Allah.

Request for fulfilment of needs has two forms: one of them may be reckoned to be *'ibadah* and the second to be having no relation with *'ibadah*. This explanation is not only a limit of demarcation between *'ibadah* and non-*'ibadah* concerning this action but is a general rule which separates monotheism and polytheism from each other in all the causes and effects.

The belief in the effect of antibiotics in killing the microbes and curing the sick can be one of the two ways. If we imagine it to be independent in life and existence or independent in its action and effect and reckon it to be needless in a superior being (i.e. Allah) then in such a case we have imagined it as a small god which is independent in its actions. And if we unknowingly respect and honor it, we have considered it as Allah and our actions will be *'ibadah*. And asking any help from it will be *shirk* and amount to worshiping it.

However, if we consider it as a possible being whose life, effects and actions are dependent on a superior one and a being which gives life and does not accomplish any task without His Wise Will, then our belief will be exactly *tawhid*. In the realm of existence no one is effective except Him (*la muathar fil Wujud illa hua*).

Thus we have reminded you that the solution to the disputes and the disarming the opposite person in most of the matters concerning monotheism (*tawhid*) and polytheism (*shirk*) is dependent on the analysis of *'ibadah* and sometimes the meaning of 'divinity' and 'lordship' and understanding the Divine actions.

Incidentally, the actions of the ignorant Arabs were linked all in all with the belief in the divinity and lordship of the idols and they considered them as the absolute authority in some of the divine actions. They believed that God had handed over the reins of these affairs to them and if they wished, they could give intercession to any one or can reject intercession of anyone they wished so.

This is the abstract of our discussion. For a more detailed explanation interested readers can refer to the books:

1. معالم التوحيد (Ma'alim al-Tawhid)[16] and
2. التوحيد والشرك في القرآن (al-Tawhid wa al-Shirk fi al-Qur'an)[17].

---

[16] معالم التوحيد في القران الكريم محاضرات الشيخ جعفر السبحاني *Ma'alim al-Tawhid fi al-Qur'an al-Karim – Muhazirat al-Sheikh Ja'far Subhani* by Ja'far Ilhadi (vol. 1) published by Mo'assasa Imam al-Sadiq, Qom, 2000.

[17] Written by Ja'far Subhani. Published by Mo'assasa Imam al-Sadiq, Qom, 2005.

11

Seeking Help from *Awliya Allah* during Their Lifetime

The request for something from the '*Awliya Allah*' takes place in various ways which we shall mention as under:

1. We request a living personality to assist us in building a house or ask him to quench our thirst by handing over the vessel of water which lies next to him.

2. We request a living personality to pray for us and seek forgiveness for us from God.

Both these cases are common, in that, we ask the person to do a work that is fully within his natural capability to fulfil it. However, the first request is related to the worldly affair and the second one to religious and heavenly affair.

3. We request a living personality to perform a task without utilizing any common and natural means. For example, we ask him to cure the sick without treatment, find our lost one or repay our debt.

In other words, we ask him to fulfil our needs through miracle or wonder without having recourse to the ordinary and natural tools.

4. The person whom we ask is not alive but since we believe that he is alive in another abode and is receiving his sustenance, we request from such a person to pray for us.

5. We request from such a person to cure our sick and find our lost ones and through utilizing the spiritual powers bestowed upon him by Allah.

These two cases, similar to the second and third one are a request to a living person except that in those cases, the responsible authority is alive in this physical and material world and in these last two cases the responsible authority is physically dead but in reality is alive. We can never request from such a person to help us in the material affairs through the ordinary channels. This is because it is presumed that he has left this world and he is cut off from the normal channels of this world.

In this way, there are five types amongst which, three of them are related to request from the living ones in the material world and two are related to the living ones in another world.

We shall discuss in this chapter, request to a living person in the material world and discuss in the next chapter, request (for help) to the *Awliya Allah* who are living in another world.

Here is the description of each of the three cases of the first type:

First Case

Requesting for work and help from a living person in the ordinary affairs of life that have natural and ordinary causes, forms the basis of human civilization. The life of human beings is established in this material world on the basis of cooperation. All those in this world, who possess intellect, seek mutual assistance in their worldly affairs. This matter is so obvious that nobody has ever found fault with it and because our discussion is based on Qur'an and traditions, we shall restrain ourselves at this point by quoting a verse. Zul-Qarnain while building the dam against the oppression of *Ya'juj* and *Ma'juj* turned towards the people of that place and said:

فَأَعِينُونِي بِقُوَّةٍ أَجْعَلْ بَيْنَكُمْ وَبَيْنَهُمْ رَدْمًا

"Thus you only help me with workers; I will make a fortified barrier between you and them. (Al-Kahf:95)"

Second Case

Requesting someone to pray for good or seeking forgiveness from living persons in this material world; the correctness and firmness of such a request from the living is from the necessities related to the Holy Qur'an. Anyone having a little acquaintance with the Holy Qur'an is aware that the ways of the Prophets was to seek forgiveness for their *ummah* (nation) and or the *ummah* themselves were placing such a request before the Prophets. Now we shall bring here all the verses which have come down in this regard.

Of course, the verses concerning this section are of several categories where, for the sake of simplicity of the matter, we shall number them as follows:

1. Sometimes, God orders His Prophet to seek forgiveness for his people such as:

فَاعْفُ عَنْهُمْ وَاسْتَغْفِرْ لَهُمْ وَشَاوِرْهُمْ فِي الْأَمْرِ

"Pardon them therefore and ask pardon for them, and take counsel with them in the affair. (Aale Imran:159)"

$$فَبَايِعْهُنَّ وَاسْتَغْفِرْ لَهُنَّ اللَّهَ إِنَّ اللَّهَ غَفُورٌ رَحِيمٌ$$

"Accept their pledge, and ask forgiveness for them from Allah, surely Allah is Forgiving, Merciful. (Mumtahina:12)"

$$خُذْ مِنْ أَمْوَالِهِمْ صَدَقَةً تُطَهِّرُهُمْ وَتُزَكِّيهِم بِهَا وَصَلِّ عَلَيْهِمْ إِنَّ صَلَاتَكَ سَكَنٌ لَّهُمْ وَاللَّهُ سَمِيعٌ عَلِيمٌ$$

"Take alms out of their property, you would cleanse them and purify them thereby, and pray for them, surely your prayer is a relief to them, and Allah is Hearing, Knowing. (Tawbah:103)"

In this verse, Allah directly commands the Holy Prophet (s) to pray for them and the effect of his prayers is so quick that one feels comfort in one's heart after the prayers of the Holy Prophet (s).

2. Sometimes, the Prophets themselves used to promise the sinners that they would seek forgiveness for them under special circumstances.

For example:

$$إِلَّا قَوْلَ إِبْرَاهِيمَ لِأَبِيهِ لَأَسْتَغْفِرَنَّ لَكَ$$

"But not in what Ibrahim said to his father: I would certainly ask forgiveness for you, (Mumtahina:4)"

$$سَأَسْتَغْفِرُ لَكَ رَبِّي إِنَّهُ كَانَ بِي حَفِيًّا$$

"I will pray to my Lord to forgive you, surely He is ever kind to me, (Maryam:47)"

$$وَمَا كَانَ اسْتِغْفَارُ إِبْرَاهِيمَ لِأَبِيهِ إِلَّا عَن مَّوْعِدَةٍ وَعَدَهَا إِيَّاهُ$$

"And Ibrahim asking forgiveness for his sire was only owing to a promise which he had made to him. (Tawbah:114)"

These verses show that the Prophets used to promise and give glad tidings to the sinners just as Ibrahim too had given such glad tidings to Azar. But when he saw him persisting in idol-worshiping, he stopped from seeking forgiveness for him because, one of the conditions for acceptance of prayers is that the person for whom the forgiveness is sought should be a monotheist and not a polytheist.

3. Allah commands a group of sinful believers to approach the Holy Prophet (s) for seeking forgiveness from Allah and to request the Prophet (s) to seek forgiveness on their behalf and if the Prophet (s) seeks forgiveness for them, then Allah would forgive their sins.

وَلَوْ أَنَّهُمْ إِذْ ظَلَمُوا أَنْفُسَهُمْ جَاءُوكَ فَاسْتَغْفَرُوا اللَّهَ وَاسْتَغْفَرَ لَهُمُ الرَّسُولُ لَوَجَدُوا اللَّهَ تَوَّابًا رَحِيمًا

"And had they, when they were unjust to themselves, come to you and asked forgiveness of Allah and the Apostle had (also) asked forgiveness for them, they would have found Allah Oft returning, Merciful. (Nisa:64)"

Which verse can be clearer than this one where Allah orders the sinful *ummah* to approach the Holy Prophet (s) for acquiring the forgiveness of Allah and requesting him to pray for them? Going to the Holy Prophet (s) and asking for forgiveness has two obvious benefits:

A. Requesting for forgiveness from the Holy Prophet (s) enlivens the essence of obedience to the Prophet in sinful persons and due to their feeling of the Holy Prophet's position, they will sincerely follow and obey the Holy Prophet (s).

Basically, such goings and comings creates a special state of humility in a person towards the Holy Prophet (s) and prepares him to sincerely act upon the verse of:

أَطِيعُوا اللَّهَ وَأَطِيعُوا الرَّسُولَ

"Obey Allah and obey the Apostle. (Nisa:59)"

B. This action clearly illustrates the position and status of the Holy Prophet (s) in the minds of the *ummah* and makes them understand that just as the material bounties are received through special means by the servants of God, the spiritual bounties which is the same forgiveness of Allah, is received through fixed channels such as the *du'a* of the Holy Prophet (s) and His beloved ones.

If the sun is the cause of flow of calories, heat and energy and these benefits are received by the people through the sun then in the same way the spiritual bounties and divine grace is received through the sun of *risalat* (messengership) and the universe in both the stages is the world of cause and causation and the material and spiritual bounties in both the worlds are received through (some) cause.

4. Some of the verses indicate that the Muslims were frequently approaching the Holy Prophet (s) and requesting him to pray for them. Thus, when the Muslims were advising the hypocrites to do the same, they were met with refusal and denial. As Qur'an says

وَإِذَا قِيلَ لَهُمْ تَعَالَوْا يَسْتَغْفِرْ لَكُمْ رَسُولُ اللَّهِ لَوَّوْا رُءُوسَهُمْ وَرَأَيْتَهُمْ يَصُدُّونَ وَهُم مُّسْتَكْبِرُونَ

"And when it is said to them: Come the Apostle of Allah will ask forgiveness for you, they turn back their heads and you may see them turning away while they are big with pride. (Munafiqun:5)"

5. Some of the verses bear witness to the fact that the people, by inspiration from their pure innate nature, were aware that the prayers of the Holy Prophet (s) for them in the court of God had a special effect and were surely acceptable. For this reason, they would approach the Prophet and request him to seek forgiveness from Allah on their behalf.

The pure nature of human being was a sort of inspiration for him that the divine bounties are received by the people through the Prophets, just as they receive the divine guidance through the Prophets. Therefore they were approaching the Prophets and requesting them to pray for their forgiveness before God.

Here is a verse about this matter:

قَالُوا يَا أَبَانَا اسْتَغْفِرْ لَنَا ذُنُوبَنَا إِنَّا كُنَّا خَاطِئِينَ قَالَ سَوْفَ أَسْتَغْفِرُ لَكُمْ رَبِّي إِنَّهُ هُوَ الْغَفُورُ الرَّحِيمُ

"They said: O our father! ask forgiveness of our faults for us, surely we were sinners. He said: I will ask for you forgiveness from my Lord, surely He is the Forgiving, the Merciful. (Yusuf:97 & 98)"

6. Verses which notify the Prophet (s) that seeking forgiveness for the hypocrites who still persist in their idol-worshipping will bear no result. This verse is one kind of exception to the previous verses and shows that other than this instance, the prayers of a Prophet has a special effect as mentioned in the following verses

إِنْ تَسْتَغْفِرْ لَهُمْ سَبْعِينَ مَرَّةً فَلَنْ يَغْفِرَ اللَّهُ لَهُمْ

"Even if you ask forgiveness for them seventy times, Allah will not forgive them. (Tawbah:80)"

سَوَاءٌ عَلَيْهِمْ أَسْتَغْفَرْتَ لَهُمْ أَمْ لَمْ تَسْتَغْفِرْ لَهُمْ لَنْ يَغْفِرَ اللَّهُ لَهُمْ

"It is alike to them whether you beg forgiveness for them or do not beg forgiveness for them, Allah will never forgive them. (Munafiqun:6)"

وَلَمَّا وَقَعَ عَلَيْهِمُ الرِّجْزُ قَالُوا يَا مُوسَى ادْعُ لَنَا رَبَّكَ بِمَا عَهِدَ عِنْدَكَ لَئِنْ كَشَفْتَ عَنَّا الرِّجْزَ لَنُؤْمِنَنَّ لَكَ وَلَنُرْسِلَنَّ مَعَكَ بَنِي إِسْرَائِيلَ

"And when the plague fell upon them, they said: O Musa! pray for us to your Lord as he has promised with you, if you remove the plague from us, we will

certainly believe in you and we will certainly send away with you the children of Israel. (A'raf:134)"

Here the sinners are asking Musa bin 'Imran (a) to pray for them and according to the sentence بِمَا عَهِدَ عِنْدَكَ they were aware that God had bestowed such a promise to Musa.

If the sentence ادْعُ لَنَا رَبَّكَ is a testimony to this point that the nation wanted Musa (a) to avert the punishment and they also traced in him the power of doing so, then in such a case, this verse will be an evidence for the third instance (Is it correct or not to ask the Prophets to perform some extraordinary acts by means of their divine powers?) But the sentence ادْعُ لَنَا رَبَّكَ makes this probability weak because, this sentence apparently shows that the work of Musa (a) was only 'to pray' and not to dominate in this world and avert punishments. Therefore the verse is related to this same instance.

That the prayers of Kalimullah Musa (a) with regard to the polytheists were not accepted has not been specified in this verse but in some other verses.

7. Verses which show that a group of believers were always praying for another group of believers such as,

وَالَّذِينَ جَاءُوا مِنْ بَعْدِهِمْ يَقُولُونَ رَبَّنَا اغْفِرْ لَنَا وَلِإِخْوَانِنَا الَّذِينَ سَبَقُونَا بِالْإِيمَانِ

"And those who come after them say: Our Lord! forgive us and those of our brethren who had precedence of faith. (Hashr:10)"

8. It is not only they who pray for the believers but the carriers of 'arsh (throne) and those besides them too, seek forgiveness for the believers. As the Holy Qur'an says:

الَّذِينَ يَحْمِلُونَ الْعَرْشَ وَمَنْ حَوْلَهُ يُسَبِّحُونَ بِحَمْدِ رَبِّهِمْ وَيُؤْمِنُونَ بِهِ وَيَسْتَغْفِرُونَ لِلَّذِينَ آمَنُوا رَبَّنَا وَسِعْتَ كُلَّ شَيْءٍ رَحْمَةً وَعِلْمًا فَاغْفِرْ لِلَّذِينَ تَابُوا وَاتَّبَعُوا سَبِيلَكَ وَقِهِمْ عَذَابَ الْجَحِيمِ

"Those who bear the power and those around Him celebrate the praise of their Lord and believe in Him and ask protection for those who believe: Our Lord! Thou embracest all things in mercy and knowledge, therefore grant protection to those who turn (to Thee) and follow Thy way, and save them from the punishment of the hell. (Ghafir:7)"

Therefore, how good it is that we too, follow this God-loving practice of this group and always seek forgiveness for the believers.

Till here, the decree of two out of the five cases of seeking help from someone other than Allah has been clarified from the viewpoint of Qur'an and out of the three cases pertaining to seeking help from a living person only one case has remained to which we shall now refer.

Third Case

We seek help from a living person who has power over extraordinary affairs and ask him to perform an act through extra ordinary ways, examples include, curing the sick, making a spring flow, and other things through a miracle.

Some of the Islamic writers reckon this kind of request to be the same as the second case and say that the aim (of the person making the request) is only to ask them to request Allah to cure his sickness, to repay his loan, etc., etc. This is because such works are the works of Allah and since the channel (of such works) is the *du'a* of the Prophet and Imams, the work of God is metaphorically attributed to the person reciting the *du'a*.[1]

However, the verses of Qur'an clearly testify that asking the prophets for fulfilment of such actions is absolutely correct and is not something metaphorical. That is to say, we sincerely want *ma'sum* (the inerrant) to do us a favor and / or through the door of miracle, cure our incurable diseases by the divine strength and power.

It is true that Qur'an attributes *shifa'* (cure) to God and says:

$$وَإِذَا مَرِضْتُ فَهُوَ يَشْفِينِ$$

"And when I am sick, then He restores me to health. (Ash Shu'ra:80)"

But in other verses, Qur'an ascribes *shifa'* (cure) to honey, or even to Quran itself, such as:

$$يَخْرُجُ مِنْ بُطُونِهَا شَرَابٌ مُخْتَلِفٌ أَلْوَانُهُ فِيهِ شِفَاءٌ لِلنَّاسِ$$

"There comes forth from within it a beverage of many colors, in which there is cure for men. (Nahl:69)"

$$وَنُنَزِّلُ مِنَ الْقُرْآنِ مَا هُوَ شِفَاءٌ وَرَحْمَةٌ لِلْمُؤْمِنِينَ$$

"And We reveal of the Qur'an that which is a healing and a mercy to the believers. (Bani Israel:82)"

---

[1] *Kashf al-'Irtiyaab*, page 274.

قَدْ جَاءَتْكُمْ مَوْعِظَةٌ مِنْ رَبِّكُمْ وَشِفَاءٌ لِمَا فِي الصُّدُورِ

"There has come to you indeed an admonition from your Lord and a cure for what is in the breasts. (Yunus:57)"

The way of reconciling these two set of verses (confinement and earmarking of *shifa'* to Allah and its verification for honey, the Qur'an and the divine admonitions) is this that Allah is 'efficient independently' and is self-dependent whereas other agents are effective by the permission of Allah and are dependent upon Him.

In Islamic world view and philosophy, all the factors and elements are the *causative* act of Allah and the causes are not having the least independence in themselves. Therefore, from the logical viewpoint and Qur'anic verses, there cannot be any objection to the fact that the same God Who has placed the power of cure in honey and has bestowed the power of cure and recovery in the chemical and herbal medicines gives the same power and ability to the Prophets and Imams.

If the meditators can acquire great spiritual powers through asceticism then what is wrong if due to Divine Grace or man's devotion and servitude, God grants them power and ability so that under special circumstances, they are able to perform the astounding acts without the natural means.[2]

Shifa' bestowed by the Prophet and Imams and performing the extraordinary acts is not inconsistent with this that the actual '*Shaaf'ee*' (curer), the true finder of the lost one, etc. is Allah Who has given these agents power and strength so that they can, by His permission, control the affairs of this world.

Incidentally, the verses of Qur'an bear testimony that the people wanted and expected such acts from the Prophets and sometimes from others too. Here we shall mention some of them.

The following mentioned verse reveals that Bani Israel requested water from their Prophet during the year of famine and that too, not through natural channels, but through some extraordinary means. They did not say: '*you pray so that God sends water for us*' but said: '*you satiate us and give us water*'. As the verse says:

وَأَوْحَيْنَا إِلَى مُوسَى إِذِ اسْتَسْقَاهُ قَوْمُهُ أَنِ اضْرِبْ بِعَصَاكَ الْحَجَرَ

---

[2] For explanation of this part and acquaintance with the verses of Qur'an, refer to the book '*Spiritual powers of Prophets*'. In this book, reader will find references from Qur'an about their spiritual powers.

"And We revealed to Musa when his people asked him for water: Strike the rock with your staff. (A'raf:160)"

A clearer verse to this one is the verse which speaks about Sulayman (a) asking those present in the gathering to bring the throne of Bilqis which was hundreds of miles away and un-free from barriers and obstacles.

$$\text{أَيُّكُمْ يَأْتِينِي بِعَرْشِهَا قَبْلَ أَنْ يَأْتُونِي مُسْلِمِينَ}$$

"Which of you can bring to me her throne before they come to me in submission? (Naml:38)"

The aim was to bring the throne of Bilqis through extraordinary means as indicated by the replies given by Afrit[3] and Asif bin Barkhiya[4] that have come down in *Surah al-Namal* verses 39 and 40.

The most significant point is that people imagine that simple and ordinary works are not Divine acts and the extraordinary ones which are not within the scope of ordinary people are the work of Allah.

Actually, the measure of Divine and non-divine acts is the matter of independence and non-independence. The divine act is one in which the doer performs the act independently without seeking the help of any power and source. In other words, the divine acts are those in which the doer is the absolute authority in performing that action and is dependent on Himself and no one else.

However, the non-divine acts, whether simple and ordinary or difficult and unusual, are those acts wherein the doer is not independent in performing that action but does so under the influence and help of an independent power.

Therefore, there is no objection to this fact that Allah bestows upon His beloved ones, the power to perform extraordinary acts which are not within the scope of ordinary people and there is no objection if we too request them to perform such acts.

The Holy Qur'an addresses 'Isa (a) very explicitly and says:

$$\text{وَتُبْرِئُ الْأَكْمَهَ وَالْأَبْرَصَ بِإِذْنِي وَإِذْ تُخْرِجُ الْمَوْتَىٰ بِإِذْنِي}$$

---

[3] Or Ifrit is a powerful jinn or mysterious creature.

[4] Asif bin Barkhiya was court vizier of Prophet Sulayman (a). He was not a Prophet but a true believer who was bestowed by God with the "knowledge of the book" [Qur'an, 27:40]. He brought Queen Bilqis's throne in the twinkling of an eye by divinely bestowed powers.

"And you healed the blind and the leprous by My permission, and when you brought forth the dead by My permission. (Maida:110)"

The total sum of these verses shows that the divine leaders possessed such powers and that requesting extraordinary works from them was a common practice and Qur'an too bears testimony to the rightness of such requests.

Till here, the decree of all the three cases of asking from the living ones has been clarified from the viewpoint of Qur'an and we saw that verses of Qur'an have clearly approved their legitimacy.

It is now time to clarify the decree of the remaining two cases (i.e. asking from the holy spirits) from the viewpoint of Qur'an and traditions (*hadiths*). We shall discuss this in the next chapter.

12

Seeking Help from the Spirits of *Awliya Allah*

The most important issue with regards to seeking help from the *Awliya Allah* (the friends or beloved of Allah) is when they have died or so to say, living in another world, whether this act of seeking help is in the form of *du'a* (invocation) or asking for some extraordinary acts to be performed. This is because the Muslims of today are not in the presence of the Holy Prophet (s) or an Imam so that they can approach them and ask them to do something in their presence. Rather, most often, their questions and requests are put before the pure spirits of the Prophets and *awliya*. For this reason, analyzing the Islamic decree with regards to these two situations is very important.

Investigation on this matter depends on the analytical study of four topics and by becoming fully aware of them, one can acknowledge the correctness of such imploration and beseeching. These four topics are:

1. Eternity of soul and spirit of man after death
2. The reality of man is his very soul and spirit
3. Relationship with the world of souls is possible
4. The authentic traditions which the Islamic traditionists have narrated bear witness to the genuineness of such implorations and the practice of the Muslims has been the same in all the ages. Now we shall describe each of these four topics.

1. Death is not Annihilation of Man

The verses of Qur'an bear a clear witness to the fact that death is not the end of life but a window for a new life. By passing from this passage, man steps into a new life, a world completely new to him and much superior than this material world.

Those who take death to be the end of life and believe that with death, everything of man is finished and nothing remains of him except one lifeless body which (even that) after some time is changed to soil and destroyed, follow the philosophy of materialism.

Such a reflection shows that a person with such a view thinks life to be nothing but a part of material effects of the organs of body and the physical and chemical reactions of the brain and nerves and with the subsiding of the heat of body and stoppage of the cells from activity and production, the life of man comes to a halt and he turns into an inanimate object. Soul and spirit in this school of thought is nothing but reflection of materialism and its properties and with the nullification of these properties and domination of reciprocal effects of the organs of body over each other, the soul and spirit become completely void and there no longer remains anything by the name of spirit, its eternity and a world related to spirits.

Such a view about the soul and spirit of man is inspired by the principles of Materialism. In this school of thought, man is nothing more than a machine where he is formed from different tools and components and the reciprocal effects of those components give the power of thought and perception to the brain, and with the dispersion of these components the effects of thought, perception and in short, life gets completely destroyed at death.

The views of materialists about soul and spirit were completely discarded by the great philosophers of the world and the divine scholars. The theologians believe that apart from the material system of body, the nervous system and its reciprocal material reactions there exists for man, a real substance by the name of soul and spirit which remains with the body for some period and then cuts off its relation with the body and lives in a special world with a much more delicate body. The continuity of soul after the death of a person is not a matter which can be established and proved in these pages because today the eternity of soul and spirit has been proven by verses of Qur'an, precise philosophical reasoning and convincing spiritual experiences. We shall now narrate the verses of Qur'an that bear testimony to the matter of eternity of spirit after death.

Qur'an and Eternity of Spirits

Verses of the Qur'an clearly indicate that the spirit continues to live after its separation from the body. For the sake of brevity, we bring here only the text of the verses and postpone its analysis for some other proper time.

$$\text{وَلَا تَقُولُوا لِمَنْ يُقْتَلُ فِي سَبِيلِ اللَّهِ أَمْوَاتٌ ۚ بَلْ أَحْيَاءٌ وَلَٰكِنْ لَا تَشْعُرُونَ}$$

"And do not speak of those who are slain in Allah's way as dead, nay, (they are) alive, but you do not perceive. (Baqarah:154)"

$$\text{وَلَا تَحْسَبَنَّ الَّذِينَ قُتِلُوا فِي سَبِيلِ اللَّهِ أَمْوَاتًا ۚ بَلْ أَحْيَاءٌ عِنْدَ رَبِّهِمْ يُرْزَقُونَ}$$

"And reckon not those who are killed in Allah's way as dead, nay, they are alive (and) are provided sustenance from their Lord. (Aale Imran:169)"

$$\text{فَرِحِينَ بِمَا آتَاهُمُ اللَّهُ مِنْ فَضْلِهِ وَيَسْتَبْشِرُونَ بِالَّذِينَ لَمْ يَلْحَقُوا بِهِمْ}$$

"Rejoicing in what Allah has given them out of His grace, and they rejoice for the sake of those who, (being left) behind them, have not yet joined them. (Aale Imran:170)"

$$\text{يَسْتَبْشِرُونَ بِنِعْمَةٍ مِنَ اللَّهِ وَفَضْلٍ}$$

"They rejoice on account of favor from Allah and (His) grace. (Aale Imran:171)"

$$\text{إِنِّي آمَنْتُ بِرَبِّكُمْ فَاسْمَعُونِ قِيلَ ادْخُلِ الْجَنَّةَ ۖ قَالَ يَا لَيْتَ قَوْمِي يَعْلَمُونَ بِمَا غَفَرَ لِي رَبِّي وَجَعَلَنِي مِنَ الْمُكْرَمِينَ}$$

"Surely I believe in your Lord, there for hear me. It was said: Enter the garden. He said: O would that my people had known of that on account of which my Lord has forgiven me and made me of the honored ones! (Yasin:25-27)"

The Paradise which he is told to enter therein is the Paradise of *barzakh* and not of the Hereafter because he wishes that his people knew and were aware that God has forgiven and honored him. Such a wish is not compatible with the world of the Hereafter, where the curtains will be removed from the eyes of the people and their condition will not be hidden from each other. Rather such unawareness is befitting with this world where the people of this abode are unaware of the condition of the people living in another world (*barzakh*) and the verse of Qur'an bears witness to this fact.

Moreover, the next verse clarifies that after his death, when man is forgiven and he enters the Paradise, the light of his people's life will be extinguished by one heavenly cry. As verse says:

$$\text{وَمَا أَنْزَلْنَا عَلَىٰ قَوْمِهِ مِنْ بَعْدِهِ مِنْ جُنْدٍ مِنَ السَّمَاءِ وَمَا كُنَّا مُنْزِلِينَ إِنْ كَانَتْ إِلَّا صَيْحَةً وَاحِدَةً فَإِذَا هُمْ خَامِدُونَ}$$

"And We did not send down upon his people after him any hosts from heaven, nor do We ever send down. It was naught but a single cry, and lo! they were still. (Yasin:28-29)"

From these two verses we come to know that after entering Paradise, his people were still living in this world till death suddenly overtook them and, this Paradise cannot be anything other than Paradise of *barzakh*.

النَّارُ يُعْرَضُونَ عَلَيْهَا غُدُوًّا وَعَشِيًّا وَيَوْمَ تَقُومُ السَّاعَةُ أَدْخِلُوا آلَ فِرْعَوْنَ أَشَدَّ الْعَذَابِ

"The fire, they shall be brought before it (every) morning and evening and on the day when the hour shall come to pass: Make Firawn's people enter the severest chastisement. (Ghafir:46)"

By paying attention to the contents of the two verses, the matter of continuity of life in the world of *barzakh* becomes clear and obvious because, before the approach of *qiyama*, the Fire will be presented to them morning and evening but after the *qiyama* they will be given the worst punishment.

If the later part of the verse ويوم تقوم الساعة was not there, then the beginning contents would not have been so clear. But by paying attention to the verse it becomes obvious that the objective is the same period of *barzakh*; otherwise the reciprocity of the two sentences would have been incorrect.

Moreover, the matter of morning and evening too bears witness that it does not refer to the world of the Hereafter since, mornings and evenings do not exist in that world.

So far, the first of the four topics has been made clear from the viewpoint of Qur'an. Now it's time to refer to the second topic.

2. The Reality of Man is his very Spirit

Man in the outset seems to be formed of body and spirit. However, the reality of man is his same spirit which is accompanied with the body.

We shall not discuss this matter from the view point of philosophy and at present we are not concerned with the Greek and Islamic philosophy. Rather we shall discuss this matter only from the viewpoint of Qur'an. By examining the verses that have come down with regards to man, this fact can easily be seen that the reality of man is his very soul and spirit. Here, we shall ponder over the contents of this verse:

قُلْ يَتَوَفَّاكُمْ مَلَكُ الْمَوْتِ الَّذِي وُكِّلَ بِكُمْ ثُمَّ إِلَىٰ رَبِّكُمْ تُرْجَعُونَ

"Say: The angel of death who is given charge of you shall cause you to die, and then to your Lord you shall be brought back. (Sajdah:11)"

Contrary to what we believe, the word of توفّى does not mean 'to cause to die'. Rather it means 'to take' or 'to seize'.[1]

Therefore, the purpose of the sentence يتوفاكمُ is: "He will seize you all". When the reality of man is his very soul and spirit, the interpretation of the verse will be correct.

However, if the soul and spirit forms a portion of man's personality and the other half is formed by his external body, then in such a case such an interpretation will not be permissible because the Angel of Death never seizes our external body. Rather, the body remains in its same condition and what the Angel seizes is only our soul.

The verses which clarify the reality of soul and spirit with regards to man are not confined to this verse and as an example; we content ourselves with one verse.

This fact that 'the reality of man and center of his spiritual excellences is his very spirit and the body is (only) a covering which has been put over it' becomes evidently clear by paying attention to the matter of eternity of spirit after death which was discussed in the first topic. Qur'an does not recognize death to be the annihilation of man and the end of his life.

Rather, it believes that life exists for the martyrs, the pious and the oppressors before the approach of *qiyama*, a life accompanied with joy and happiness, (or) accompanied with torment and punishment and if the reality of man is his fundamental body then, undoubtedly the body gets destroyed after a few days and changes to different elements and in such a case the matter of eternity of man or the life of *barzakh* becomes meaningless.

3. Qur'an and the Possibility of Connection with another World

Proving eternity of spirit is not enough for the purpose of recommending and proving (beseeching) to be useful. Rather, apart from its eternity, the possibility of establishing relationship with it should be proved from the viewpoint of reason and Qur'an.

---

[1] Allama Balaghi has presented his valuable research about the word of توفّى in his introduction to *Tafsir Aala al-Rahman*", page 34.

We have talked about this matter in detail in the book 'Originality of the Spirit'.

Here, we shall mention in brief, some of those verses which prove that the relationship of man continues with his past ones and is not yet disconnected.

A. Salih (a) Speaks with the Souls of His People

فَعَقَرُوا النَّاقَةَ وَعَتَوْا عَنْ أَمْرِ رَبِّهِمْ وَقَالُوا يَا صَالِحُ ائْتِنَا بِمَا تَعِدُنَا إِنْ كُنْتَ مِنَ الْمُرْسَلِينَ

"So they slew the she-camel and revolted against their Lord's commandment, and they said: O Salih! Bring us what you threatened us with, if you are one of the apostles. (A'raf:77)"

فَأَخَذَتْهُمُ الرَّجْفَةُ فَأَصْبَحُوا فِي دَارِهِمْ جَاثِمِينَ

"Then the earthquake overtook them, so they became motionless bodies in their abode. (A'raf:78)"[2]

فَتَوَلَّىٰ عَنْهُمْ وَقَالَ يَا قَوْمِ لَقَدْ أَبْلَغْتُكُمْ رِسَالَةَ رَبِّي وَنَصَحْتُ لَكُمْ وَلَٰكِنْ لَا تُحِبُّونَ النَّاصِحِينَ

"Then he turned away from them and said: O my people, I did certainly deliver to you the message of my lord, and I gave you advice, but you do not love those who give advice. (A'raf:79)"

Pay careful attention to the contents of these three verses.

The first verse shows that when they were alive they demanded the punishment of Allah.

The second verse shows that the divine punishment overtook and destroyed each one of them.

The third verse shows that Salih (a) spoke to them after their death and destruction and said: *"I presented you the divine messages but you disliked someone giving you advice."*

---

[2] In some of the verses the cause of their destruction is said to be a heavenly cry (*Surah Hud* verse 6) and some other verses mention the cause as thunderbolt (*Surah Fussilat* verse 17). In these two verses, earthquake is mentioned and the total of verses is such that there was a severe cry along with thunderbolt and earthquake.

A clear witness to this fact that he spoke to them after their death are the following two points:

1. The order of verses in the aforementioned form.
2. The alphabet of فا in the word of فتولى which denotes an order. i.e. after their destruction, he turned towards them and spoke in such words.

The sentence of (ولكن لا تُحبون الناصحين) shows that they were so much sunk in obstinacy and wretchedness that even after death, they possessed wicked mentality so much so that they did not like people who gave advices and warnings.

The expression of Qur'an is in such manner that, he speaks to his peoples' souls with sincerity and considers them as his audience, and reminds them of their permanent obstinacy which was present in them even after death and says: "Now too, you do not like an advisor."

B. Shu'ayb (a) Speaks with the Souls of the Deceased Ones

فَأَخَذَتْهُمُ الرَّجْفَةُ فَأَصْبَحُوا فِي دَارِهِمْ جَاثِمِينَ

"Then the earthquake overtook them, so they became motionless bodies in their abode. (A'raf:91)"

الَّذِينَ كَذَّبُوا شُعَيْبًا كَأَنْ لَمْ يَغْنَوْا فِيهَا ۚ الَّذِينَ كَذَّبُوا شُعَيْبًا كَانُوا هُمُ الْخَاسِرِينَ

"Those who called Shu'ayb a liar were as though they had never dwelt therein, those who called Shu'ayb a liar, they were the losers. (A'raf:92)"

فَتَوَلَّىٰ عَنْهُمْ وَقَالَ يَا قَوْمِ لَقَدْ أَبْلَغْتُكُمْ رِسَالَاتِ رَبِّي وَنَصَحْتُ لَكُمْ ۖ فَكَيْفَ آسَىٰ عَلَىٰ قَوْمٍ كَافِرِينَ

"So he turned away from them and said: O my people! certainly I delivered to you the messages of my Lord and I gave you good advice, how shall I then be sorry for an unbelieving people? (A'raf:93)"

The method of reasoning in this verse is the same as the verses related to Salih (a).

C. The Holy Prophet (s) of Islam Speaks with the Souls of Prophets

وَاسْأَلْ مَنْ أَرْسَلْنَا مِنْ قَبْلِكَ مِنْ رُسُلِنَا أَجَعَلْنَا مِنْ دُونِ الرَّحْمَٰنِ آلِهَةً يُعْبَدُونَ

"And ask those of Our Apostles whom We sent before you: Did We ever appoint gods to be worshipped besides the Beneficent God? (Zukhruf:45)"

This verse shows that the Prophet (s) can establish a connection from this very world with the prophets who live in another world till it becomes clear that the order of God in all the ages and to all the Prophets was not to worship anyone other than Allah.

D. Qur'an Sends Salutations upon the Prophets

The Holy Qur'an has on occasions sent peace and salutations on Prophets and these salutations were not meaningless compliments or some kind of formalities.

Great! it is far from justice if we wish to put down the sublime meanings of the beloved Qur'an to the level that has taken the tinge of staleness. It is true that today, the materialists who do not believe in the validity of spirit, send in their speeches, peace and salutations upon their leaders and founders of this school of thought as a form of respect and honor. But is it fair that we put aside the sublime meanings of Qur'an which reveals facts and realities and bring them down to low level and say that all these salutations which Qur'an has sent upon the prophets (and we Muslims too recite them day and night) are just some dry and meaningless compliments? The Holy Qur'an says:

سَلَامٌ عَلَىٰ نُوحٍ فِي الْعَالَمِينَ

1. *Peace be upon Nuh, in the Universe.*

سَلَامٌ عَلَىٰ إِبْرَاهِيمَ

2. *Peace be upon Ibrahim.*

سَلَامٌ عَلَىٰ مُوسَىٰ وَهَارُونَ

3. *Peace be upon Musa and Harun.*

سَلَامٌ عَلَىٰ إِلْ يَاسِينَ

4. *Peace be upon Aal Yasin.*

سَلَامٌ عَلَى الْمُرْسَلِينَ

5. *Peace be upon the Messengers.*[3]

---

[3] *Surah al-Saffat*: verses 79, 109, 120, 130, 181.

Salutations upon the Holy Prophet (s) in the State of *Tashahhud*:

All the Muslims of the world irrespective of the differences which they have in the principles of jurisprudence address the glorious Messenger of Allah in the *tashahhud* of their *salat* every morning and night and say:

السلام عليك أيها النبيّ ورحمة الله وبركاته

The only thing is that the Shafi'ites and some others reckon this to be obligatory in *tashahhud* whereas other sects think it to be *mustahab* (recommendable). However all of them are unanimous in their opinion that the Holy Prophet (s) has taught the Muslims as such and the *sunnah* of the Prophet (s) remains the same during life and death.

If really our link and connection with the Holy Prophet (s) is cut-off and disconnected, then such a salutation and that too in the form of address (to the Prophet) is of what benefit?

The proofs of possibility of such connections and their occurrences are not confined to what we have said till now. Rather, we have other verses too in this regard which, for the sake of brevity, have not been discussed. For a more detailed discussion, interested readers can refer to the book of 'Originality of spirit from the viewpoint of Qur'an'. In this book, a section of verses dealing with the topic are mentioned.

In the end, we remind you that the rationalization of *salam* in *tashahhud* was discussed due to its decisiveness among the verses.[4]

Conclusion of Our Discussion

For the first point, it was proved that death is not the end of life and the destruction of man. Rather, it is a window for getting transferred to another world.

On the second point, it was clarified that the reality of man is his very soul and spirit and his body is a dress covering his spirit. And if his soul and spirit remain, then naturally his reality, personality and all the other abilities (not the type of ability which is related to the material body) too remain. Therefore, if in

---

[4] Refer to the book of *Tadhkirat al-Fuqaha'*, vol. 3, page 232 and the book of *al-Khilaf* by Sheikh al-Tusi, vol.1 page 47. In this book, he has narrated *tashahhud* in various forms from 'Umar bin al-Khattab and 'Abdullah bin Mas'ud which all of them have such *salam* and the jurists of Ahl al-Sunnah such as Abu Hanifa, Malik and Shafi'i have each taken one of these forms of *tashahhud* and given *fatwa* (verdict) upon them.

this world his soul had the power to pray and eulogize or had the ability to perform some extraordinary actions by the Will of God, his holy *nafs* possesses by the Will of God, the same power and ability in that world and except for those acts which require the material body, it is capable of performing all the other actions.

On the third point, it was proved that it is possible for the people of this world to have relationship with the people of the next world and that the holy spirits can hear our words and sayings.

By paying attention to these three points, the philosophical possibility of the matter is proved i.e. it has been proved that the awliya Allah can listen to our talks and also reply to them by the Will of Allah. However, whether such a thing is lawful from the viewpoint of Islamic regulations or not, will be discussed in the fourth point to which we shall now refer.

1. Muslims and Asking for the Fulfilment of Their Needs from the Holy Spirits

Ibn Taymiyyah and his followers with their unusual trait of opinionated judgements, deny the fact that the companions of the Holy Prophet (s) and those after them had asked the Prophet (s) for their needs to be fulfilled. Regarding this matter they say:

ولم يكن أحد من سلف الأمة في عصر الصحابة ولا التابعين ولا تابعي التابعين يتخيرون الصلاة والدعاء عند قبور الأنبياء ويسألونهم ولا يستغيثون بهم لا في مغيبهم ولا عند قبورهم.

"No one from the past ummah either at the time of the Companions nor the period after the tabi'in (disciples of companions) have performed salat and du'a near the graves of prophets. Never has anyone asked anything from them nor has anyone beseeched them either in their absence or near their graves."[5]

Perhaps a person unacquainted with the history of the Companions (of the Holy Prophet) and the *tabi'in* may imagine such an attribution to be true. However, referring to history will prove contrary to that. As an example, we narrate some instances:

---

[5] Treatise of *al-Hadiyyat al-Saniyya*, page 162 (Egyptian edition).

أصاب الناس قحط في زمان عمر بن الخطاب فجاء رجل إلى قبر النبيّ فقال يا رسول الله استسق الله لأمتك فإنهم قد هلكوا فأتاه رسول الله صلى الله عليه وأله في المنام فقال: أنت عمر ، فاقرنه وأخبره إنهم مسقون.

"During the Caliphate of 'Umar, when there was a famine, a person came near the grave of the Holy Prophet (s) and said: 'O Prophet, ask water for your people as they are being destroyed.' Thereafter the Holy Prophet (s) appeared in his dream and told him as such: 'Go to 'Umar and send salam upon him and, inform him that all will soon be satiated with water.'"[6]

A. Al-Samhudi continues as such:

ومحل الإستشهاد طلب الإستسقاء منه صلى الله عليه وأله وهو في البرزخ ودعاؤه لربه هذه الحالة غير ممتنع وعلمه بسؤال من يسأله قد ورد فلا مانع من سؤال الإستسقاء وغيره كما كان في الدنيا.

"This incident shows that though the Prophet (s) is in barzakh, one can ask him to pray for us. This matter is of no objection because he (i.e. the Prophet) is aware of the requests of the people. Thus there is no hindrance if one requests him to pray for us just as he was doing in this life."[7]

B. al-Samhudi narrates from al-Hafiz Abu 'Abdullah Muhammad bin Musa bin al-Nu'man with the chain of narrators ending in Ali bin Abi Talib (a) that three days had passed after the burial of the Holy Prophet (s) when an Arab from outside Medina came and sprinkled the soil of the Prophet's grave over his head and said:

يا رسول الله قلت فسمعنا قولك ووعيت عن الله سبحانه ما وعينا عنك ، وكان فيما انزل عليك (ولو أنهم إذ ظلموا أنفسهم جاؤك فاستغفروا الله...) وقد ظلمت وجئتك نستغفر لي

"O Prophet! you spoke and we listened to your sayings. You received from God what we received from you. Among those things which was revealed upon you is this particular verse. 'If among them anyone who has done injustice upon themselves comes to you and seeks forgiveness from Allah and you too seek forgiveness for them, then they will find Allah most -Merciful and Forgiving.' I have done injustice upon myself and I have come to you (so that) you seek forgiveness for me."[8]

The writer of *Wafa' al-Wafa'*, at the end of chapter eight, narrates many incidents which show that pleading and asking for one's need from the Holy Prophet (s) has been the constant practice of the Muslims. He even mentions that

---

[6] *Wafa' al-Wafa'*, vol. 2, page 1371.
[7] *Ibid.*
[8] *Wafa' al-Wafa'*, vol. 2, page 1361

Imam Muhammad bin Musa bin al-Nu'man has written a book in this regard under the title of *Misbah al-Zalam fi al-Mustaghithin bi Khayr al-An'am fi al-Yaqzah wa al-Manam*.

C. Muhammad bin Munkadar says:

"A man gave my father 80 dinars as a trust while he was leaving for jihad and said: "You may spend this money if you fall in need". Incidentally due to high cost of living, my father utilized that money. Finally its owner came and demanded back his money. My father told him to come the next day and the same night my father went to the mosque and pointing to the grave and pulpit of the Prophet (s), he implored and pleaded till the early dawn. At that moment, a man appeared from the dark and said "O Aba Muhammad take this." He gave a purse to my father which contained 80 dinars." [9]

D. Abu Bakr al-Muqri says:

Hunger overtook al-Tabarani, Abu al-Sheikh and myself and we were close to the grave of the Holy Prophet (s). When night approached I went near the grave of the Prophet (s) and said:

يا رسول الله الجوع...

Moments later, a person from the Alawites entered the mosque with two young men and each of them was holding a bag full of food.... When we finished eating the 'Alawi man said.... "I saw the Holy Prophet (s) in my dream and he commanded me to bring food for you." [10]

E. Ibn al-Jallad says:

"Poverty-stricken, I entered Medina and went near the grave of the Holy Prophet (s) and said: O Prophet I am your guest. Suddenly I fell asleep and saw in my dream that the Holy Prophet (s) gave bread in my hands." [11]

Right now we are not concerned with the verity or inaccuracy of those incidents. Our point is that these incidents whether true or false prove that such an affair was a common one and if it was innovation or forbidden or polytheism and blasphemy than the fabrication and the enactors of such matters would not have narrated such matters which would lower them in the eyes of the people.

---

[9] *Wafa' al-Wafa'*, vol. 2, page 1380 (Egyptian print). He has described example of these implorations till page 1385.
[10] *Ibid*.
[11] *Wafa' al-Wafa'*, vol. 2, page 1361.

We have narrated in the book *Asalat al-Ruh (The Originality of Spirit)*[12] in the section of 'Connection (with) Spirits', traditions that prove the authenticity of asking the holy spirits to pray.

Here, we are bound to mention a few points:

1. In as much as these kinds of decrees and incidents are incompatible with the temperament of a group, they therefore declare all to be unknown without investigating into their references and narrations. Does such inadmissible denial bring harm to our reasoning?

Answer: Such an encounter with the historical events becomes the cause of interpolation of history because the number of these kinds of pleadings for fulfilment of needs is so numerous that one cannot consider all of them to be false and baseless. If someone intends to collect such narrations or stories he will be able to compile a thick book.

Now let us suppose that these stories and narrations are false and baseless. But these same baseless claims in the entire history inform us of one fact and it is as follows:

If these implorations and beseeching were unlawful, they would not have been fabricated and enacted such unlawful action in the form of honor and glorification as otherwise, their status would be lowered and they would be subject to the wrath and anger of the people.

The fabrication and enactors of tradition and history strive to fabricate and enact those things which suit the taste of the common people. If such an action was against Qur'an and *Sunnah*, then it would be considered as polytheism and *'ibadah* by the Muslims and the fabricators would never have enacted them and lowered their status in the eyes of the people.

2. Seeking help from the holy spirits either in the form of request for *du'a* or in the form of fulfilling an action (Curing the sick, returning the lost one, etc.) is without any objection considering the four principles which we have discussed.

The thing which was in vogue among the Muslims at the time of seeking *tawassul* of the holy spirits was the very request for *du'a* or so to say, requesting the holy spirit of the Prophet to seek forgiveness for them from Allah and pleading for the fulfilment of their worldly and heavenly affairs. From the

---

[12] اصالت روح از نظر قرآن *Asalat al-Ruh az Nazare Qur'an (The Originality of Spirit from the viewpoint of Qur'an)* by Ja'far Subhani. Published by Mo'assasa Imam al-Sadiq, Qom, 1999.

viewpoint of logic, request for fulfilment of actions like curing of the sick, freeing of the captive; solving of problems in life is the same as request for *du'a*.

3. By paying attention to the measure which we reminded you about *'ibadah*, such requests and pleadings are never considered as *'ibadah* of the holy spirits. This is because the person making the request neither believes in their divinity nor in their lordship and neither considers them as God nor as the one who manages the world or part of it. He also does not believe that some of the actions of God have been entrusted to them. Rather, they consider them to be the pure servants of Allah who have never committed the least offence in their worldly life.

By paying attention to the four basic facts, one cannot doubt their power and *barzakhi* ability in fulfilling the requests of the pleaders. They are living creatures and our relation with them is well established. The only point is that every action and affair either in the form of *du'a* or other than that it is dependent on the Will of Allah and they are clear evidence to:

$$وَمَا تَشَاءُونَ إِلَّا أَن يَشَاءَ اللَّهُ$$

...but you will not wish unless it is wished by Allah... (Insan:30 and Takwir:29)

Just as in this world, 'Isa (a) could pray to God for goodness for someone or could cure by the Will of Allah, those who were born blind and those who suffered from leprosy, in the same manner, considering the fact that these powers and abilities are related to his soul and spirit and not his body, he can perform these same two actions (even) after his transfer to another world. However, in both the stages, the permission of Allah and His will is a necessary condition for receiving Grace through this channel.

4. Even though such humility and humbleness in connection to the inerrant leaders are apparently for paying attention to them, yet if we tear open the inner portion of this attentiveness and the *tawassul*, we will find which really is desired and demanded by God Himself. In reality, paying attention to the cause is like paying attention to the 'Causer of the causes' and those who are having a firm step in the matter of behavior and dealing with the people are aware and conscious of this reality with a conscious and enlightened heart.

Those who seek *tawassul* do not believe in the originality and independence of these causes and agents. Rather, they are means which God, the Causer has made them a channel and a route for receiving His Grace and Mercy and He, Himself, has ordered the believers for attaining as such. As verse says:

يَا أَيُّهَا الَّذِينَ آمَنُوا اتَّقُوا اللَّهَ وَابْتَغُوا إِلَيْهِ الْوَسِيلَةَ وَجَاهِدُوا فِي سَبِيلِهِ لَعَلَّكُمْ تُفْلِحُونَ

"O you who believe! be careful of (your duty to) Allah and seek means of nearness to Him and strive hard in His way that you may be successful. (Maida:35)"

If *salat*, fasting and all the divine duties are وسيلة means, then in the same manner, the pure *du'a* of Prophets and *awliya* too, by decree of the previous verse (verse related to asking for forgiveness), is وسيلة means and paying attention to these means is like paying attention to the Creator of these means and our action is in accordance to the command of the afore-mentioned verse.

13

Seeking *Shafa'a* (Intercession) from *Awliya Allah*

All of us are well acquainted with the term *shafa'a*. When the discussion of crime, sin and guilt of a person is brought up and someone else intercedes and mediates for him in order to save him from death and execution or imprisonment and detention, we say so and so has done *shafa'a* for him.

The word of *shafa'a* has been taken from the root word شفع which means 'even' as against وتر which means 'odd'. The reason that the mediation of a person for saving a sinner is known as *shafa'a* is that the status and position of the one doing *shafa'a* and his effective powers get attached (and become even) with the factors of salvation which is present in the person receiving the *shafa'a* (even though it may be a little). Both these, with the help of one another become the cause of release of the sinful person.

The *shafa'a* of the beloved ones of Allah for the sinners is apparently because of their proximity and position which they have before Allah, (of course by the will of Allah and under special norms which have general and not personal aspects) they can mediate for the criminals and the sinners and through (invocation), and pleadings ask God to forgive their crimes and sins. Of course, *shafa'a* and its acceptance depend on a series of conditions of which some are related to the sinful person and some to the circumstances of *shafa'a* of sins.

Shafa'a in other words is the help of the beloved ones of Allah (by His will) to the one who in spite of being sinful has not disconnected his spiritual relation with Allah and the beloved ones of Allah. Moreover, this standard should always be safeguarded.

According to one of the meanings, *shafa'a* is: One inferior person who has the aptitude for leaping forward and progressing seeks help from a superior person in the form of one lawful order. However, the person seeking help should not, from the viewpoint of spiritual perfections, fall to such extent that he loses the power of advancing and the possibility of changing into a pious man.

Right from the time of the Holy Prophet (s) till the later periods it had been the practice of the Muslims to seek *shafa'a* from the true intercessors. They were always asking in their lifetime or in their death and such *shafa'a* had never been objected by any of the Islamic scholars on any ground or Islamic principles.

It was only in the 7th century A.H. that Ibn Taymiyyah with his special way of thinking, opposed this and many other lasting customs and traditions that were in vogue among the Muslims. Three centuries after him, Muhammad bin 'Abd al-Wahhab once again raised the flag of opposition and enlivened Ibn Taymiyyah's school of thought with much more vigor.

One of the point of differences of the Wahhabis with the other Islamic sects is that although they have accepted *shafa'a* as an Islamic principle (like the other Muslims) and say that on the Day of Judgement (*qiyama*) the intercessors will intercede for the sinners and in this matter the Holy Prophet (s) will play a greater role, yet they say that no one has the right to seek *shafa'a* from them in this world. In this matter they have gone to such an extreme that narrating the text of their sayings will be the source of spiritual discomfort. In short, they say:

The Holy Prophet (s), the other Prophets, the angels and the beloved ones of Allah have the right of doing *shafa'a* on the Day of Judgement but one should ask for *shafa'a* from the Master of *shafa'a* and the One who gives permission for that i.e. Allah and say:

اللهم شفع نبينا محمد فينا يوم القيامة أو اللهم شفع فينا عبادك الصالحين أو ملائكتك أو نحو ذلك مما يُطلب من الله لا منهم فلا يُقال يا رسول الله أو يا وليَّ الله أسألك الشفاعة أو غيرها مما لا يقدر عليه إلا الله فإذا طلبت ذلك في أيام البرزخ كان في اقسام الشرك.

"O God, make the Holy Prophet (s) and your virtuous servants and the Angels as our intercessors on the Day of Judgement." However we are not having the right to say, "O Prophet of Allah" or "O wali of Allah, we ask you to seek shafa'a for us. This is because shafa'a is something which no one is capable of doing except Allah. Asking such a thing from the Holy Prophet (s) who is living in barzakh will be a kind of polytheism (shirk)."[1]

The Wahhabis have, with a series of notions, forbidden the seeking of *shafa'a* from the true intercessors and have labelled the one who does so as a polytheist and his action as polytheism.

---

[1] *al-Hadiyyat al-Saniyya*, 2nd treatise, page 42.

Before looking into their reasoning, we shall discuss the matter from the viewpoint of Qur'an, *sunnah* and the practice of the Muslims in this regard. After that, we will examine their reasoning.

Our reasoning on the logical firmness of seeking *Shafa'a*

Our reasoning for the permissibility of seeking intercession *(shafa'a)* is a combination of two matters which by proving them, the matter of intercession will become clear. These two matters are:
1. Asking for *shafa'a* is the same as asking for *du'a*.
2. Requesting for *du'a* from some worthy person is a recommended *(mustahab)* order.

1. Asking for *Shafa'a* is the same as asking for *Du'a*

The intercession of the Holy Prophet (s) and other true intercessors is nothing but *du'a* and eulogy before Allah owing to the proximity and the position which they have before Allah. It is due to their *du'a* that Allah bestows His mercy and Grace upon the sinners and forgives them. Asking for *du'a* from one believer (what if it is asked from the Holy Prophet) is an approved affair and none amongst the Islamic scholars whether Wahhabis or Non-Wahhabis have doubt in its authenticity.

Of course it cannot be said that the reality of *shafa'a* in all the stations of *mahshar* is this very *du'a* before Allah. But one can say that one of its clear meanings is *du'a* and the one who says:

يا وجيهاً عند الله اشفع لنا عند الله

"O the one who has a position before Allah intercede for us from Allah."
denotes the same meaning.

Nizamuddin al-Nishapuri[2] while interpreting the verse

من يشفع شفاعة سيّئة يكن له كفل منها

"And whoever joins himself (to another) in an evil cause shall have the responsibility of it. (Nisa:85)"

---

[2] Nizamudddin Hasan al-Nishapuri (d. 1328 A.H. / 1910 A.D.) was a Persian mathematician, astronomer, jurist, exegete, and poet originally from Qom. He wrote many famous books including exegesis of Qur'an *Tafsir al-Gharaeb al-Qur'an* (تفسير الغرائب القرآن) which is a commentary on the wonders of Qur'an in exegesis a.k.a. Tafsir Nishapuri.

It is narrated from *Muqatil* as such:

الشفاعة إلى الله إنما هى الدعوة لمُسلم

"The reality of shafa'a is performing du'a for the Muslims."

It is also narrated from the Holy Prophet (s) that anyone who performs *du'a* for his Muslim brother will be accepted and an angel will cry out: "The same shall be for you too."

Ibn Taymiyyah is one of those who believed that the request for *du'a* from a living person is correct. Therefore, asking for *shafa'a* is not confined to the Holy Prophet (s) but one can make such a request from any believer who possesses value and esteem before Allah.

Al-Fakhruddin al-Razi[3] is one of those who have interpreted *shafa'a* as *du'a* and eulogy before Allah. In interpreting the verse:

وَيَسْتَغْفِرُونَ لِلَّذِينَ آمَنُوا رَبَّنَا وَسِعْتَ كُلَّ شَيْءٍ رَّحْمَةً

"And ask protection for those who believe: Our Lord! Thou embracest all things in mercy. (Ghafir:7)"

He says: "This verse shows that the *shafa'a* performed by the carriers of *'arsh* (Throne) is only in connection with the sinners." [4]

Similarly, the *shafa'a* of the Holy Prophet (s) and other Prophets (s) with regards to the same group (i.e. the sinners) is the same because Allah commands as such:

وَاسْتَغْفِرْ لِذَنبِكَ وَلِلْمُؤْمِنِينَ وَالْمُؤْمِنَاتِ

"And, ask protection for your fault and for the believing men and the believing women. (Muhammad:19)"[5]

And Nuh (a) sought forgiveness for himself, his parents, those who had faith in him and all the believers who are to come till *qiyama* and in this way he has fulfilled his mission of *shafa'a*.[6]

---

[3] Fakhruddin Razi (1150 - 1210 A.D.) was a famous Sunni Shafi'i Ash'ari Muslim theologian and philosopher from Khorasan. He was born in Rey and died in Herat. He was known as Sultan al-Mutakallimin (Prince of the Rhetoricians) and Imam al-Mushakkikin (Leader of the Skeptics). He wrote several books including *Tafsir al-Kabir* a.k.a. *Mafatih al-Ghayb* and *'Aja'ib al-Qur'an*.

[4] Since the end of the verse says: "وقهم عذاب الجحيم" *and protect them from the torment of Hell.*

[5] *Surah Muhammad*, Ayah 19, as a decisive evidence bears witness to the inerrancy of the Holy Prophet (s) and other Prophets, naturally the word sin means something else for them. We have written the description of this section in Vol. 5 of the exegesis of *Manshur Javid* which is the first topic wise exegesis in Persian.

[6] *Surah Nuh*: verse 28. رَبِّ اغْفِرْ لِي وَلِوَالِدَيَّ وَلِمَن دَخَلَ بَيْتِيَ مُؤْمِنًا وَلِلْمُؤْمِنِينَ وَالْمُؤْمِنَاتِ *"My Lord! Forgive me and my parents, and whoever enters my house in faith, and the faithful men and women."*

This description from al-Fakhruddin al-Razi bears witness that he has presented *shafa'a* to be the same as *du'a* of the intercessor for the sinner and has reckoned the request for *shafa'a* to be the same as request for *du'a*.

In the Islamic traditions (hadiths), there are clear indications that the 'Dua' of one Muslim for another Muslims is 'Shafa'at'.

Ibn 'Abbas narrates from the Holy Prophet (s) as such:

ما من رجل مسلم يموت فيقول على جنازته اربعون رجلاً لا يُشركون بالله شيئاً إلا شفعهم الله فيه

"If one Muslim dies and forty men who are not polytheist, recite salat over his dead body, then Allah will accept their shafa'a which was done in his favor." [7]

In this tradition, the person reciting the *du'a* is introduced as an intercessor. Now, if someone in his life-time requests forty of his loyal friends to be present after his death and perform *salat* and *du'a* upon his dead body, he has in reality sought *shafa'a* from them and has prepared the premises of *shafa'a* of the servants of Allah.

In *Sahih al-Bukhari* there is a chapter entitled as:

إذا استشفعوا إلى الإمام ليستسقى لهم لم يرُدهم

"When the people would ask their Imam to intercede (do shafa'a) and plead before Allah to descend rain, he (i.e. the Imam) would not reject their demands."

Also, there is a chapter entitled as:

إذا إستشفع المُشركون بالمسلمين عند القحط

"Occasions when the polytheists demanded shafa'a from Muslims at times of famine." [8]

Narration of these two chapters is evidence that request for *shafa'a* is the same as request for *du'a* and it should not be interpreted in another way.

Till here, one pillar of reasoning has been clarified and that is, the reality of seeking *shafa'a* is nothing but requesting *du'a*. Now we should engage ourselves in describing the second pillar of reasoning and that is asking from one brother-in-faith (what if it is asking the *Awliya Allah*) is a desirable and recommended action.

2. Qur'an and Request for *du'a* from Worthy People

The verses of Qur'an bear witness that when the Prophets seek forgiveness for the people it is very effective and beneficial such as the following verses:

---

[7] *Sahih Muslim*, vol. 3, page 54.
[8] *Sahih al-Bukhari*, vol. 1.

$$\text{وَاسْتَغْفِرْ لِذَنبِكَ وَلِلْمُؤْمِنِينَ وَالْمُؤْمِنَاتِ}$$

"And ask protection for your fault and for the believers. (Muhammad:19)"

$$\text{وَصَلِّ عَلَيْهِمْ إِنَّ صَلَاتَكَ سَكَنٌ لَهُمْ}$$

"And pray for them, surely your prayer is a relief to them. (Tawbah:103)"

If the *du'a* of Prophet (s) has such benefit for man then what is the harm if one requests him to pray as such for him? On the other hand, request for *du'a* is nothing but request for *shafa'a*.

$$\text{وَلَوْ أَنَّهُمْ إِذْ ظَلَمُوا أَنفُسَهُمْ جَاءُوكَ فَاسْتَغْفَرُوا اللَّهَ وَاسْتَغْفَرَ لَهُمُ الرَّسُولُ لَوَجَدُوا اللَّهَ تَوَّابًا رَحِيمًا}$$

"And had they, when they were unjust to themselves, come to you and asked forgiveness of Allah and the Apostle had (also) asked forgiveness for them, they would have found Allah Oft-returning (to mercy), Merciful. (Nisa:64)"

By جاءوك (they come to you) it means that they would come and ask the Prophet (s) to pray and seek forgiveness. If it means something else then their coming will be useless and in vain. Moreover, the honor of meeting the Prophet (s) and asking him to pray is itself a witness of the spiritual transformation which prepares the ground for acceptance of prayers. The Holy Qur'an narrates from the sons of Ya'qub (a) that they requested their father to seek forgiveness for them and Ya'qub (a) too accepted their request and acted upon his promise.

$$\text{قَالُوا يَا أَبَانَا اسْتَغْفِرْ لَنَا ذُنُوبَنَا إِنَّا كُنَّا خَاطِئِينَ قَالَ سَوْفَ أَسْتَغْفِرُ لَكُمْ رَبِّي}$$

"They said: O our father! ask forgiveness of our faults for us, surely we were sinners. He said: I will ask for you forgiveness from my Lord. (Yusuf:97)"

All these verses show that requesting the Prophet (s) and other virtuous ones to perform *du'a* which is the same as requesting *shafa'a*, is not having the least objection from the viewpoint of Islamic standards. For the sake of brevity, we have not narrated the traditions regarding request of *du'a* from the virtuous ones.

Islamic Traditions (*hadiths*) and the Path of Companions

The famous traditionist, al-Tirmidhi and the writer of one of the *Sihah* of the *Ahl al-Sunnah* narrates from Anas as such:

Seeking *Shafa'a* (Intercession) from *Awliya Allah*

سألت النبيّ أن يشفع لي يوم القيامة فقال أنا فاعل قلت فأين أطلبك فقال على الصراط

(Anas says): "I requested the Holy Prophet (s) to ask shafa'a for me on the day of Judgement and he accepted and said, "I shall request your shafa'a. I asked: "Where should I find you? The Prophet said: "Find me near Sirat (bridge over Hell)." [9]

With his mild disposition, Anas requests for *shafa'a* from the Holy Prophet (s) and he too accepts it and gives him glad tidings. Sawad bin Qarib was one of the Companions of the Holy Prophet (s). In the contents of one of his poems, he seeks intercession from the Prophet (s) and says:

فكن لي شفيعاً يوم لا ذو شفاعة بمُغنٍ قتيلاً عن سواد بن قارب

"O' the honorable Prophet! you be my intercessor on the Day of Judgment, the day when the shafa'a of no one will be useful and beneficial to Sawad bin Qarib."[10]

Before the Holy Prophet's (s) birth, a person by the name of Tubba' from the tribe of al-Himyar had heard that soon a Prophet was going to be appointed by God in the Arab territory. Before dying, he wrote one letter and requested his near ones that if the day came when such a prophet was sent, then they should hand over his letter to him. In this letter, he had written as such:

وإن لم أدركك فاشفع لي يوم القيامة ولا تُنسِني

"Though my age was not loyal and I died before seeing you, ask my shafa'a on the Day of qiyama and do not forget me."

When the letter was handed to the Holy Prophet (s) he said thrice:

مرحباً بتبع الأخ الصالح

"Congratulations to Tubba', my pious brother." [11]

If request for *shafa'a* was polytheism then Holy Prophet (s) would never have addressed him as his brother and would not have thrice congratulated him.

Seeking *Shafa'a* from the Dead

Last section of traditions indicated that seeking *shafa'a* from the true intercessors in their lifetime is absolutely correct.

Now, we shall mention two traditions that show that the companions of the Holy Prophet (s) used to seek *shafa'a* from him even after his demise.

---

[9] *Sunan al-Tirmidhi*, vol. 4, p. 42. Chapter of: "ما جاء في شأن الصراط"
[10] *Qamus al-Rijal*, under the section سواد (Sawad).
[11] *Manaqib Ibn Shahr Ashub*, vol.1, p. 12; *Bihar al-Anwar*, vol.15, p. 314.

1. Ibn 'Abbas says: When Amir al-mu'minin (a) finished giving *ghusl* (ablution) and *kafan* (shroud) to the Holy Prophet (s), he uncovered the face (of the Prophet) and said:

بأبي أنت وأمي طبت حياً وطبت ميتاً...واذكرنا عند ربك

"May my mother and father be sacrificed; you are chaste and pure in life and in death. Remember us near your Lord."[12]

2. When the Holy Prophet (s) passed away, Abu Bakr uncovered his face and kissed him and said:

"May my father and mother be sacrificed; you are chaste and pure in life and death. Remember and think of us near your Lord." [13]

The aforesaid traditions show that seeking *shafa'a* of the intercessor makes no difference whether the intercessor is alive or dead. Thus, by paying attention to these verses, traditions and the continuing custom of the Muslims in all the ages, the matter of seeking *shafa'a* becomes self-evident and one should never be in slightest doubt with regards to its integrity. Moreover, the companions of the Holy Prophet (s) were requesting the Holy Prophet (s) to pray for them even after his demise and if request for *du'a* (prayers) after his demise is correct, then request for *shafa'a* too which is one kind of request for *du'a* is proper and correct.[14]

---

[12] *Nahj al-Balagha*, Sermon no. 230.
[13] *Kashf al-'Irtiyab*, page 265 narrated from *Khulasat al-Kalam*.
[14] For more details refer to the book *Shafa'a in the realm of Reason, Qur'an and Traditions* written by (this) author. In this book, you will find 100 traditions (45 traditions from *Ahl al-Sunnah* and 55 traditions from Shi'a books).

14

Examining the Reasoning of Wahhabis about the Prohibition of Seeking *Shafa'a*

In the previous chapter, we became acquainted with the permissibility of seeking *shafa'a* with logical reasons. Now it is time to learn about the reasoning of the opponents with regards to such request for *shafa'a*. The group of opposition has prohibited seeking of *shafa'a* with their particular way of thinking which we shall now discuss in brief.

1. Seeking *shafa'a* is *shirk* (Polytheism)

By *shirk* they mean *shirk* in *'ibadah* and present seeking of *shafa'a* to be *'ibadah* of the intercessor. In chapter 9 we had discussed in detail about *'ibadah* and have clarified that requesting and asking someone and or seeking *shafa'a* will be counted as *'ibadah* only when we believe the other person to be الله God, رب (Lord) and the one who is managing the world or is the source and master of divine affairs. If it is not as such then any kind of request and asking any kind of respect and honor will never be counted as *'ibadah*.

The one who seeks *shafa'a* from the true intercessors before Allah (where Allah has permitted them to do *shafa'a*) consider them as an intimate and chosen servants of Allah where they are neither God nor the divine affairs such as forgiveness and *shafa'a* have been transferred to them so that they are able to willfully and without the permission of Allah, do *shafa'a* and forgive whomsoever they wish.

Within the framework of 'Permission of Allah', these divine people can seek forgiveness and mercy for those particular people who still have spiritual relation with God and their spiritual connection with the divine intercessors has not yet been discontinued. And such a request from someone who does not reckon the intercessor to be more than an intimate servant can never be considered as *'ibadah*.

Of course, we remind you that if such a request (of intercession) to the intercessor who is dead amounts to *'ibadah* then the same request to a living intercessor too should be counted as *'ibadah*.

However, in the previous discussion we pointed out that Qur'an and traditions command the Muslims to approach the Holy Prophet (s) and request him to seek forgiveness for themselves. And such a request is nothing but seeking *shafa'a* from him in his life-time and it is impossible that one action which is polytheism in one period turns into a monotheistic action in another period.

To elaborate further, they say: *Shafa'a* is the act of God and in better terms, is the right of God and asking others about something which is related to His action will amount to *'ibadah* of that person. They speak the same about asking for *shifa'* (cure) of the sick and other similar things from the beloved ones of God and say: Such kinds of requests are requests for the acts of God and naturally it will be like doing his *'ibadah*.

By paying attention to the previous discussions, the reply to this reasoning becomes absolutely clear and it is as such: None amongst the Muslims have differences in this general rule and universal measure and all agree that asking others about the actions of Allah will be counted as *'ibadah* and involves the belief in divinity and Lordship. But the main point of our discussion is: What is meant by 'action' of God? The Wahhabi writers during these three centuries have not explained the standard for the 'acts' or 'action' of God without which the reasoning will be brought to naught.

In the discussion about the definition and limitation of *'ibadah* we reminded you that in many verses of Qur'an, the actions which are specific to God have also been attributed to other than Him. For example, giving death which is a specific action of God as mentioned in *Surah al-Mu'minun* verse 80.

$$\text{وَهُوَ الَّذِي يُحْيِي وَيُمِيتُ}$$

"He is one who gives life and Death" is also attributed to (someone) other than Him as mentioned in another verse as such:

$$\text{حَتَّى إِذَا جَاءَ أَحَدَكُمُ الْمَوْتُ تَوَفَّتْهُ رُسُلُنَا}$$

"Until when death comes to one of you, our messengers cause him to die. (An'am:61)"

Until the time death overtakes one of them, our messengers take away their souls. It is not only this action (i.e. 'giving death') that is specifically the action of God and is attributed to (someone) other than Him but in fact, a portion of the actions of God and those things that should be asked only from God have been permitted to be asked from someone other than Him.

For example: Qur'an commands the Muslims to say day and night (in ritual prayers while reciting *Surah Fatihah*: *Only from Thee do we seek help*...) but at the same time in another verse it commands us to seek help from (something) other than Him like *salat* and patience, as verse says:

وَاسْتَعِينُوا بِالصَّبْرِ وَالصَّلَاةِ ۚ وَإِنَّهَا لَكَبِيرَةٌ إِلَّا عَلَى الْخَاشِعِينَ

"And seek assistance through patience and prayer, and most surely it is a hard thing except for the humble ones. (Baqarah:45)"

If we wish to narrate those verses that are specific to Allah, but are attributed to other than Him, then our discussion will lengthen.[1] What is necessary is to solve the controversy through Qur'anic insight and acquire the actual meaning of Qur'an and it is as such:

Each of these affairs irrespective of our request has two forms:

1. A 'doer' performs an action without relying on a creature, without acquiring power from any position and without obtaining the will of anybody, For example, he gives death to a living creature or helps a creature.

2. A 'doer' performs the same action by relying on a superior being, by acquiring power from a higher position and obtaining His permission. The first affair is the affair of God and the second a human or non-divine affair. This is a general yardstick for distinguishing the divine action from the non-divine ones.

The divine actions such as giving life, death, cure, sustenance etc., are invariably those actions for which the doer is needless of anything in performing them.

On the other hand, a non-divine action is that action which the doer has to depend on a superior and higher creature than him and without His Power and Will, is not able to perform that action.

---

[1] Refer to the book *Manshur Javid*, vol. 2, Section of "Limitation of *'ibadah*".

By paying attention to this principle, it becomes clear that the *shafa'a* which is the special right of Allah is different from that *shafa'a* which is sought from the virtuous people.

Allah is needless from all angles in these actions whereas the virtuous one put them into operation only under the light of His wise Will and Permission.

Whenever *shafa'a* is sought from the *Awliya Allah* in the first sense, then in such a case, the divine action is asked from someone other than God and such an asking will be reckoned as *'ibadah*.

However, if *shafa'a* is sought from them in the second sense i.e. a limited and permitted *shafa'a* which is in the form of one acquired right, then in such a case, a non-divine action is asked from them.

By paying attention to this yardstick, the fists of the fallacious writers of Wahhabis will open up and it becomes clear that such kind of requests, most common being request for *shafa'a* and others such as *shifa'* (cure) and the like of it takes place under two forms and no virtuous monotheist will request such an action in the first form and no one, no matter how little Islamic knowledge he possesses, will ever reckon them to be the ones managing this world or the ones in charge of the system of creation.

Moreover, they do not (even) reckon them to be such creatures to whom God has entrusted His position and His actions and do not imagine that in the actions of *shafa'a* and fulfilment of needs they are unlimited and unconditional.

In short, asking for a limited and authorized *shafa'a* is the action of a man from man himself and is not asking for the Acts of God from someone other than Him.

We shall speak about the 'action of God' and its special features in the near future.

2. The *Shirk* (Polytheism) of the Polytheists was due to Their Seeking of *Shafa'a* from the Idols

The second reasoning which the Wahhabis give for the prohibition of *shafa'a* is this that God has labelled the idol-worshippers of Hijaz as polytheists because of their seeking of *shafa'a* from the idols; their crying and wailing before them and their request (to them) to act as mediators, The following verse bears testimony to this:

وَيَعْبُدُونَ مِنْ دُونِ اللَّهِ مَا لَا يَضُرُّهُمْ وَلَا يَنْفَعُهُمْ وَيَقُولُونَ هَٰؤُلَاءِ شُفَعَاؤُنَا عِنْدَ اللَّهِ

"And they serve beside Allah what can neither harm them nor profit them, and they say: These are our intercessors with Allah. (Yunus:18)"

Therefore, any kind of *shafa'a* from other than God will be polytheism and worshipping of the intercessor.

Reply

Firstly, this verse is never an indication of what they say and if the Qur'an calls them as polytheists it is not because they were seeking *shafa'a* from the idols but because they worship them (idols) and finally reaching the stage of seeking *shafa'a* from them.

If seeking *shafa'a* from the idols did really amount to their worship then, in addition to the sentence ويعبدون there was no reason to bring the sentence:

ويقولون هؤلاء شفعاؤنا

That these two sentences have come in a parataxis form in this verse shows that the matter of *'ibadah* (worship) of the idols was different from the matter of seeking *shafa'a* from them. Worshipping of the idols is the sign of polytheism and dualism and seeking *shafa'a* from the stones and wood is reckoned to be a foolish act, devoid of any logic or reason.

This verse never shows that seeking *shafa'a* from the idols amounts to worshipping them so that we may say that seeking *shafa'a* from the true beloved ones of Allah is the sign of worshipping them.

Secondly, even if we assume that the reason of their polytheism was due to their seeking of *shafa'a'* from the idols yet, there exists a vast difference between their seeking *of shafa'a* and the seeking of *shafa'a* of the Muslims. They reckoned the idols to be the masters of *shafa'a* and the absolute authorities in the matters related to *shafa'a* and 'forgiveness of sins'. Perhaps God has discharged Himself from these affairs and has entrusted them to the idols.

Such a *shafa'a* will naturally be (like) worshipping them because they were seeking *shufu'a* from them by having belief in their divinity, lordship and their being the source of divine affairs. On the other hand, a Muslim seeks *shafa'a* and requests for *du'a* from the beloved ones of Allah as one esteemed and honorable one (of Allah) and as one authorized servant of Allah in the matter of *shafa'a*.

Thus, considering these two forms as one and the same is far from justice and realism.

3. Request for Fulfilment of Need from Someone other than Allah is Forbidden

The third reason which the Wahhabis give for the prohibition of the matter of seeking *shafa'a* from the divine leaders is this that by specific decree of Qur'an, we should not, in the position of *du'a*, call anyone other than Allah. And asking for *shafa'a* from other than God is one kind of asking (for fulfilment of needs).

The Holy Qur'an says:

فَلَا تَدْعُوا مَعَ اللَّهِ أَحَدًا

"Then do not call anyone with Allah (Jinn:18)"

If on the one hand it is said that calling someone other than Allah is forbidden and on the other hand the matter of *shafa'a* of the *Awliya Allah* has been established, then the way of concluding is to say that we should seek *shafa'a* of the divine leaders from God and not from themselves.

The proof that such callings is *'ibadah* and worship is the following verse of Qur'an:

ادْعُونِي أَسْتَجِبْ لَكُمْ ۚ إِنَّ الَّذِينَ يَسْتَكْبِرُونَ عَنْ عِبَادَتِي سَيَدْخُلُونَ جَهَنَّمَ دَاخِرِينَ

"Call upon Me, I will answer you; surely those who are too proud for My service shall soon enter hell abased. (Ghafir:60)"

Attention is required in the beginning of the verse; the word and in the end the word has come which shows that 'calling' and worship give one and the same meaning. In the books of traditions too, we find as such:

الدعاء مخ العبادة

"Du'a is the brain of 'ibadah (worship)."[2]

Reply

Firstly, the verse which has prohibited دعوت (calling) of someone other than God in the sentence فلا تدعوا does not refer to absolute calling and requesting. Instead, this prohibition (of دعوت) refers to the prohibition of worshipping someone other than God; the reason being the preceding verse which says وأن

---

[2] Reported from Prophet (s). *Bihar al-Anwar*, vol. 93, page 300.

المساجد لله. This sentence shows that by دعوت (in this verse) is meant some specific دعوت which is accompanied by worship and a rising which is mixed with unlimited humility and lowliness in front of the one whom they consider as God of the Universe, Lord of the worlds and the absolute authority in creation.³

And such a bond does not exist in the matter of seeking *shafa'a* from someone in whom Allah has bestowed such a right to give *shafa'a* by His will.

Secondly, what has been prohibited in the verse is 'calling someone along with Allah' and 'considering him at His level', as the word of مع الله is a clear evidence to this fact. If someone requests the Holy Prophet (s) to pray for him, that Allah may forgive his sins or fulfil his needs, then he has not called anyone along with Allah. Rather, the reality of this calling is nothing but the calling of Allah.

If asking for fulfilment of needs from the idols is introduced as polytheism in some of verses, it is because they reckoned them to be the small gods, the authorities in all or some of the divine affairs and the ones who are powerful enough to fulfil their needs. Therefore, the Qur'an criticizes such ideas and says:

وَالَّذِينَ تَدْعُونَ مِنْ دُونِهِ لَا يَسْتَطِيعُونَ نَصْرَكُمْ وَلَا أَنْفُسَهُمْ يَنْصُرُونَ

"And those whom you call upon besides Him are not able to help you, nor can they help themselves. (A'raf:197)"

The Qur'an also says:

إِنَّ الَّذِينَ تَدْعُونَ مِنْ دُونِ اللَّهِ عِبَادٌ أَمْثَالُكُمْ

"Surely those whom you call on besides Allah are in a state of subjugation like yourselves. (A'raf:194)"

In short, the polytheists imagined the idols to be small gods and believed them to be absolute possessors of divine actions. However, asking *'shafa'a* and *du'a* from someone whom God has granted such a right and position is devoid of such stipulations.

Thirdly, calling is having a much wider and comprehensive meaning and is occasionally used metaphorically in *'ibadah* (worship) such as the verse of ادعوني استجب لكم *"Call Me, and I will hear you!"* (Ghafir:60) and the tradition الدعاء مع العبادة. However, such partial usages in metaphorical form is no reason

---

³ In fact the meaning of the verse is والذين لا يدعون مع الله إلهاً as mentioned in another verse فلا تعبدوا مع الله أحداً أخر *"Those who do not invoke another deity besides Allah.."* (Surah al-Furqan verse 68).

that we always interpret دعوت in the meaning of worship and condemn the request for fulfilment of need and *du'a* from someone (in a reasonable manner) as polytheism.

Moreover, the actual meaning of دعوت is 'to call' which sometimes takes the shape of *'ibadah* and mainly gives the meaning of calling others (and not *'ibada*).

Later, we shall have a chapter on the meaning of دعوت in Qur'an and will prove that every دعوت (calling) and pleading is not accompanied with *'ibadah* and worship.

4. *Shafa'a* is the Special Right of Allah

The following verse shows that *shafa'a* is the right of Allah and as such, what meaning can we derive other than this?

أَمِ اتَّخَذُوا مِنْ دُونِ اللَّهِ شُفَعَاءَ ۚ قُلْ أَوَلَوْ كَانُوا لَا يَمْلِكُونَ شَيْئًا وَلَا يَعْقِلُونَ قُلْ لِلَّهِ الشَّفَاعَةُ جَمِيعًا

"Or have they taken intercessors besides Allah? Say: what! even though they did not ever have control over anything, nor do they understand. Say: Allah's is the intercession altogether. (Zumar:43-44)"

Reply

The sentence لِلَّهِ الشَّفَاعَةُ جَمِيعًا does not mean that only God gives *shafa'a* and that no one else is having the right of *shafa'a*. This is because undoubtedly, God never asks anyone to do *shafa'a* for someone else. Rather, it means that God is the original Owner of *shafa'a* and not the idols; since the one who possesses wisdom and ownership of all things becomes the owner of *shafa'a* and not the idols whom they worship which are devoid of both these qualifications. As Qur'an says:

قُلْ أَوَلَوْ كَانُوا لَا يَمْلِكُونَ شَيْئًا

"Say, "Even though they do not possess [power over] anything, (Zumar:43)

Therefore, the pivot of discussion of this verse is that God is the Owner of *shafa'a* and not the idols and in whomsoever He sees worth and merit, He gives the right of *shafa'a* (and not to the idols). Therefore, this verse has no relation with the topic of our discussion because the Muslims consider only God as the Owner of *shafa'a* and not the beloved ones of God. They believe that only those who are having His permission can do *shafa'a* and not everybody. They also believe that by the decree of verses and traditions, God has authorized the Holy

Prophet (s) to do *shafa'a*. Thus, they seek *shafa'a* from him as one authorized person (and not as the Owner of *shafa'a*). As such, what is the relation between the discussion and the contents of this verse?

5. Seeking *Shafa'a* from the Dead is Useless

Their last reasoning is that seeking *shafa'a* from the *Awliya Allah* is (like) seeking fulfilment of needs from the dead who are lacking the hearing sense. The Holy Qur'an explains the dead to be unworthy. As it says:

إِنَّكَ لَا تُسْمِعُ الْمَوْتَىٰ وَلَا تُسْمِعُ الصُّمَّ الدُّعَاءَ إِذَا وَلَّوْا مُدْبِرِينَ

"Surely you do not make the dead to hear, and you do not make the deaf to hear the call when they go back retreating. (Naml:80)"

In this verse, the Holy Qur'an likens the polytheists to the dead and informs us that just as the dead are not capable of understanding, in the same manner; it is not possible for you to make this group to understand. If the dead were capable of speaking and hearing, then it was not proper to compare the dead-hearted polytheists to the group of dead people.

إِنَّ اللَّهَ يُسْمِعُ مَنْ يَشَاءُ وَمَا أَنْتَ بِمُسْمِعٍ مَنْ فِي الْقُبُورِ

"Surely Allah makes whom He pleases hear, and you cannot make those hear who are in the graves. (Fatir:22)"

The analysis of this verse is the same as the analysis of the previous verse. Thus, seeking *shafa'a* from a person is like seeking (something) from an inanimate object.

Reply

This group always finds fault with the other sects of Islam through the door of *shirk* (polytheism) and as supporters of monotheism, they seek to label others as *kafir* (unbelievers). But, in this analysis, they have changed the form of this discussion and have presented the matter of uselessness of paying attention to the *awliya*. However, they are completely unaware that:

The *Awliya Allah* by the blessings of rational[4] and narrative[5] reasoning, are alive and living. The objective of this verse is not to prove that the bodies which have been laid to rest are not capable of understanding and anybody from which the soul has been detached, is unable to perceive and understand and turns into an inanimate object.

However, it should be known that what we address is not the hidden body inside the grave but the pure and living spirits which are living with *barzakhi* bodies in the world of *barzakh* and are, as per the Qur'an, alive. We seek *shafa'a* from these spirits and not the concealed bodies in the soil.

If the dead and the hidden bodies inside the soil are not capable of understanding, it does not mean that the spirits (and their good influence) which according to Qur'an are alive and receiving their sustenance in another world are incapable of understanding.

If we say salutations or seek *shafa'a* and or speak to them, our attention is directed to those holy and living spirits and not the hidden bodies inside the soil. If we go for *ziyarat* (visit) of their graves, houses or place of living, it is because we wish by this way, to prepare ourselves for establishing a spiritual relationship with them. Even if we become aware that their bodies have changed to soil (though the Islamic traditions prove contrary to that) still we will seek of reach such instances so that in this way, we prepare for our relationship with these pure spirits.

---

[4] The reasons for abstraction (non-material existence) of soul from matter after the separation of body and its needlessness from material body demands that the soul of man continues and enjoys perception after death too. By providing several reasons, the great Islamic philosophers have proved the eternity of the soul and its superiority over matter and have not left any ambiguity for any impartial person.

[5] The verses of Qur'an, for example, *Surah Aale Imran*: 169, 170; *Surah Nisa*: 41, *Surah Ahzab*: 45, *Surah al-Mu'minun*: 100 and *Surah Ghafir*: 46 prove that life after death continues and we have discussed this matter in the earlier text and chapters.

15

Is Belief in Invisible Power the Basis of *Shirk* (Polytheism)?

There is no doubt that a sincere request for fulfilment of needs is possible only when the person making the request reckons the requested person or entity to be powerful and capable enough to fulfil his need. Sometimes, this power is an apparent and a physical one such as when we ask someone for water and he fills the vessel with it and hands it over to us.

Sometimes too, this power is an invisible power, far from the natural channels and beyond the domain of physical laws. For example, a person believes that Imam Ali (a) could lift the door of the fort of Khaybar which was not within the power of an ordinary man and pull it off not by human power but by an unseen power. Or that 'Isa (a) could, by his curative healing, cure the incurable disease without the use of medicine or any kind of operation.

If belief in this unseen power is such that it is supported by the Power and Will of Allah, it will be similar to the belief in the physical power which does not involve *shirk* (polytheism). This is because the same God who has placed the physical power in that particular person also gives the unseen power to another person but without assuming the creature to be the Creator and without taking that person to be independent of God.

The Views of Wahhabis

They say: If someone asks one of the *Awliya Allah*, whether dead or alive, to cure his sick ones or to find his lost ones or to help him in repaying his debt, such requests involve the belief in the sovereignty and power (of the one whom he asks) where he is prevailing over the natural system and the laws in force in the world of creation. Belief in such sovereignty and power of someone other than God is the same as the belief in the divinity (Godliness) of that person and asking something from him under this bond will be *shirk* (polytheism).

If a thirsty person in the desert asks for water from his servant, he has observed the order prevailing over the laws of nature and such an asking will not be *shirk* (polytheism). However, if he asks water from a Prophet (s) or an Imam who is concealed under the soil or lives in some other place, then such a request involves the belief in his unseen sovereignty (of providing him with water without the physical causes and means) and such a belief is exactly the same as the belief in the divinity of that person.

Abu al-'A'la al-Mawdudi[1] is the one who has emphasized this matter and says:

إن التصوّر الذي لأجله ندعو الإنسان الاله وتستغيثه ويتصرغ إليه هو لا حرم تصور كونه مالكاً للسلطة المهيمنة على قوانين الطبيعة.

"The reason that man calls God and beseeches Him is because he thinks Him as the One possessing sovereignty over the laws of nature and dominance over such power which is outside the scope of the influence and limits of physical laws."[2]

Our Viewpoint

Their basic mistake is that they imagine the belief in the unseen power of someone to be absolute source of polytheism and dualism. They have neither wished nor have been able to differentiate between the power which is dependent on the sovereignty of God and the power which is independent and separate from God. The *shirk* (polytheism) which they speak about is related to the second one.

The Holy Qur'an very explicitly mentions the names of some personalities who all possessed unseen powers and command of their will was dominant over the laws of nature. We shall mention here, from the viewpoint of Qur'an, the names of those *Awliya Allah* who possessed such powers.

1. Unseen Sovereignty of Yusuf (a)

Yusuf (a) tells his brothers as such:

اذْهَبُوا بِقَمِيصِي هَٰذَا فَأَلْقُوهُ عَلَىٰ وَجْهِ أَبِي يَأْتِ بَصِيرًا

---

[1] Syed Abu al-'A'la al-Mawdudi (1903 – 1979 A.D.) was a Pakistani Sunni Hanafi scholar, journalist, imam and political activist and head of Jamaat-e-Islami. His numerous works covered a wide range of topics such as Qur'anic exegesis, hadith, law, philosophy, politics and history.

[2] *Al-Mustalahat al-Arba'a*, page 18.

"Take this my shirt and cast it on my father's face, he will (again) be able to see." (Yusuf:93)

And so when his command was carried out:

فَلَمَّا أَنْ جَاءَ الْبَشِيرُ أَلْقَاهُ عَلَىٰ وَجْهِهِ فَارْتَدَّ بَصِيرًا

Then, as the harbinger of happy news arrived and put the garment over his face his eyesight was restored. (Yusuf:96)"

Apparently, this verse shows that Ya'qub (a) regained his sight owing to the will and acquired power of Yusuf and this action was not the direct act of Allah. Rather, it was the act of Allah through some channel; otherwise there was no reason for Yusuf to order his brothers to put his shirt over their father's face. Instead, it was enough for him to just pray. This action is nothing but the appropriation of the representative of Allah over a part of the world but by the Will of Allah and such a representative is the possessor of unseen sovereignty which Allah gives in special circumstances.

2. Unseen Sovereignty of Musa (a)

Musa (a) is ordered by Allah to strike his staff upon a mountain so that twelve fountains i.e. the number of tribes of the sons of Israel, come out of it. As the Qur'an says:

اضْرِبْ بِعَصَاكَ الْحَجَرَ ۖ فَانْفَجَرَتْ مِنْهُ اثْنَتَا عَشْرَةَ عَيْنًا

"Strike the rock with your staff. So there gushed from it twelve springs. (Baqarah:60)"

In another place he is charged with striking his staff over the sea so that every drop of it becomes the size of mountain for the Bani Israel to pass. As Qur'an says:

فَأَوْحَيْنَا إِلَىٰ مُوسَىٰ أَنِ اضْرِبْ بِعَصَاكَ الْبَحْرَ ۖ فَانْفَلَقَ فَكَانَ كُلُّ فِرْقٍ كَالطَّوْدِ الْعَظِيمِ

"Then we revealed to Musa: Strike the sea with your staff. So it had cloven as under, and each part was like a huge mound. (Ash-Shu'ara:63)"

Here, one cannot imagine that the will and wish of Musa (a) and the striking of his staff played no role in the appearance of the fountains and mountains.

3. Unseen Sovereignty of Sulayman (a)

Prophet Sulayman (a) is a great beloved one of Allah who possessed wide unseen Powers and because of this great divine bounty, he has been described with the sentence وأوتينا من كل شئ in *Surah Naml*, verse 16 and the details of these bounties and talents have come down in *Surah Naml*, verse 17 to 44, *Surah Saba*, verse 12, *Surah Anbiya*, verse 81 and *Surah Sa'ad*, verse 36-40. Referring to these verses will acquaint us with the magnificence of the gifted powers of Sulayman. In order that the readers become aware of these powers, we shall mention some of the verses related to this *wali Allah* so that it becomes clear that belief in the unseen power of the servant of Allah is a matter which Qur'an itself has pointed out.

From the viewpoint of Qur'an, Sulayman (a) had dominancy over the *Jinns* and birds and was aware of the languages of the birds and insects; as Qur'an says:

وَوَرِثَ سُلَيْمَانُ دَاوُودَ وَقَالَ يَا أَيُّهَا النَّاسُ عُلِّمْنَا مَنْطِقَ الطَّيْرِ وَأُوتِينَا مِنْ كُلِّ شَيْءٍ إِنَّ هَذَا لَهُوَ الْفَضْلُ الْمُبِينُ وَحُشِرَ لِسُلَيْمَانَ جُنُودُهُ مِنَ الْجِنِّ وَالْإِنْسِ وَالطَّيْرِ فَهُمْ يُوزَعُونَ حَتَّى إِذَا أَتَوْا عَلَى وَادِ النَّمْلِ قَالَتْ نَمْلَةٌ يَا أَيُّهَا النَّمْلُ ادْخُلُوا مَسَاكِنَكُمْ لَا يَحْطِمَنَّكُمْ سُلَيْمَانُ وَجُنُودُهُ وَهُمْ لَا يَشْعُرُونَ فَتَبَسَّمَ ضَاحِكًا مِنْ قَوْلِهَا وَقَالَ رَبِّ أَوْزِعْنِي أَنْ أَشْكُرَ نِعْمَتَكَ الَّتِي أَنْعَمْتَ عَلَيَّ وَعَلَى وَالِدَيَّ

"And Sulayman was Dawud's heir, and he said: O men! we have been taught the language of birds, and we have been given all things; most surely this is manifest grace. And his hosts of the jinn and the men and the birds were gathered to him, and they were formed into groups. Until when they came to the valley of the Naml, an ant said: O Naml! enter your houses, (that) Sulayman and his hosts may not crush you while they do not Know. So he smiled, wondering at her word, and said: My Lord! grant me that I should be grateful for Thy favor which Thou hast bestowed on me and on my parents. (Naml:16-19)"

If you refer to the story of 'Hud' in Qur'an which was given charge by Sulayman to deliver his message to the Queen of Saba, you will be astonished by the unseen power of Sulayman. Therefore it is requested that you kindly refer and ponder deeply over *Surah Naml*, verses 20-44.

According to the specification of Qur'an, Sulayman possessed unseen dominancy and the movement of the wind took place as per his wish and command. As the verse says:

$$\text{وَلِسُلَيْمَانَ الرِّيحَ عَاصِفَةً تَجْرِي بِأَمْرِهِ إِلَى الْأَرْضِ الَّتِي بَارَكْنَا فِيهَا ۚ وَكُنَّا بِكُلِّ شَيْءٍ عَالِمِينَ}$$

"And (We made subservient) to Sulayman the wind blowing violent, pursuing its course by his command to the land which We had blessed, and We are Knower of all things. (Anbiya:81)"

The point which is worthy of attention is the sentence تجري بأمره which shows that the wind was blowing as per his command.

4. 'Isa (a) and His Unseen Sovereignty

By examining the verses of Qur'an, one can follow the unseen power of 'Isa (a). For indicating his power and position, we present here some verses. The Holy Qur'an narrates from 'Isa (a) as such:

$$\text{أَنِّي أَخْلُقُ لَكُم مِّنَ الطِّينِ كَهَيْئَةِ الطَّيْرِ فَأَنفُخُ فِيهِ فَيَكُونُ طَيْرًا بِإِذْنِ اللَّهِ ۖ وَأُبْرِئُ الْأَكْمَهَ وَالْأَبْرَصَ وَأُحْيِي الْمَوْتَىٰ بِإِذْنِ اللَّهِ ۖ وَأُنَبِّئُكُم بِمَا تَأْكُلُونَ وَمَا تَدَّخِرُونَ فِي بُيُوتِكُمْ ۚ إِنَّ فِي ذَٰلِكَ لَآيَةً لَّكُمْ إِن كُنتُم مُّؤْمِنِينَ}$$

"I create you out of dust like the form of a bird, then I breathe into it and it becomes a bird with Allah's permission and I heal the blind and the leprous, and bring the dead to life with Allah's permission and I inform you of what you should eat and what you should store in your houses, most surely there is a sign in this for you, if you are believers. (Aale Imran:49)"

If 'Isa (a) relates his actions to the Will of God, it is because no Prophet is the possessor of such authority without the Will of God. As verse says:

$$\text{وما كان لرسول أن يأتي بآية إلا بإذن الله}$$

"And it is not in (the power of) an apostle to bring a sign except by Allah's permission. (Ra'd:38)"

On the other hand, 'Isa (a) attributes the unseen actions to himself and says: I cure, I make alive, I give the news. The words أبرئ، أحيي، أنبئكم which are all صيغة مثلكم (the first person) bear witness to this fact, it is not only Yusuf, Musa, Sulayman and 'Isa (a) who possessed unseen powers and supernatural sovereignty but a group of prophets[3] and angels possessed and still possess unseen sovereignty and Qur'an describes Jibra'eel as شديد القوى (mighty in power) and the Angels as فالمدبرات أمراً (regulator of affairs).

---

[3] The discussion about unseen sovereignty of Prophets and *Awliya Allah* is sufficient in this treatise and we have discussed them in detail in our book *'Spiritual power of the Prophets'* and this book (in Persian) has been printed several times.

In Qur'an, the Angels have been introduced as the managers of the affairs of the world, the takers of the lives of people, the protectors and guards of the people, the writers of deeds, the destroyers of sinful nations and tribes, etc., etc. Those who have the basic knowledge of Qur'an are aware that the Angels possess unseen power and by relying on the Will and power of Allah, they perform extra ordinary acts.

If belief in unseen sovereignty involves (belief of) divinity in that person, then, as far as the Qur'an is concerned, all of these prophets and angels should be introduced as الهة gods.[4]

As mentioned before, the solution to this dilemma lies in this that one should differentiate between 'independent power' and 'acquired power'. Belief in independent power (of a creature) is the source of *shirk* (polytheism) in all the circumstances whereas belief in acquired power with regards to any action is monotheism.

So far, it has been clarified that belief in the unseen power of the awliya Allah along with this belief that they are dependent on the eternal Power of God and are only the channels appointed by God, is not only far from *shirk* (polytheism) but is purely *(tawhid)* monotheism. The basis of *tawhid* is not this that the actions which are dependent on the natural powers are related to man and the actions that are dependent on the unseen powers are related to God. Rather, the reality of *tawhid* is to believe that all the powers whether dependent on natural powers or dependent on unseen powers are all related to God and manifest Him to be the prime source of all types of powers and strength.

Now it's time to discuss the matter of asking extraordinary actions from the *Awliya Allah*.[5]

Is it Shirk (Polytheism) to request for Extra-Ordinary Actions?

Any phenomenon, as per the laws of cause and effect, has a cause for itself and the existence of such a phenomenon is not possible without that cause. As a result, no phenomenon remains without a cause in this Universe. Miracles and wonders of the Prophets and other awliya too are not without a cause. The only

---

[4] *Surah al-Najm*: verse 5.
[5] *Surah al-Nazi'at*: verse 5.

thing being that there is no natural and physical cause for them and this differs from saying that there is no cause (at all) for them.

If the staff of Musa (a) is changed into a snake, or the dead are made alive by 'Isa (a) or the moon is cut into two halves by the Holy Prophet (s) of Islam and the pebbles start glorification of God in the hands of the Holy Prophet (s), etc., are all with some cause. The only point is that in these cases, the natural causes or the well-known physical causes are not at work and it is not that they are basically without a cause.

Sometimes it is thought that asking natural actions from someone is not polytheism but asking some extraordinary acts from him is polytheism. Now we shall examine this very view.

Reply

The Holy Qur'an mentions instances where in the Prophets and others have been asked to perform a series of extraordinary acts which are outside the scope of natural and physical laws. The Holy Qur'an narrates these requests without criticizing any of them. For example, the tribe of Musa (a), as per the stipulation of Qur'an, turned towards Musa (a) and asked water and rain from him so that they could be saved from the severe famine. As the Qur'an says:

وَأَوْحَيْنَا إِلَى مُوسَى إِذِ اسْتَسْقَاهُ قَوْمُهُ أَنِ اضْرِب بِعَصَاكَ الْحَجَرَ

"......And we revealed to Musa when his people asked him for water: strike the rock with your staff...." (A'raf:160)"[6]

It is possible that it may be said that there is no objection in asking extraordinary acts from a living person but our point concerns such request from dead people. However the reply is obvious since, life and death cannot bring any change in any action which is in accordance with the principle of monotheism such that we declare one to be polytheism and the other as monotheism. Life and death can have effect on usefulness or un-usefulness but not on polytheism and monotheism.

---

[6] Also refer to *Surah al-Baqarah* verse 60.

Sulayman (a) Seeks the Throne of Bilqis

In summoning the throne of Bilqis, Sulayman (a) asked an extraordinary act from those present in his gathering. He said:

أَيُّكُمْ يَأْتِينِي بِعَرْشِهَا قَبْلَ أَنْ يَأْتُونِي مُسْلِمِينَ قَالَ عِفْرِيتٌ مِنَ الْجِنِّ أَنَا آتِيكَ بِهِ قَبْلَ أَنْ تَقُومَ مِنْ مَقَامِكَ وَإِنِّي عَلَيْهِ لَقَوِيٌّ أَمِينٌ قَالَ الَّذِي عِنْدَهُ عِلْمٌ مِنَ الْكِتَابِ أَنَا آتِيكَ بِهِ قَبْلَ أَنْ يَرْتَدَّ إِلَيْكَ طَرْفُكَ فَلَمَّا رَآهُ مُسْتَقِرًّا عِنْدَهُ قَالَ هَذَا مِنْ فَضْلِ رَبِّي

"Which of you can bring to me her throne before they come to me in submission?' One audacious among the jinn said: 'I will bring it to you before you rise up from your place, and most surely I am strong (and) trusty for it.' One who had the knowledge of the Book said: 'I will bring it to you in the twinkling of an eye.' Then when he saw it settled beside him, he said: 'This is by the grace of my Lord.'" (Naml:38-40)

If such views (asking for extraordinary acts is polytheism) are true, then asking miracles in all ages and times from the claimants of Prophethood is blasphemy and polytheism. This is because the people asked for miracles (which required extraordinary acts) from those claiming to be prophets; not from God who has sent them. They were told as such:

إِنْ كُنْتَ جِئْتَ بِآيَةٍ فَأْتِ بِهَا إِنْ كُنْتَ مِنَ الصَّادِقِينَ

"If you have come with a sign, then bring it, if you are of the truthful ones. (A'raf:106)"

All the nations of the world used to employ this method in recognizing the true prophets from the false ones and the prophets were always inviting the nations to come and see their miracles. The Qur'an too narrates, without objection, the people's demand for miracles from the Prophets which shows its acceptance of this matter.

If people wishing to investigate come to 'Isa (a) and say: 'If you are truthful in your claim, then you cure this blind or that one suffering from leprosy'. Then, not only has he not become a polytheist but he will be counted amongst the holy men and will be praised in this action. Now, if after the (apparent) demise of 'Isa (a), his people ask his holy soul to cure another sick one amongst them, then why should he be regarded as polytheist when the life and death of that person plays no role in polytheism and monotheism.[7]

---

[7] For more information about the miracles of 'Isa (a), refer to *Surah Aale 'Imran:* verse 49 and *Surah Ma'idah:* verses 100 and 110.

In short, as per the specification of Qur'an, a group of selected servants of Allah possessed the power of performing extraordinary acts. They would utilize these powers in certain circumstances and sometimes too, the people would approach and ask them to put these powers into action. If the Wahhabis say that no one possesses the power to fulfil these affairs, then these verses bear witness contrary to their saying.

If they reckon such asking to be polytheism, then why did Sulayman and the others make such a request? If they say: Asking for fulfilment of one's need from the *awliya* through extraordinary means involves the belief in their unseen sovereignty then our reply is that unseen sovereignty is of two types; one is pure monotheism and the other the source of polytheism.

If they say that asking miracles only from the divine living personalities is proper and not from the dead, then we reply that life and death are not the basis of polytheism or monotheism.

If they say that asking cure for the sick by unusual means is (like) asking for the actions of Allah from someone other than Him. We say that the basis of polytheism is to consider that person as God and that he is source of divine activities. Asking for some unnatural act is not similar to asking for the acts of Allah from someone other than Him. This is because the standard to judge an Act of Allah is not that it should be above the limits of ordinary laws so that such requests becomes (the same as) requests for His Acts from someone else. Rather, the criterion for an Act of Allah is this that the doer should be independent in performing that act. If a doer performs an act relying on the divine power, then to ask such an act will not be considered as asking for the Act of Allah from someone other than Him and it makes no difference whether that act is ordinary or unusual.

Regarding specific request for cure from the servants of Allah, we say: Sometimes it is imagined that asking for cure and the like of it from the *awliya* is (the same as) asking for the Acts of Allah from someone other than Him and the Qur'an says:

وَإِذَا مَرِضْتُ فَهُوَ يَشْفِينِ

"And when I am sick, then He restores me to health. (Ash-Shu'ara:80)"

So, how can we say: "O Prophet of Allah, cure my sickness! The same is true for all that we ask which are of extraordinary nature."

Reply

This group has still not been able to differentiate the divine acts from the human acts. They imagine that any act which is not by natural way should be called as the divine act and any act which is having natural aspect and physical cause should be called as human act.

This group does not wish and is unable to compare the scale or measure of divine act from the human act. The measure for divine and human acts is never to see whether that act is ordinary or not; otherwise we have to consider the works of magicians as divine acts and consider themselves as Gods.

Rather, the measure in the divine acts is this that the doer depends on Himself in His actions and does not seek help from anyone. Such an act is a divine act. However, if a doer who performs his acts under the light of divine power will be a non-divine one, whether that act is having a physical and ordinary aspect or is something extraordinary.

While performing any act whether ordinary or outside the scope of laws of nature, man always depends on God and seeks help from His power and any act which he performs is fulfilled under the light of such power which is acquired from God. Therefore, possessing such power and similarly, the ability to fulfil our wishes and requests by them are never a source of polytheism because in all the stages we say that God has given them such power and God has authorized them to utilize it.

The great teacher, Imam Khomeini (ra)[8] says about divine acts as such:

"The divine act is that act where its performer performs it without interference from outside and without seeking help from another power."

In other words, the divine act is that act which is performed independently and its performer is needless of others. Non-divine act is exactly opposite to this.

---

[8] For more discussion and details on such topics, refer to two books by Imam Khomeini (ra) (1902 -1989 A.D.): *Forty Hadith- An exposition* available at: https://www.al-islam.org/forty-hadith-exposition-second-revised-edition-sayyid-ruhullah-musawi-khomeini and *Adab as-Salat: The Disciplines of the Prayer* available at: https://www.al-islam.org/adab-salat-disciplines-prayer-second-revised-edition-sayyid-ruhullah-musawi-khomeini

God creates the Universe, gives sustenance and cures the sick without seeking help from any power. No one interferes in His affairs either wholly or partially and His Power and Strength is not acquired from anyone.

However, if someone other than God performs an act, whether ordinary and simple or extraordinary and difficult, his power is not from himself. He does not perform that action by his own power.[9]

In other words, whenever we believe a being to be independent either from the viewpoint of existence or influence, we will deviate from the path of monotheism. This is because belief in independence in the original existence is similar to his being needless of God in existence. Such a being can be no one except Allah Who is needless of anything in life and His existence is related only to Himself.

Similarly, if we consider his existence to be created by Allah but believe that he is independent in his actions whether ordinary and simple or extraordinary and difficult then in such a case, we have inclined towards polytheism. This is because independence in action finally leads to independence in the original life and existence and if we consider an ignorant Arab to be polytheist it is because they believed that the charge of running the affairs of the world and or the affairs of the people have been transferred and entrusted to their gods and they are independent in them.

Such was the belief of most of the polytheists during the period of ignorance and at the time of the advent of Islam. They believed that the angels and or the stars (which are created ones) were managing the affairs[10] or that at least some of the divine affairs like *shafa'a* and 'forgiveness' were entrusted to them and they were having complete freedom in them.

If the group of Mu'tazalites[11], who reckon man to be the creation of God (from the viewpoint of existence) but believe him to be independent in actions

---

[9] *Kashf al-Asrar*, page 51.
[10] When 'Amr bin Lahi asked the Syrians the reason for worshipping idols they replied: *"We ask rain from them and they send rain for us, we seek help and they help us"*. With this belief, he took the idol of Habal to Mecca. (Refer to *Sira Ibn Hisham*, vol. 1 page 77).
[11] Mu'tazila is a school of Islamic theology that flourished in the cities of Basra and Baghdad, during 8th to 10th centuries A.D. It was founded in 8th century in Basra by Waṣil ibn 'Ata' (d. 748 A.D.). Mu'tazila school of theology was opposed to Ash'arism or Ash'ari theology which was theological school of Sunni Islam founded by the Arab theologian Abu al-Hasan al-Ash'ari (d. 936 A.D.).

and efficacy, ponder deeply over their own sayings, then surely they will realize that such a belief is one kind of hidden *shirk* (polytheism) even though it is not equal to the *shirk* of the polytheists. The difference between these two types of *shirk* is clear. One claims independence in managing the affairs of the world and the divine affairs while the other claims independence of man in his own affairs.

16

Pleading Allah by the Right and Position of *Awliya*

One of the point of differences between the Wahhabi sect and the other sects of Islam is this that the former manifest two kinds of pleading as *harām* (forbidden) and occasionally as *shirk* (polytheism) in *'ibadah*.

These two kinds of pleading are:

1. Pleading Allah by the right and position of *awliya*
2. Pleading to someone other than Allah.

Now, we shall discuss both of these topics in this chapter.

Pleading Allah by the Position of *Awliya*

The Holy Qur'an praises different groups under such titles as:

الصَّابِرِينَ وَالصَّادِقِينَ وَالْقَانِتِينَ وَالْمُنْفِقِينَ وَالْمُسْتَغْفِرِينَ بِالْأَسْحَارِ

"The patient, and the truthful, and the obedient, and those who spend (benevolently) and those who ask forgiveness in the morning times. (Aale Imran:17)"

Now, if someone in the middle of the night, after the mid-night prayers, turns towards his Lord and pleads God by the right and position of this group and says:

اللهم إني أسئلك بحق المستغفرين بالأسحار اغفر لي ذنوبي

"O Allah, I ask Thee by the right of those asking forgiveness at twilight to forgive my sins."

How can one call this action as *shirk* in *'ibadah* since *shirk* in *'ibadah* is this when we worship someone other than Allah and consider him as God or the source of divine affairs? While, in this benediction, we have not paid attention to other than Allah and we have asked only from Allah and nobody else.

Therefore, if such an action is forbidden, it should have some other reason than *shirk*. At this stage, we shall remind the Wahhabi writers of one point and it is the fact that the Holy Qur'an has mentioned as a criterion for differentiating a polytheist (of course *shirk* in *'ibadah*) from a monotheist and with this explanation, has closed any kind of interpretation of the word of polytheist according to one's personal opinion. This criterion is as follows:

وَإِذَا ذُكِرَ اللَّهُ وَحْدَهُ اشْمَأَزَّتْ قُلُوبُ الَّذِينَ لَا يُؤْمِنُونَ بِالْآخِرَةِ وَإِذَا ذُكِرَ الَّذِينَ مِنْ دُونِهِ إِذَا هُمْ يَسْتَبْشِرُونَ

"And when Allah alone is mentioned, the hearts of those who do not believe in the hereafter shrink, and when those besides Him are mentioned, lo! they are joyful. (Zumar:45)"

In another verse it describes the offenders who are the same polytheists as such:

إِنَّهُمْ كَانُوا إِذَا قِيلَ لَهُمْ لَا إِلَهَ إِلَّا اللَّهُ يَسْتَكْبِرُونَ وَيَقُولُونَ أَئِنَّا لَتَارِكُو آلِهَتِنَا لِشَاعِرٍ مَجْنُونٍ

"Surely they used to behave proudly when it was said to them: there is no god but Allah; And to say: What! shall we indeed give up our gods for the sake of a mad poet? (Safaat:35-36)"

According to the contents of these two verses, a polytheist is the one whose heart gets disgusted by remembering the Unique God and becomes happy in remembering the others (false gods) and or behaves proudly if asked to confess in the Oneness of God.

As per this criterion, can we label the one who in the middle of the night, calls nobody but Allah and takes pleasure from His remembrance to such extent that he forbids upon himself the sweet and pleasant sleep and instead, beseeches Him and pleads to Him by the position of the monotheist servants who are His beloved ones as a polytheist? Has he, in such a situation, turned away from the remembrance of Allah or has he acted with haughtiness from confessing His Oneness!?

Why have the Wahhabi writers with unknown and imaginary norms, named all the monotheists as polytheists and reckoned themselves to be the beloved ones of Allah?

By paying attention to this criterion, one cannot call ninety-nine percent of the people of *qibla* as polytheists and reckon only the group of Najdi's to be monotheists.

The interpretation of *shirk* in *'ibadah* has not been left to our discretion and we have no authority to interpret it in the way we like and label any group that we assume as polytheists!

Amir al-Mu'minin and His Pleading to God by the Position of the Holy Ones

In the prayers of Amir al-mu'minin Ali (a) we can find such pleadings very clearly.

After finishing the night *'Nafila'* (Supererogatory) prayers, Imam (a) would recite this dua:

اللَّهُمَّ إِنِّي أَسْأَلُكَ بِحُرْمَةِ مَنْ عَاذَ بِكَ وَلَجَأَ إِلَى عِزِّكَ واسْتَظَلَّ بِفَيْنِكَ واعْتَصَمَ بِحَبْلِكَ وَلَمْ يَثِقْ إِلَّا بِكَ

"O Allah, I ask Thee by the honor of the one who seeks refuge in Thy repentance (he thinks of no shelter other than thee) and who seeks protection in Thy Honor and who is under the shadow of Thy protection and who has seized Thy rope and has not attached himself to anyone except Thee." [1]

In another invocation too, which Imam Ali (a) taught one of his followers, he says as such:

وبحق السائلين عليك ، والراغبين إليك ، والمُتعوذين بك ، والمُتصغرين إليك ، وبحق كل عبدٍ متعبد لك في كل برٍ أو بحرٍ أو سهلٍ أو جبل أدعوك دعاء من اشتدّت فاقته

"O Allah, by the right of the questioners and those who turn their attention and seek refuge in Thee; and those who are humble before Thee; and by the right of every worshipper who worships Thee in land and in sea, in desert and in the mountains, we call Thee; like the calling of the one whose helplessness has reached the extremes."[2]

Is it not that such soul provoking prayers and expression of such feelings before Allah brings no result other than strengthening monotheism! (except for Allah there is no other refuge) and what else can we derive from expression of affection for the friends of Allah which itself is one way of paying attention to Allah!?

Therefore, we should overlook the charge of blasphemy and polytheism which can be found more than any other thing in the 'kit' of the Wahhabis and the matter should be looked from another angle.

On this basis, some of the moderates amongst them have mooted the matter of 'pleading Allah by the *awliya*' within the limits of prohibition and aversion. Contrary to the extreme al-San'ani who ruled the matter of pleading within the circle of blasphemy and polytheism, they do not talk about it as blasphemy and polytheism.

---

[1] *Sahifah al-'Alawiyya*, Islamic Publications, page 370.
[2] *Sahifah al-'Alawiyya*, page 51.

Now that the main theme of discussion has been made clear and it is known that the matter should be discussed within the framework of *harām* (forbidden) and *makruh* (abominable) it is necessary to prove the authenticity of such *tawassul* (recourse).

Occurrence of such pleadings in Islam

In Islamic traditions too, one can find such type of pleadings and with the presence of such firm traditions that have come down partly from the Holy Prophet (s) and partly from his Ahl al-Bayt (a), one cannot consider such pleadings as *harām* or *makruh*.

The Holy Prophet (s) trained that blind person to say as such:

اللهم إني أسألك وأتوجه إليك بنبيك محمد نبيّ الرحمة

"Oh God, I ask you and seek your attention for the sake of your prophet Muhammad, the merciful Prophet."[3]

Abu Sa'eed al-Khudri has narrated from the Holy Prophet (s) the following *du'a*:

اللهم إني أسألك بحق السائلين عليك وأسألك بحق ممشاي هذا

"Oh God I ask for the sake of those who ask for and I ask you for the sake of the followers of this matter."[4]

Adam (a) repented as such:

أسألك بحق محمد إلا غفرت لي

"I ask you by the right of Muhammad to forgive me."[5]

When the Holy Prophet (s) buried the mother of Ali (a), he recited this invocation for her:

اغفر لأمي فاطمة بنت أسد ووسّع عليها مدخلها بحق نبيك والأنبياء الذين من قبلي

"Forgive my mother Fatima the daughter of Asad and by the right of your Prophet and the Prophets before him and make her place vast and wide (and save her from the torment of grave)."[6]

---

[3] *Sunan Ibn Majah*, vol.1, page 441; *Musnad Ahmad*, vol. 3, page 1388; *Mustadrak al-Hakim*, vol.1, page 313; and others.
[4] *Sunan Ibn Majah*, vol.1, page 261, 262; *Musnad Ahmad*, vol. 3, hadith no. 21.
[5] *Al-Durr al-Manthur*, vol.1, page 59; *Mustadrak al-Hakim*, vol. 2, page 615; *Ruh al-Ma'ani*, vol. 1, page 217. (In the chapter of *tawassul*, this tradition was mentioned with greater context).
[6] *al-Fusul al-Muhimma*, page 31 by Ibn al-Sabbagh al-Maliki (d. 855 AH).

Although in these types of sentences the word of pleading has not been explicitly mentioned yet, the true purpose of them, by the decree of باء refers to pleading to Allah by the rights (بحق) of the *awliya*. When they say *"O God, I ask You by the right of the questioners"* it means *"I plead You by their rights."*

The supplications that have been narrated from the fourth Imam (a) in *al-Sahifa al-Sajjadiyya* is itself a clear proof upon the authenticity and soundness of such *tawassul*. The splendid meanings of the supplications in *al-Sahifa* and the eloquence and meanings of sentences makes us needless to mention its authenticity and its attribution to Imam.

Imam al-Sajjad (a) used to secretly converse with Allah on the day of Arafat as such;

بحق من أنتجبت من خلقك وبمن اصطفيته لنفسك بحق من اخترت ، من بريّتك ، ومن إجتبيت لشأنك ، بحق من وصلت طاعته ومن نُطت معاداته بمعاداتك

"O God, by the right of those whom You have selected from Your other creatures; by the right of those people whom You have vested authority and have created them for acquainting (the people) of Your position; by the right of those pure ones whom You have connected their obedience to Your obedience and their enmity to Your enmity."[7]

When Imam al-Sadiq (a) performed *ziyarat* of his great grandfather Amir al-mu'minin (a), he concluded his prayers as such:

اللَّهُمَّ فَاسْتَجِبْ دُعَائِي وَ اقْبَلْ ثَنَائِي وَ اجْمَعْ بَيْنِي وَ بَيْنَ أَوْلِيَائِي بِحَقِّ مُحَمَّدٍ وَ عَلِيٍّ وَ فَاطِمَةَ وَ الْحَسَنِ وَ الْحُسَيْنِ

"O God respond to my prayers and accept my glorification (of You) and by the right of Muhammad, 'Ali, Fatima, al-Hasan and al-Husayn (a) unite us with Thy beloved ones."[8]

It is not only Imam al-Sajjad (a) and Imam al-Sadiq (a) who in their invocations pleaded to Allah by the right of His beloved ones but, in the supplications of other Shi'a Imams too, one can find such *tawassul*.

The noble leader, Imam Husayn ibn Ali (a) in one of the supplications says:

---

[7] *Sahifah al-Sajjadiyya*, du'a no. 47. Accessible with English translation at: https://www.al-islam.org/sahifa-al-kamilah-sajjadiyya-imam-zain-ul-abideen

[8] *Ziyarat* of Aminullah. It is ziyarat of Imam Ali (a). Accessible with English translation at: https://www.al-islam.org/supplications-month-ramadhan/ziyarat-ameenullah

اَللّٰهُمَّ اِنّی اَسْأَلُکَ بِکَلِماتِکَ وَ مَعاقِدَ عَرْشِکَ وَ سُکّانِ سَماواتِکَ وَ اَرْضِکَ وَ اَنْبِیائِکَ وَ رُسُلِکَ اَنْ تَسْتَجیبَ لی، فَقَدْ رَهَقَنی مِنْ أمری عُسراً ، فَأسْألُکَ اَنْ تُصَلِّیَ عَلی مُحَمَّدٍ وَ الِ مُحَمَّدٍ وَ اَنْ تَجْعَلَ لی مِن عُسْری یُسْراً

"O Allah, I ask You by Your words and the center of Your honor; and by the inhabitants of the heavens and the land; and by your Prophets and Messengers that You answer my prayers for my affairs have become difficult. I ask You to send salutations upon Muhammad and his progeny and to make my affairs easy."

These kinds of supplications are so numerous that narrating all of them will lengthen our discussion. It is better that we cut short our discussion here and mention the reasoning and objections of the opposition.

First Objection

The scholars of Islam are unanimous in their decision that pleading to Allah by the way of a creature or by the right of a creature is *harām* (forbidden).[9]

Reply

The meaning of unanimity or rather consensus is this that the scholars of Islam in every period of history or in all the eras are unanimous in their opinion over a decree derived from the commandments.

In such a case, the viewpoint of the scholars of Ahl al-Sunnah and their consensus of opinion is itself one of the divine proofs. The Shi'a scholars consider this to be a divine proof from this viewpoint that it is springs from the Infallible Imam's counsel (who lives among the people) and his approval.

Now we ask whether such type of consensus of opinion exists in this matter. We keep aside the Shi'a and other Ahl al-Sunnah scholars and consider the opinion of the leaders of the four schools of thought only. Have the leaders of these four schools of thought given *fatwa* (verdict) that the matter of pleading is forbidden? If they have given such verdict, we request them to produce the text of their verdicts along with the name of the book and the page number.

Basically, such type of *tawassul* has not been propounded in the books of *fiqh* (jurisprudence) and *hadith* belonging to the scholars of Ahl al-Sunnah so that they can express their opinion about them. In such a case, how can there be

---

[9] *Kashf al-'Irtiyab*, page 32 narrated from *al-Hadiyyat al-Saniyya*.

unanimity and consensus as claimed by the author of *al-Hadiyyah al-Saniyyah*?[10] The only person whom he says has prohibited this matter is an unknown figure by the name of al-'Izz bin 'Abd al-Salam. As if the opinions of all the scholars of Islam is considered by the author of *al-Hadiyyah al-Saniyyah* into the single opinion of al-'Izz bin 'Abd al-Salam.

Thereafter, he has narrated from Abu Hanifa and his student Abu Yusuf that both of them too have said that it is *makruh* (abominable) to say 'by the right of so and so'.

In short, there does not exist any proof in the name of consensus (اجماع) in this matter. What worth can the *fatwa* (verdict) of these two persons have in comparison to the firm tradition of the Holy Prophet (s) and his Ahl al-Bayt which according to the consensus of the traditionists of Ahl al-Sunnah are and their sayings a proof.[11] Moreover, the authenticity of attributing this *fatwa* to Abu Hanifa is also not proved.

Second Objection

إن المسألة بحق المخلوق لا تجوز لأنه لا حق للمخلوق على الخالق

"Asking Allah by the right of a creature is not permissible because the one who is created has no right before the Creator."[12]

Reply

Such reasoning is nothing but *ijtihad* (independent reasoning) compared to explicit text. If really a creature has no right before the Creator then why in the previous traditions, Adam (a) and the Holy Prophet (s) of Islam (s) pleaded o Allah by such rights and asked Allah by these same rights?

Besides, how should we justify the verses of the Qur'an? In certain instances, the Qur'an has explicitly indicated that the servants of Allah to possess a right upon Allah. The same is mentioned in Islamic traditions (hadiths).

These are the verses:

وَكَانَ حَقًّا عَلَيْنَا نَصْرُ الْمُؤْمِنِينَ

---

[10] *al-Hadiyyah al-Saniyyah wa-al-Tuhfah al-Wahhabiyyah al-Najdiyyah* written by Sulayman bin Sihman al-Najdi, published by the orders of the ruler of Najd, 'Abdul 'Aziz al-Sa'ud in 1342 A.H.

[11] *Hadith al-Thaqalayn* is an authentic tradition and none denies its authenticity except for the obstinate. For its authenticity kindly see: https://www.al-islam.org/hadith-al-thaqalayn

[12] *Kashf al-'Irtiyab*, p.331, narrated from al-Qaduri.

"And helping the believers is ever incumbent on Us. (Rum:47)"

وَعْدًا عَلَيْهِ حَقًّا فِي التَّوْرَاةِ وَالْإِنْجِيلِ

"A promise which is binding on Him in the Torah and the Injil (Tawbah:111)"

كَذَٰلِكَ حَقًّا عَلَيْنَا نُنْجِ الْمُؤْمِنِينَ

"It is binding on us (that) We deliver the believers. (Yunus:103)"

إِنَّمَا التَّوْبَةُ عَلَى اللَّهِ لِلَّذِينَ يَعْمَلُونَ السُّوءَ بِجَهَالَةٍ

"Repentance with Allah is only for those who do evil in ignorance. (Nisa:17)"

Is it proper to interpret so many of these verses just for the sake of propagation of groundless dogmatic ideas?

Now some examples from traditions:

حقٌّ على الله عون من نكح إلتماس العفاف مما حرَّم الله

"It is a right upon Allah to help the one who marries because of protecting his chastity from the forbidden acts."[13]

قال رسول الله : ثلاثة حق على الله عونُهم: الغازي في سبيل الله والمكاتب الذي يريد الأداء ، والناكح الذي يريد التعنف

"The Holy Prophet (s) said: "There are three groups of people to whom help is an obligation upon Allah. A warrior in the path of Allah, a servant who agrees to pay a sum to his master for his release and a youth who wishes to protect his honor by way of marriage."[14]

أتدري ما حق العباد على الله...

"Do you not see the obligation which is upon Allah with regards to His slaves?"[15]

Let it not remain unmentioned here that, essentially, no person is having any right even though he may worship God and remain humble before him for ages. This is because whatever a person possesses is from Allah and he has not used any of his own resources in the way of Allah so that it can be compensated in the form of reward.

---

[13] al-Suyuti, *al-Jami' al-Saghir*, vol. 2 page 33.
[14] *Sunan Ibn Majah*, vol. 2 page 841.
[15] *Al-Bidayah wal Nihayah*, Ibn Kathir, under "حق".

Therefore, the meaning of this right in such cases is the very divine rewards and positions which Allah, due to His special favors has bestowed upon them and entrusted (these favors) upon Himself. Such a right (or obligation) upon Allah is the sign of His Greatness and Magnificence.

No creature has any right upon Allah except if Allah, due to His Mercy and Favor, justifies it upon Himself and shows that His creatures as creditors and Himself as debtor.

This matter that a creature possesses a right upon Him is similar to seeking of loan by Allah from His poor servants. These commitments and obligations which He has promised is due to His Grace and Honor. Moreover, with utmost Grace, He has considered Himself to be indebted to His virtuous servants and has presented them as owners of rights and Himself as and an obligor.[16]

Swearing Upon Other Than Allah

Swearing (someone or something) upon other than Allah is a matter which is very sensitive for the Wahhabis.

One of their writers by the name of al-San'ani[17] in his book *Tathir al-I'tiqad*[18] has reckoned it to be the source of *shirk* (polytheism)[19] and the author of *al-Hadiyyah al-Saniyyah* has called it as minor *shirk*.[20]

However we shall, by the Grace of God, discuss the matter without any prejudice and will take into account the Qur'an and the true *sunnah* of the Prophet (s) and inerrant Imams as the radiant of source for our guidance in this matter.

Our Proofs for Permissibility of Swearing upon Other than Allah
First Proof

Qur'an is the leader, the *al-Thaql al-Akbar* (Greater Weight) and the living symbol of every Muslim. In this book, one can find tens of swearings upon other

---

[16] *Surah al-Baqarah*: 245. "مَّن ذَا الَّذِي يُقْرِضُ اللَّهَ قَرْضًا حَسَنًا فَيُضَاعِفَهُ لَهُ أَضْعَافًا كَثِيرَةً"
[17] Muhammad ibn Isma'il al-San'ani
[18] *Tathir i'tiqad 'an adran al-Ilhad* published by Dar al-Kutub al-'Ilmiyah, Beirut, 1994.
[19] *Kashf al-'Irtiyab*, page 336 narrated from the book *Tathir al-I'tiqad*, p. 14.
[20] Above reference, narrated from the book *al-Hadiyyat al-Saniyya*, p. 25.

than Allah which, if we were to gather all of them in this book, it would lengthen our discussion.

In *Surah al Shams* alone, Allah Himself swore by eight things from His creation. They are: Sun, its light, moon, day, night, heavens, earth and the human soul.[21]

Similarly, in *Surah al-Nazi'at*, one can find such swearing for three things[22] and in *Surah al-Mursalat* for two things[23]. In the same manner, such swearings have been mentioned in *Surah al-Buruj, Surah al-Tariq, Surah al-Qalam, Surah al-'Asr,* and *Surah al-Balad*.

Once more, we remind you of some examples from the Qur'an.

وَالتِّينِ وَالزَّيْتُونِ وَطُورِ سِينِينَ وَهَٰذَا الْبَلَدِ الْأَمِينِ

"I swear by the fig and the olive, and Mount Sinai, and this city made secure." (Teen:1-3)

وَاللَّيْلِ إِذَا يَغْشَىٰ وَالنَّهَارِ إِذَا تَجَلَّىٰ

"I swear by the night when it draws a veil, and the day when it shines in brightness. (Lail:1-2)"

وَالْفَجْرِ وَلَيَالٍ عَشْرٍ وَالشَّفْعِ وَالْوَتْرِ وَاللَّيْلِ إِذَا يَسْرِ

"I swear by the daybreak, And the ten nights, And the even and the odd, And the night when it departs. (Fajr:1-4)"

وَالطُّورِ وَكِتَابٍ مَسْطُورٍ فِي رَقٍّ مَنْشُورٍ وَالْبَيْتِ الْمَعْمُورِ وَالسَّقْفِ الْمَرْفُوعِ وَالْبَحْرِ الْمَسْجُورِ

"I swear by the Mountain, And the Book written. In an outstretched fine parchment. And the House (Ka'ba) that is visited, and the elevated canopy, and the swollen sea. (Tur:1-6)"

لَعَمْرُكَ إِنَّهُمْ لَفِي سَكْرَتِهِمْ يَعْمَهُونَ

"By your life! they were blindly wandering on in their intoxication. (Hijr:72)"

---

[21] *Surah al-Shams* verse: 1 to 7.
[22] *Surah al-Nazi'at* verse: 1 to 3.
[23] *Surah al-Mursalat* verse: 1 to 3.

With such successive swearings in Qur'an, can one say that it is polytheism and (*harām*) forbidden?

Qur'an is the book of guidance and it is an example to follow and a model to adopt. If such a matter was forbidden for the people it was necessary for it (i.e. Qur'an) to mention that such swearings are the specific to Allah only.

Some of the ungifted men who are unaware of the Qur'anic aims, reply in this manner that it is possible that a thing issued from God's side is good but the same thing issued from someone other than God may not be good.

However the reply is obvious. Because truly, if the reality of swearing upon someone or something other than God is polytheism and same as likening that person to God, then why such an absolute or a minor polytheism has been committed by God? Is it right that God practically considers a partner for Himself but forbids others from considering such a partner to Him!?

Second Proof

In certain instances, the Holy Prophet (s) has sweared upon someone other than Allah.

1. Tradition from *Sahih Muslim*

جاء رجل إلى النبيّ فقال يا رسول الله أي الصدقة أعظم اجراً؟ فقال أما وابيك لتنبأنه ، أن تصدق وأنت صحيح شجيح تخشى الفقر وتأمل البقاء

"A person approached the Holy Prophet (s) and said: 'O Prophet of Allah, which charity bears the greatest reward?' The Holy Prophet (s) replied: 'I swear by your father that very soon, I will inform you about it. The charity which bears the greatest reward is the charity that you give when you are healthy and in need of it and when you fear from poverty and think of your future life.'"[24]

2. Another Tradition from *Sahih Muslim*

جاء رجل إلى رسول الله مِن نجد يسأل عن الإسلام فقال رسول الله (صلى الله عليه وأله): خمس صلوات في اليوم والليل فقال: هل عليَّ غيرهم؟ قال: لا إلا أن تطوَّع وصيام شهر رمضان فقال: هل عليَّ غيره؟ قال لا أن تطوَّع وذكر له رسول الله (صلى الله عليه وأله) الزكاة فقال: هل عليَّ غيره قال لا إلا أن تطوَّع فأدبر الرجل وهو يقول والله لا أزيد على هذا ولا أنقص منه فقال رسول الله أفلح إن صدق أو دخل الجنة وأبيه إن صدق.

"A person from Najd approached the Holy Prophet (s) and questioned him about Islam. The Holy Prophet (s) replied: 'The foundations of Islam are the following: The daily five

---

[24] *Sahih Muslim*, Book of zakat part 3; chapter of 'Best charity' page 94.

prayers. The Najdi man said: 'Is there any other salat other than these salat?' The Holy Prophet (s) replied: 'Yes they are mustahab (recommendable).' Fasting in the month of Ramadan. The man said: 'Is there any other fasting other than these fasting?' The Holy Prophet (s) replied: 'Yes they are mustahab.' Zakat. The man said: 'Is there any other zakat?' The Holy Prophet (s) replied? 'Yes they are mustahab.' The Najdi man left the Holy Prophet (s) while saying: 'I shall neither add nor deduct.' The Holy Prophet (s) said: 'I swear by his father that he will be successful if he speaks the truth; I swear by his father that he will enter paradise if he speaks the truth.'[25]

3. Tradition from *al-Musnad* of Ahmad ibn Hanbal:

فلعمري لأن تكلم بمعروف وتنهى عن مُنكر خير من أن تسكت

"I swear by my life that 'enjoining good and forbidding evil' is better than silence."[26]

There are many other similar traditions and it will get very lengthy if we were to narrate all of them.[27]

Amir al-mu'minin Ali bin Abi Talib (a) who is an esteemed example of Islamic training has repeatedly sweared by his life in his sermons, letters and sayings.[28] Even the first Caliph swears in his conversations by the father of the addressee.[29]

The Four Schools of Thought and the Matter of Swearing upon other than Allah

Before examining the reasoning of the Wahhabis, it is necessary to know the *fatawa* (verdicts) of the leaders of the four schools of thought.[30]

The Hanafis believe that swearing such as "I swear by your father and your life" and the like of it are *makruh* (abominable).

The Shafi'is believe that swearing by someone other than Allah is abominable but not similar seeking partner for Him and not as a trust.

The Malikis say: "Swearing by the great and holy existences like Prophet, Ka'ba and the like of them has two interpretations: *makruh* and *haram* and what is famous is to honor."

---

[25] *Sahih Muslim*, part 1 chapter of 'What is Islam and its qualities' page 32.
[26] *Musnad Ahmad ibn Hanbal*, vol. 5, page 225.
[27] Refer to *Musnad Ahmad*, vol. 5, p. 212; and *Sunan Ibn Majah* vol. 4, p. 995 and vol.1, p. 255.
[28] *Nahj al-Balagha*, sermons 23, 25, 56, 85, 161, 168, 182, 187 and letters no. 6, 9 and 54.
[29] Malik bin Anas, *al-Muwatta'*, (along with commentary of al-Zurqani), vol. 4, page 159.
[30] *Al-Fiqh 'ala al-Madhahib al-Arba'ah*, book of al-Yamin, vol. 1, page 75 (Egyptian print).

The Hanbali's believe that swearing by someone other than Allah and His qualities is forbidden even though the swearing may be in the name of Prophet or *wali* from one of his *awliya*.

Let us overlook this fact that all these *fatawa* (verdicts) are a kind of *ijtihad* in the face of the clear texts of Qur'an and *sunnah* of prophet and *awliya* Allah and due to the closure of the door of *ijtihad* for the Ahl al-Sunnah, the contemporary scholars have no option but to follow their views.

Let us overlook the fact that al-Qastallani has narrated in (*al-Irshad al-Sari*, vol. 9, page 358) from Malik ibn Anas about the matter of being abominable. And let us once more overlook this fact that attributing prohibition of such a swearing according to the Hanbalis is not certain because, Ibn Qudama[31] in *al-Mughni'* that was written with the aim of reviving the Hanbali *fiqh* (jurisprudence) writes: "A group among our companions have said that swearing by the Holy Prophet (s) is a promise which if not fulfilled would invite *kaffara* (atonement). It has been narrated from Ahmad ibn Hanbal that anyone who swears by the right of Messenger of Allah and then breaks it, has to pay *kaffara* since the right of the Holy Prophet (s) is one of the pillars of *shahada* (profession of Islam). Therefore, swearing in his name is (like) swearing by Allah and both invite *kaffara*.[32]

From these narrations, it is obvious that it can never be said that any of the Imam of the four schools of thought have decisively given any verdict on the prohibition of this matter.

After getting acquainted with the views and opinions of the jurisprudents of the four schools of thought, we shall now discuss two traditions which the Wahhabis have used as a pretext for unjustly shedding innocent blood[33] and accusing millions of Muslims with blasphemy.

---

[31] Abdullah Ibn Ahmad Ibn Qudama al-Maqdisi (1146 – 1223 A.D.) was a famous Palestinian Syrian Sunni Hanbali Scholar and expert in the Hanbali *fiqh* (jurisprudence) and law. He compiled the first famous and complete book of Hanbali jurisprudence, *Al-Mughni*.

[32] *Al-Mughni*, vol. 9, p. 517. Published by Darul Kutub al-'Ilmiyah, Beirut, 2013.

[33] The Wahhabis first attacked Karbala in the year 1216 A.H. / 1801 A.D. and again in the year 1259 A.H. / 1843 A.D. and in these attacks, they did not spare the young and the old. Within three days, they killed 6000 people and like the army of Yazid, they plundered the precious things inside the shrine. Why? Just because they were seeking *tawassul* by the progeny of the Holy Prophet (s) and were expressing their love towards them!

First Tradition

إن رسول الله سمع عمر وهو يقول: وأبي فقال إن الله ينهاكم أن تحلفوا بآبائكم ومن كان حالفاً فليحلف بالله أو يسكت

"The Holy Prophet (s) heard 'Umar swearing by his father. The Holy Prophet (s) said: 'God has forbidden you (all) from swearing by your fathers. Anyone who wishes to swear should swear by God or else should keep silent.'"[34]

Firstly, swearing by their fathers was prohibited because of the fact that they were polytheists and idol-worshippers and such people did not hold any esteem or honor so that one could swear by them. As it has come down in some of the traditions that one should not swear either by the fathers or by the devils (the idols of the Arab).[35]

Secondly, the prohibition to swear by the father is at times of judgement and hostilities. This is because as per the consensus of the Islamic scholars, at times of hostilities, no swearing is allowed except for the swearing by Allah and His attributes which are a reference to His Essence.

By paying attention to what has been said, how can one dare to say that the Holy Prophet (s) has prohibited and restrained us from swearing by the holy personalities like the Prophets and *awliya*. His prohibition was only under special circumstances and was not having a general application.

Second Tradition

جاء ابن عمر رجل فقال: احلف بالكعبة قال لا ولكن احلف برب الكعبة فإن عمر كان يحلف بأبيه فقال رسول الله (صلى الله عليه وآله): لا تحلف بأبيك فإن من حلف بغير الله فقد اشرك.

"A person approached the son of 'Umar and said: 'I swear by the Ka'ba.' The son of 'Umar said: 'You should swear by the Lord of the Ka'ba because when 'Umar swore by his father, the Prophet (s) ordered him not to do so since anyone who swears by someone other than Allah has considered a partner for Allah.'"[36]

---

[34] *Sunan Ibn Majah*, vol. 1, p. 277; *Sunan al-Tirmidhi*, vol. 4, p. 109; *Sunan al-Nasa'i*, vol. 7, p. 485; *Sunan al-Kubra*, vol. 10, p. 29.

[35] *Sunan al-Kubra*, vol.1, p. 29 narrated from *Sahih Muslim*, *Sunan al-Nasa'i* vol.7, p. 7 and *Sunan Ibn Majah*, vol. 1, p. 278. In another tradition it has come as: لا تحلفوا بآبائكم ولا بأمهاتكم ولا بالأنداد (*Sunan al-Nasa'i* vol.7, p. 6).

[36] *Sunan al-Kubra*, vol.1, p. 29 narrated from *Sahih Muslim*, *Sunan al-Nasa'i* vol.7, p. 7 and *Sunan Ibn Majah*, vol. 1, p. 278. In another tradition it has come as: لا تحلفوا بآبائكم ولا بأمهاتكم ولا بالأنداد (*Sunan al-Nasa'i* vol.7, p. 6).

Reply

By paying attention to the previous reasoning that recommends swearing to someone other than Allah, this tradition should be described in the following manner.

This tradition consists of three parts:

1. A person approached Ibn 'Umar and wished to swear by the *Ka'ba* but the latter prevented him from doing so.
2. 'Umar swears by his father in the presence of the Holy Prophet (s) and the latter prevents him from doing so as it was the source of *shirk*.
3. The *Ijtihad* (independent reasoning) of Ibn 'Umar covered the Holy Prophet's saying and included swearing by the holy things such as *Ka'ba* too in the Prophet's saying.

Under these circumstances, the way of reconciling this tradition and the previous traditions (where the Holy Prophet (s) and others have sworn by someone other than God without any apprehension) is this that the saying of the Prophet, (that anyone who swears by someone other than God has committed *shirk*) is confined to instances where that person who is sworn by, is a polytheist and not a Muslim and holy like the Qur'an, *Ka'ba* or the Prophet. Thus the *ijtihad* of Ibn 'Umar who has derived a wider meaning from the saying of the Prophet is an argument only for himself and not for others.

The reason that swearing by the 'polytheist father' is one kind of *shirk* is because such swearing is apparently considered to be an approval of their ways and means.

This was an explanation of the *ijtihad* of Ibn 'Umar who derived a wider meaning from the tradition which has come down in the case of swearing by the polytheists. Moreover, he has also applied this to holy things too (for example, *Ka'ba*). So, there's another analysis for this tradition which is much clearer and more evident than the analysis of Ibn 'Umar.

Now, we shall discuss his second analysis.

Second Analysis

The saying of the Holy Prophet (s), that من حلف بغير الله فقد أشرك is related to swearing by the devil's gods such as Lat and 'Uzza and not swearing by the polytheist father; leaving aside the matter of swearing by the holy things like

Ka'ba. It is the *ijtihad* of Ibn 'Umar who adopted this rule (which is exclusively related to the idols) to the two cases (swearing by the polytheist and swearing by the Ka'ba) or else, there was no such extension in the Holy Prophet's saying, the proof being that in another tradition, the Prophet (s) says:

من حلف فقال في حلفه بالات والعزى فليقل: لا إله إلا الله

"Anyone who swears and swears by Lat and 'Uzza and then immediately says "There is no god except Allah.........."³⁷

This tradition shows that the sediment of the period of ignorance was still prevailing in the minds of the people who were yet following the ancient habits like the practice of swearing by the idols and it was for the eradication of this ugly practice that the Holy Prophet (s) uttered such a general statement. But Ibn 'Umar has applied this to both swearing by the holy thing as well as swearing by a polytheistic father.

The proof that the saying of the Holy Prophet (s) is neither connected to swearing by the holy thing nor connected to swearing by a polytheist father and the evidence that it is Ibn 'Umar who has combined the Prophet's saying with two cases and even to the swearing of 'Umar by his father. The following is the text of another hadith:

Imam Hanbal in his *al-Musnad* vol. 2, page 34 has narrated the second tradition in such a manner that it shows that such comparison is the work of Ibn 'Umar. Here is the text of the tradition:

كان يحلف أبي فنهاه النبيّ قال: من حلف بشئ دون الله فقد أشرك

"'Umar swore by his father; then the Holy Prophet (s) prohibited him from doing so and said: 'The one who swears by someone other than Allah has adopted polytheism.'"

Just as you can see, the sentence من حلف has come without واوعاطفه(parataxis) or فاء and if the second tradition was below the tradition of 'swearing by the father', then it was necessary for the second tradition to come with the word of عطف (parataxis).

Again the writer of *al-Musnad* in vol. 2, page 67 has narrated the tradition of من حلف in an independent form without the incident of 'Umar swearing. It is as such.

من حلف بغير الله قال فيه قولاً شديداً

---

³⁷ *Sunan al-Nasa'i*, vol. 7, page 8

"The one who swears by someone other than God has said an unfair thing and or the Prophet (s) has said something severe about him for example 'has adopted polytheism.'"

17

Nadhr (Vow) to the People in Grave

People in difficulties and pain customarily make a *nadhr* (vow) that if their difficulty is solved and if their so and so work is made easy, they will donate a certain sum of money for one of the shrines over the grave and / or will sacrifice a goat for preparing food for the pilgrims. They say:

لله عليَّ كذا إن كان كذا

"By God it is on me (to perform) so and so, if so and so happens."

This matter is prevalent among all the Muslims of the world especially at those centers where the graves of *Awliya Allah* and virtuous personalities are present.

The Wahhabis are sensitive to these types of vows and the most abusive writer amongst them, Abdullah al-Qasimi writes as such:

"The Shi'a, because of their belief in the divinity (Godliness) of Ali and his sons, worship them in their graves and it is for this reason that they have built their graves and populated near them. From every nook and corner of the world, they go for their ziyarat and present their vows and sacrifices to them and shed tears and blood over their graves."[1]

This shameless and foul-mouthed writer whose basic culture and manners is apparent from the title of his book[2] has reckoned this matter to be related to the Shi'a whereas, the founder of Wahhabism, Ibn Taymiyyah has discussed the matter in a wider scope and has believed it to be related to the common Muslims. As he says:

---

[1] *Al-Sira'*, vol. 1, page 54.
[2] He has named this book, so to speak, as a rebuff to *Kashf al-'Irtiyab* written by Allama Sayyid Mohsin al-Amin and given the title of *"Battle between Islam and Idol-worshipping"* and in this way has called the Shi'a, who form one-fourth of Muslim population in the world, as Idol-worshippers.

من نذر شيئاً للنبيّ أو غيره من النبيّين والأولياء من أهل القبول أو ذبح ذبيحة كان كالمشركين الذين يذبحون لأوثانهم و ينذرون لها فهو عابد لغير الله فيكون بذلك كافراً

"Anyone who has a nadhr (vow) to make and sacrifice for the Holy Prophet (s), other Prophets and other awliya is similar to the polytheists who were doing vows and sacrifices for their idols. Such a person is same as the one worshipping someone other than God and he will be called an infidel (kafir)."[3]

The master and student have both been deceived by apparent (appearances) similarity. By the decree of this apparent similarity, they have attacked both with one stick, whereas in the case of common actions, the criterion and basis of judgement is not to be looked in its apparent form but what is important is the intention by heart.

If apparent similarities suffice in a judgement then we have to say that many of the obligatory Hajj actions are similar to the actions of the idol-worshippers who used to circumambulate around the stones and mud and worship their wooden and metallic idols. The same actions are performed by us. We circumambulate around the Holy *Ka'ba* which is made of stone and mud; we kiss the *Hajar al-Aswad* (stone) and shed blood in Mina.

The basis of judgements and arbitrations in apparently similar affairs are the motives and the intentions and one can never pass a similar judgement only because the two actions are apparently the same.

Regarding this matter, the author of *Sulh al-'Ikhwan* has given a statement which can clarify this matter. He says:

إن المسألة تدور مدار نيات الناذرين وإنما الأعمال بالنيات فإن كان قصد الناذر الميت نفسه والتقرب إليه بذلك لم يجُز قولاً واحداً وإن كان قصد وجه الله تعالى وانتفاع الأحياء بوجه من الوجوه وثوابه لذلك المنذور له الميت فيجب الوفاء بالنذر

This Sunni scholar who is himself a critic of the beliefs of Wahhabis has, in this short statement discussed the matter from the viewpoint of the intentions and motives. He says:

---

[3] *Furqan al-Qur'an*, page 132 written by al-'Azami narrated from Ibn Taymiyyah.

"If the intention of nadhr (vow) is to gain proximity to the dead, then undoubtedly such an act is not permissible (for nadhr should be for Allah and His proximity). If it is for the sake of Allah and His proximity and consequently a section of people benefit from it and its reward is presented to the dead, then there is no objection to it and one should in such a case, fulfil his nadhr (vow)."[4]

The truth is what this scholar has said in these sentences and the motive of *nadhr* among the Muslims is exactly the same as what has come in the second phase of his statement. It is here that the difference (in essence) between the action of the Muslims and the action of the idol-worshippers becomes obvious. Their intention in presenting gifts and sacrificing animals was to seek proximity to their idols. They even slaughtered animals in their names and their aim was only the idols and seeking their proximity and nothing else. On the other hand, the aim of the Muslims is to seek the satisfaction of Allah and present its reward to the dead. Therefore, they bring the word of Allah in their vows and say:

لله عليَّ إن قضيت حاجتي ان افعل كذا

"The purpose of nadhr in reality is seeking proximity to Allah and presenting its reward to the one in grave and the beneficiaries of these nadhr are the poor and the indigent."

In such a case, how can one consider this action as *shirk* and place it on par with the action of the polytheists!?

In short, these kinds of *nadhr* are one type of charity given on behalf of the Prophets (s) and virtuous people the reward of which goes to them and none of the Islamic scholars have objected to such a charity given on behalf of the dead.

For acquainting the respected readers with the fallacious thinking of the Wahhabis, we shall discuss this matter in greater length.

In Arabic language, the matter of charity is presented with لام but sometimes, this letter is taken in the sense of aim, goal and motive, like; لله عليَّ and sometimes it is meant to describe its usage likeإنما الصدقات للفقراء and while carrying out the paradigm of *nadhr* (vow) they use both kinds of لام and say:

نذرت لله إن قُضيت حاجتي أن أذبح للنبيَّ

The first لام is the same لام of goal and motive and it implies that the aim of this *nadhr* is seeking the satisfaction of Allah and gaining His proximity whereas

---

[4] *Sulh al-Ikhwan*, page 102 and ...

the second لام indicates the very object which derives benefit from this *nadhr* and the reward is presented to him.

While the لام in صليت لله and or نذرت لله is for expressing goal and motive i.e. I recited *salat* and I did *nadhr* because of obeying the commands of Allah and seeking His satisfaction and proximity.

On the other hand لام in لوالدتي او اذبح للنبيّ اولوالدئ is for clarifying the beneficiary and showing that this action takes place on his behalf and it is he who reaps the benefits of its reward.

Such *nadhr* not only is not an *'ibadah* (worship) of that person but rather, it is *'ibadah* of Allah for the sake of benefit of the creatures of Allah.

In Islamic traditions, there are many instances regarding this matter where we shall hereunder mention a few of them.

1. One of the companions of the Holy Prophet (s) by the name of Sa'd told the Prophet: "My mother has died and if she was alive today, she would be giving charity. Supposing that I give charity on her behalf, will she derive any benefit from it?" The Holy Prophet (s) replied: "Yes". Thereafter, he asked the Prophet (s) that amongst all the charities which charity was the most useful and the Prophet (s) replied: "Water". Sa'd dug a well and said:

هذه لإم سعد

As you must have noticed, the لام of this sentence is different from the لام that is present in the sentence نذرت لله the first لام is for expression of motive and the second لام shows the object deriving the gain.[5]

2. During the time of the Holy Prophet (s), a person made a *nadhr* to sacrifice a camel at place called Bavana. For this reason, he approached the Holy Prophet (s) and informed him of his intentions, the Prophet (s) asked: "During the era of paganism, was there any idol at that place for the people to worship?" He replied "No." The Prophet (s) asked: "Was any congregation held in any of the ignorant festivals in that place?" He replied "No." At that moment, the Prophet (s) said:

اوفِ بنذرك فإنه لا وفاء لنذرٍ في معصية الله ولا فيما لا يملك ابن أدم

---

[5] *Furqan al-Qur'an*, page 133 narrated from *al-Ghadir*, vol. 5, page 181.

"Fulfill your vow (nadhr) as nadhr is not correct in two instances: (a) In case of sins and disobedience of Allah and (b) In things which he is not the owner." [6]

3. A woman told the Holy Prophet (s) as such: I have made a *nadhr* to slaughter an animal at one particular place. The Holy Prophet (s) asked: "Have you made a *nadhr* for an idol? She replied "No.": The Holy Prophet (s) said: Fulfil your *nadhr*.[7]

4. The father of Maymuna said: I have done *nadhr* to slaughter 50 sheep at Bavana. The Holy Prophet (s) said:

"*Is there any idol in that place?*" He replied "*No.*" The Prophet (s) said: "*You may fulfil your nadhr.*"

The successive questionings by the Prophet (s) about the existence of idols in the past and present and or about the presence of any congregations in the form of festivals at those places was due to the fact that under such situations, the sacrifice took place for those idols and for gaining their proximity whereas sacrifices should be only for Allah and not for the idols. In fact, one of the forbidden acts from the viewpoint of Qur'an is to slaughter in the name of an idol. As the Holy Qur'an says:

وَمَا ذُبِحَ عَلَى النُّصُبِ

"And what is sacrificed on stones set up (for idols). (Maida:3)"

The reason that the questioners were fixing the place of slaughter was because of the presence of poor and needy people and or the easiness in performing the deed in those places. Those who are having connection with the pilgrims to the holy graves are fully aware that *nadhr* is made for the sake of Allah and His satisfaction and sacrifice is done in His name. However, as far as the benefits are concerned its rewards go to the *awliya* Allah and its material gains to the poor and / or to the holy shrine itself.

---

[6] *Sunan Abu Dawud*, vol. 2, page 80.
[7] *Sunan Abu Dawud*, vol. 2, page 81.

18

'Calling' the Divine Personalities

One of the matters of disputes between the Wahhabis and other Islamic sects is the matter of pleading and calling the pious personalities and *awliya Allah* in the times of hardship and difficulties.

Pleading and asking help from the Prophets (s) and *awliya Allah* near their graves or otherwise is completely in vogue among the Islamic sects and they consider it neither to be *shirk* (polytheism) nor contradicting the Islamic foundations. On the other hand, the Wahhabis have strongly rejected such pleadings and for intimidating their opponents, they set forth some verses of Qur'an that are not having the least connection to what they claim and always raise the following verse as their slogan.

وَأَنَّ الْمَسَاجِدَ لِلَّهِ فَلَا تَدْعُوا مَعَ اللَّهِ أَحَدًا

"The mosques belong to Allah; do not call anyone with Allah. (Jinn:18)"

For acquainting the respected readers with all such verses that are the greatest excuse in the hands of the Wahhabis, we shall present them here and then explain their contents. The Wahhabis prove their point by producing the afore-mentioned and the following verses.

لَهُ دَعْوَةُ الْحَقِّ وَالَّذِينَ يَدْعُونَ مِنْ دُونِهِ لَا يَسْتَجِيبُونَ لَهُمْ بِشَيْءٍ

"To Him is due the true prayer; and those whom they pray to beside Allah give them no answer. (Ra'd:14)"

وَالَّذِينَ تَدْعُونَ مِنْ دُونِهِ لَا يَسْتَطِيعُونَ نَصْرَكُمْ وَلَا أَنْفُسَهُمْ يَنْصُرُونَ

"And those whom you call upon besides Him are not able to help you, nor can they help themselves. (A'raf:197)"

وَالَّذِينَ تَدْعُونَ مِنْ دُونِهِ مَا يَمْلِكُونَ مِنْ قِطْمِيرٍ

"And those whom you call upon besides Him do not control a straw. (Fatir:13)"

$$\text{إِنَّ الَّذِينَ تَدْعُونَ مِنْ دُونِ اللَّهِ عِبَادٌ أَمْثَالُكُمْ}$$

"Surely those whom you call on besides Allah are in a state of subjugation like yourselves. (A'raf:194)"

$$\text{قُلِ ادْعُوا الَّذِينَ زَعَمْتُم مِّن دُونِهِ فَلَا يَمْلِكُونَ كَشْفَ الضُّرِّ عَنكُمْ وَلَا تَحْوِيلًا}$$

"Say: Call on those whom you assert besides Him, so they shall not control the removal of distress from you nor (its) transference. (Bani-Israel:56)"

$$\text{أُولَٰئِكَ الَّذِينَ يَدْعُونَ يَبْتَغُونَ إِلَىٰ رَبِّهِمُ الْوَسِيلَةَ}$$

"Those whom they call upon, themselves seek the means of access to their Lord. (Bani-Israel:57)"

$$\text{وَلَا تَدْعُ مِن دُونِ اللَّهِ مَا لَا يَنفَعُكَ وَلَا يَضُرُّكَ}$$

"And do not call besides Allah on that which can neither benefit you nor harm you. (Yunus:106)"

$$\text{إِن تَدْعُوهُمْ لَا يَسْمَعُوا دُعَاءَكُمْ}$$

"If you call on them they shall not hear your call. (Fatir:14)"

$$\text{وَمَنْ أَضَلُّ مِمَّن يَدْعُو مِن دُونِ اللَّهِ مَن لَّا يَسْتَجِيبُ لَهُ إِلَىٰ يَوْمِ الْقِيَامَةِ}$$

"And who is in greater error than he who calls besides Allah upon those that will not answer him till the day of resurrection. (Ahqaf:5)"

The Wahhabis conclude from these verses that calling the *awliya* and virtuous people after their death is *'ibadah* and their worship, and that anyone who says, "O Muhammad" either near his grave or from far off, this calling itself is *'ibadah* and therefore an act of *shirk* (polytheism).

Kashf al-'Irtiyab on page 274, citing al-San'ani[1], narrates from book *Tanzih al-I'tiqad*[2] as such:

وقد سمّى الله الدعاء عبادة بقوله: ادعوني استجب لكم إن الذين يستكبرون عن عبادتي ، ومن هتف باسم نبي أو صالح بشئ أو قال اشفع لي إلى الله في حاجتي أو استشفع بك إلى الله في حاجتي أو نحو ذلك أو

---

[1] Muhammad ibn Isma'il al-San'ani (1688-1768 A.D.) was a Yemeni Salafi scholar specialized in the Science of hadith.

[2] *Tanzih al-I'tiqad 'an al-Hulul wa al-Itihad* authored by Jalal al-Din al-Suyuti.

قال إقض ديني أو إشف مريضي أو نحو ذلك فقد دعا النبي والصالح والدعاء عبادة بل مُخّها فيكون قد بد غير الله وصار مشركاً إذ لا يُتمّ التوحيد إلا بتوحيده تعالى في الإلهية بإعتقاد أن لا خالق ولا رازق غيره العبادة بعدم عبادة غيره ولو ببعض العبادات وعُباد الأصنام إنما اشركوا لعدم توحيد الله في العبادة.

"The Holy Qur'an has unconditionally declared pleadings and callings towards someone other than Allah as 'ibadah; the reason being that in the beginning of verse, it says ادعوني *and following that it says:* أستجب لكم

يستكبرون عن عبادتي

Therefore, anyone who calls the Prophet (s) and or a pious person or asks to intercede for fulfilling his or her needs, or says "You help in repaying my debt", or says "You cure my sickness", then in these cases this person has, with such sayings, worshipped them because the reality of worship is nothing but calling someone. As a result of such calling, he has worshipped (someone) other than Allah and has become a polytheist since monotheism of divinity[3] (i.e. there is no Creator and Sustainer except Allah) should be accompanied with monotheism of worship which means not worshipping anyone except Him."

Reply

There is no doubt about this fact that the word of دعا in Arabic means 'to call' and the term عبادات means 'to worship' and one can never reckon these two words to be synonymous to each other; and say that both give the same meaning. In other words, one cannot say that every call and plead is 'ibadah (worship) because: Firstly, in the Holy Qur'an, the word of دعوت (calling) has been used in instances where it does not give the meaning of 'worship' at all.

Like:

قَالَ رَبِّ إِنِّي دَعَوْتُ قَوْمِي لَيْلًا وَنَهَارًا

"He said: 'O Lord! I called my nation (towards Thee) day and night. (Nuh:5)'"

Can we say that the intention of Nuh was to say "I worshipped my nation day and night!"?

The Qur'an quotes Satan as saying:

كَانَ لِيَ عَلَيْكُمْ مِنْ سُلْطَانٍ إِلَّا أَنْ دَعَوْتُكُمْ فَاسْتَجَبْتُمْ لِي

"I did not have any authority upon you except that I called you (towards evil deeds) and you obliged. (Ibrahim:22)"

---

[3] Contrary to the terminology of the Wahhabis, al-San'ani has used the word of "الوهي" whereas he should have, from their viewpoint, used the word of "ربوني".

Is it possible for anyone to interpret Satan's calling to mean that he has worshipped his followers!? If it was an act of worship it was from the side of the followers of Satan and not from Satan himself.

In this verse and tens of other un-mentioned verses, the word of دعوت (calling) has not been used in the meaning of عبادات (worship). Therefore, one cannot say that دعوت and عبادات are synonymous to each other and based on this, conclude that if anyone seeks help and calls the Prophets or the virtuous people, he has worshipped them.[4]

Secondly, by دُعا in these verses is not meant as absolute calling but refers to some special calling which can be synonymous to the word of عبادات because, all these verses have come down with regard to the idol-worshippers who believed their idols to be small gods who were entrusted with some of the divine ranks and who possessed some kind of independence in their affairs.

Let it not be unsaid that humbleness and humility or any kind of utterance or behavior in front of a creature either as a big God or small god if it is with this intention that he is God, Lord, and the Owner of affairs like *shafa'a* and forgiveness, then it will be *'ibadah* or worship. There is no doubt that the humility of the idol-worshippers and their pleading and calling were before those idols which they depicted as the owners of the right of intercession etc., and considered them as the independent authority in the affairs of this world and the Hereafter.

It is apparent that under these circumstances, any kind of pleading and calling towards these creatures is *'ibadah* or worship. The most obvious witness to the fact that their pleadings and callings were accompanied with the belief in their divinity is this verse:

فَمَا أَغْنَتْ عَنْهُمْ آلِهَتُهُمُ الَّتِي يَدْعُونَ مِنْ دُونِ اللَّهِ مِنْ شَيْءٍ

"So their gods whom they called upon besides Allah did not avail them ought. (Hud:101)"

---

[4] From the viewpoint of relationship, calling and worship (general and special) is in one direction. In case of asking help from someone other than Allah but as a doer depending on God, it shows calling and not worship. But in practical glorifications like *ruku'* and *sajdah* which is accompanied with the belief in the divinity of the opposite person it denotes 'worship' and not دُعا. In some instances, such as *salat*, both دُعا and عبادات are applicable.

Therefore, the verses under discussion have no relation to the main point of our discussion.

The topic of our discussion is pleading of one slave to another slave who neither considers him as God nor Lord nor as the Owner and independent authority in the worldly and heavenly affairs. Rather, he reckons him to be a beloved servant of Allah who has appointed him to the position of Prophethood and Imamate and promised to accept his prayers with regards to His slaves. As verse says:

وَلَوْ أَنَّهُمْ إِذْ ظَلَمُوا أَنْفُسَهُمْ جَاءُوكَ فَاسْتَغْفَرُوا اللَّهَ وَاسْتَغْفَرَ لَهُمُ الرَّسُولُ لَوَجَدُوا اللَّهَ تَوَّابًا رَحِيمًا

"And had they, when they were unjust to themselves, come to you and asked forgiveness of Allah and the Apostle had (also) asked forgiveness for them, they would have found Allah Oft-returning (to mercy), Merciful. (Nisa:64)"

Thirdly, in the aforementioned verses itself, there is a clear evidence that by دعوت is not meant absolute asking for one's affairs and needs but refers to asking and calling in the sense of *'ibadah* and worship. For this reason, in one of the verses, the word of *'ibadah* immediately follows the word of دعوت giving the same meaning. Like:

وَقَالَ رَبُّكُمُ ادْعُونِي أَسْتَجِبْ لَكُمْ إِنَّ الَّذِينَ يَسْتَكْبِرُونَ عَنْ عِبَادَتِي سَيَدْخُلُونَ جَهَنَّمَ دَاخِرِينَ

"And your Lord says: Call upon Me, I will answer you, surely those who are too proud for My service shall soon enter hell abased. (Ghafir:60)"

Just as you must have noticed, in the beginning of the verse the word of ادعوني and following the same verse the word of عبادتي has come and this clearly shows that by this دعوت is meant some special pleading and beseeching before a creature whom they recognized by the divine qualities.

The master of the prostrators, Imam Zayn al-'Abidin (a) says in his supplication as such:

فسميت دعاءك عبادة وتركه استكباراً وتوعّدت على تركه دخول جهّنم داخرين

"Thou have named Thy calling as worship and its abandonment as pride and Thou have promised a miserable entry into the fire for those who abandon it."[5]

And sometimes in two verses where the contents are similar, we see in one place the word of عبادات and in another place the word of دعوت such as:

قُلْ أَتَعْبُدُونَ مِنْ دُونِ اللَّهِ مَا لَا يَمْلِكُ لَكُمْ ضَرًّا وَلَا نَفْعًا

---

[5] *al-Sahifa al-Sajjadiyya*, supplication No. 45 and what is meant is *Surah Ghafir* verse 60.

"Say: Do you serve besides Allah that which does not control for you any harm, or any profit? (Maida:76)"

In another verse it says:

قُلْ أَنَدْعُو مِنْ دُونِ اللَّهِ مَا لَا يَنْفَعُنَا وَلَا يَضُرُّنَا

"Say: Shall we call on that besides Allah, which does not benefit us nor harm us. (An'am:71)"

In *Surah Fatir*, verse 13 it says:

وَالَّذِينَ تَدْعُونَ مِنْ دُونِهِ مَا يَمْلِكُونَ مِنْ قِطْمِيرٍ

"And those whom you call upon besides Him do not control a straw."

In this verse, the word of تدعون is used whereas in another verse which contains the same contents the word of تعبدون is used.

إِنَّ الَّذِينَ تَعْبُدُونَ مِنْ دُونِ اللَّهِ لَا يَمْلِكُونَ لَكُمْ رِزْقًا

"Surely they whom you serve besides Allah do not control for you any sustenance. (Ankabut:17)"

Sometimes, in one verse, both the words have appeared and has been used in the same meaning:

قُلْ إِنِّي نُهِيتُ أَنْ أَعْبُدَ الَّذِينَ تَدْعُونَ مِنْ دُونِ اللَّهِ

"Say: I am forbidden to serve those whom you call upon besides Allah. (An'am:56)"

"Say, I am forbidden from worshipping those which you call them (i.e. worship them)"[6]

Respected readers are requested to refer to *al-Mu'jam al-mufahras*[7] under the words عبد and دعا so that they will witness as to how in on verse the word of عبادات has come and in another verse the word of دعوت has come giving the same meaning. This itself shows that the meaning of دعوت in this verse, is *'ibadah* and worship and not absolute calling.

If you carefully pay attention to the whole set of verses wherein the word of دعوت has been used in the sense of عبادات you will realize that these verses either refer to the Great God of the Universe whom all the monotheist believe in His Divinity, Lordship and Mastership or refers to the idols where its

---

[6] The same is the content of *Surah Ghafir*, verse 66.
[7] *Al-Mu'jam Al-Mufahras li alfaz al-Qur'an al-Karim* compiled by Muhammad Fu'ad 'Abd al-Baqi (1882 – 1968 A.D.) an Egyptian Islamic scholar.

worshippers considered them as small gods and masters of intercession. Under these circumstances, reasoning out with these verses for discussing about دعوت (calling) one of the *awliya* and beseeching one of them who doesn't have any of these qualities is really astonishing.

19

Political and Social Dimensions of Hajj

Like Marxism, the school of Wahhabism too, when coming across the events and phenomenon which go against the aim of their school of thought, tend to draw a new line and issue some new commandments for the Muslims in the course of time.

The victory of Islamic revolution in Iran brought up an extraordinary fear in hearts of the political leaders of Wahhabi ideology. They became very anxious from its influence over the neighbouring regions and the very thought of awakening of their nations brought them pain and agony.

In the Hajj season, when our dear and noble country of Iran would, as a revolutionary duty, engage in demonstrations and invite the Islamic nations towards unity and cooperation against the blood-thirsty Americans and international Communism and Zionism, the politicians of Saudi Arabia stretched their hands towards the clergy for conjuring up a solution about this matter so that they could finally prohibit such demonstrations.

'Abd al-'Aziz bin Baz[1], the Grand *Mufti* of Saudi Arabia, prohibited demonstrations under the pretext that Hajj is a devotional deed and should not be mingled with the other matters. As a result, the police attacked the pilgrims and the honorable guests to the House of Allah with whips and arms. They entertained the pilgrims to the House of Allah with curses, blows and bullets and instigated other people against them and this incident continues every year.

This part of the book has been written in reply to the *fatwa* (verdict) of the Mufti of Saudi Arabia and the political and social dimensions of this duty have

---

[1] 'Abdul 'Aziz ibn Abdullah ibn Baz (1910-1999 A.D.), also known as Bin Baz, was born in Nejd, was a Saudi Arabian Wahhabi scholar. He was the Grand Mufti of Saudi Arabia from 1993 until his death in 1999. He was main architect of Saudi state policies and legitimizing them on the basis of Wahhabism. His views and *fatwas* (rulings) were controversial and condemned by Muslim scholars and intellectuals worldwide including the decision to permit U.S. troops to be stationed in Saudi Arabia in 1991.

been explained from the viewpoint of verses, traditions and the common practice of the Muslims.

The aim of performing Hajj duties is to call for humility before God and this matter is clear and apparent by paying attention to the Hajj rituals.

'Ibadah and worship of the Lord and non-worship of other than Him is evident right from the beginning of the deeds till the last of them and it is needless to mention them, especially if these actions are accompanied with recommended prayers. We derive the following conclusions from all such deeds:

Hajj is *'ibadah* and worship of the true Lord in the best possible circumstances.

Hajj is expressing humility with honor before God in the best form.

Hajj is beseeching and weeping before God in its deepest form.

Hajj is such an *'ibadah* where all kinds of elements of expression of devotion and bondage have been collected and one can clearly witness humility, submission, piety, deliverance from desires and attachments of this world.

The pilgrims to the House of Allah exhibit their deliverance from material manifestations by wearing two pieces of cloths and in this way, show that except for Allah, they have no interest in anything even to their sons, family and relatives. The only thing which preoccupies the minds of the pilgrims to the House of Allah is the saying of *labbayk* in one harmonious voice.

This matter is completely evident and clear by paying attention to the obligatory acts of Hajj, the places where these acts are to be performed and the stops where the pilgrims have to make a halt. Therefore, one should consider Hajj to be the greatest devotional act and the greatest religious obligation.

However, apart from this matter, there is another matter to be looked into and that is whether this act, apart from *'ibadah*, has any political and social dimensions or not? Or is it that, like the midnight prayers, it ends only and only in *'ibadah* and worship without having any relation with the common Islamic problems!

In other words, has God made Hajj obligatory upon all the Muslims whether men or women and young or old so that with such deeds they worship their Lord and except for this worship it does not hold any political and social dimensions.

Or is it that this obligation is the point of combination for *'ibadah* and politics and is the center of relating worship of God with the other social and economic matters. It is this matter which we are going to discuss and we shall see that what the Qur'anic verses, the Islamic traditions (*hadiths*) and the practice of virtuous companions approve is the second point.

Observing the Benefits of Hajj

The Holy Qur'an describes the Hajj of Ibrahim (a) as follows:

وَأَذِّن فِي النَّاسِ بِالْحَجِّ يَأْتُوكَ رِجَالًا وَعَلَىٰ كُلِّ ضَامِرٍ يَأْتِينَ مِن كُلِّ فَجٍّ عَمِيقٍ لِيَشْهَدُوا مَنَافِعَ لَهُمْ وَيَذْكُرُوا اسْمَ اللَّهِ فِي أَيَّامٍ مَعْلُومَاتٍ عَلَىٰ مَا رَزَقَهُم مِّن بَهِيمَةِ الْأَنْعَامِ ۖ فَكُلُوا مِنْهَا وَأَطْعِمُوا الْبَائِسَ الْفَقِيرَ ثُمَّ لْيَقْضُوا تَفَثَهُمْ وَلْيُوفُوا نُذُورَهُمْ وَلْيَطَّوَّفُوا بِالْبَيْتِ الْعَتِيقِ ذَٰلِكَ وَمَن يُعَظِّمْ حُرُمَاتِ اللَّهِ فَهُوَ خَيْرٌ لَّهُ عِندَ رَبِّهِ ۗ وَأُحِلَّتْ لَكُمُ الْأَنْعَامُ إِلَّا مَا يُتْلَىٰ عَلَيْكُمْ ۖ فَاجْتَنِبُوا الرِّجْسَ مِنَ الْأَوْثَانِ وَاجْتَنِبُوا قَوْلَ الزُّورِ حُنَفَاءَ لِلَّهِ غَيْرَ مُشْرِكِينَ بِهِ ۚ وَمَن يُشْرِكْ بِاللَّهِ فَكَأَنَّمَا خَرَّ مِنَ السَّمَاءِ فَتَخْطَفُهُ الطَّيْرُ أَوْ تَهْوِي بِهِ الرِّيحُ فِي مَكَانٍ سَحِيقٍ ذَٰلِكَ وَمَن يُعَظِّمْ شَعَائِرَ اللَّهِ فَإِنَّهَا مِن تَقْوَى الْقُلُوبِ لَكُمْ فِيهَا مَنَافِعُ إِلَىٰ أَجَلٍ مُّسَمًّى ثُمَّ مَحِلُّهَا إِلَى الْبَيْتِ الْعَتِيقِ

"And proclaim among men the pilgrimage: they will come to you on foot and on every lean camel, coming from every remote path, that they may witness benefits for them and mention the name of Allah during stated days over what He has given them of the cattle quadrupeds, then eat of them and feed the distressed one, the needy. Then let them accomplish their needful acts of shaving and cleansing, and let them fulfil their vows and let them go around the Ancient House. That (shall be so); and whoever respects the sacred ordinances of Allah, it is better for him with his Lord; and the cattle are made lawful for you, therefore avoid the uncleanness of the idols and avoid false words, Being upright for Allah, not associating aught with Him and whoever associates (others) with Allah, it is as though he had fallen from on high, then the birds snatch him away or the wind carries him off to a far-distant place. That (shall be so); and whoever respects the signs of Allah, this surely is (the outcome) of the pity of hearts. You have benefits in them till a fixed time, then their place of sacrifice is the Ancient House. (Hajj: 27-33)"

From among all these verses consider the second verse and ponder deeply over this sentence, ليشهدوا منافع للناس so that it becomes clear that:

Firstly, what is meant by these benefits where the pilgrims to the House of Allah should be a witness. The fact that this sentence has come before the sentence وليذكروا اسم الله somewhat shows that Hajj possesses two dimensions, a devotional dimension which is embodied in praise and remembrance of Allah and the social dimension which ends in the witness of the benefits and;

Secondly: in this verse, منافع (benefits) which is an indicator to social and political dimension is prior to ذكر الله (remembrance of Allah).

Thirdly, the Holy Qur'an has brought the word of منافع in absolute terms and without any restrictions so that it includes every kind of benefits; economic, political and social and we have no right to adopt this word and restrict its meaning to a particular benefit. We should include in it, the economic benefits or social and political benefits. This word, by decree of the next sentence وليذكروا اسم الله shows that apart from devotion, Hajj possesses another domain which one should benefit from and we should not consider it to be a dry *'ibadah* having no relation with the lives of the Muslims.

It is advisable at this stage to know in what manner, the former head of al-Azhar, Shaikh Mahmud Shaltut[2] has interpreted this sentence.

He says: The منافع (benefits), where Hajj is the perceptional and acquirable channel for that and which has been set forth as the foremost philosophy of Hajj, is having a wide and comprehensive meaning which cannot be concluded in any special forms. Rather, this sentence, with all the universality and commonness it possesses, contains all personal and social benefits. If purification of the soul and seeking proximity of Allah are benefits, then seeking advice too is benefit. If these two are reckoned to be benefits then, inviting the Muslims for centralizing their forces for the spread of Islam too is a benefit. Therefore, according to the necessities of time and the conditions of the Muslims, these benefits differ in every era.[3]

In another place too, the former Sheikh of Al-Azhar says:

---

[2] Sheikh Shaltut (Shaltoot) (1893 – 1963 A.D.) was a prominent Egyptian Sunni scholar and Islamic theologian best known for his work in Islamic reform and unity of all five (Hanafi, Maliki, Hanbali, Shafi'i and Shia (Ja'fari)) Islamic Schools of thought. He was Grand Imam of Al-Azhar from 1958 until his death in 1963. In 1953, Sheikh Shaltut issued his famous fatwa on the legitimacy of Shia Ja'fari School of Thought. Online at: https://www.icit-digital.org/articles/shaykh-mahmud-shaltut-s-fatwa-about-shia-madhab-1959

[3] *Al-Shari'a wa al-'Aqida*, page 151.

'By paying attention to the special position which Hajj enjoys in Islam and the aims which have been set forth in it for one individual and one society, it is worthy that people of knowledge, wisdom and culture, (the responsible persons in charge of administrative and political affairs, the experts in financial and economic affairs, the teachers in laws and religion and the people in the battle-front) give special importance to it (and a group derives its benefits from Hajj).

It is worthy that people from all walks of life make haste towards this divine House. It is worthy that people of knowledge, insight, *ijtihad* and faith and the ones possessing lofty aims gather over there so that it is seen as to how Mecca spreads its wings of mercy over them and how it collects their slogan of *tawhid* in and around the House and (so that) they finally engage in seeking recognition, advice and help from each other and then they leave for their respective countries as one nation and with a single heart and united goals and outlook.[4]

The point which is worthy of attention is this that just after the aforesaid verses (which all manifested the position and benefits of Hajj) the Holy Qur'an concludes the discussion with verses about *jihad* and safeguarding of Islamic frontiers. As the Holy Qur'an says:

إِنَّ اللَّهَ يُدَافِعُ عَنِ الَّذِينَ آمَنُوا ۗ إِنَّ اللَّهَ لَا يُحِبُّ كُلَّ خَوَّانٍ كَفُورٍ أُذِنَ لِلَّذِينَ يُقَاتَلُونَ بِأَنَّهُمْ ظُلِمُوا ۚ وَإِنَّ اللَّهَ عَلَىٰ نَصْرِهِمْ لَقَدِيرٌ الَّذِينَ أُخْرِجُوا مِنْ دِيَارِهِمْ بِغَيْرِ حَقٍّ إِلَّا أَنْ يَقُولُوا رَبُّنَا اللَّهُ ۗ وَلَوْلَا دَفْعُ اللَّهِ النَّاسَ بَعْضَهُمْ بِبَعْضٍ لَهُدِّمَتْ صَوَامِعُ وَبِيَعٌ وَصَلَوَاتٌ وَمَسَاجِدُ يُذْكَرُ فِيهَا اسْمُ اللَّهِ كَثِيرًا ۗ وَلَيَنْصُرَنَّ اللَّهُ مَنْ يَنْصُرُهُ ۗ إِنَّ اللَّهَ لَقَوِيٌّ عَزِيزٌ الَّذِينَ إِنْ مَكَّنَّاهُمْ فِي الْأَرْضِ أَقَامُوا الصَّلَاةَ وَآتَوُا الزَّكَاةَ وَأَمَرُوا بِالْمَعْرُوفِ وَنَهَوْا عَنِ الْمُنْكَرِ ۗ وَلِلَّهِ عَاقِبَةُ الْأُمُورِ

"Surely Allah will defend those who believe; surely Allah does not love anyone who is unfaithful, ungrateful. Permission (to fight) is given to those upon whom war is made because they are oppressed, and most surely Allah is well able to assist them, those who have been expelled from their homes without adjust cause except that they say: Our Lord is Allah. And had there not been Allah's repelling some people by others, certainly there would have been pulled down cloisters and churches and synagogues and mosques in which Allah's name is much remembered; and surely Allah will help him who helps His cause; most surely Allah is Strong, Mighty. Those who, should We establish them in the

---

[4] *Al-Shari'a wa al-'Aqida*, page 150.

land, will keep up prayer and pay the poor-rate and enjoin good and forbid evil; and Allah's is the end of affairs. (Hajj: 38-41)"

Is it that the presentation of verses of *jihad* and defense just after the verses of Hajj or so to say, the coming together of verses of Hajj and Jihad is accidental and without any reason? Never! Qur'an never brings together in one place the nonproportional verses and then fails to observe their relation.

In accordance with the unity and necessity of relation between these two sets of verses, we realize that there exists a special relation between Hajj and *jihad*; between the field of intellect and the field of defense and for such a relationship, the place of Hajj is the best place where the Muslims can prepare themselves mentally and spiritually so much so that they can rub the nose of the proud to the ground and pull down the knees of colonization.

Yes, this great Divine Congress where the representatives of every nation gather is the best opportunity for the intellectuals amongst them to come together and discuss their political and defensive matters and form a united row before the enemies and teach them an unforgettable lesson. Even though this duty is not confined to the time and place of Hajj and rather the Muslims should face the enemies under any given situation and time, yet the time of Hajj and the gathering of Muslims at that place is the best opportunity for fulfilling this divine obligation.

It is not only Sheikh Shaltut who has interpreted منافع (benefits) which has come down in the verses in the general sense but the old exegetist of *Ahl al-Sunnah*, al-Tabari, after commenting a few words on this matter, specifies that the most worthy utterance in the interpretation of this verse is to say: God has meant a general concept from this sentence. That is to say, the Muslims should perceive every kind of benefits which is possible at any time or to derive every kind of worldly and heavenly benefits and no tradition or rational decree has assigned any special meaning for this sentence (which is having a comprehensive meaning).[5]

---

[5] *Tafsir al-Tabari*, vol.17, page 108 (Beirut print).

Ka'ba is the Existence of Life

The Holy Qur'an describes *Ka'ba* and *Bayt al-harām* by the following sentence:

جَعَلَ اللَّهُ الْكَعْبَةَ الْبَيْتَ الْحَرَامَ قِيَامًا لِلنَّاسِ وَالشَّهْرَ الْحَرَامَ وَالْهَدْيَ وَالْقَلَائِدَ ۚ ذَٰلِكَ لِتَعْلَمُوا أَنَّ اللَّهَ يَعْلَمُ مَا فِي السَّمَاوَاتِ وَمَا فِي الْأَرْضِ وَأَنَّ اللَّهَ بِكُلِّ شَيْءٍ عَلِيمٌ

"Allah has made the Ka'ba, the sacred house, maintenance for the people, and the sacred month and the offerings and the sacrificial animals with garlands, this is that you may know that Allah knows whatever is in the heavens and whatever is in the earth, and that Allah is the Knower of all things. (Maida:97)"

The word of قيام which has come down in this verse, can be seen in another verse too. As:

وَلَا تُؤْتُوا السُّفَهَاءَ أَمْوَالَكُمُ الَّتِي جَعَلَ اللَّهُ لَكُمْ قِيَامًا

"And do not give away your property which Allah has made for you a (means of) support. (Nisa:5)"

Here, gives the meaning of existence and in fact is synonymous with pillar and the meaning of the verse is this that the Hajj ceremonies and the *ziyarat* of *Ka'ba* and one's presence near the House of Allah is the mainstay for the existence of worldly and heavenly life of the Islamic community.

Gathering during Hajj season, not only ensures the spiritual life of the Muslims but is the source of making secure every kind of element that has a great influence in one's individual and social life. Pondering over the meaning of this verse, guides us to a more comprehensive meaning i.e. whatever is related to the interests of the Muslims and are reckoned to be their life and existence is ensured in this Hajj season. With such general application and extensive saying, is it possible to conclude and limit this matter to only and only the interests related to *'ibadah* and worship?

What better expediency is superior to one political platform that organizes and unites the Muslims against the colonists and the exploiters and makes them steadfast and encourages them to stand united in the battle against them. The Holy Qur'an does not allow the parents or guardians of the insane to give their wealth which is the source of their living and existence to them. It emphatically says:

وَلَا تُؤْتُوا السُّفَهَاءَ أَمْوَالَكُمُ الَّتِي جَعَلَ اللَّهُ لَكُمْ قِيَامًا

"And do not give away your property which Allah has made for you a (means of) support. (Nisa:5)"

Considering the contents of this verse, is it proper that the Hajj formalities should fall in the hands of those who are unaware of it and are fully heedless of the role it plays in the lives of the Muslims!

To acquaint the respected readers with the views of the commentators who focused on the same axis, we present here some of their views regarding the sentence of قياماً للناس.

Al-Tabari says: "God has bestowed *Ka'ba* and *Bayt al-Harām* as a life for the people!

Moreover, he later says:

وجعلها معالم لدينهم ومصالح أمورهم

"He has made Ka'ba the place of signs of people's beliefs and the base for their interests and affairs."[6]

The author of *Al-Manar*[7] while interpreting the afore-mentioned verse, says: *"God has made the Ka'ba a pillar for the people's religious affairs in such manner that it refines their morals and trains them. These are achieved through the Hajj obligations which is the greatest foundation of our religion and it is an 'ibadah which is spiritual (but) containing the economic and social dimensions."*

Then, he continues and says: "This جعل in the verse جعل الله refers to both تكويني (creation) and تشريعي (laws) which guarantees every kind of worldly and heavenly interests of the people."[8]

Expression of Aversion on the Occasion of Hajj

Even if you doubt in the generality of the sentence ليشهدوا منافع لهم and or قياماً للناس yet you cannot doubt in the action of the Holy Prophet's (s) representative in the Hajj season which was totally a political affair.

Because, in the year 9th Hijri, the Holy Prophet (s) gave charge to Ali (a) to readced out a letter which contained expression of disgust towards the polytheists.

---

[6] *Tafsir al-Tabari*, vol. 7, p. 49.
[7] *Tafsir al-Manar*, written by Muhammad Rashid Rida (1865 – 1935 A.D.). He was a Sunni Salafi Egyptian scholar whose ideas influenced 20th-century Islamist thinkers in developing a political philosophy of an Islamic state.
[8] *Al-Manar*, vol. 7, p. 11

This was at the time when 16 verses from the beginning of *Surah Bara'a* (*Tawbah*) were revealed to the Prophet (s) which comprises of the following:

بَرَاءَةٌ مِنَ اللَّهِ وَرَسُولِهِ إِلَى الَّذِينَ عَاهَدْتُمْ مِنَ الْمُشْرِكِينَ فَسِيحُوا فِي الْأَرْضِ أَرْبَعَةَ أَشْهُرٍ وَاعْلَمُوا أَنَّكُمْ غَيْرُ مُعْجِزِي اللَّهِ ۙ وَأَنَّ اللَّهَ مُخْزِي الْكَافِرِينَ وَأَذَانٌ مِنَ اللَّهِ وَرَسُولِهِ إِلَى النَّاسِ يَوْمَ الْحَجِّ الْأَكْبَرِ أَنَّ اللَّهَ بَرِيءٌ مِنَ الْمُشْرِكِينَ ۙ وَرَسُولُهُ ۚ فَإِنْ تُبْتُمْ فَهُوَ خَيْرٌ لَكُمْ ۖ وَإِنْ تَوَلَّيْتُمْ فَاعْلَمُوا أَنَّكُمْ غَيْرُ مُعْجِزِي اللَّهِ ۗ وَبَشِّرِ الَّذِينَ كَفَرُوا بِعَذَابٍ أَلِيمٍ

"(This is a declaration of) immunity by Allah and His Apostle towards those of the idolaters with whom you made an agreement. So go about in the land for four months and know that you cannot weaken Allah and that Allah will bring disgrace to the unbelievers. And an announcement from Allah and His Apostle to the people on the day of the greater pilgrimage that Allah and His Apostle are free from liability to the idolaters, therefore if you repent, it will be better for you, and if you turn back, then know that you will not weaken Allah; and announce painful punishment to those who disbelieve. (Tawbah:1-3)"

After reciting these verses, Amir al-mu'minin (a) issued a four-point resolution as such:

Behold O polytheists!

1. The idol-worshippers have no right to enter the House of Allah.
2. Circumambulation in the state of uncovered body is prohibited.
3. Henceforth, no idol-worshipper will take part in the Hajj ceremony.
4. Those that have signed a non-aggression treaty with the Holy Prophet (s) and have been loyal in their treaty will be faithfully respected. However, for those polytheists who are not having any pact with the Muslims or have intentionally dishonored their pact, they will be given from this date (10th *Dhu'l hijjah*) four months to clarify their stance before the Islamic Government or will have to join the monotheists and break-off from polytheism and dualism or prepare themselves for war.[9]

What deed can be more political than this action where, in the midst of Hajj duties when the Muslims and polytheists were engaged in circumambulation, Ali (a) climbs a high place and starts nullifying some of the points of treaty and gives a four month deadline to either discard polytheism and join the ranks of the monotheists or face the consequences of a war.

---

[9] *Tafsir al-Tabari*, vol. 10, p. 47; *Sirah Ibn Hisham*, vol. 4, p. 545.

Political Elegy of Farazdaq in Masjid al-Harām

Once, during Hajj time, when Hisham son of 'Abdul Malik[10] was circumambulating the *Ka'ba* amidst a huge crowd, he tried many times to kiss *al-Hajar al-Aswad*. However, due to the enormous crowd, Hisham did not get a chance and helplessly sat at one corner and glared at the people. Suddenly he saw a thin, good-looking, divinely-bright personality gradually advancing towards *al-Hajar al-Aswad*. The people respected him and involuntarily moved back so that he could easily reach *al-Hajar al-Aswad*. The people of Syria who were around Ibn 'Abdul Malik asked him: 'Who is this man?' Hisham, even though he knew that personality very well refrained from introducing Imam and instead lied and said: 'I don't know him.'

At this moment, a poet by the name of Farazdaq[11] who enjoyed special freedom and liberty un-hesitantly recited some poems and in this way, introduced Imam al-Sajjad (a) very nicely. Some of the verses of his poem are as follows:

والبيت يعرفه والحِل والحرم	هذا الذي تعرف البطحاء وطأته
هذا التقي النقيّ الطاهر العلم	هذا ابن خير عباد الله كلهم
بجده انبياء الله قد خُتم	هذا ابن فاطمة إن كنت جاه
رُكن الحطيمم إذا ما جاء يستلم	تكاد يُمسكه عِرفان راحته

"He is someone who, the soil of Batha' is aware of his footprints and Ka'ba, the House and its exterior are well-acquainted with him; He is the son of the best servants of Allah; He is pious, pure, holy and well-known. If you are unaware of him, he is the son of Fatima, (daughter of the Holy Prophet (s). Soon, when he will touch al-Hajar al-Aswad, it will not release his well-recognized hand."[12]

The poem of Farazdaq had such far-reaching effect that Hisham became wild and angry and immediately ordered for his arrest. When Imam (a) became aware of this matter, he consoled Farazdaq very much.

---

[10] Hisham ibn Abd al-Malik ibn Marwan (691 – 743 A.D.) was the 10th Umayyid caliph who ruled from 724 until his death in 743. He like most of his ancestors had bitter enmity towards Bani Hashim and specially Ahlul Bayt (as).

[11] Hammam ibn Ghalib (641- 730 A.D.), also known as Al-Farazdaq or Abu Firas, was a famous Iraqi poet.

[12] *Al-Aghani* 5 vol. 21, p. 376-377; *Manaqib Ibn Shahr Ashub*, vol. 4, p. 169. The aforementioned elegy of Farazdaq has come in most of the historical and literary books. To doubt in the authenticity of this poem is one kind of opposition with the reliable traditions.

Political and Social Dimensions of Hajj in Islamic Traditions

So far, it has somewhat become clear from the verses and ways of the Holy Prophet (s) that Hajj, while being one devotional deed, is evidently having a political aspect too where sometimes the Holy Prophet (s) himself considered them as identical. The Holy Prophet (s) has also referred to this aspect in traditions which we shall now mention a few of them:

In the book of *Al-Taj al-Jami' li al-Usul fi Ahadith al-Rasul*[13], vol. 2, pages 98-99, one can find the Holy Prophet (s) narrating as such:

افضل الجهاد حج مبرور

The best jihad is the Hajj which has been accepted.

جهاد الكبير والصغير والضعيف والمرأة الحج والعمرة

Hajj and 'Umra is a universal jihad and in that, men, women, the weak and the powerful participate.

نعم عليهم جهاد لا قتال فيه الحد والعمرة

Is there a jihad for women? Yes! there is jihad for women wherein there is no battle but taking part in the Hajj ceremony.

وقَّد الله ثلاثة الغارى والحاج والمُعتمر

The chosen ones before Allah are these: Those participating in jihad and the pilgrims to the House of God for Hajj and for 'Umra.

In this tradition, Hajj has been introduced as universal *jihad* and as *jihad* for women and in the last part of the tradition, those participating in *jihad* and those participating in Hajj are introduced as the chosen ones whom Allah has invited.

If in this tradition, Hajj has been called as *jihad*, (then) there should exist a kind of sign and similarity between these two that one can apply the word of *jihad* to another. One of the reasons why Hajj is called a *jihad* is because Hajj is similar to *jihad* in its objectives and effects. This divine obligation, apart from being *'ibadah*, is also an occasion for special endeavor in pre-determined matters. The strategies for practical *jihad* and the means and method of cooperation between the Muslims are set forth on this very occasion.

---

[13] Written by Sheikh Mansur Ali Nasif, a famous Egyptian scholar from Al-Azhar University. Published by Dar al-Fikr, Beirut, 2000.

Political Speech of the Holy Prophet (s) at the Time of Hajj

A great and splendid gathering had taken place in Masjid al-Harām around the House of God. The Muslims and polytheists, the friends and foes had all come together and an aura of greatness had surrounded the environment of the mosque due to the magnificence of Islam and the greatness of Holy Prophet (s)

At such a moment, the Holy Prophet (s) began to speak by describing for the people the actual visage of his invitation which had taken twenty years from the date of its commencement. We bring here some of those historical sayings:

1. O people, under the light of Islam, God took away from you the (so called) glories and the impunable acts attributed to your genealogy which was prevalent during the period of ignorance (*jahiliyyah*). All have come into existence from Adam and he too has been created from soil. The best of the people is he who refrains from sins and disobedience.[14]

2. O people, being an Arab is not a part of your nature. Rather, it is only a lip-service. Anyone who is negligent in his duties then the glories of his fathers and forefathers will be of no avail and will not make any amends for his shortcomings.[15]

3. All the people of the past and present are similar and equal like the teeth of a comb and no Arab is having preference over non-Arab nor the white over the black. The standard for excellence is piety and fear of God.[16]

4. I abrogate all the claims related to life and property and all the delusive glories of the pars period and declare all of them as baseless.[17]

5. A Muslim is the brother of another Muslim and all the Muslims are brothers to each other and before the strangers they have one common order. Their blood is the same as each other and the lowest amongst them can make a commitment on behalf of the Muslims.[18]

6. After accepting this religion, do not take an about turn where in such instances has resulted in the deviation of some and caused them to become the owners of each other.[19]

---

[14] ايها الناس إن الله قد أذهب عنكم نحوة الجاهلية وتفاخرها بابائها ألا أنكم من أدم وأدم من طين إلا أن خير عبد اتقاه
[15] ألا أن العربية ليست "اب" والد ولكنها لسان ناطق فمن قصر عمله لم يبلغ به حسبه.
[16] إن الناس من لدن أدم إلى يومنا هذا مثل اسنان المشط لا فضل للعربي على العجمي ولا للأحمر على الأسود إلا بالتقوى
[17] ألا إن كان مالٍ كان مال ومائرة ودم في الجاهلية تحت قدمي هاتين
[18] المسلم أخ المسم والمسلمون اخوة وهم يد واحدة على من سواهم تتكافور مائهم يسعى بذمتهم ادناهم
[19] ا ترجعوا بعدي كفار مضلين يملك بعضكم رقاب بعض

7. Your blood and your property are forbidden for you and are honorable like the honor of this day, this month and this city.[20]

8. All the blood which has been shed in the period of ignorance is declared to be in vain and the first blood which I keep under my foot is the blood of Rabie son of Harith.[21]

9. Every Muslim is the brother of another Muslim and all the Muslims are brothers (to each other). Nothing from his property is permissible for another except if he gives him as a good-will.[22]

10. There are three things which the heart of a believer is never disloyal to:

    1. Sincerity in action for the sake of God.

    2. Wishing goodness for the true leaders.

    3. Attending the gathering of the believers.[23],[24]

Political Poems at the Time of Victory of Mecca

At the time of victory of Mecca, the Muslims, before the very perplexed eyes of the polytheists were ordered, apart from performing their Hajj obligation, to call out and say the following *du'a* which is full of monotheism and epic.

لا إله إلا الله وحده لا شريك له وله المُلك وله الحمد يُحيي ويُميت وهو على كل شئ قدير.

لا إله إلا الله وحده أنجز وعده ونصر عبده وهزم الأحزاب وحده.

"There is no god except Allah; there is no partner for Him and the Kingdom belongs to Him. (All) Praise is for Him; He gives life and causes death and He is Powerful over all things. There is no god except Allah; He is alone. He has fulfilled His promise and helped His servant and alone He has destroyed the collective powers."[25]

Signals and Implications

The Holy Prophet (s) has not restrained himself with such type of expressions in determining the political dimension of Hajj. Sometimes, through signs and indication, he showed that the most trivial actions of Hajj are not far from political dimensions.

---

[20] إن دماءكم وأموالكم عليكم حرام كحُرمة يومكم هذا في شهركم هذا في بلدكم هذا.

[21] ودماء الجاهلية موضوع وأول دم أضعه دم ربيعة بن حارث.

[22] إن كل مسلم أخ المسلم وإن المسلمين اخوة فلا يحل لا مرئ من أخيه إلا ما أعطا عن طيب نفسه منه.

[23] ثلاث لا يغل عليهن قلب امرئ مسلم: إخلاص العمل لله، والنصح لأئمة المسلمين، ولزوم جماعتهم.

[24] Our references for these are: *Rawdat al-Kafi*, page 246; *Sirah Ibn Hisham*, vol. 2 page 412; *al-Manar, al-Waqidi* vol. 2, page 826 and others.

[25] Refer to the books of Hajj of *Sahih al-Bukhari*, *Sahih Muslim* and others.

In so much as in the endeavor between Safa and Marwa at one particular place, he increased his speed in walking so that in this way he wanted to reject the gossip of the polytheists who spread rumors that due to the inclemency of the weather of Medina, the *Muhajirs* (immigrants) and helpers of Prophet (s) had become weak. Therefore in "*Umra-Qadha*" he ordered the people to walk faster in the endeavor (between Safa and Marwa) and while circumambulating in order to show their strength to the polytheists.[26]

In the prayers of *tawaf* the Holy Prophet (s) recited *Surah al-Tawhid* in the first unit and *Surah al-Kafirun* in the second unit. All are aware what dimensions, the contents of these two Surahs have and how they refute and forbid every kind of non-monotheistic thoughts or unity with any side from the camps of disbelief (*kufr*).

It is seen in history that at the time of touching or kissing *al-Hajar al-Aswad*, the Muslims used to recite the following:

بسم الله والله أكبر على ما هدانا لا إله إلا الله لا شريك له أمنت بالله وكفرت بالطاغوت

"*In the name of God, and God is great for He guides us, there is no God save Allah, there is no partner to Him, I believe in God and I deny Taghut (Tyrant).*"[27]

Political Dimensions of Hajj in the Words of Infallible Leaders

1. Imam al-Sadiq (a): About the philosophy of Hajj and the secrets of its legislations Imam al-Sadiq (a) say as such:

وجعل فيه الإجتماع من المشرق والمغرب ليتعارفوا ولتُعرف اثار رسول الله وتُعرف اخباره ولا تُنسى ولوكان كلُّ قوم إنما يتكلون على بلادهم وما فيها هلكُوا وخربت البلاد وسقط الجَلب والأرباح وعميت الأخبار ولم يقفوا على ذلك وذلك علة الحج.

"*In the land of Mecca, there manifested a gathering from East and West so that the people recognize each other and the effects of the Holy Prophet's works (traditions) are recognized and not forgotten. If every group depended upon what was taking place in their own lands, they would be destroyed, the cities would head towards ruin, the trade and economic affairs would collapse and the news and information would not reach the people. This is the philosophy of Hajj.*"[28]

---

[26] *Jami' al-'Usul*, vol. 4, Book of Hajj.
[27] Abu Walid al-'Azarqi, *Ta'rikh Makka*, vol.1, p. 339.
[28] *Bihar al-Anwar*, vol. 99, p. 33, narrated from '*Ilal al-Shara'i*', by al-Sadduq.

This sentence shows that Hajj possesses scientific, economic and political aspects. In fact, Hajj is a connecting chain between the Muslims of the world who in this way engage in exchange of news and current situation of the world and acquire knowledge of the life and *Sunnah* (practices) of the Prophet (s) which has been disseminated through the companions, disciples of the companions and the scholars of *hadith* from the East and West. Meanwhile, every group presents its goods over there and the method of trade and commerce is acquired and recognized.

2. Again Imam al-Sadiq (a) says:

ما مِن بُقعة أحب إلى الله مِن المسعى لأنه يُذل فيه كل جبار

"No spot of the world is more lovable to Allah than the place of endeavor between Safa and Marwa because in this place all the stubborn people become abject and miserable and exhibit their servitude and bondage."[29]

3. History, very clearly reports that the companions and the disciples of the companions derived benefits from this occasion to the advantage of Islam and the Muslims. The seed of most of the uprisings and movement for freedom originated from here and on such an occasion the nations would be invited to fight and combat the unjust rulers. Suffice it is in this case to listen to the words of al-Husayn ibn Ali (a) on the day of Mina. At Hajj time, he called together the names of the sons of Ibn Hisham, the great personalities, their women and even the *Ansars* (helpers) who had interest in him such that more than one thousand people attended his speech. At this moment, when the companions and their sons were listening to his speech, he began his speech as such:

أما بعد فإن هذا الطاغية قد صنع بنا ما قد علمتم ورأيتهم وشهدتم وبلغنكم وإني أريد أن أسئلكم عن أشياء فإن صدفت فصدقوني وإن كذبت فكذبوني اسمعُوا مقالتي واكتُموا قولي ثم إرجعوا إلى امصاركم وقبائلكم من امّنتُموه ووثقتم به فادعُوهم إلى ما تعلمون فإني اخاف أن يندرس هذا الحق ويذهب والله مُتِم نُوره ولو كره الكافرون

"After praising Allah and sending salutations upon the Holy Prophet (s), he said: O people, Know that what evils this tyrant (Mu'awiyah) has committed against us to which you are all knowing and are aware about. I ask you of some affairs which if you find truth in them, then approve my saying and if I speak false, then reject my sayings. Now, listen to my talks and keep them hidden in your hearts and thereafter return back

---

[29] *Bihar al-Anwar*, vol.19, p. 49.

to your towns and among your tribes. You invite every person whom you trust and have confidence towards what you have knowledge (religious duty). I fear that the true religion gets eroded and nullified even though God is the terminator of His light and the unbelievers dislike it."[30]

Thereafter, Husayn ibn Ali (a) recited some verses which has been revealed in favor of the Household of the Prophet and promised the people that when they returned back to their home-towns, they should relate his speech to the people whom they trust. Then he descended from his pulpit and the people dispersed.

It was not only Husayn ibn Ali (a) who had taken advantage of this great gathering. Even the Christians and Jews who were living under the protection of Islamic Government would, at times when their rights were violated, plead for justice on such an occasion and demand back their right from the Islamic ruler. This is a witness to the presence of such a *Sunnah* (practice) amongst the Muslims. History has recorded it:

One of the Coptics of Egypt, during the time of governorship of 'Amr bin al-'As, entered into a competition with the son of the ruler and won the competition. The victory of one Coptic over the son of ruler who was dear to 'Amr bin al-'As and his son finally lead to his beating through the son of 'Amr bin al-'As.

The Coptic related the matter to the ruler of the time ('Umar bin al-Khattab) during Hajj time and explained his innocence. 'Umar called for the 'Amr bin al-'As and accounted a famous sentence in this regard:

متى استعبدتم الناس وقد ولدتهم أمهاتهم أحرارٌ

"Since when you have taken the people as your slaves whereas they have been born free from their mothers!?"[31]

Thereafter he took revenge for the beaten one from the one who had beaten him.

---

[30] *Kitab Sulaym b. Qays al-Kufi*, p. 18. Sulaym ibn Qays al-Hilali (630 – 689 A.D.) was one of the Tabi'un (the second generation of companions of Prophet (s)) and companions of Imam Ali (as). *Kitab Sulaym b. Qays al-Kufi* is the oldest Islamic text on hadithes and traditions as it was written in the first century after Prophet's death, much earlier than the *Sahih al-Bukhari* and *Sahih Muslim*.

[31] *Da'irat al-ma'arif* of Farid Wajdi, Book of Hajj vol. 3, p. 350.

History has narrated such incidents on so many occasions that it itself is a witness to the fact that Hajj is not only for worship and *'ibadah* and void of other dimensions. When Hajj is the center of setting forth complaints, then why it cannot be the center of setting forth complaints about the tyrant rulers of the East and West.

Sayings of Contemporary Thinkers about the Philosophy of Hajj

Now it is proper to narrate few sayings of the Islamic researchers about Hajj responsibilities. We shall narrate three sayings from three contemporary writers and one of them is the member of advisory board of King Abdul Aziz University in Saudi Arabia. Here are some portions of their sayings:

1. Farid Wajdi in the Islamic *Da'irat al-Ma'arif* (Encyclopedia) writes about the matter of Hajj as such:

"The philosophy of divine legislation of Hajj is not something which can be explained in this book. What passes in one's mind is this that if all the Islamic Governments take advantage from this occasion in establishing Islamic unity amongst the Muslim nations, they will achieve a perfect result because a gathering of tens of thousands of people from different places in one common place and the attentiveness of their hearts to those things which are inspired to them in this place creates a special kind of impression in them and all return back to their respective countries with one heart and there, they propagate to their brothers whatever they have heard and learnt.

The example of this group is like the example of members of one big congress which gather from all corners of the world and after the termination of the congress disperse to different parts of the world carrying a message. Whatever may be the result of this magnificent Congress, gatherings on such occasions and later, the dispersion to the home-towns bears the same result.

2. Doctor al-Qardawi, the contemporary writer, writes in the book *al-'Ibadah fi al-Islam* as such:

The greatest result which can be achieved from this gathering is that Hajj is the most important factor for awakening the Islamic *Ummah* from its long sleep. For this reason, some of the puppet governments and invaders of Islamic states have become an obstacle for the Muslims from visiting the House of Allah since they know that if the slightest movement is set up amongst the Muslims, then no factor can stop them from such a movement.

He writes in the book: *al-Din wa al-Hajj 'ala al-Madhahib al-Arba'a*, on page 51 as such:

"Hajj is a means of acquaintance among the Muslims and the source of forming affection and relation among the various kinds of people who live under the banner of monotheism. This is because at such times their hearts become one and their voice becomes united. Then, they embark on rectifying their own condition and setting right the defects of their own society."

Doctor Muhammad Mubarak, advisor to King Abdul Aziz University writes as such:

"Hajj is a world congress where all the Muslims gather in one line for worshipping God. But this worship is not un-mixed and separate from their lives. Rather, it possesses a special relation with their lives."

In this regard, the Holy Qur'an says:

$$...لِيَشْهَدُوا مَنَافِعَ لَهُمْ وَيَذْكُرُوا اسْمَ اللَّهِ فِي أَيَّامٍ مَعْلُومَاتٍ$$

"That they may witness advantages for them and mention the name of Allah during stated days ….. (Hajj:28)"

By witness of the benefits and perception of the benefits nothing is meant but a common purpose encompassing all the aspects of the affairs of the Muslims.

Conclusion

If truly the obligatory act of Hajj possesses such a high place and position towards which the Holy Qur'an and *Sunnah*, the past practices of the Muslims and the views of the contemporary writers guide us then why should we be negligent in making use of it?

If Hajj is the means of attracting hearts, monotheistic expression and forming a global united front for the Muslims, then why shouldn't we mobilize through this means, the Islamic forces and powers against the aggressors who have committed oppression in the Islamic lands such as occupied Palestine and Afghanistan?[1] If Hajj has scientific, social, cultural and economic dimensions, then why shouldn't the Muslims during such an occasion find solution to improve their economic conditions, make efforts to resolve their difficult problems and unsolved matters and come out of the miserable current situation?

Why shouldn't the oppressed people of Palestine, Iraq, Afghanistan, Africa and Lebanon be given the opportunity to openly demonstrate and mention their problems to inform and awaken their brethren Muslims from other countries and why shouldn't they seek help from them in defending their just and legal rights?

During Hajj, why shouldn't vast and extensive gatherings, conferences, seminars and congregations be held against the Eastern and Western arrogant powers and to expose their crimes and plots so that the Muslims return back to their respective countries with illuminated thoughts and united plans and coordinated programs to implement solutions? For how long should we lose such golden opportunities and continue to bear these losses?

We hope for the day when the foreign hands, who are at work behind the scenes, are cut-off from the two holy shrines and the sacred tombs and the historic places of Islam are taken care of by a responsible group selected from the International Islamic Community so that the real objectives of Hajj and its valuable fruits are achieved and materialized.

---

[1] Recently several other Islamic countries including Yemen, Syria, Iraq, Bahrain, Libya, Rohingya Muslims in Myanmar, Muslims in Nigeria, etc. have witnessed aggression and invasion, massacres and brutal inhumane crimes committed against innocent civilians with the support of world arrogant powers such as USA, Zionist entity, Europeans and their allied Arab countries such as Saudi Arabia. Wahhabi extremist ideology is the basis of these crimes.

Wahhabism

Glossary of Important Terms

Awliya Allah: Divine personalities such as Prophets, Imams and Saints who by the virtue of their purity of soul and sincere worship of Allah are bestowed by Him with miracles and feats that a normal human being cannot perform. Such miracles or feats are for the guidance of or for helping human beings.

Du'a: Seeking help from Allah either directly or through *Awliya Allah*.

Fatiha: Reciting Surah Fatiha (the first Surah of Qur'an), commonly over the grave or a dead person for seeking the mercy of Allah.

'Ibadah (Worship): Any act that is done sincerely for the sake of seeking nearness to Allah and for His pleasure.

Kufr (Disblief): Denial of the existence of Allah or creator of the universe.

Nadhr: Making a vow to carryout a good and logical act for relief from a disease or hardship by seeking nearness to Allah and / or through a divine personality.

Nida: Calling upon God or a divine personality.

Rububiyyat (Lordship): Taking care of all the affairs of creatures by Allah or by His authority through creatures such a parents. Thus, belief in lordship of parents and thanking them for their hardships doesn't make a person *mushrik* (polytheist) as they are only responsible for nurturing their children while they didn't create them.

Sajdah (Prostration): Bowing down either for the worship of God or for the sake of respect of a divine personality. Respect doesn't mean worship.

Shahada (Testimony): Verbal utterance of the belief in *Tawhid* (One God, Allah), denial of every other God and belief in messengetship of Prophet Muhammad (s). By the utterance of *Shahada*, harming and shedding blood of Muslim becomes forbidden (*harām*) on other Muslims.

Shifa: Seeking benediction through *tabarruk* of divine personalities for cure of illness or for relief from disability or difficulty.

Shirk (Polytheism): Belief that there is more than one creator of Universe.

Sunnah: The way of life of Prophet (s), either in intentions, words or deeds.

Tabarruk: Remnants or traces of divine personalities such as Prophets, Imams and saints. *Tabarruk* of divine personalites have miraculous powers.

Takfir: Wrongfully accusing Muslim or a person who belieives in Allah of being a *Kafir* (unbeliever or denier of God).

Tawassul: Seeking intercession through divine personalities for the forgiveness of sins or for seeking help in worldly matters.

Tawhid (Monotheism): Belief in one God (i.e. Allah).

Tazallul (Submisiveness): Showing utmost humbles or humility to God or a divine personality. Doesn't mean worship when practiced for a divine personality.

Ta'zim (Respect, honor): Respecting a divine personality. It doesnot mean worship.

Ubudiyyat (Submission): Carrying out all the acts for the sake of worship of Allah. Utmost submission means that a person becomes totally gives up his personal desires and performs all the acts sincerely as a bondsman of Allah.

Ziyarat: Visitation of the grave of a divine personality and / or reciting greetings (*salams*) and honoring them with words of praise and remembering their services for the sake of Allah and His religion on their birth or death anniversary.

APPENDIX

APPENDIX

APPENDIX I

List of *Ayahs* of Holy Qur'an used by Wahhabi Scholars to prove their deviant ideology and the rebuttal of their argument

#	Ayah	Rebuttal
1	He makes the night pass into the day and makes the day pass into the night, and He has disposed the sun and the moon, each moving for a specified term. That is Allah, your Lord; to Him belongs all sovereignty. As for those whom you invoke besides Him, they do not control so much as the husk of a date stone. [*Surah Fatir:*13]	These ayahs pertain to authority of God over universe, His exclusive worship and faith in Him. All Muslims or followers of any monotheistic divine religions believe that the whole universe is created by God and all its affairs are under the total authority of God. No follower of monotheistic divine religion takes anyone besides God as a partner in His authority. Paying respect to Prophets and *awliya* (saints or divine personalities) doesn't mean worshipping them. Any authority exercised or miracle shown by Prophets and *awliya* is because God has bestowed them special powers and they are not independent in their authority or power. These miracles include giving *shifa* (restoring health), *shaqq al-qamar*, dividing the moon into two halves, *shafa'a* (interceding for the sins), bringing dead to life again etc. Visiting the graves of dead and addressing them is the sunnah of Prophet (s). Remembering the dead and saluting them is the sunnah of Prophet and Ayahs of Qur'an mention those who have passed before. Commemorating the days of birth and death of Prophet and *awliya* is mentioned in Qur'an and sunnah of Prophet. Seeking help from creatures of God either alive or those who are bestowed with life after death such martyrs doesn't mean worshipping them or taking them as partners in the authority of God. Weeping over dead relatives or beloved of God such as Prophets, *awliya* and martyrs is mentioned in Qur'an and is a sunnah of prophet.
2	They worship besides Allah that which neither causes them any harm, nor brings them any benefit, and they say, 'These are our intercessors with Allah.' Say, 'Will you inform Allah about something He does not know in the heavens or on the earth?' Immaculate is He and exalted above [having] any partners that they ascribe [to Him]! [*Surah Yunus:*18]	
3	Indeed, only exclusive faith is worthy of Allah, and those who take other as *awliya* besides Him [claiming,] 'We only worship them so that they may bring us near to Allah,' Allah will judge between them concerning that about which they differ. Indeed Allah does not guide someone who is a liar and an ingrate. [*Surah Zumur:*3]	

APPENDIX II

Najd[1] and Wahhabi *fitna* as mentioned in the hadithes of Prophet Muhammad (s)

Following are selected few hadithes from authentic sources of hadith books about the sedition predicted by Prophet Muhammad (s) that will emerge from Najd.

Hadith # 1

حَدَّثَنَا عَلِيُّ بْنُ عَبْدِ اللَّهِ، حَدَّثَنَا أَزْهَرُ بْنُ سَعْدٍ، عَنِ ابْنِ عَوْنٍ، عَنْ نَافِعٍ، عَنِ ابْنِ عُمَرَ، قَالَ ذَكَرَ النَّبِيُّ صلى الله عليه وسلم "اللَّهُمَّ بَارِكْ لَنَا فِي شَأْمِنَا، اللَّهُمَّ بَارِكْ لَنَا فِي يَمَنِنَا". قَالُوا وَفِي نَجْدِنَا. قَالَ "اللَّهُمَّ بَارِكْ لَنَا فِي شَأْمِنَا، اللَّهُمَّ بَارِكْ لَنَا فِي يَمَنِنَا". قَالُوا يَا رَسُولَ اللَّهِ وَفِي نَجْدِنَا فَأَظُنُّهُ قَالَ فِي الثَّالِثَةِ "هُنَاكَ الزَّلاَزِلُ وَالْفِتَنُ، وَبِهَا يَطْلُعُ قَرْنُ الشَّيْطَانِ".

Narrated Ibn 'Umar:

The Prophet (s) said, "*O Allah! Bestow Your blessings on our Sham! O Allah! Bestow Your blessings on our Yemen.*" The People said, "And also on our Najd." He said, "*O Allah! Bestow Your blessings on our Sham (north)! O Allah! Bestow Your blessings on our Yemen.*" The people said, "O Allah's Apostle! And also on our Najd." I think the third time the Prophet (s) said, "*There (in Najd) is the place of earthquakes and afflictions and from there comes out the side of the head of Satan.*"

[*Sahih al-Bukhari*, Vol. 9, Book 88, Chapter: "The Fitnah will appear from the east", Hadith 214]

Hadith # 2

حَدَّثَنَا مُحَمَّدُ بْنُ الْمُثَنَّى، قَالَ حَدَّثَنَا حُسَيْنُ بْنُ الْحَسَنِ، قَالَ حَدَّثَنَا ابْنُ عَوْنٍ، عَنْ نَافِعٍ، عَنِ ابْنِ عُمَرَ، قَالَ اللَّهُمَّ بَارِكْ لَنَا فِي شَامِنَا وَفِي يَمَنِنَا. قَالَ قَالُوا وَفِي نَجْدِنَا قَالَ قَالَ اللَّهُمَّ بَارِكْ لَنَا فِي شَامِنَا وَفِي يَمَنِنَا. قَالَ قَالُوا وَفِي نَجْدِنَا قَالَ قَالَ هُنَاكَ الزَّلاَزِلُ وَالْفِتَنُ، وَبِهَا يَطْلُعُ قَرْنُ الشَّيْطَانِ.

Narrated Ibn 'Umar:

(The Prophet) said, "*O Allah! Bless our Sham and our Yemen.*" People said, "Our Najd as well." The Prophet again said, "*O Allah! Bless our Sham and Yemen.*" They said

---

[1] Najd is the geographically central region of present Saudi Arabia that has about a third of the population of the country. Najd consists of the modern administrative regions of Riyadh, Al-Qassim, and Ha'il. Najd was a part of Hijaz in the time of Prophet Muhammad (s).

again, "Our Najd as well." On that the Prophet (s) said, "*There will appear earthquakes and afflictions, and from there will come out the side of the head of Satan.*"

[*Sahih al-Bukhari*, Vol. 2, Book 17, Chapter: "Invoking Allah for Rain (*Istisqaa*)", Hadith 147]

Hadith # 3

قَالَ وَقَالَ ابْنُ كَثِيرٍ عَنْ سُفْيَانَ، عَنْ أَبِيهِ، عَنِ ابْنِ أَبِي نُعْمٍ، عَنْ أَبِي سَعِيدٍ ـ رضى الله عنه ـ قَالَ بَعَثَ عَلِيٌّ ـ رضى الله عنه ـ إِلَى النَّبِيِّ صلى الله عليه وسلم بِذُهَيْبَةٍ فَقَسَمَهَا بَيْنَ الأَرْبَعَةِ الأَقْرَعِ بْنِ حَابِسٍ الْحَنْظَلِيِّ ثُمَّ الْمُجَاشِعِيِّ، وَعُيَيْنَةَ بْنِ بَدْرٍ الْفَزَارِيِّ، وَزَيْدٍ الطَّائِيِّ ثُمَّ أَحَدِ بَنِي نَبْهَانَ، وَعَلْقَمَةَ بْنِ عُلاَثَةَ الْعَامِرِيِّ ثُمَّ أَحَدِ بَنِي كِلاَبٍ، فَغَضِبَتْ قُرَيْشٌ وَالأَنْصَارُ، قَالُوا يُعْطِي صَنَادِيدَ أَهْلِ نَجْدٍ وَيَدَعُنَا. قَالَ " إِنَّمَا أَتَأَلَّفُهُمْ ". فَأَقْبَلَ رَجُلٌ غَائِرُ الْعَيْنَيْنِ مُشْرِفُ الْوَجْنَتَيْنِ، نَاتِئُ الْجَبِينِ، كَثُّ اللِّحْيَةِ، مَحْلُوقٌ فَقَالَ اتَّقِ اللَّهَ يَا مُحَمَّدُ. فَقَالَ " مَنْ يُطِعِ اللَّهَ إِذَا عَصَيْتُ، أَيَأْمَنُنِي اللَّهُ عَلَى أَهْلِ الأَرْضِ فَلاَ تَأْمَنُونِي ". فَسَأَلَهُ رَجُلٌ قَتْلَهُ ـ أَحْسِبُهُ خَالِدَ بْنَ الْوَلِيدِ ـ فَمَنَعَهُ، فَلَمَّا وَلَّى قَالَ " إِنَّ مِنْ ضِئْضِئِ هَذَا ـ أَوْ فِي عَقِبِ هَذَا ـ قَوْمٌ يَقْرَءُونَ الْقُرْآنَ، لاَ يُجَاوِزُ حَنَاجِرَهُمْ، يَمْرُقُونَ مِنَ الدِّينِ مُرُوقَ السَّهْمِ مِنَ الرَّمِيَّةِ، يَقْتُلُونَ أَهْلَ الإِسْلاَمِ، وَيَدَعُونَ أَهْلَ الأَوْثَانِ، لَئِنْ أَنَا أَدْرَكْتُهُمْ لأَقْتُلَنَّهُمْ قَتْلَ عَادٍ ".

Narrated Abu Sa`eed:

'Ali sent a piece of gold to the Prophet (s) who distributed it among four persons: al-Aqra' bin Habis al-Hanzali from the tribe of Mujashi, 'Uyaina bin Badr al-Fazari, Zaid al-Ta'i who belonged to (the tribe of) Bani Nahban, and 'Alqama bin Ulatha al-`Amir who belonged to (the tribe of) Bani Kilab. So the Quraish and the Ansar became angry and said, "He (i.e. the Prophet) gives the chief of Najd and does not give us." The Prophet (s) said, "*I give them) so as to attract their hearts (to Islam).*" Then a man with sunken eyes, prominent checks, a raised forehead, a thick beard and a shaven head, came (in front of the Prophet (s) and said, "Be afraid of Allah, O Muhammad!" The Prophet (s) said "*Who would obey Allah if I disobeyed Him? (Is it fair that) Allah has trusted all the people of the earth to me while, you do not trust me?*" Somebody who, I think was Khalid bin Al-Walid, requested the Prophet (s) to let him chop that man's head off, but he prevented him. When the man left, the Prophet (s) said, "*Among the off-spring of this man will be some who will recite the Qur'an but the Qur'an will not reach beyond their throats (i.e. they will recite like parrots and will not understand it nor act on it), and they will renegade from the religion as an arrow goes through the game's body. They will kill the Muslims but will not disturb the idolaters. If I should live up to their time' I will kill them as the people of 'Ad were killed (i.e. I will kill all of them).*"

[*Sahih al-Bukhari*, Vol. 4, Book 55, Chapter: "Prophets", Hadith 558]

APPENDIX II

Hadith # 4

حَدَّثَنَا هَنَّادُ بْنُ السَّرِيِّ، حَدَّثَنَا أَبُو الأَحْوَصِ، عَنْ سَعِيدِ بْنِ مَسْرُوقٍ، عَنْ عَبْدِ الرَّحْمَنِ، بْنِ أَبِي نُعْمٍ عَنْ أَبِي سَعِيدٍ الْخُدْرِيِّ، قَالَ بَعَثَ عَلِيٌّ - رضى الله عنه - إِلَى رَسُولِ اللَّهِ صلى الله عليه وسلم - وَهُوَ بِالْيَمَنِ بِذُهَيْبَةٍ فِي تُرْبَتِهَا إِلَى رَسُولِ اللَّهِ صلى الله عليه وسلم فَقَسَمَهَا رَسُولُ اللَّهِ صلى الله عليه وسلم بَيْنَ أَرْبَعَةِ نَفَرٍ الأَقْرَعِ بْنِ حَابِسٍ الْحَنْظَلِيِّ وَعُيَيْنَةَ بْنِ بَدْرٍ الْفَزَارِيِّ وَعَلْقَمَةَ بْنِ عُلاَثَةَ الْعَامِرِيِّ ثُمَّ أَحَدِ بَنِي كِلاَبٍ وَزَيْدِ الْخَيْرِ الطَّائِيِّ ثُمَّ أَحَدِ بَنِي نَبْهَانَ - قَالَ - فَغَضِبَتْ قُرَيْشٌ فَقَالُوا أَتُعْطِي صَنَادِيدَ نَجْدٍ وَتَدَعُنَا فَقَالَ رَسُولُ اللَّهِ صلى الله عليه وسلم " إِنِّي إِنَّمَا فَعَلْتُ ذَلِكَ لأَتَأَلَّفَهُمْ " فَجَاءَ رَجُلٌ كَثُّ اللِّحْيَةِ مُشْرِفُ الْوَجْنَتَيْنِ غَائِرُ الْعَيْنَيْنِ نَاتِئُ الْجَبِينِ مَحْلُوقُ الرَّأْسِ فَقَالَ اتَّقِ اللَّهَ يَا مُحَمَّدُ . - قَالَ - فَقَالَ رَسُولُ اللَّهِ صلى الله عليه وسلم " فَمَنْ يُطِعِ اللَّهَ إِنْ عَصَيْتُهُ أَيَأْمَنُنِي عَلَى أَهْلِ الأَرْضِ وَلاَ تَأْمَنُونِي " قَالَ ثُمَّ أَدْبَرَ الرَّجُلُ فَاسْتَأْذَنَ رَجُلٌ مِنَ الْقَوْمِ فِي قَتْلِهِ - يُرَوْنَ أَنَّهُ خَالِدُ بْنُ الْوَلِيدِ - فَقَالَ رَسُولُ اللَّهِ صلى الله عليه وسلم " إِنَّ مِنْ ضِئْضِئِ هَذَا قَوْمًا يَقْرَءُونَ الْقُرْآنَ لاَ يُجَاوِزُ حَنَاجِرَهُمْ يَقْتُلُونَ أَهْلَ الإِسْلاَمِ وَيَدَعُونَ أَهْلَ الأَوْثَانِ يَمْرُقُونَ مِنَ الإِسْلاَمِ كَمَا يَمْرُقُ السَّهْمُ مِنَ الرَّمِيَّةِ لَئِنْ أَدْرَكْتُهُمْ لأَقْتُلَنَّهُمْ قَتْلَ عَادٍ ".

Abu Sa'eed al-Khudri reported that 'Ali (Allah be pleased with him) sent some gold alloyed with dust to the Messenger of Allah (s), and the Messenger of Allah (s) distributed that among four men, al-Aqra bin Habis Hanzali and Uyaina bin Badr al-Fazari and 'Alqama bin 'Ulatha al-'Amiri, then to one person of the tribe of Kilab and to Zaid al-Khair al-Ta'i, and then to one person of the tribe of Nabhan. Upon this the people of Quraish felt angry and said:

He (the Holy Prophet) gave to the chiefs of Najd and ignored us. Upon this the Messenger of Allah (s) said: *"I have done it with a view to conciliating between them."* Then there came a person with thick beard, prominent cheeks, deep sunken eyes and protruding forehead and shaven head. He said: Muhammad, fear Allah. Upon this the Messenger of Allah (s) said: *"If I disobey Allah, who would then obey Him? Have I not been (sent as the) most trustworthy among the people of the world? But you do not repose trust in me."* That person then went back. A person among the people then sought permission (from the Holy Prophet) for his murder. According to some, it was Khalid bin al-Walid who sought the permission. Upon this the Messenger of Allah (s), said: *"From this very person's posterity there would arise people who would recite the Qur'an, but it would not go beyond their throat; they would kill the followers of Islam and would spare the idol-worshippers. They would glance through the teachings of Islam so hurriedly just as the arrow passes through the pray. If I were to ever find them I would kill them like 'Ad."*

[*Sahih Muslim*, Book 5, "The Book of Zakat", Hadith 2318]

Hadith # 5

أَخْبَرَنَا مَحْمُودُ بْنُ غَيْلاَنَ، قَالَ حَدَّثَنَا عَبْدُ الرَّزَّاقِ، قَالَ أَنْبَأَنَا الثَّوْرِيُّ، عَنْ أَبِيهِ، عَنِ ابْنِ أَبِي نُعْمٍ، عَنْ أَبِي سَعِيدٍ الْخُدْرِيِّ، قَالَ بَعَثَ عَلِيٌّ إِلَى النَّبِيِّ صلى الله عليه وسلم وَهُوَ بِالْيَمَنِ بِذُهَيْبَةٍ فِي تُرْبَتِهَا فَقَسَمَهَا بَيْنَ الأَقْرَعِ بْنِ حَابِسٍ الْحَنْظَلِيِّ ثُمَّ أَحَدِ بَنِي مُجَاشِعٍ وَبَيْنَ عُيَيْنَةَ بْنِ بَدْرٍ الْفَزَارِيِّ وَبَيْنَ عَلْقَمَةَ بْنِ عُلاَثَةَ الْعَامِرِيِّ

ثُمَّ أَحَدِ بَنِي كِلَابٍ وَبَيْنَ زَيْدِ الْخَيْلِ الطَّائِيِّ ثُمَّ أَحَدِ بَنِي نَبْهَانَ ۔ قَالَ ۔ فَغَضِبَتْ قُرَيْشٌ وَالْأَنْصَارُ وَقَالُوا يُعْطِي صَنَادِيدَ أَهْلِ نَجْدٍ وَيَدَعُنَا فَقَالَ " إِنَّمَا أَتَأَلَّفُهُمْ " . فَأَقْبَلَ رَجُلٌ غَائِرُ الْعَيْنَيْنِ نَاتِئُ الْوَجْنَتَيْنِ كَثُّ اللِّحْيَةِ مَحْلُوقُ الرَّأْسِ فَقَالَ يَا مُحَمَّدُ اتَّقِ اللَّهَ قَالَ " مَنْ يُطِعِ اللَّهَ إِذَا عَصَيْتُهُ أَيَأْمَنُنِي عَلَى أَهْلِ الْأَرْضِ وَلَا تَأْمَنُونِي " . فَسَأَلَ رَجُلٌ مِنَ الْقَوْمِ قَتْلَهُ فَمَنَعَهُ فَلَمَّا وَلَّى قَالَ " إِنَّ مِنْ ضِئْضِئِ هَذَا قَوْمًا يَخْرُجُونَ يَقْرَءُونَ الْقُرْآنَ لَا يُجَاوِزُ حَنَاجِرَهُمْ يَمْرُقُونَ مِنَ الدِّينِ مُرُوقَ السَّهْمِ مِنَ الرَّمِيَّةِ يَقْتُلُونَ أَهْلَ الْإِسْلَامِ وَيَدَعُونَ أَهْلَ الْأَوْثَانِ لَئِنْ أَنَا أَدْرَكْتُهُمْ لَأَقْتُلَنَّهُمْ قَتْلَ عَادٍ".

It was narrated that Abu Sa'eed al-Khudri said:

"When 'Ali was in Yemen, he sent some gold that was still enclosed in rock to the Prophet (s), who distributed it among al-Aqra' bin Habis al-Hanzali, who belonged to Banu Mujashi', 'Uyaynah bin Badr al-Fazari, 'Alqamah bin 'Ulathah al-'Amiri, who belonged to Banu Kilab and Zaid al-Khail al-Ta'i, who belonged to Banu Nabhan. The Quraish and the Ansar became angry and said: 'He gives to the chiefs of Najd and ignores us!' He said: 'I am seeking to win them over (firmly to Islam).' Then a man with sunken eyes, a bulging forehead, a thick beard and a shaven head came and said: 'O Muhammad, fear Allah!' He said: 'Who will obey Allah if I do not? He trusts me with the people of this Earth but you do not trust me.' A man among the people asked for permission to kill him, but he did not let him do that. When (the man) went away, he (the Prophet (s) said: *'Among the offspring of this man there will be people who will recite the Qur'an but it will not go beyond their throats, and they will go out of Islam as an arrow goes through the target. They will kill the Muslims and leave the idol-worshippers alone. If I live to see them, I will kill them as the killing of 'Ad'*".

[*Sunan al-Nasa'i*, Vol. 5, Book 37, "The Book of Fighting [The Prohibition of Bloodshed]" Hadith 4106]

Hadith # 6

حَدَّثَنَا مُحَمَّدُ بْنُ كَثِيرٍ، أَخْبَرَنَا سُفْيَانُ، عَنْ أَبِيهِ، عَنِ ابْنِ أَبِي نُعْمٍ، عَنْ أَبِي سَعِيدٍ الْخُدْرِيِّ، قَالَ : بَعَثَ عَلِيٌّ عَلَيْهِ السَّلَامُ إِلَى النَّبِيِّ صلى الله عليه وسلم بِذُهَيْبَةٍ فِي تُرْبَتِهَا، فَقَسَّمَهَا بَيْنَ أَرْبَعَةٍ بَيْنَ : الْأَقْرَعِ بْنِ حَابِسٍ الْحَنْظَلِيِّ ثُمَّ الْمُجَاشِعِيِّ، وَبَيْنَ عُيَيْنَةَ بْنِ بَدْرٍ الْفَزَارِيِّ، وَبَيْنَ زَيْدِ الْخَيْلِ الطَّائِيِّ ثُمَّ أَحَدِ بَنِي نَبْهَانَ وَبَيْنَ عَلْقَمَةَ بْنِ عُلَاثَةَ الْعَامِرِيِّ ثُمَّ أَحَدِ بَنِي كِلَابٍ قَالَ فَغَضِبَتْ قُرَيْشٌ وَالْأَنْصَارُ وَقَالَتْ : يُعْطِي صَنَادِيدَ أَهْلِ نَجْدٍ وَيَدَعُنَا . فَقَالَ : " إِنَّمَا أَتَأَلَّفُهُمْ " . قَالَ : فَأَقْبَلَ رَجُلٌ غَائِرُ الْعَيْنَيْنِ مُشْرِفُ الْوَجْنَتَيْنِ نَاتِئُ الْجَبِينِ كَثُّ اللِّحْيَةِ مَحْلُوقٌ قَالَ : اتَّقِ اللَّهَ يَا مُحَمَّدُ . فَقَالَ : " مَنْ يُطِعِ اللَّهَ إِذَا عَصَيْتُهُ أَيَأْمَنُنِي اللَّهُ عَلَى أَهْلِ الْأَرْضِ وَلَا تَأْمَنُونِي " . قَالَ : فَسَأَلَ رَجُلٌ قَتْلَهُ أَحْسِبُهُ خَالِدَ بْنَ الْوَلِيدِ ۔ قَالَ ۔ فَمَنَعَهُ . قَالَ : فَلَمَّا وَلَّى قَالَ : " إِنَّ مِنْ ضِئْضِئِ هَذَا أَوْ فِي عَقِبِ هَذَا قَوْمًا يَقْرَءُونَ الْقُرْآنَ لَا يُجَاوِزُ حَنَاجِرَهُمْ يَمْرُقُونَ مِنَ الْإِسْلَامِ مُرُوقَ السَّهْمِ مِنَ الرَّمِيَّةِ، يَقْتُلُونَ أَهْلَ الْإِسْلَامِ وَيَدَعُونَ أَهْلَ الْأَوْثَانِ لَئِنْ أَنَا أَدْرَكْتُهُمْ قَتَلْتُهُمْ قَتْلَ عَادٍ".

Abu Sa'eed al-Khudri said:

'Ali sent some gold-mixed dust to the prophet (May peace be upon him). He divided it among the four: al-Aqra b. Habis al-Hanzall and then al-Mujashi, Uyainah bin Badr al-Fazari, Zaid al-Khail al-Ta'i, next to one of Banu Nabhan, and 'Alqamah b. 'Ulathat al-Amiri (in general), next to one of Banu Kulaib. The Quraish and the ansar became angry and said: He is giving to the chiefs of the people of Najd and leaving us. He said: I am giving them for reconciliation of their hearts. Then a man with deep-seated eyes, high cheek-bones, a projecting brow, a thick beard and a shaven head came forward and said: For Allah, Muhammad! He said: *"Who will obey Allah if I disobey Him? Allah entrusts me with power over the inhabitants of the earth, but you do not."* A man asked to be allowed to kill him and I think he was Khalid bin al-Walid but he prevented him. Then when the man turned away, he said: *"From this one's stock there will be people who recite the Quran, but it will not pass down their throats. They will sever from Islam and leave the worshippers of Idols alone; but if I live up to their time, I shall certainly kill them as 'Ad were killed."*

[*Sunan Abu Dawud*, Book 41, "Chapter: Fighting Against The Khawarij" Hadith 4746]

APPENDIX III

List and brief description of few books written by leading Muslim scholars in rebuttal of Wahhabism

[Book title (bold text) and author names are mentioned in Arabic]

1.**تطهير الفؤاد من دنس الاعتقاد**: للشيخ محمد بخيت المطيعي الحنفي، من علماء الأزهر، مطبوع.

Tatheer al-Fuad min dins al E'tiqad written by Sheikh Mohammad Bakheet Al-Mutee'i al-Hanafi (d. 1935 A.D.). The author was a famous Sunni Hanafi Ash'ari Scholar from Egypt. He was senior faculty at Al-Azhar University, Cairo. Published by Maktab al-Haqeeqah, Istanbul, Turkey (2003).

2. **التوسّل بالنبي والصالحين**: لأبي حامد بن مرزوق الدمشقي الشامي، مطبوع.

Al-Tawassul bi al-Nabi wa al-Salihin written by Abu Hamid bin Marzuq al-Dimishqi (d. 1872 A.D.). Published by Isık Kitabevi, Hakikat Kitabevi, Istanbul, Turkey (2005).

3. **جلال الحقّ في كشف أحوال أشرار الخلق**: للشيخ إبراهيم حلمي القادري الاسكندري، مطبوع.

Jalal al-Haq fi Kashf Ahwal Ashrar al-Khalq written by Sheikh Ibrahim Hilmi al-Qadri (d. 1970 A.D.). The author was Sunni scholar belonged to Sufi Tariqah al-Qadriyah from Alexandria, Egypt. Published by Maktab al-Ghaza al-Arwah, Alexandria, Egypt (1936).

4.**الحقائق الإسلامية في الردّ على المزاعم الوهّابية بأدلّة الكتاب والسنة النبوية**: لمالك ابن الشيخ محمود، مدير مدرسة العرفان بمدينة كوتبالي بجمهورية مالي الأفريقية، مطبوع.

Al-Haqaiq al-Islamiyyah fi al-Radd 'ila al-maza'im al-Wahhabiyyah bi Dalla al-Kitab wa al-Sunnah Al-Nabawiyyah written by Al-Haj Malik Ibn Sheikh Dawood. The author was a famous Sunni Scholar from Koutiala city Mali. Published by Maktab al-Haqeeqah, Istanbul, Turkey (2014).

5.**الحقيقة الإسلامية في الردّ على الوهّابية**: لعبد الغني بن صالح حمادة، مطبوع.

Al-Haqeeqah al-Islamiyyah fi Radd 'ala al-Wahhabiyyah written by Abd al-Ghani bin Salih Hammadah (d. 1894 A.D.). The author was a Syrian Sunni scholar. Printed in Idlib, Syria, 1894.

6.الدرر السنيّة في الردّ على الوهّابية: للسيد أحمد بن زيني دحلان. مفتي مكة الشافعي، المتوفى سنة 1304هـ، مطبوع.

Al-Durar al-Saniyyah fi al-Radd 'ala al-Wahhabiyyah written by Seyyid Ahmad bin Zayni Dahlan (d. 1886 A.D.). The author was a famous Sunni Shafi'i scholar. He was the Grand Mufti of Mecca and Shaykh al-Islam in the Hijaz region during Ottoman rule. Published by Mustafa al-Babi al-Halabi, Egypt (1989).

7. فتنة الوهابية : للسيد أحمد بن زيني دحلان. مفتي مكة الشافعي، المتوفى سنة 1304هـ، مطبوع.

Fitnat al-Wahhabiyyah written by Seyyid Ahmad bin Zayni Dahlan (d. 1886 A.D.). Published by Isık Kitabevi, Hakikat Kitabevi, Istanbul, Turkey (1978).

8. الدليل الكافي في الرد على الوهابي: للشيخ مصباح بن أحمد شبقلو البيروتي، مطبوع.

Al-Dalil al-Kafi fi al-Radd 'ala al-Wahhabi written by Sheikh Misbah bin Ahmad Shabaqlu. published by Matb'ah al-Wataniyyah Beirut, 1923.

9. ردّ المحتار على الدر المختار: لمحمد أمين الشهير بابن عابدين الحنفي الدمشقي، مطبوع.

Radd al-Muhtar al-Dar al-Mukhtar written by Muhammad Amin al-Shaheer bi Ibn Abidin (d. 1836 A.D.). The author was a famous Syrian Sunni Hanafi Scholar and Jurist from Damascus during the Ottoman era. Published by Darul Fiqr, Beirut. 1992.

10.الردّ على ابن عبد الوهاب: لشيخ الإسلام إسماعيل التميمي المالكي بتونس، المتوفى سنة 1248هـ، وهو في غاية التحقيق والإحكام. مطبوع في تونس.

Al-Radd 'ala Ibn al-Wahhab written by Sheikh al-Islam Ismaeel al-Tamimi al-Maliki (d. 1832 A.D.). The author belonged to Tunis where he was a famous scholar and a mufti (judge). The book has been published by Dar al-Sahar, Tunis.

11.الردّ على محمد بن عبد الوهاب: للشيخ عبد الله القدومي الحنبلي النابلسي، عالم الحنابلة بالحجاز والشام المتوفى سنة 1331هـ . رد عليه في مسئلة الزيارة ومسئلة التوسل بالأنبياء والصالحين، وقال: إنه مع مقلديه من الخوارج، وقد ذكر ذلك في رسالته "الرحلة الحجازية والرياض الأنسية في الحوادث والمسائل ، مطبوع.

Al-Radd 'ala Muhammad bin 'Abdul Wahhab written by Sheikh 'Abdullah Sufan al-Qadumi (d. 1912 A.D.). The author was a famous Sunni Hanbali scholar from Nablus who travelled to Syria and Hejaz and was mufti of Hanbalis in Syria. He has extensively written on rebuttal of Abdul Wahhab's views on *ziyarah* and *tawassul*. He was of the view that 'Abdul Wahhab was from Khawarij.

12. **رسالة في حكم التوسّل بالأنبياء والأولياء:** للشيخ محمّد حسنين مخلوف العدوي المصري وكيل الجامع الأزهر، مطبوعة.

Risalah fi Hukm al-Tawassul bil Anbiya' wal Awliya written by Sheikh Muhammad Hasnain Makhluf al-'Adwi (d. 1990 A.D.). The author was a famous Egyptian Sunni Maliki scholar and was ranked among the top leaders of Al-Azhar University. Published by Kishidah lil Nashr wa al-Tawzih al-Silsilah Turath al-Azharin, Cairo, 2017.

13. **سعادة الدارين في الردّ على الفرقتين الوهابية ومقلّدة الظاهرية:** لإبراهيم بن عثمان بن محمّد السمنودي المنصوري المصري، مطبوع في مصر سنة 1320 هـ، في مجلدين.

Sa'adah al-Darayn fi al-Radd 'ala al-Fariqatayn al-Wahhabiyyah wa Muqalladah al-Zahiriyyah written by Ibrahim bin Uthman Muhammad al-Samnudi al-Mansuri al-Misri (d. 1908 A.D.). The author was a famous Egyptian Shafi'i scholar. Published by Dar al-Khulud al-Turath, Cairo, 2008.

14. **صدق الخبر في خوارج القرن الثاني عشر في إثبات أن الوهّابية من الخوارج:** للشريف عبد الله بن حسن باشا بن فضل باشا العلوي الحسيني الحجازي، أمير ظفار، طبع باللاذقية.

Sidq al-Khabar fi Khawarij al-Qarn al-Thani al-'Ashr fi Asbat an al-Wahhabiyyah min al-Khawarij written by Seyyid Sharif Abdullah bin Hassan Pasha bin Fazl Pasha al-Alawi al-Husayni al-Hejazi (d. 1854 A.D.). Published by Komayn Publishers, Syria.

15. **صلح الإخوان في الردّ على من قال على المسلمين بالشرك والكفران: في الردّ على الوهّابية لتكفيرهم المسلمين.** للشيخ داود بن سليمان النقشبندي البغدادي الحنفي، المتوفى سنة 1299هـ.

Sulh al-Ikhwan fi al-Radd 'ala man Qal 'ala al-Muslimin bil Shirk wa al-Kufran – fi al-Radd 'ala al-Wahhabiyyah li Takfir hum al-Muslimeen written by Sheikh Dawood bin Sulayman al-Naqshbandi (d. 1881 A.D.). The author is a famous Sunni Hanafi Scholar born in Baghdad then he travelled to Mecca where he witnessed growth of Wahhabism and preached against it. Published from Bombay in 1888.

16. **الصواعق الإلهية في الردّ على الوهّابية:** للشيخ سليمان بن عبد الوهاب شقيق المبتدع محمّد بن عبد الوهاب، مطبوع.

Al-Sawa'iq al-Ilahiyya fi al-Radd 'ala al-Wahhabiyyah written by Sheikh Sulayman bin 'Abd al-Wahhab (d. 1795 A.D.), a Sunni Hanbali scholar. The author was brother of Muhammad Ibn 'Abd al-Wahhab. This was the first book written against the Wahhabism. The English translation of the book entitled *"The Divine Lightning"* published by Spire Publishing 2011 is available at amazon.com.

17. ضياء الصدور لمنكر التوسل بأهل القبور: ظاهر شاه ميان بن عبد العظيم ميان، طبع.

Ziya' al-Sudur li Munkar al-Tawassul bi Ahlal al-Qubur written by Zahir Shah Mian bin Abdul Azim Mian al-Madini. The author was an Indian Sunni Hanafi scholar. Published by Huseyin Hilmi, Istanbul, 1985.

18. العقائد الصحيحة في ترديد الوهّابية النجدية: لحافظ محمّد حسن السرهندي المجددي، مطبوع.

Al-'Aqaid al-Sahihah fi Tardid al-Wahhabiyyah al-Najdiyah written by Hakim al-Ummat Khawaja Muhammad Hassan Jan Sahib al-Sarhindi al-Mujaddadi (d. 1931 A.D.). The author was a Sunni Hanafi scholar from Qandahar, Afghanistan. Published by Maktab al-Haqeeqah, Istanbul, Turkey (2000).

19. غوث العباد ببيان الرشاد: للشيخ مصطفى الحمامي المصري، مطبوع.

Ghaus al-Ibad bi Bayan al-Rishad written by Sheikh Mustafa al-Hamami al-Misri (d. 1949 A.D.). The author was an Egyptian Sunni Shafi'i scholar. Published by Mustafa al-Babi al-Halabi, Egypt (1950).

20. فصل الخطاب من كتاب الله وحديث الرسول وكلام العلماء في مذهب بن عبد الوهاب: للشيخ سليمان بن عبد الوهاب شقيق محمّد مؤسس الوهّابية، وهذا أول كتاب ألف ردّا على الوهّابية.

Fasl al-Khitab min Kitab Allah wa Hadith al-Rasul wa Kalam al-'Ulama fi Mazhab bin 'Abdul Wahhab written by Sheikh Sulayman bin 'Abd al-Wahhab (d. 1795 A.D.), a Sunni Hanbali scholar. The author was brother of Muhammad Ibn 'Abd al-Wahhab. Published by Isık Kitabevi, Hakikat Kitabevi, Istanbul, Turkey (1978).

21. المدارج السنيّة في ردّ الوهّابية: للشيخ عامر القادري، معلّم بدار العلوم القادرية-كرا تشي، الباكستان، مطبوع.

Al-Madarij al-Sunniyyah fi al-Radd al-Wahhabiyyah written by Sheikh 'Amir al-Qadri (d. 1977 A.D.), a Sunni Hanafi scholar. Published by Maktab al-Haqeeqah, Istanbul, Turkey (2000).

22. مصباح الأنام وجلاء الظلام في ردّ شبه البدعي النجدي التي أضل بها العوام: للسيد علوي بن أحمد الحداد، المتوفى سنة 1232 هـ ، مطبوع.

Misbah al-'anam wa Jila' al-Zalam fi Radd Shubah al-Bid'ah al-Najdi allati 'zalla biha al-Awam written by Seyyid Alawi Ahmad al-Haddad (d. 1817 A.D.), a Yemeni Sunni Shafi'i scholar. Published by Maktab al-Haqeeqah, Istanbul, Turkey (1996).

23. المقالات الوفيّة في الردّ على الوهّابية: للشيخ حسن قزبك، مطبوع بتقريظ الشيخ يوسف الدجوي.

Al-Maqalat al-Wafiyyah fi al-Radd 'ala al-Wahhabiyyah written by Sheikh Hassan bin Hassan Qazbak Sharqawi (d. 1999 A.D.), an Egyptian Sunni Shafi'i Ash'ari scholar. Published by Sheikh Yusuf al-Dajawi.

24.النقول الشرعية في الردّ على الوهّابية: للشيخ مصطفى بن أحمد الشطي الحنبلي، الدمشقي. طبع في إستانبول 1406 هـ.

Al-Nuqul al-Shari'ah fi al-Radd 'ala al-Wahhabiyyah written by Sheikh Mustafa bin Ahmad al-Shatti al-Hanbali al-Dimishqi (d. 1929 A.D.), a Syrian Sunni Hanbali Asha'ari scholar. Published by Dar Ghar al-Hira' publishers, Damascus, 1997.

25. البراهين الساطعة في رد بعض البدع الشائعة: للشيخ سلامة العزامي ، طبع.

Al-Barahin al-Sati'ah fi Radde Ba'z al-Bid'a al-Shai'ah written by Sheikh Salamah al-Azzami (d. 1956 A.D.), famous Egyptian Sunni Shafi'i scholar. Published by Maktabah al-Adab, Cairo, 1985.

26. كشف الارتياب في أتباع محمد بن عبد الوهّاب: السيد محسن الأمين العاملي ، مطبوع.

Kashf al-'Irtiyab fi Atba' Muhammad ibn 'Abd al-Wahhab written by 'Allama Sayyid Mohsin al-Amin (d. 1952 A.D.). Published by Mo'assasa Dar al-Kitab al-Islami, Qom, 2004.

27.الوهابية مذهب الكراهية : دكتر سعد الشريف ، مطبوع.

Al-Wahhabiyyah Mazhab al-Karahiyah written by Dr. Sa'd Sharif. Published by Dar al-Mizan, Beirut, 2012.

28. نهج الرشاد لمن أراد السداد: جعفر كاشف الغطاء ، مطبوع.

Manhaj al-Rashad li man Arad al-Sadad written by Sheikh Ja'far Kashif al-Ghita (d. 1812 A.D.). Published by Mo'assasa Da'ira al-Ma'arif al-Fiqh al-Islami, Qom, 2005.

29. الإغاثة بأدلة الإستغاثة : سيد حسن بن على بن هاشم السقاف ، مطبوع.

Al-Ighatha bi'dillah al-Istighatha written by Seyyid Hasan bin 'Ali bin Hashim as-Saqqaf (b. 1960 A.D.). the author is a Jordanian Sunni Shafi'i Ash'ari scholar who has extensively written on Wahhabism. Published by Dar al Imam Nawawi, Beirut, 2013.

30. فتنة التكفير : شيخ دكتر احمد محمود كريمه ، مطبوع.

Fitnah al-Takfir written by Sheikh Dr. Ahmad Mahmoud Karimah. He is a famous Egyptian Sunni scholar from Al-Azhar University. Published by Al-Azhar University, Cairo, 2013.

31.السلفية الوهابية أفكارها الأساسية وجذورها التاريخية : سيد حسن بن على بن هاشم السقاف ، مطبوع.

Al-Salafiyyah al-Wahhabiyyah Afkaruha al-Asasiyyah wa Jazurha al-Tarikhiyyah written by Seyyid Hasan bin 'Ali bin Hashim as-Saqqaf (b. 1960 A.D.). the author is a Jordanian Sunni Shafi'i Ash'ari scholar who has extensively written on Wahhabism. Published by Dar al Imam Nawawi, Jordan, 2002.

32. مخالفة الوهابية للقرآن والسّنة : عمر عبد السلام ، مطبوع.

Mukhalafatul Wahhabiyyah lil Qur'an wa al-Sunnah written by Umar Abd al-Salam. The author is a famous Sunni scholar from Palestine. He was motivated to write this book because of his own experience during Hajj and harsh and humiliating attitude of Wahhabis in Mecca and Medina. Published by Darul Siddiq al-Akbar, Beirut, 2006.

33. *Wahhabis Fitna Exposed* written by Sayyid Saeed Akhtar Rizvi (d. 2002). Published by Bilal Muslim Mission of Tanzania, 1997.

34. *A New Analysis of Wahhabi Doctrines* written by Muhammad Husayn Ibrahimi. Published by CreateSpace Independent Publishing Platform, 2017.

35. *Wahabism at the Crossroads* written by Ayatullah Nasir Makarim Shirazi. Published by ABWA Publishing and Printing Center, Qom, 2011.

APPENDIX IV

A description of Ibn Taymiyyah by the famous Muslim scholar and explorer Ibn Battuta

Ibn Battuta[1] is his book of journey *Rihla Ibn Battuta*[2] writes: "In Damascus I saw great Hanbali *faqih* (jurisprudent) Taqi al-Din Ibn Taymiyyah. He used to give lectures on different topics, however, he had something in his intellect.[3] Mentioning further, he writes: "He was busy giving sermon in a mosque on Friday and I also attended the gathering."

"He was speaking as:

'God [from '*Arsh*] comes down from the first heaven in the same way as I come down from pulpit (*mimber*). After saying it, he came one step down from the pulpit. At that moment, a Maliki *faqih* by the name of 'Ibn Zahra' confronted him and rebutted his speech. People attending the sermon sided with Ibn Taymiyyah and started hitting that Maliki *faqih* with fists and their shoes.'"

This firsthand account of Ibn Taymiyyah's views comes from a person who was totally unbiased.

---

[1] Complete name: Abu Abdullah Muhammad Ibn Battuta (1304 – 1368 A.D.) was a Muslim Moroccan scholar, and explorer who widely travelled the medieval world. Over a period of thirty years, Ibn Battuta visited most of the Islamic world and many non-Muslim lands, including Central Asia, Southeast Asia, South Asia and China.

[2] *The Travels of Ibn Battuta* (رحلة ابن بطوطة, or *Rihla Ibn Battuta*), p. 95-96, published 1384 S.H.

[3] Translated word for word from Arabic to avoid confusion.

APPENDIX V

Wahhabism in Contemporary Western Literature

A. Books on Wahhabism and its various forms and aspects published by international publishers

1. Y. H. Aboul-Enein, *Militant Islamist ideology: Understanding the global threat*, Annapolis, MD. Naval Institute Press, 2010.

2. Z. Abuza, *Militant Islam in Southeast Asia: Crucible of terror*, Lynne Rienner Publishers, 2003.

3. L. Addi, and A. Roberts, *Radical Arab nationalism and political Islam*, Washington, D.C: Georgetown University Press, 2017.

4. V. D. Aghai, *Terrorism, an Unconventional Crime: Do We Have the Wisdom and Capability to Defeat Terrorism?* Xlibris Corporation, 2011.

5. S. Ahmad, *ISIS: The Rise of New Terror*, Book Around Publishing, 2014.

6. N. Alaolmolki, *Militant Islamists: Terrorists Without Frontiers: Terrorists Without Frontiers*, ABC-CLIO, 2009.

7. M. K. Al-Atawneh, *Wahhabi Islam facing the challenges of modernity: Dar al-Ifta in the modern Saudi State*, Leiden; Boston: Brill, 2010.

8. H. Algar, *Wahhabism: a critical essay*, 1st ed., Oneonta, N.Y. Islamic Publications International, 2002.

9. T. Ali, *The clash of fundamentalisms: crusades, jihads and modernity*, Pbk. ed., London; New York: Verso, 2003.

10. C. Allen, *God's terrorists: The Wahhabi cult and the hidden roots of modern Jihad*, Da Capo Press, Inc., 2006.

11. M. Al-Rasheed, *Transnational connections and the Arab Gulf*, London; New York: Routledge, 2005.

12. M. Al-Rasheed, *Kingdom without borders: Saudi political, religious and media frontiers*, New York: Columbia University Press, 2008.

13. M. Al-Rasheed, *Salman's legacy: the dilemmas of a new era in Saudi Arabia*, Oxford; New York, NY: Oxford University Press, 2018.

14. F. Armanios, and Library of Congress. Congressional Research Service., "*The Islamic traditions of Wahhabism and Salafiyya*," CRS report for Congress RS21695, Congressional Research Service Library of Congress, Distributed by Penny Hill Press, 2003.

15. A. B. Atwan, *Islamic State: the digital caliphate*, Oakland, California: University of California Press, 2015.

16. M. Ayoob, and H. Kosebalaban, *Religion and politics in Saudi Arabia: Wahhabism and the state*, Boulder, CO: Lynne Rienner Publishers, 2009.

17. P. Bascio, *Defeating Islamic terrorism: an alternative strategy*, Wellesley, MA: Branden Books, 2007.

18. G. Beck, *It is about Islam: exposing the truth about ISIS, Al Qaeda, Iran, and the Caliphate, (The Control Series, Book 3)* Threshold Editions, 2015.

19. M. Benjamin, *Kingdom of the unjust: behind the U.S.-Saudi connection*, New York: OR Books, 2016.

20. R. B. Betts, *The Sunni-Shi'a divide: Islam's internal divisions and their global consequences*, Potomac Books Inc. 2013.

21. J. Birt, "*Wahhabism in the United Kingdom: Manifestations and Reactions*," Transnational connections and the Arab Gulf, pp. 168-182, Routledge, 2005.

22. G. Bonacina, *The Wahhabis seen through European Eyes (1772-1830)*, Brill, 2015.

23. D. Byman, *Al Qaeda, the Islamic State, and the global jihadist movement: What everyone needs to know*, New York, New York: Oxford University Press, 2015.

24. P. Cockburn, *The rise of Islamic State: ISIS and the new Sunni revolution*: Verso Books, 2015.

25. D. Commins, and M. Ruthven, *Islam in Saudi Arabia*: Cornell University Press, 2015.

26. D. Commins, *The Wahhabi Mission and Saudi Arabia*, I. B. Tauris, 2006.

27. R. Davis, *Western imaginings: the intellectual contest to define Wahhabism*, Cairo; New York: The American University in Cairo Press, 2018.

28. N. DeLong-Bas, *Wahhabism: Oxford Bibliographies Online Research Guide*: Oxford University Press, 2010.

29. N. J. DeLong-Bas, *Wahhabi Islam: From revival and reform to global Jihad*, New York: Oxford University Press, 2004.

30. N. J. DeLong-Bas, *Wahhabism*, New York: Oxford University Press, 2009.

31. H. A. El-Hasan, *Killing the Arab Spring*, New York: Algora Publishing, 2019.

32. H. Erlikh, *Saudi Arabia and Ethiopia: Islam, Christianity, and politics entwined*, Boulder, CO: Lynne Rienner Publishers, 2007.

33. J. L. Esposito, *Unholy war: Terror in the name of Islam*: Oxford University Press, USA, 2003.

34. T. K. Firro, *Wahhabism in tribal Arabia: politics, power and religion in the rise of Al-Saud*, London: I.B. Tauris, 2013.

35. T. K. Firro, *Wahhabism and the rise of the House of Saud*, Brighton; Portland: Sussex Academic Press, 2018.

36. B. H. Fishman, *The Master Plan: ISIS, Al-Qaeda, and the Jihadi Strategy for Final Victory*, Yale University Press, 2016.

37. S. Gale, *The War on Terrorism: 21st-century Perspectives*, Routledge, 2017.

38. F. A. Gerges, *ISIS: A History*, Princeton University Press, 2017.

39. D. Gold, *Hatred's kingdom: Saudi Arabia, Wahhabism, and the rise of global terrorism*, Washington, DC: Regnery Publishing, 2003.

40. D. Gold, *Hatred's kingdom: How Saudi Arabia supports the new global terrorism*: Regnery Publishing, 2004.

41. B. Heing, *ISIS Brides*, Enslow Publishing, LLC, 2017.

42. B. Heing, *Cultural Destruction by ISIS*, Enslow Publishing, LLC, 2017.

43. C. Hellmich, *Knowing al-Qaeda: the epistemology of terrorism*, Routledge, 2016.

44. A. Ibrahim, *Radical origins: Why we are losing the battle against Islamic extremism--and how to turn the tide*, First Pegasus books edition. ed., New York: Pegasus Books, 2017.

45. A. Iddrisu, *Contesting Islam in Africa: homegrown Wahhabism and Muslim identity in northern Ghana, 1920-2010*, Durham, NC: Carolina Academic Press, 2013.

46. D. M. Jones, *Globalisation and the new terror: the Asia Pacific dimension*: Edward Elgar Publishing, 2004.

47. P. Kamolnick, *The Al-Qaeda Organization and the Islamic State Organization: History, Doctrine, Modus, Operandi, and US Policy to Degrade and Defeat Terrorism Conducted in the Name of Sunni Islam*: Strategic Studies Institute, United States Army War College, 2017.

48. R. Labeviere, and R. Labévière, *Dollars for Terror: The United States and Islam*, Algora Publishing, 2000.

49. J. R. Macris, *Investigating the ties between Muhammed ibn Abd al-Wahhab, early Wahhabism, and ISIS*, Routledge, 2016.

50. C. D. Malbouisson, *Focus on Islamic issues*, New York: Nova Science Publishers, 2007.

51. C. Mallampalli, *A Muslim Conspiracy in British India?*, Cambridge University Press, 2017.

52. P. Margulies, *Al Qaeda: Osama bin Laden's Army of Terrorists*: The Rosen Publishing Group, Inc, 2002.

53. T. Matthiesen, *The Other Saudis: Shiism, Dissent and Sectarianism*, Cambridge University Press, 2014.

54. J. McBrien, "Extreme conversations: secularism, religious pluralism, and the rhetoric of Islamic extremism in Southern Kyrgyzstan" *The Postsocialist Religious Question: Faith and Power in Central Asia and East-Central Europe* (Halle Studies in the Anthropology of Eurasia), pp. 47-73. LIT Verlag Münster, 2006.

55. K. Morrison, *Wahhabism in the Balkans*, Shrivenham: Defence Academy of the United Kingdom, Advanced Research and Assessment Group, 2008.

56. N. Mouline, *The clerics of Islam: Religious authority and political power in Saudi Arabia*, Yale University Press, 2014.

57. L. Murawiec, *Princes of darkness: The Saudi assault on the West*, Rowman & Littlefield Publishers, Inc., 2005.

58. D. R. Nagunian, *Saudi Arabia: A hotbed of unrest?* New York: Nova Science Publishers, 2009.

59. N. Nahouza, *Wahhabism and the rise of the new Salafists: theology, power and Sunni Islam*, London: I.B. Tauris & Co. Ltd, 2018.

60. N. Nahouza, and E. University of, *Contemporary Wahhabism rebranded as Salafism: the issue of interpreting the Qur'anic verses and hadith on the Attributes of God and its significance*: University of Exeter, 2009.

61. L. Napoleoni, *Merchants of Men: How Jihadists and ISIS Turned Kidnapping and Refugee Trafficking into a Multi-Billion Dollar Business*: Seven Stories Press, 2016.

62. A. S. Pasha, *Wahhabism and its refutation by the Ahl As-Sunna*, S.N. Publishers, 1977.

63. A. Perkins, *Trailblazers in politics*, First edition. ed., New York: Rosen Publishing, 2015.

64. D. Perlmutter, *Investigating religious terrorism and ritualistic crimes*: CRC Press, 2003.

65. E. Peskes, *Wahhabism: doctrine and development*, Berlin, Germany: Gerlach Press, 2016.

66. S. K. Rath, *Fragile Frontiers: The Secret History of Mumbai Terror Attacks*: Routledge India, 2015.

67. M. R. Ronczkowski, *Terrorism and organized hate crime: Intelligence gathering, analysis and investigations*: CRC Press, 2017.

68. S. Schwartz, *The two faces of Islam: Saudi fundamentalism and its role in terrorism*: Anchor, 2003.

69. M. J. Sedgwick, *Islam & Muslims: A guide to diverse experience in a modern world*, Boston: Nicholas Brealey Publishing, 2006.

70. A. Shahi, *The politics of truth management: the case of Wahhabism in Saudi Arabia*, Routledge, 2013.

71. S. Shay, *Islamic terror and the Balkans*: Routledge, 2017.

72. K. E. Shienbaum, and J. Hasan, *Beyond jihad: Critical voices from inside Islam*, Bethesda, MD: Academica Press, LLC, 2006.

73. G. L. Simpson, *Force and Fanaticism: Wahhabism in Saudi Arabia and Beyond, by Simon Ross Valentine*, Routledge, 2016.

74. H. Solomon, *Terrorism and Counter-Terrorism in Africa: Fighting Insurgency from Al Shabaab, Ansar Dine and Boko Haram*, Palgrave Macmillan, 2015

75. C. Townsend, *ISIS Hostages*: Enslow Publishing, LLC, 2017.

76. H. Turku, *The Destruction of Cultural Property as a Weapon of War: ISIS in Syria and Iraq*, Springer, 2017.

77. U. Ulutaş, *The State of Savagery: ISIS in Syria*: SET Vakfı İktisadi İşletmesi, 2016.

78. S. R. Valentine, *Force and fanaticism: Wahhabism in Saudi Arabia and beyond*, Oxford University Press, 2015.

79. A. M. Vasilev, *The history of Saudi Arabia*, London: Saqi Books, 1998.

80. E. R. Wald, *Saudi, Inc.: The Arabian kingdom's pursuit of profit and power*, New York: Pegasus Books, 2018.

81. J. Warrick, Black flags: *The rise of ISIS*, Anchor Publishers, 2016.

82. M. Weiss, and H. Hassan, *ISIS: Inside the Army of Terror* (updated edition): Simon and Schuster, 2016.

83. R. Wise, *al Shabaab*, Case Study Series, Center for Strategic and International Studies, 2011.

84. L. Zoja, and D. L. Williams, *Jungian reflections on September 11: A global nightmare*, Einsiedeln Switzerland: Daimon Verlag, 2002.

85. A. H. Al-Fahad, "The `Imama vs. the `Iqal: Hadari—Bedouin Conflict and the Formation of the Saudi State," *Counter-Narratives*, pp. 35-75, New York, Palgrave Macmillan, 2004.

86. K. M. Bakke, and J. T. Checkel, "Copying and learning from outsiders? Assessing diffusion from transnational insurgents in the Chechen wars," *Transnational Dynamics of Civil War*, pp. 31-62, Cambridge University Press, 2014.

87. D. Commins, "Saudi Arabia, southern Arabia and the Gulf states from the First World War," *The New Cambridge History of Islam*, pp. 451-480, Cambridge University Press, 2000.

88. D. Commins, B. Haykel, T. Hegghammer et al., "From Wahhabi to Salafi," *Saudi Arabia in Transition, Insights on Social, Political, Economic and Religious Change*, pp. 151-166, New York: Cambridge University Press, 2015.

89. P. Dresch, "Arabia to the end of the First World War," *The New Cambridge History of Islam*, pp. 134-153, Cambridge University Press, 2000.

90. R. Geaves, "Learning the lessons from the neo-revivalist and Wahhabi movements: The counterattack of new Sufi movements in the UK," *Sufism in the West*, pp. 142-159, Routledge, 2006.

91. M. R. Habeck, "Knowing the enemy: Jihadist ideology and the war on terror," *The Theory and Practice of Islamic Terrorism*, pp. 65-68, Springer, 2008.

92. J. Hanssen, "History, heritage and modernity: cities in the Muslim world between destruction and reconstruction," *The New Cambridge History of Islam*, pp. 521-548, Cambridge University Press, 2000.

93. R. Marchal, and Z. M. Sheikh, "Ahlu Sunna wal-Jama'a in Somalia," *Muslim Ethiopia*, pp. 215-239, New York, Palgrave Macmillan, 2013.

94. J. Maskivker, C. López-Guerra, and J. Maskivker, "A Social-Psychological Theory for Female Suicide Bombings," *Rationality, Democracy, and Justice*, pp. 115-142, Cambridge University Press, 2014.

95. J. McMillan, "Saudi Arabia and Iraq - Oil, religion, and an enduring rivalry," *Regional Influences on Iraq (Politics and Economics of the Middle East Series)*, pp. 269-291, Nova Science Pub Inc., 2010.

96. L. G. Mincheva, and T. R. Gurr, "Unholy alliances: Evidence on linkages between trans-state terrorism and crime networks: The case of Bosnia," *Transnational Terrorism, Organized Crime and Peace-Building*, pp. 190-206: Springer, 2010.

97. N. Mouline, B. Haykel, T. Hegghammer et al., "Enforcing and Reinforcing the State's Islam," *Saudi Arabia in Transition, Insights on Social, Political, Economic and Religious Change*, pp. 48-68, New York: Cambridge University Press, 2015.

98. S. S. Pattanaik, "Islamist extremism and the terror network in Bangladesh," *Religion and Security in South and Central Asia*, pp. 108-126: Routledge, 2010.

99. O. Roy, "Islamic revival and democracy: The case in Tunisia and Egypt," *Arab Society in Revolt: The West's Mediterranean Challenge*, pp. 47-52, Brookings Institution Press, 2012.

100. A. Siddiqa, M.A. Hassan, A. Khan. *Saudi–Israeli Nexus: Implications for Iran.* Monograph. Center for Iranian Studies in Ankara. 2019.

101. D. Simeunović, and A. Dolnik, "Security Threats of Violent Islamist Extremism and Terrorism for South East Europe and Beyond," *Shaping South East Europe's Security Community for the Twenty-First Century*, pp. 87-113: Springer, 2013.

102. A. Speckhard, and K. Akhmedova, "Black widows and beyond: Understanding the motivations and life trajectories of Chechen female terrorists," *Female Terrorism and Militancy*, pp. 114-135: Routledge, 2007.

103. R. Spencer, *The History of Jihad: From Muhammad to ISIS*, Bombardier Books, 2019.

104. Z. E. Ünsal, "Terrorism, radicalism and IS in the case of Muslim population in SEEC," *Countering Terrorist Activities in Cyberspace*, pp. 63-80, IOS Press, 2018.

105. A. Wahid, "Right Islam vs. wrong Islam: Muslims and non-Muslims must unite to defeat the Wahhabi ideology," *The Theory and Practice of Islamic Terrorism*, pp. 113-117: Springer, 2008.

106. B. G. Williams, "Crushing Wahhabi fundamentalists in central Asia and the Caucasus: Subplot to the global struggle against al Qaida or suppression of legitimate religious opposition?" *New Religious Movements in the Twenty-First Century: Legal, Political, and Social Challenges in Global Perspective*, pp. 129-148, Routledge, 2004.

B. Scholarly articles on Wahhabism and its various aspects published in peer reviewed international journals

1. A'la A. The genealogy of Muslim radicalism in Indonesia: A study of the roots and characteristics of the padri movement. *Journal of Indonesian Islam* 2008; 2 2:267-99.

2. Abuza Z. Tentacles of Terror: Al Qaeda's Southeast Asian Network. *Contemporary Southeast Asia: A Journal of International & Strategic Affairs* 2002; 24 3:7-18.

3. Abuza Z. Funding terrorism in Southeast Asia: the financial network of Al Qaeda and Jemaah Islamiya. *Contemporary Southeast Asia: A Journal of International and Strategic Affairs* 2003; 25 2:169-99.

4. Akaev V. Religious and political elites in the Northern Caucasus: Formation, ideological contradictions, and practical opposition. *Central Asia and the Caucasus* 2013; 15 1:77-89.

5. Al-Atawneh M. Wahhabi Legal Theory as Reflected in Modern Official Saudi Fatwas: Ijtihad, Taqlid, Sources, and Methodology. *Islamic Law and Society* 2011; 18 3-4:327-55.

6. Al-Atawneh M. Wahhabi Self-Examination Post-9/11: Rethinking the 'Other', 'Otherness' and Tolerance. *Middle Eastern Studies* 2011; 47 2:255-71.

7. Al-Fahad AH. From exclusivism to accommodation: Doctrinal and legal evolution of Wahhabism. *New York University Law Review* 2004; 79 2:485-519.

8. Al-Ibrahim B. ISIS, Wahhabism and Takfir. *Contemporary Arab Affairs* 2015; 8 3:408-15.

9. Al-Jarbou A. The Role of Traditionalists and Modernists on the Development of the Saudi Legal System. *Arab Law Quarterly* 2007; 21 3:191-229.

10. Allen C. The hidden roots of Wahhabism in British India. *World Policy Journal* 2005; 22 2:87-93.

11. Alonso R, García Rey M. The evolution of jihadist terrorism in Morocco. *Terrorism and Political Violence* 2007; 19 4:571-92.

12. Alvi H. The diffusion of intra-Islamic violence and terrorism: The impact of the proliferation of Salafi/Wahhabi ideologies. *Middle East Review of International Affairs (Online)* 2014; 18 2:38.

13. Antúnez JC, Tellidis I. The power of words: the deficient terminology surrounding Islam-related terrorism. *Critical Studies on Terrorism* 2013; 6 1:118-39.

14. Antwi-Boateng O. The Rise of Pan-Islamic Terrorism in Africa: A Global Security Challenge. *Politics & Policy* 2017; 45 2:253-84.

15. Azumah J. Boko Haram in Retrospect. *Islam and Christian–Muslim Relations* 2014; 26 1:33-52.

16. Bagby I. The American Mosque in Transition: Assimilation, Acculturation and Isolation. *Journal of Ethnic and Migration Studies* 2009; 35 3:473-90.

17. Bahari B, Ahmad MBS. Neo-Wahhabism: Ideological basis of Islamic Military Groups. *GSTF Journal of Law and Social Sciences (JLSS)* 2017; 1 1:20-23.

18. Balci B. Between Sunnism and Shiism: Islam in post-Soviet Azerbaijan. *Central Asian Survey* 2004; 23 2:205-17.

19. Bardos GN. Terror Crossroads. *World Affairs* 2016; 179 1:81-8.

20. Barnett C. Islam in Saudi Arabia. *Political Science Quarterly* 2016; 131 4:893-5.

21. Bendle MF. Secret Saudi funding of radical Islamic groups in Australia. *National Observer* 2007; 72:7-18.

22. Benthall J. Puripetal Force in the Charitable Field. *Asian Ethnology* 2016; 75 1:29-51.

23. Bobrovnikov V. 'Ordinary Wahhabism' versus 'Ordinary Sufism'? Filming Islam for Postsoviet Muslim Young People. *Religion, State and Society* 2011; 39 2-3:281-301.

24. Botha A. Terrorism in the Maghreb: The transnationalisation of domestic terrorism. *Institute for Security Studies Monographs* 2008; Series 144: pp.236

25. Brigaglia A. A Contribution to the History of the Wahhabi 'Da'wa' in West Africa: The Career and the Murder of Sheikh Ja'far Mahmoud Adam (Daura, ca. 1961/1962–Kano 2007). *Islamic Africa* 2012; 3 1:1-23.

26. Bröning M. Don't fear the Shiites the idea of a Teheran-controlled 'Shiite crescent' over the greater Middle East is at odds with reality. *Internationale Politik und Gesellschaft* 2008; 3:60-75.

27. Brown LC. Religion and Politics in Saudi Arabia: Wahhabism and the State. *Foreign Affairs* 2009; 88 3:179-80.

28. Bryden M. No quick fixes: coming to terms with terrorism, Islam, and statelessness in Somalia. *Journal of Conflict Studies* 2003; 23 2:24-56.

29. Burki SK. Ceding the Ideological Battlefield to Al Qaeda: The Absence of an Effective U.S. Information Warfare Strategy. *Comparative Strategy* 2009; 28 4:349-66.

30. Burki SK. The Creeping Wahhabization in Pukhtunkhwa: The Road to 9/11. *Comparative Strategy* 2011; 30 2:154-76.

31. Byman D. Passive sponsors of terrorism. *Survival* 2005; 47 4:117-44.

32. Byrd AR. Interpreting ISIS: Four Recent Works on the History and Strategy of the Islamic State. *Review of Middle East Studies* 2017; 51 2:240-8.

33. Camara MS. Nation building and the politics of Islamic internationalism in Guinea: toward an understanding of Muslims' experience of globalization in Africa. *Contemporary Islam* 2007; 1 2:155-72.

34. Chelin R, Mngomezulu BR. Unravelling Al Qaeda terrorism in the Maghreb region. *African Renaissance* 2015; 12 1:107-28.

35. Choksy CE, Choksy JK. The Saudi connection: Wahhabism and global jihad. *World Affairs* 2015; 178 1:23-35.

36. Cordesman AH. Saudi Arabia: friend or foe in the war on terror? *Middle East Policy* 2006; 13 1:28-41.

37. Crawford MJ. The Daʿwa of Ibn ʿAbd al-Wahhab before the Al Saʿud. *Journal of Arabian Studies* 2011; 1 2:147-61.

38. Crawford MJ, Facey WHD. ʿAbd Allah Al Saʿud and Muḥammad ʿAli Pasha: The Theatre of Victory, the Prophet's Treasures, and the Visiting Whig, Cairo 1818. *Journal of Arabian Studies* 2017; 7 1:44-62.

39. Crooke, A, You Can't Understand ISIS If You Don't Know the History of Wahhabism in Saudi Arabia, *New Perspectives Quarterly*, 2015; 32 1:56–70.

40. Darboe M. Gambia. *African Studies Review* 2014; 47 2:73-82.

41. Darwich M. The Ontological (In)security of Similarity Wahhabism Versus Islamism in Saudi Foreign Policy. *Foreign Policy Analysis* 2016; 12 3:469-88.

42. Dekmejian R. The liberal impulse in Saudi Arabia. *The Middle East Journal* 2003; 57 3:400-13.

43. Diagne SB. Of Reciting and Reading. *Comparative Studies of South Asia, Africa and the Middle East* 2015; 35 3:666-71.

44. Dobaev I. Radical Wahhabism as an extremist religious-political ideology. *Central Asia and the Caucasus* 2002; 16 4:128-38.

45. Dogra SA. Living a piety-led life beyond Muharram: Becoming or being a South Asian Shia Muslim in the UK. *Contemporary Islam* 2019; 13 3:307-24.

46. Dorsey JM. Saudi Arabia and Iran: The Battle for Hegemony that the Kingdom Cannot Win. *Przegląd Strategiczny* 2016; 9 9:357-73.

47. Eden J. Did Ibn Saud's militants cause 400,000 casualties? Myths and evidence about the Wahhabi conquests, 1902–1925. *British Journal of Middle Eastern Studies* 2018; 46 4:519-34.

48. Emerson S, Levin J. Terrorism financing: origination, organization, and prevention: Saudi Arabia, terrorist financing and the war on terror. *United States Senate Committee on Governmental Affairs, The Investigative Project Report*, July 31, 2003; pp. 45.

49. Evered EO. Rereading Ottoman Accounts of Wahhabism as Alternative Narratives: Ahmed Cevdet Pasa's Historical Survey of the Movement. *Comparative Studies of South Asia, Africa and the Middle East* 2012; 32 3:622-32.

50. Farquhar M. Saudi Petrodollars, Spiritual Capital, and the Islamic University of Medina: A Wahhabi Missionary Project in Transnational Perspective. *International Journal of Middle East Studies* 2015; 47 4:701-21.

51. Fedorov E. The Islamic State of Iraq and Al-Sham: The Group's Nation-Building Project through the Instrumental Use of Violence. *McGill Journal of Political Studies* 2016; 7:32-9.

52. Firro TK. The Political Context of Early Wahhabi Discourse of Takfir. *Middle Eastern Studies* 2013; 49 5:770-89.

53. Furlan M. Israeli–Saudi Relations in a Changed and Changing Middle East: Growing Cooperation? *Israel Journal of Foreign Affairs* 2019; 13 2:173-87.

54. Fürtig H. Saudi Arabia: Giving in to terror? *Geographische Rundschau* 2005; 57 11:48-51.

55. Garner DW, McFarland RL. Suing Islam: Tort, Terrorism and the House of Saud. *Oklahoma Law Review* 2007; 60 2:223-281.

56. Geaves R. 'That which we have forgotten': The emergence of 'Traditional Islam' as a new movement in global Muslim religious contestation. *Journal for the Academic Study of Religion* 2013; 26 1:29-50.

57. Gomes ADT, Mikhael MM. Terror or Terrorism? Al-Qaeda and the Islamic State in Comparative Perspective. *Brazilian Political Science Review* 2018; 12 1:1-27.

58. Gould R. The modernity of premodern Islam in contemporary Daghestan. *Contemporary Islam* 2010; 5 2:161-83.

59. Gould R. Secularism and Belief in Georgia's Pankisi Gorge. *Journal of Islamic Studies* 2011; 22 3:339-73.

60. Gregory S. The ISI and the War on Terrorism. *Studies on Conflict and Terrorism* 2007; 30 12:1013-1031.

61. Hadler J. A Historiography of Violence and the Secular State in Indonesia: Tuanku Imam Bondjol and the Uses of History. *The Journal of Asian Studies* 2008; 67 03:971-1010.

62. Hamdan AM. Secularism in the Middle East, Palestine as an Example. *Comparative Studies of South Asia, Africa and the Middle East* 2011; 31 1:120-3.

63. Hamid AFA, Fauzi A. ISIS in Southeast Asia: Internalized Wahhabism is a major factor. *ISEAS Perspective* 2016; 16:1-10.

64. Haron Z, Hussin N. A study of the Salafi jihadist doctrine and the interpretation of jihad by al jama'ah al islamiyah. *Kemanusiaan* 2013; 20 2:15-37.

65. Hasan N. The Failure of the Wahhabi Campaign. *South East Asia Research* 2018; 18 4:675-705.

66. Hegghammer T. Terrorist recruitment and radicalization in Saudi Arabia. *Middle East Policy* 2006; 13 4:39-60.

67. Helfont S. Islam in Saudi Foreign Policy: The Case of Ma'ruf al-Dawalibi. *The International History Review* 2019:1-16.

68. Hellmich C. Al-Qaeda—terrorists, hypocrites, fundamentalists? The view from within. *Third World Quarterly* 2005; 26 1:39-54.

69. Hellmich C. Creating the ideology of al Qaeda: from Hypocrites to Salafi-Jihadists. *Studies on Conflict and Terrorism* 2008; 31 2:111-24.

70. Hitman G. Saudi Arabia's Wahhabism and Nationalism: The Evolution of Wataniyya into Qawmiyya. *Digest of Middle East Studies* 2018; 27 1:79-96.

71. Horsman S. Themes in official discourses on terrorism in Central Asia. *Third World Quarterly* 2005; 26 1:199-213.

72. Hussain I. Fundamentalism and Bangladesh. *South Asian Survey* 2016; 14 2:207-229.

73. Jackson R. Constructing enemies: 'Islamic terrorism' in political and academic discourse. *Government and Opposition* 2007; 42 3:394-426.

74. Jamilah M, Fikra HU, Harza Z. Facilitating Conditions of Saudi Arabia–Israel Normalization in 2015-2018. *Journal of Diplomacy and International Studies* 2019; 2 01:38-51.

75. Jordan J, Horsburgh N. Mapping jihadist terrorism in Spain. *Studies on Conflict and Terrorism* 2005; 28 3:169-91.

76. Kabha M, Erlich H. Al-Ahbash and Wahhabiyya: Interpretations of Islam. *International Journal of Middle East Studies* 2006; 38 4:519-38.

77. Karabulatova I, Polekhina M, Lyausheva S, Dubinina N. How the discourse of Sufism became the expressive discourse of Islamic radicalism in the regions of "popular Islam" in Russia. *Central Asia and the Caucasus* 2017; 18 4:92-8.

78. Karagöz M. September 11: A New Type of Terrorism. *Journal of International Affairs,* VII 2002;25-33.

79. Kayaoglu T. Explaining Interfaith Dialogue in the Muslim World. *Politics and Religion* 2015; 8 2:236-62.

80. Kepel G. The Arab world in turmoil. A conversation with Gilles Kepel. *Herodote* 2016; 160-161:85-96.

81. Khan M. The Globalization of Wahhabism- A Theology of Hate. *Fellowship* 2003; 69 7-8:14-15.

82. Khashan H. The spiritual Utopia of Islamic historical determinism. *Arab World Geographer* 2006; 9 3:155-67.

83. Klass D, Goss R. The politics of grief and continuing bonds with the dead: the cases of Maoist China and Wahhabi Islam. *Death Studies* 2003; 27 9:787-811.

84. Knysh A. A clear and present danger:" Wahhabism" as a rhetorical foil. *Die Welt des Islams* 2004; 44 1:3-26.

85. Kobo O. The Development of Wahhabi Reforms in Ghana and Burkina Faso, 1960–1990: Elective Affinities between Western-Educated Muslims and Islamic Scholars. *Comparative Studies in Society and History* 2009; 51 3:502-532.

86. Kotovcevski M. Wahhabism in The Balkans-Islamic threat or threat to the Islam. *Security Dialogues* 2013; 4 1:11-23.

87. Kovács A. The 'new jihadists' and the visual turn from al-Qa'ida to ISIL/ISIS/Da'ish. *Bitzpol Affairs* 2014; 2 5:47-69.

88. Lacroix S. Between Islamists and Liberals: Saudi Arabia's New "Islamo-Liberal" Reformists. *The Middle East Journal* 2004; 58 3:345-65.

89. Lanskoy M. Daghestan and Chechnya: The Wahhabi challenge to the State. *SAIS Review* 2002; 22 2:167-92.

90. Lewis P. Only connect: Can the ulema address the crisis in the transmission of Islam to a new generation of South Asians in Britain? *Contemporary South Asia* 2006; 15 2:165-80.

91. Liu JH, Woodward M. Towards an indigenous psychology of religious terrorism with global implications: Introduction to AJSP's Special Issue on Islamist terrorism in Indonesia. *Asian Journal of Social Psychology* 2013; 16 2:79-82.

92. Lohlker R. Excluding the Other: Wahhabism, Salafism, Jihadism, and Political Islam. *Totalitarismus und Demokratie* 2017; 14 2:265-89.

93. Lopez KJ, Schwartz S. Roots of "Islamic" Terrorism. *Crime and Justice International* 2003; 1970:23-6.

94. Low MC. Ottoman Infrastructures of the Saudi Hydro-State: The Technopolitics of Pilgrimage and Potable Water in the Hijaz. *Comparative Studies in Society and History* 2015; 57 4:942-74.

95. Lynch III TF. The Impact of ISIS on Global Salafism and South Asian Jihad. *Current Trends in Islamist Ideology* 2015; 19:85-120.

96. Macris JR. Investigating the ties between Muhammed ibn Abd al-Wahhab, early Wahhabism, and ISIS. *The Journal of the Middle East and Africa* 2016; 7 3:239-55.

97. Mahendrarajah S. Saudi Arabia, Wahhabism, and the Taliban of Afghanistan: 'Puritanical reform' as a 'revolutionary war' program. *Small Wars & Insurgencies* 2015; 26 3:383-407.

98. Mallampalli C. "A Fondness for Military Display": Conquest and Intrigue in South India during the First Anglo-Afghan War, 1839–40. *The Journal of Asian Studies* 2018; 77 1:139-59.

99. Matthiesen T. Shi'i Historians in a Wahhabi State: Identity Entrepreneurs and the Politics of Local Historiography in Saudi Arabia. *International Journal of Middle East Studies* 2015; 47 1:25-45.

100. Michel T. Implications of the Islamic revival for Christian-Muslim dialogue in Asia. *International Journal for the Study of the Christian Church* 2003; 3 2:58-76.

101. Mouline N. Ulamas of the palace: Journey of the Committee of Senior Ulama members. *Archives de Sciences Sociales des Religions* 2010; 149 1:229-53.

102. Mustafa D, Brown KE. The Taliban, public space, and terror in Pakistan. *Eurasian Geography and Economics* 2010; 51 4:496-512.

103. Nafi BM. Salafism Revived: Nu'man al-Alusi and the Trial of Two Ahmads. *Die Welt des Islams* 2009; 49 1:49-97.

104. Öktem K. Global Diyanet and Multiple Networks: Turkey's New Presence in the Balkans. *Journal of Muslims in Europe* 2012; 1 1:27-58.

105. Oliver-Dee S. Started but Contested: Analyzing US and British Counter-Extremism Strategies. *The Review of Faith & International Affairs* 2018; 16 2:71-83.

106. Osaherumwen IS, Mutunrayo AK. International Terrorism in the Middle East: ISIS as a Case Study. *Science and World* 2013; 7 35:59-65.

107. Osella F, Osella C. Islamism and Social Reform in Kerala, South India. *Modern Asian Studies* 2008; 42 2-3:317-46.

108. Otterbeck J. Wahhabi ideology of social control versus a new publicness in Saudi Arabia. *Contemporary Islam* 2012; 6 3:341-53.

109. Pack J, Smith R, Mezran K. The Origins and Evolution of ISIS in Libya. *The Atlantic Council* 2017.

110. Pavlik MY. The influence of Wahhabism on the commission of crimes of a terrorist nature in Russia: Criminological aspects. *Journal of Legal, Ethical and Regulatory Issues* 2017; 20 Special issue 1. [published online]

111. Peil F. The seizure of the Mecca's Grand Mosque in 1979 - The social profile and ideology of the Ihwãn. *Orient* 2006; 47 3:387-408.

112. Pérouse de Montclos M-A. A Sectarian Jihad in Nigeria: The Case of Boko Haram. *Small Wars & Insurgencies* 2016; 27 5:878-95.

113. Podeh E. Saudi Arabia and Israel: From Secret to Public Engagement, 1948–2018. *The Middle East Journal* 2018; 72 4:563-86.

114. Potezica O. The Wahhabis newcomers to the Balkans. *Politics and Religion Journal* 2007; 1 1:205-28.

115. Rakic M, Jurisic D. Wahhabism as a Militant Form of Islam on Europe's Doorstep. *Studies on Conflict and Terrorism* 2012; 35 9:650-63.

116. Rezvani B. Reflections on the Chechen Conflict: Geopolitics, Timing and Transformations. *Middle Eastern Studies* 2014; 50 6:870-90.

117. Rigoulet-Roze D. The Shias of the Saudi Province of al-Ahsa: A Few "National" Strategic Issues at the Heart of Regional Ethno-Confessional Challenges. *Herodote* 2009; 133:108-135.

118. Rizvi SH. Shi'ism in Bahrain: Marja'iyya and politics. *Orient* 2009; 50 3:16-24.

119. Rusli R. Indonesian Salafism on Jihad and Suicide Bombings. *Journal of Indonesian Islam* 2014; 8 1:91-111.

120. Saikal A. How Islamic Has the "Islamic State" Been? *Journal of Muslim Minority Affairs* 2018; 38 2:143-52.

121. Salama AHY. Ideological collocation and the recontexualization of Wahhabi-Saudi Islam post-9/11: A synergy of corpus linguistics and critical discourse analysis. *Discourse & Society* 2011; 22 3:315-42.

122. Sari E, Nazaruddin T, Nurdin A, Puteh AC. The syiah stance in a sharia land: A socio-legal study of a latent syiah minority entity in contemporary Aceh. *International Journal of Recent Technology and Engineering* 2019; 7 6:1378-82.

123. Schwartz BE. America's Struggle Against the Wahhabi/Neo-Salafi Movement. *Orbis* 2007; 51 1:107-28.

124. Schwartz S. The Terrorist War against Islam: Clarifying Academic Confusions. *Academic Questions* 2011; 24 1:59-73.

125. Sedgwick M. Al-Qaeda and the nature of religious terrorism. *Terrorism and Political Violence* 2004; 16 4:795-814.

126. Shaaban B. The Rise of ISIS and Other Extremist Groups: the role of the West and Regional Powers. *The Canadian Charger*, February 2016; 19. [published online]

127. Shaffer R. Jihad and Counter-Jihad in Europe: Islamic Radicals, Right-Wing Extremists, and Counter-Terrorism Responses. *Terrorism and Political Violence* 2016; 28 2:383-94.

128. Shukla A. Wahhabism and Global Terrorism. *International Journal of Innovation and Applied Studies* 2014; 9 4:1521-1530.

129. Simeunovic D. Islamic extremism in the Western Balkans. *Revija za Kriminalistiko in Kriminologijo* 2018; 69 2:128-43.

130. Simons G. Western imaginings: the intellectual contest to define Wahhabism. *Religion, State and Society* 2019; 47 2:282-3.

131. Sirriyeh E. Modern Muslim interpretations of shirk. *Religion* 1990; 20 2:139-59.

132. Snow D, Byrd S. Ideology, framing processes, and Islamic terrorist movements. *Mobilization: An International Quarterly* 2007; 12 2:119-36.

133. Speckhard A. The emergence of female suicide terrorists. *Studies on Conflict and Terrorism* 2008; 31 11:995-1023.

134. Speckhard A. Female Terrorists in ISIS, Al Qaeda and 21st Century Terrorism. *Trends Research: Inside the Mind of a Jihadist* 2015:1-9.

135. Speckhard A, Ahkmedova K. The making of a martyr: Chechen suicide terrorism. *Studies on Conflict and Terrorism* 2006; 29 5:429-92.

136. Speckhard A, Akhmedova K. The new Chechen jihad: Militant Wahhabism as a radical movement and a source of suicide terrorism in post-war Chechen society. *Democracy and Security* 2006; 2 1:103-55.

137. Stephens J. The Phantom Wahhabi: Liberalism and the Muslim fanatic in mid-Victorian India. *Modern Asian Studies* 2012; 47 1:22-52.

138. Strobl S. Policing in the Eastern Province of Saudi Arabia: understanding the role of sectarian history and politics. *Policing and Society* 2015; 26 5:544-62.

139. Teitelbaum J. Hashemites, Egyptians and Saudis: the tripartite struggle for the pilgrimage in the shadow of Ottoman defeat. *Middle Eastern Studies* 2020; 56 1:36-47.

140. Tippee B. The editor's perspective: Attacks in Riyadh draw attention to fiery Wahhabism. *Oil & Gas Journal* 2003; 101 21:68-75.

141. Trifunović D, Mijalkovski M. Terrorist Threats by Balkans Radical Islamist to International Security. *Politics and Religion Journal* 2014; 8 2:291-326.

142. Umar MS. The popular discourses of Salafi radicalism and Salafi counter-radicalism in Nigeria: A case study of Boko Haram. *Journal of Religion in Africa* 2012; 42 2:118-44.

143. Uz I, Kemmelmeier M. Islamist terrorism as identity threat: The case of ambivalent identification and self-stereotyping among Turkish Muslims. *Journal of Applied Social Psychology* 2014; 44 10:660-71.

144. Uz I, Kemmelmeier M, Yetkin E. Effects of Islamist terror in Muslim students: Evidence from Turkey in the wake of the November 2003 attacks. *Behavioral Sciences of Terrorism and Political Aggression* 2009; 1 2:111-26.

145. Valiyev AM. Foreign Terrorist Groups and Rise of Home-grown Radicalism in Azerbaijan. *HUMSEC Journal* 2008; 2:95-112.

146. Venkatraman A. Religious basis for Islamic terrorism: The Quran and its interpretations. *Studies on Conflict and Terrorism* 2007; 30 3:229-48.

147. Vidino L. How Chechnya became a breeding ground for terror. *Middle East Quarterly* 2005;12 3:34-51.

148. vom Bruck G. Regimes of Piety Revisited: Zaydi Political Moralities in Republican Yemen. *Die Welt des Islams* 2010; 50 2:185-223.

149. Wagemakers J. Defining the Enemy: Abu Muhammad al-Maqdisis Radical Reading of Surat al-Mumtahana. *Die Welt des Islams* 2008; 48 3:348-71.

150. Wagemakers J. The Enduring Legacy of the Second Saudi State: Quietist and Radical Wahhabi Contestations of Al-Wala' Wa-L-Bara'. *International Journal of Middle East Studies* 2012; 44 1:93-110.

151. Walia F. Islamist Indoctrination: Exploring the Techniques Used by Hizb Ut-Tahrir to Radicalize Young British Muslims. *Journal for Deradicalization* 2020; 11:30-58.

152. Winsor Jr C. Saudi Arabia, Wahhabism and the Spread of Sunni Theofascism. *Mideast Monitor* 2007; 2 1:1-14.

153. Winters CA. Koranic education and militant Islam in Nigeria. *International Review of Education* 1987; 33 2:171-85.

154. Yamani M. The Two Faces of Saudi Arabia. *Survival* 2008; 50 1:143-56.

155. Yamani M. Saudi youth: The illusion of transnational freedom. *Contemporary Arab Affairs* 2010; 3 1:7-20.

156. Yemelianova GM. Islam and Nation Building in Tatarstan and Dagestan of the Russian Federation. *Nationalities Papers* 2018; 27 4:605-30.

157. Yo M. Seeking the Roots of Terrorism: An Islamic Traditional Perspective. *The Journal of Religion and Popular Culture* 2005; 10 1:2-14.

158. Zambelis C. Terror in Tehran: The Islamic State Goes to War with Islamic Republic. *Combating Terrorism Center (CTC) Sentinel* 2017; 10 6. [published online]

159. Zaytseva A. Cohesion of Religious Communities in the Situation of Conflict: A Case Study of Confrontations around Imam in a Dagestani Village. *State, Religion and Church in Russia and Worldwide* 2016; 34 2:281-309.

Selected Bibliography

1. Abd al-Rahman bin Ali al-Jawzi (d. 1201 A.D.). *al-Wafa bi Ahwal al-Mustafa*. Darul Kutub al-'Ilmiyah, Beirut, 2005.
2. Abdul Rahman al-Jaziri (d. 1941 A.D.). *Al-Fiqh 'ala al-Madhahib al-Arba'ah*. Darul Ihya Turath al-Arabi, Beirut, 1989.
3. Abu 'Abdilluh Ahmad Ibn Muhammad Ibn Ḥanbal (d. 855 A.D.). *al-Musnad*. Darul Fiqr, Beirut, 1988.
4. Abu 'Abdilluh Muḥammad ibn Yazid Ibn Majah al-Qazwini (d. 887 A.D.). *Sunan Ibn Majah*. Darul Fiqr, Beirut, 2003.
5. Abu 'Abdullah Muhammad al-Ansari al-Qurtubi (d. 1273 A.D.). *Tafsir al-Qurtubi (Al-Jami li-Ahkam Al-Qur'an)*. Darul Kutub al-'Ilmiyah, Beirut, 2014.
6. Abu 'Abdullah Muhammad al-Hakim al-Nishapuri (d. 1012 A.D.). *Al-Mustadrak alaa al-Sahihain*. Darul Kutub al-'Ilmiyah, Beirut, 1988.
7. Abu 'Abdullah Muhammad Ibn Battuta (d. 1368 A.D.) *Rihla ibn Battuta*, Dar Sadir, Beirut, 1964.
8. Abu al-Faḍl 'Abd al-Raḥman Jalal al-Din al-Suyuti (d. 1505 A.D.). *al-Durr al-Manthur*. Darul Fiqr, Beirut, 1982.
9. Abu al-Faḍl 'Abd al-Raḥman Jalal al-Din al-Suyuti (d. 1505 A.D.). *Jami' al-Saghir Fi Ahadith al-Bashir al-Nadir*. Darul Kutub al-'Ilmiyah, Beirut, 1985.
10. Abu Bakr Ahmad ibn Husayn al-Bayhaqi (d. 1066 A.D.). *Al-'Asma wa al-Sifat*. Darul Kutub al-'Ilmiyah, Beirut, 1984.
11. Abu Bakr Ahmad ibn Husayn al-Bayhaqi (d. 1066 A.D.). *Al-Sunan al-Kubra*. Darul Kutub al-'Ilmiyah, Beirut, 1994.
12. Abu Bakr Ahmad ibn Husayn al-Bayhaqi (d. 1066 A.D.). *Dala'il al-Nubuwwah Wa ma'rifat Ahwal Sahib al-Shari'ah*. Dar al-Hadith, Cairo, 2007.
13. Abu Ḥamid Muḥammad ibn Muḥammad al-Ghazali (d. 111 A.D.). *Ihya' 'Ulum al-din*. Darul Marifat, Beirut, 1983.
14. Abu Ja'far Muhammad ibn Jarir al-Tabari (d. 923 A.D.). *Tarikh al-Tabari (Tarikh al-Rusul wal Muluk)*(English Translation). SUNY Press, N.Y., 1991.
15. Abu Naṣr Taj al-Din Abd al-Wahhab ibn Ali al-Subki (d. 1370 A.D.). *Al-Tuhfat al-Mukhtara fi al-Radd 'ala Munkir al-Ziyarah*. Maṭba'at al-Sa'adah, Cairo, 1942.
16. Abu Zayd 'Abd ar-Rahman ibn Muhammad ibn Khaldun al-Hadrami (d. 1406 A.D.). *Muqaddimah*. JiaHu Books, United States, 2014.
17. Abu'l-Qawsim Sulayman al-Tabarani (d. 971 A.D.). *Al-Mu'jam al-Saghir*. Darul Kutub al-'Ilmiyah, Beirut, 1983.

18. Abul Hassan Taqi al-Din Ali Ibn Kafi al-Subki (d. 1355 A.D.). *Al-Durrat al-Mudi'a fi al-Radd 'ala Ibn Taymiyyah.* Isık Kitabevi, Hakikat Kitabevi, Istanbul, Turkey 2008.
19. Abul Hassan Taqi al-Din Ali Ibn Kafi al-Subki (d. 1355 A.D.). *Al-Sayf al-Saqil fi al-Radd 'alá ibn Zafil.* Matba'at al-Sa'adah, Cairo, 1937.
20. Abul Hassan Taqi al-Din Ali Ibn Kafi al-Subki (d. 1355 A.D.). *Shifa' al-Saqam fi Ziyarat Qabr Khayr al-Anam.* Published by the Committee of Arab Manuscripts, Beirut, 1960.
21. Abul-Hasan 'Ali ibn 'Umar al-Baghdadi al-Daraqutni (d. 995 A.D.). *Sunan al-Daraqutni.* Darul Mahasin, Cairo, 1976.
22. Aḥmad ibn 'Abdullah Abu Nu'aym al-Iṣfahani (d. 1038 A.D.). *Dala'il al-Nubuwwah.* 'Alam al-Kutub, Beirut, 1983.
23. Ahmad ibn Shu'ayb ibn Ali ibn Sinan al-Nasa'i (d. 915 A.D.). *Sunan al-Nasa'i.* Darul Kutub al-'Ilmiyah, Beirut, 2011.
24. Al-Hafiz Muhibb al-Din Ahmad ibn Abdullah al-Tabari (d. 1284 A.D.). *Dhakha'ir al-'Uqba fi Manaqib Dhawi'l Qurba.* Darul Marifat, Beirut, 1986.
25. Al-Hafiz Nur al-Din Ali ibn Abi Bakr al-Haytami (d. 1404 A.D.). *Majma' al-Zawa'id wa Manba' al-Fawa'id.* Darul Kutub al-'Ilmiyah, Beirut, 2009.
26. Ali bin Ahmad al-Samhudi (d. 1533 A.D.). *Wafa' al-Wafa' fi Akhbar dar al-Mustafa.* Al-Furqan Islamic Heritage Foundation, London, 2002.
27. Ali ibn al-Ḥasan Ibn 'Asakir (d. 1175 A.D.). *Tarikh Ibn Asakir.* Darul Fiqr, Beirut, 1981.
28. Allama 'Abd al-Ḥusayn Amini (d. 1970 A.D.). *Al-Ghadir fi al-Kitab wa al-Sunnah wa al-Adab.* Mo'assasa al-A'lami lil Matbu'aat, Beirut, 2001.
29. Allama Sayyid Mohsin al-Amin (d. 1952 A.D.). *Kashf al-'Irtiyab fi Atba' Muhammad ibn 'Abd al-Wahhab.* Mo'assasa Dar al-Kitab al-Islami, Qom, 2004.
30. Asakir ad-Din Muslim ibn al-Hajjaj ibn Muslim ibn Ward Nishapuri (d. 875 A.D.). *Sahih Muslim.* Darul Kutub al-'Ilmiyah, Beirut, 2005. [English translations available online].
31. Badr al-Din Mahmud bin Ahmad al-'Ayni (d. 1453 A.D.). *'Umdat al-Qari fi Sharh Sahih al-Bukhari.* Darul Ihya Turath al-Arabi, Beirut, 2007.
32. Hussein bin Mufaddal al-Isfahani (d. 1108 A.D.). *Al-Mufradat fi Gharib al-Qur'an* (also known as *Al-Mufradat Alfaz al-Qur'an*). Darul Shamiyyah, Beirut, 1992.
33. Ibn al-'Athir 'Izz al-Din 'Ali bin Muhammad bin Muhammad bin 'Abd al-Karim al-Jazari (d. 1232 A.D.). *Usd al-Ghabah fi Ma'rifat al-Sahaba.* Darul Ihya turath al-Arabi, Beirut, 1988.

34. Ibn al-'Athir 'Izz al-Din 'Ali bin Muhammad bin Muhammad bin 'Abd al-Karim al-Jazari (d. 1232 A.D.). *Al-Kamil fi al-Tarikh*. Darul Kitab al-Arabi, Beirut, 1986.
35. Isma'il bin 'Umar bin Kathir (d. 1373 A.D.). *Al-Bidayah wal Nihayah*. Darul Fikr, Beirut, 1981.
36. Ja'far Subhani (born 1929 A.D.). *A Teaching Course on Criticism of Wahhabism*. Mo'assasa Darul A'alam li Madressa Ahlul Bayt, Qom, 2017.
37. Ja'far Subhani (born 1929 A.D.). *Manshur Javid*. Mo'assasa Imam al-Sadiq Publications, Qom. 1993.
38. Ja'far Subhani (born 1929 A.D.). *Wahhabism – Ideological Foundations and Course of Actions*. Mo'assasa Imam al-Sadiq Publications, Qom, 2016.
39. Malik bin Anas bin Malik (Imam Malik) (d. 795 A.D.) *al-Muwatta'*. Darul Afaq al-Jadida, Beirut, 1982.
40. Mohammad Baqir Majlisi (d. 1698 A.D.). *Bihar al-Anwar*. Darul Ihya Turath al-Arabi, Beirut, 2000.
41. Muhammad bin Musa bin Nu'man al-Mazali al-Maliki (d. 1284 A.D.). *Misbah al-Zalam fi al-Mustaghithin bi Khayr al-An'am fi al-Yaqzah wa al-Manam*. Darul Kutub al-'Ilmiyah, Beirut, 2004.
42. Muḥammad ibn Abi Bakr ibn Ayyub al-Zur'i al-Dimashqi al-Ḥanbali Ibn al-Qayyim (d. 1350 A.D). *Zad al-Ma'ad fi Huda Khayr al-'Ibad*. Darul Fiqr, Beirut, 1973.
43. Muhammad ibn 'Isa as-Sulami ad-Darir al-Bughi al-Tirmidhi (d. 892 A.D.) *Jami' al-Tirmidhi (Sunan al-Tirmidhi)*. Darul Kutub al-'Ilmiyah, Beirut, 2011.
44. Muhammad ibn Isma'il al-Ju'fi al-Bukhari (d. 870 A.D.) *Sahih al-Bukhari*. Darul Kutub al-'Ilmiyah, Beirut, 2008. [with English translation].
45. Muhammad Rashid Rida (d. 1935 A.D.). *Tafsir al-Manar*. Darul Kutub al-'Ilmiyah, Beirut, 1992.
46. Ni'mat Allah al-Musawi Jaza'iri (d. 1701 A.D.). *Anwar al-Naumaniyah*. Matba'ah, Shirkat-i Chaap, Tabriz, 1959.
47. Qazi Nurullah Shustari (1542 -1610 A.D.). *al-Sawarim al-Muhriqah fi Jawab al-Sawa'iq al-Muhriqah*. Mo'assasa al-Balagh, Beirut, 2006.
48. Sa'aduddin Mas'ud bin Umar bin Abdullah Taftazani (d. 1390 A.D.). *Sharh al-Maqasid*. Darul Kutub al-'Ilmiyah, Beirut, 2011.
49. Sayyid Ahmad ibn Zayni Dahlan (d. 1886 A.D.). *Al-Durar al-Saniyya fi al-Radd 'ala al-Wahhabiyyah*. Maktabah Mustafa al-Babi al-Halabi, Cairo, 1966.
50. Sayyid Ahmad ibn Zayni Dahlan (d. 1886 A.D.). *Khulasat al-Kalam fi Bayaan Umara' al-Balad al-Ḥaraam*. Dar al-Saqi al-Ṭab'ah, Beirut, 1993.

51. Shams al-Din Muhammad bin Ahmad al-Dhahabi (d. 1348 A.D.). *Mizan al-I'tidal fi Naqd al-Rijal*. Darul Kutub al-'Ilmiyah, Beirut, 2008.
52. Sheikh Hasan al-'Adawi al-Hamzawi (d. 1885 A.D.). *Kanz al-Matalib fi Fazl al-Bayt wa fi-Hijr wa Ashshazarwan wa ma fi Ziyarah al-Qabr al-Sharif min al-Ma'arib*. Books-Publisher, Beirut, 2019.
53. Sheikh Sa'id 'Abd al-Qadir Ibn Salim Bashanfar. *Tabarruk al-Sahabah bi'l-Nabi wa Atharuh*. Sheikhy Notes Publishers, UK, 2016.
54. Shibab al-Din Ahmad ibn Muhammad ibn Hajar al-Haytami al-Makki (d. 1566 A.D.). *al-Sawa'iq al-Muhriqah*. Darul Kutub al-'Ilmiyah, Beirut, 1991.
55. Shihab ad-Din Sayyid Mahmud ibn 'Abdullah al-Alusi (d. 1854 A.D.) *Ruh al-Ma'ani fi Tafsir al-Qur'an al-'Azim wa-al-sab' al-Mathani*. Darul Ihya Turath al-Arabi, Beirut, 1977.
56. Shihab al-Din Ahmad ibn Muhammad al-Qastallani (d. 1517 A.D.). *al-Mawahib al-Ladunniyyah bil-manha al-Muhammadiyyah fil Seerat al-Nabawiyyah*. Darul Kutub al-'Ilmiyah, Beirut, 1988.
57. Shihab al-Din Ahmad ibn Muhammad al-Qastallani (d. 1517 A.D.). *Irshad al-Sari fi Sharh Sahih al-Bukhari*. Darul Kutub al-'Ilmiyah, Beirut, 1999.
58. Shihab al-Din Muhammad Ibn Hajr 'Asqalani (d. 1449 A.D.). *Al-Isaba fi Tamyiz al-Sahaba*. Darul Ihya Turath al-Arabi, Beirut, 1985.
59. Shihab al-Din Muhammad Ibn Hajr 'Asqalani (d. 1449 A.D.). *Fath al-Bari fi Sharh Sahih al-Bukhari*. Darul Kutub al-'Ilmiyah, Beirut, 1983.
60. Shihab al-Din Muhammad Ibn Hajr 'Asqalani (d. 1449 A.D.). *Lisan al-Mizan*. Darul Kutub al-'Ilmiyah, Beirut, 2010.
61. Shihab al-Din Muhammad Ibn Hajr 'Asqalani (d. 1449 A.D.). *Tahdhib al-Tahdhib*. Darul Fiqr, Beirut, 1988.
62. Taqi al-Din Abu Bakr bin Muhammad al-Hisni al-Shafi'i (d. 1425-6 A.D.). *Daf' Shubah man Shabbaha wa-Tamarrada wa-Nasaba Dhalik ila al-Sayyid al-Jalil al-Imam Aḥmad wa-yalihi al-Fatawa al-Sahmiyah fi ibn Taymiyyah*. Dar al-Muṣṭafa lil-Nashr wa-al-Tawzi', Brunei, 2003.
63. 'Uthman ibn Bishr al-Najdi (d. 1871 A.D.). *'Unwan al-majd fi tarikh Najd*. Matba'at al-Salafiyah, Mecca, 1929.
64. Sheikh Ja'far Kashif al-Ghita (d. 1812 A.D.). *Manhaj al-Rashad li man Arad al-Sadad*. Mo'assasa Da'ira al-Ma'arif al-Fiqh al-Islami, Qom, 2005.
65. Muhammad Fu'ad 'Abd al-Baqi (d. 1968 A.D.). *Al-Mu'jam Al-Mufahras li alfaz al-Qur'an al-Karim*. Darul Marifat, Beirut, 1998.

INDEX

A

A Teaching Course on Criticism of Wahhabism, 18, 326
Aala al-Rahman, 166, 191
Abbas bin 'Abd al-Muttalib, 76
Abbas bin 'Abd al-Muttalib, 139
Abbasid, 7, 117
Abbasids, 10, 53
Abd al-'Aziz ibn Sa'ud, 35
Abd al-'Aziz bin Baz, 265
Abd al-Qadir Ibn Salim Bashanfar, 157, 328
Abd al-Rahman bin Abi Bakr, 99
Abd al-Rahman bin Aswad, 67
Abd al-Wahhab, 23, 24, 26, 27, 30, 31, 34, 35, 82, 111, 123, 135, 148, 153, 204, 301, 302, 308, 318, 325, 326
Abdallah Samahiji, 135
Abdul Husayn Dastghaib Shirazi, 104
Abdul Rahman al-Jaziri, 57, 324
Abdullah bin Jahsh, 89
Abdullah bin Zubayr, 52
Abdullah ibn Baz, 145, 265
Abdullah ibn Lahi'ah, 71
Abdullah Ibn Saba, 12, 14
Abdullah-ibn-Sa'eed, 63
Abu al-'A'la al-Mawdudi, 222
Abu al-Khayr al-Baydawi, 86
Abu al-Zubayr, 62, 65, 67
Abu Ayyub al-Ansari, 157
Abu Bakr, 15, 33, 47, 52, 53, 62, 71, 125, 198, 210, 324, 328
Abu Hurayrah, 111
Abu Ja'far Al-Hanbali, 34
Abu Ja'far Al-Khutami, 125
Abu Nu'aym al-Isfahani, 129, 132
Abu Wa'il al-'Asadi, 54
Abu'l-Qawsim Sulayman al-Tabarani, 125, 325
Adam (a), 48, 128, 131, 236, 240

Afrit, 185
Ahlul Bayt (as), 7, 274
Ahmad Amin Misri, 12
Ahmad bin Hanbal, 54, 65, 66, 67, 70
al-'Aqqad, 30
al-'Asqalani, 54, 66, 71, 86
al-'Adawi al-Hamzawi, 143, 327
al-Ahsa, 24, 25, 27, 320
al-Alusi, 24, 25, 29, 129, 319, 328
al-'Asma wa al-Sifat, 143
al-'Azami al-Shafi'i al-Quda'i', 143
al-Badr ibn Jama'ah, 32
al-Bayan wa al-Ikhtisar, 142
Al-Bidayah wal Nihayah, 12, 16, 241, 326
al-Dar'iyya, 25, 26
al-Daraqutni, 66, 325
al-Dhahabi, 33, 71, 126, 327
al-Dhari'a ila Tasanif al-Shi'a, 39
al-Din wa al-Hajj 'ala al-Madhahib al-Arba'a, 282
al-Durar al-Saniyya, 131, 132
al-Durr al-Manthur, 47, 129, 324
al-Fath al-Majid, 145
Al-Fiqh 'ala al-Madhahib al-Arba'ah, 57, 61, 108, 245, 324
al-Firuzabadi, 56
al-Fusul, 27, 237
Al-Futuhat al-Islamiyyah ba'da Mudhiy al-Futuhat al-Nabawiyyah, 30
Al-Ghadir, 33, 107, 326
Al-Ghazali, 113
al-Hadiyyah al-Saniyyah, 239, 241
al-Hadiyyah al-Saniyyah wa-al-Tuhfah al-Wahhabiyyah al-Najdiyyah, 239
al-Hadiyyat al-Saniyya, 196, 204, 238, 241
al-Hasan al-Basri, 63
al-Hayyaj, 40, 41, 53, 56, 60
al-Hisni, 33, 328
al-Hujjah 'ala al-Dhahib ila Takfir Abi Talib, 134

309

Ali ibn Sinan al-Nasa'i, 58, 325
al-Isaba fi tamyiz al-Sahaba, 54
Al-Jami' al-Saghir, 126
Al-Jawhar al-Munazzam fi Ziyarati'l Qabr al-Mukarram, 137
Al-Kafi, 3, 11
al-Kasa'is al-Kubra, 118
al-Khalidi al-Baghdadi, 142
Allama al-Amini, 33, 107
Allama Majlisi, 13
al-Mansur Dawaniqi, 117
Al-Maqalat al-Mardiyya, 32
al-mash'ar, 42
al-Mawahib al-Ladunniyyah, 136, 142, 328
Al-Mawaqif, 11
al-Milal wa al-Nihal, 170
al-Mubahat al-'Awwaliyya, 74
Al-Mu'jam Al-Mufahras li alfaz al-Qur'an al-Karim, 262, 329
Al-Mu'jam al-Saghir, 129, 325
Al-Munjid, 56
al-Musnad, 65, 70, 71, 84, 120, 125, 128, 244, 249, 324
Al-Mustadrak alaa al-Sahihain, 64, 125, 126
Al-Mustalahat al-Arba'a, 222
al-Muwatta', 84, 326
al-Nasa'i, 53, 58, 64, 81, 82, 87, 89, 121, 325
al-Nawawi, 59, 114
al-Qamus, 56
al-Qastallani, 60, 86, 87, 131, 142, 245, 328
al-Qurtubi, 100, 324
al-Radd 'ala al-'Ikhna'i, 29
al-Rasa'il al-Hadiyya al-Saniyya, 111
al-Risalah al-'Aqida al–Hamawiyya al-Kubra, 29
Al-Sa'ud tribe, 25
al-Sahifa al-'Alawiyya, 135
al-Sahifa al-Sajjadiyya, 135, 237, 261
al-San'ani, 235, 241, 258, 259
al-Sawa'iq al-Ilahiyya fi al-Radd 'ala al-Wahhabiyyah, 30
al-Sawa'iq al-Muhriqah, 137, 138, 327, 328
al-Sawarim al-Muhriqah, 138, 327
al-sha'air, 42
al-Sindi, 64, 69, 87
al-Sira al-Halabiyya, 134

al-Sirat al-Mustaqim, 48
Al-Sirri, 14, 15, 17
Al-Sirri bin 'Asim, 14
al-Suyuti, 47, 60, 64, 80, 111, 114, 118, 125, 126, 129, 132, 136, 240, 258, 324
al-Tabaqat al-Kubra, 49
al-Tabarani, 125, 129, 132, 198
al-Tabarsi, 42
Al-Taj al-Jami', 105, 126, 275
Al-Taj al-Jami' li al-'Usul fi Ahadith al-Rasul, 105
al-Thaql al-Akbar, 242
al-Tirmidhi, 58, 63, 69, 71, 95, 99, 125, 126, 209, 327
Al-Tuhfat al-Mukhtara fi al-radd 'ala Munkir al-Ziyarah, 32
al-Tusi, 195
al-Wafa bi Ahwal al-Mustafa, 142, 324
al-Zamakhshari, 80, 116
al-Zurqani, 131, 137, 142, 244
Amir al-mu'minin (a), 17
Amir al-mu'minin Ali (a), 156, 235
Anas bin Malik, 47, 84, 326
Anwar al-Naumaniyah, 13, 327
Aqil bin Abi Talib, 76
Arabian Peninsula, 35, 48
Asalat al-Ruh, 199
Ashab al-Kahf, 79
Asif bin Barkhiya, 185
Awliya Allah, 6, 38, 42, 45, 46, 51, 66, 73, 79, 84, 91, 107, 123, 135, 137, 145, 174, 177, 178, 187, 203, 208, 214, 216, 219, 220, 221, 222, 225, 226, 251, 286
Ayatullah Khomeini, 166
Ayesha (r), 52, 71

B

Baitul Maqdis, 48, 52
Bani Hashim, 76, 274
Bani Kinana, 133
Baqi', 38, 39, 40, 74, 75, 76, 96, 97, 103, 119
barzakh, 189, 190, 191, 197, 220
barzakhi life, 104, 106
Basrah, 24

Battle of Harrah, 7
Bethlehem, 118
Bihar al-Anwar, 13, 209, 216, 279, 326
Bilal (r), 156
Bilqis, 185, 228
Bishr al-Najdi, 25, 26, 328
bi'that, 148, 151
Building of tombs in the light of Qur'an and Hadith, 72
Bulugh al-Maram, 101
Burhan al-Din al-Halabi, 134

C

Companions of *Kahf*, 79, 80

D

Da'wat dhul-'Ashirah, 9
Da'irat al-Ma'arif al-Qarn al-'Ishrin, 23
Daesh, 5
Daf' Shubah, 32, 33
Da'irat al-Ma'arif, 23, 281
Damascus, 16, 24, 32, 33, 38, 299, 302, 304
Danial (a), 48
Dhakha'ir al-'Uqba fi Manaqib Dhawi'l Qurba, 141, 325
Dhu'l Kifl (a), 48
Douzi, 13
Dr. 'Abd al-Jawad al-Kalidar, 27
du'a 'Arafa, 135

E

Egypt, 4, 11, 19, 31, 32, 33, 48, 51, 54, 60, 69, 98, 134, 137, 154, 281, 298, 299, 301, 311
Ehsan Elahi Zaheer, 8, 11, 12
Eid al-Ghadir, 28

F

Fajr al-Islam, 12
Fakhar bin Ma'ad, 134
Fakhr bin Mu'allim al-Qurashi, 32
Fakhruddin Razi, 206
Farazdaq, 274, 275

Farid Wajdi, 23, 281
Fath al-Bari, 54, 86, 137, 140, 328
Fatiha, 51, 100, 286
Fatima (a), 100, 156
Fatima bint Asad, 76, 89
Fitnat al-Wahhabiyyah, 30, 299
Forty Hadith- An exposition, 230
Furqan al-Qur'an, 143, 252, 254

G

Ghara'ib al-Qur'an, 80
Gharqad, 75, 97

H

Habib bin Abi Thabit, 55
Habib bin Abi Thabit, 53, 54
Hadith al-Thaqalayn, 135, 239
Hadithe Qudsi, 28
Hajar al-Aswad, 163, 172, 252, 274, 278
Hakim al-Nishapuri, 64, 69, 120, 324
Hamza (r), 73, 89, 100, 119
Hanbali jurisprudence, 23, 245
Hanbalis, 6, 245, 299
Haram, 3, 4, 5, 310, 313, 319, 321
harām, 61, 68, 69, 72, 73, 76, 83, 87, 88, 89, 91, 98, 113, 114, 116, 121, 138, 145, 146, 233, 236, 238, 243, 245, 271
Hasan ibn Ali (a), 106, 119
Hassan bin Thabit, 136
Hassan bin Thabit, 140
Hawwa, 48
Hizbullah movment, 17
Holy Harams, 5, 20
Holy Imams (a), 39
Hud (a), 48
Huraymala, 24
Husayn ibn Ali (a), 106, 238, 279, 280

I

Ibn Abi al-Hadid, 56, 134
Ibn Abi al-Hadid al-Mu'tazili, 56
Ibn Aflah, 76

Ibn al-'Athir, 136, 156, 326
Ibn al-Athir al-Jazari, 16
Ibn al-Jawzi, 142
Ibn al-Qayyim, 31, 33, 38, 72, 89, 118, 327
Ibn al-Sabbagh al-Maliki, 237
Ibn Bulayhid, 76
Ibn Dawud al-Maliki al-Shadhili, 142
Ibn Hajar al-Haythami, 137
Ibn Ḥanbal, 65, 324
Ibn Hibban, 55, 66, 101, 132
Ibn Jurayh, 62, 63, 65, 66
Ibn Kathir, 12, 14, 241
Ibn Khaldun, 12, 14, 16
Ibn Majah al-Qazwini, 63, 128, 324
Ibn Qayyim, 6, 31
Ibn Taymiyyah, 7, 6, 28, 29, 31, 32, 33, 34, 38, 48, 72, 82, 109, 113, 115, 118, 123, 125, 135, 143, 196, 204, 206, 251, 252, 304, 325
Ibn 'Umar, 247, 248, 249
Ibrahim (a), 48, 117, 172, 267
Ihya' 'Ulum al-din, 113, 324
Ikhwan al Muslimeen, 4
ilm al-'usul, 80
Ilm al-Kalam, 11
Imam Abu Hanifah, 55
Imam al-'Askari (a), 46
Imam al-Hadi (a), 46
Imam al-Humaydi, 71
Imam Ali (a), 8, 9, 12, 17, 18, 124, 221, 235, 237
Imam al-Sadiq (a), 3, 11, 21, 117, 237, 238, 279
Imam al-Sajjad (a), 237, 238, 274
Imam Bukhari, 63, 81
Imam Hafiz Ibn al-'Arabi, 99
Imam Husayn (a), 27, 28
Imam Khomeini, 230
Imam Malik, 84, 117, 118, 131, 143, 326
Imam Muslim, 58
Imamat, 10, 172
Indonesia, 11, 312, 316, 318
Iraq, 6, 26, 35, 48, 51, 60, 166, 284, 310, 311, 315
Irshad al-Sari, 60, 86, 245, 328
Isa (a), 150, 151, 172, 186, 200, 221, 225, 227, 228

Ishaq (a), 48
ISIS, 5, 306, 307, 308, 309, 310, 312, 313, 314, 315, 316, 318, 319, 320, 321
Islamic Revolution of Iran, 5
Islamic sects, 5, 6, 11, 13, 18, 19, 20, 31, 160, 204, 257
Isma'il (a), 48
Isma'il ibn Kathir, 16
Isma'il Kufi, 14
Israel, 4, 17, 160, 162, 167, 182, 183, 184, 223, 258, 315, 317, 319
Isra'iliyyat, 14

J

Ja'far Ilhadi, 20, 176
Ja'far Kashif al-Ghita, 35, 302, 329
Ja'far Subhani, 4, 1, 20, 176, 199, 326
Jabir Ibn Abdullah, 65
Jala' al-Afham fi Salat wa al-Salam 'ala Khayr al-An'am, 118
Jazirat al-'Arab fi al-Qarn al-'Ishrin, 27
Jeddah, 48
Jesus Christ (a), 49

K

Ka'ba, 3, 4, 5, 6, 35, 43, 46, 61, 73, 85, 243, 245, 247, 248, 252, 271, 272, 274
Kanz al-Matalib, 143, 327
Karbala, 27, 28, 246
Kashf al-'Irtiyab, 39, 49, 52, 131, 132, 210, 238, 239, 241, 251, 258, 302, 326
Khadimayn Harmayn Sharifayn, 4
Khalilullah, 3, 5
Khulasat al-Kalam, 125, 132, 210, 327
Kitab Sulaym b. Qays al-Kufi, 280

L

Lisan al-Mizan, 15, 54, 328
Lothrop Stoddard, 29

M

Mafaheem al-Qur'an, 20

Index

Mafatih al-Jinan, 135
Magus, 5
Mahmud bin Ahmad al-'Ayni, 134, 326
Majma' al-Bayan, 130
Majma' al-Zawa'id, 141, 325
Majma' al-Bayan, 42
Majmu' al-Rasa'il al-Kubra, 29
makruh, 61, 62, 69, 70, 87, 88, 89, 98, 99, 236, 239, 245
Malaysia, 11
Malik ibn Anas, 245
Manhaj al-Rashad li man Arad al-Sadad, 35, 302, 329
Manshur Javid, 206, 213, 326
Maqam Ibrahim, 117
Ma'qil bin Yasar (r), 101
Marwan bin al-Hakam, 157
Mary (a), 49
Masdar al-Wujud, 7
Masjid al-Harām, 4, 46, 111, 274, 276
Masjid al-Kufa, 18
Masjid al-Nabi, 88
Masjid Quba, 114
mawadda fi al-qurba, 45
Mecca, 4, 5, 30, 34, 38, 39, 48, 67, 71, 99, 141, 173, 231, 269, 277, 279, 299, 300, 303, 319, 328
Medina, 7, 24, 30, 34, 38, 39, 40, 52, 53, 59, 64, 74, 75, 77, 99, 115, 118, 137, 156, 173, 197, 198, 278, 303, 315
Miftah al-haja fi Sharh Sahih Ibn Majah, 98
Miftah al-Kirama, 28
Miller, 12
Misbah al-Zalam fi al-Mustaghithin bi Khayr al-An'am, 139, 142, 198, 327
Mizan al-I'tidal, 15, 71, 327
Mohammad bin 'Abd al-Wahhab, 6
Mohammad Husayn Mozaffari, 8
mount of Hira, 50
Mount Sinai, 118, 242
Mu'awiyah, 17, 18, 280
Mufradat al-Raghib, 148
Mughira ibn Shu'ba, 18
Muhammad al-Busti, 55
Muhammad Ali Chenarani, 7

Muhammad bin Munkadar, 198
Muhammad bin Muslim al-'Asadi, 65
Muhammad Fu'ad 'Abd al-Baqi, 262, 329
Muhammad Hamid al-Faqi, 145
Muhammad ibn Isma`il al-San`ani, 52
Muhammad ibn Nasr al-Marwazi, 55
Muhammad ibn Sa'ud, 25
Muhammad Jawad al-'Amili, 28
Muhammad Jawad al-Balaghi, 166
Muhammad Jawad Maghniyyah, 19
Muhammad Nasib al-Rifa`i al-Salafi, 125
Muqaddimah, 12, 16, 325
Mus'ab bin 'Umayr, 89
Musa (a), 48, 172, 182, 223, 227
mustahab, 46, 57, 70, 111, 114, 115, 123, 138, 195, 205, 244
Mu'tazilites, 159

N

Nadhr, 6, 251, 286
Nafila, 235
Nahj al-Balagha, 56, 210, 244
Najaf, 28, 35, 134
Najd, 7, 5, 23, 24, 25, 26, 29, 34, 35, 39, 51, 61, 239, 244, 292, 293, 294, 295, 296, 328
Najm al-Muhtadi wa Rajm al-Muqtadi, 32
Ni'mat Allah al-Musawi Jaza'iri, 13, 327
Nizamuddin Hasan al-Nishapuri, 205
Nuh (a), 3, 172, 207
Nu'man al-Mazali al-Maliki, 139, 327
Nu'man al-Mazali al-Marakishi, 142
Nurullah al-Shustari, 137

O

occupied Quds, 48
One Hundred and fifty fictitious Companions of Prophet, 15
Ottoman Empire, 34, 134

P

Palestine, 60, 284, 303, 316
Palestinians, 4
petrodollars, 5

Prophet of God (s), 9, 62, 105

Q

Qadhi Ezzuddin Aiji, 11

R

Raghib Isfahani, 148
Riyadh, 5, 20, 23, 24, 25, 35, 292, 321
Rohingya Muslims, 284
Ruh al-Ma'ani, 25, 129, 236, 328

S

Sa'd bin Mu'adh, 76
Sa'eed bin Muhammad bin Jubayr, 76
Safa and Marwa, 42, 118, 172, 278, 279
Safiyyah, 141
Sahih al-Bukhari, 23, 54, 60, 64, 80, 81, 87, 89, 99, 114, 134, 136, 139, 140, 154, 155, 207, 278, 280, 292, 293, 294, 326, 327, 328
Sahih Muslim, 53, 58, 59, 62, 64, 69, 82, 84, 87, 95, 96, 97, 98, 114, 154, 155, 207, 243, 244, 246, 247, 278, 280, 294, 326
Saif Ibn Umar, 14
Salih (a), 48, 192, 193
Samhudi, 53, 75, 76, 89, 100, 105, 106, 108, 110, 131, 132, 142, 156, 157, 197, 325
Saudi Arabia, 4, 5, 6, 7, 8, 10, 11, 12, 19, 23, 24, 35, 155, 265, 266, 281, 284, 292, 306, 307, 308, 309, 310, 311, 313, 314, 315, 316, 317, 318, 319, 321, 322
Sawad bin Qaa'reb, 135
Sayf Ibn 'Umar, 15
Sayyid Mohsin al-Amin, 39, 49, 251, 302, 326
Sayyid Murtaza Al-Askari, 14, 15, 16
sha'air, 42, 43, 45
Shafa'a, 6, 175, 203, 205, 210, 211, 212, 214, 218, 219
Shaikh Mahmud Shaltut, 268
Sharh al-Jami' al-Saghir, 121
Sharh al-Maqasid, 11, 327
Sharh al-Mawahib, 131, 137, 142
Sharh Nahj al-Balagha, 56, 134
Sheikh al-Sadduq, 13

Sheikh Dawud al-Khalidi, 157
Sheikh Mansur Ali Nasif, 105, 275
Sheikh Mufid, 13
Shias and Shiaism, 8, 12, 13, 14, 17, 18
shifa', 174, 175, 183, 184, 212
Shifa' al-Saqam fi Ziyarat Qabr Khayr al-Anam, 31, 108, 325
Shuayb bin Ibrahim Kufi, 15
Sihah al-Sittah, 56, 58, 154
Sira Ibn Hisham, 231
South Lebanon, 4
Spiritual powers of Prophets, 184
Sufyan al-Thawri, 54, 55
Sufyan bin 'Anbar, 105
Sulaym ibn Qays al-Hilali, 280
Sulayman (a), 172, 185, 224, 228
Sulayman ibn 'Abd al-Wahhab, 30, 34
Sulayman Ibn Musa, 63
Sulh al-'Ikhwan, 142, 143, 156, 157, 252
Sultan Abdul Hamid, 53
Sunan Abu Dawud, 64, 96, 98, 99, 100, 101, 105, 111, 255, 296
Sunan al-Bayhaqi, 120, 125
Sunan al-Daraqutni, 66, 325
Sunan al-Nasa'i, 96, 97, 111, 114, 119, 120, 121, 246, 247, 248, 295
Sunan al-Tirmidhi, 53, 63, 99, 209, 246, 327
Sunan Ibn Majah, 63, 64, 70, 92, 95, 96, 98, 125, 126, 128, 236, 240, 244, 246, 247, 324
Sunan of Abu Dawud, 64
Syria, 6, 16, 26, 31, 32, 51, 60, 125, 134, 156, 274, 284, 298, 299, 300, 310

T

Tabari, 10, 12, 13, 14, 15, 16, 17, 141, 270, 272, 273, 324, 325
tabarruk, 73, 80, 83, 86, 113, 116, 117, 118, 120, 135, 136, 153, 154, 155, 157
Tabarruk al-Sahabah bi'l-Nabi wa Atharuh, 157, 328
Tadhkirat al-Fuqaha', 195
Tafsir al-Baydawi, 86, 92
Tafsir al-Burhan, 130, 131
Tafsir al-Jalalayn, 80, 125
Tafsir al-Kashshaf, 80

Tafsir al-Qurtubi, 100, 324
Tafsir al-Sahih Ayatul Mushkilah al-Qur'an, 128
Taftazani, 11, 327
Tahdhib al-Tahdhib, 15, 54, 55, 66, 71, 328
Tahfiz al-Qur'an al-Kareem, 4
Taj al-Din al Subki, 32
Talkhis al-Mustadrak, 126
Taqi al-Din Abi 'Abdillah al-'Ikhna'i, 32
Taqi al-Din al-Hisni, 32, 33
Taqi al-Din al-Subki, 31, 32, 105, 108, 109, 142
Tarikh al-Khatib, 15
Tarikh al-Mamlakat al-'Arabiyya al-Sa'udiyya, 27
Tarikh al-Tabari, 10, 12, 13, 14, 15, 16, 324
Tarikh Baghdad, 25
Tarikh Ibn 'Asakir, 16
Tarikh Kamil Ibn Athir, 16
Tathir al-I'tiqad, 52
Tathir al-I'tiqad, 241
Tawassul, 6, 20, 105, 107, 123, 124, 125, 127, 128, 131, 133, 134, 135, 138, 142, 286, 298, 300, 301
Tawassul with the Holy Spirits, 20
Tawhid, 6, 3, 8, 20, 143, 159, 160, 176, 278, 286
The Divine Lightening, 34
The Five Schools of Islamic Law, 19
The New World of Islam, 29
tradition of Burayda, 95
Tunisia, 51, 311

U

Umar ibn al-Khattab, 129, 132
Umayyid, 7, 10, 274
Umdat al-Qari, 134, 326
Umm al-mu'minin, 85, 86, 87
Umm al-Qura, 39, 41
Umm Salama, 41, 82
Umme Habiba, 82
Umra mufarrada, 4
umrat al-tamattu, 4
United States, 5, 308, 315, 325
Usd al-Ghabah fi Ma'rifat al-Sahaba, 136, 326

Uthman, 15, 25, 26, 63, 75, 124, 126, 300, 328
Uthman ibn Hamd, 25
Uthman ibn Hunayf, 124, 126
Uyayna, 23, 24, 25

W

Wafa' al-Wafa', 53, 75, 89, 100, 105, 106, 108, 109, 110, 118, 131, 132, 137, 140, 142, 156, 157, 197, 198, 325
Wafa' al-Wafa' fi Akhbar dar al-Mustafa, 53, 75, 89, 106, 108, 109, 325
Wahhabi ideology, 5, 30, 265, 312, 319
Wahhabism – Ideological Foundations and Course of Actions, 18, 326
Wellhausen, 13

Y

Yahya al-Qattan, 55
Yahya bin Sa'eed, 71
Yahya bin Yahya, 53
Ya'qub (a), 48, 148, 149, 153, 162, 174, 208, 223
Yawm al-Inzar, 9
Yazid al-Faq'asi, 15
Yazid Ibn Mu'awiyah, 6
Yemen, 6, 26, 60, 72, 284, 292, 293, 295, 322
Yunus (a), 48
Yusuf (a), 48, 148, 153, 162, 222

Z

Zad al-Ma'ad fi Huda Khayr al-'Ibad, 38, 327
Zayni Dahlan, 30, 125, 131, 132, 134, 135, 299, 327
Zionist, 5, 17, 284
ziyarat, 3, 4, 6, 41, 79, 91, 92, 94, 95, 96, 97, 98, 99, 100, 101, 102, 104, 105, 107, 108, 109, 110, 111, 112, 113, 114, 220, 237, 251, 271
Ziyarat al-Qubur, 82, 115
Zoroastrianism, 5
Zuhayr bin Harb, 53
Zul-Qarnain, 178

www.ingramcontent.com/pod-product-compliance
Lightning Source LLC
LaVergne TN
LVHW061249060426
835507LV00017B/1983